Rethinking Climate Policy

Policies designed to address climate change have been met with limited success. Multilateral treaties, agreements and frameworks linked to the UN and COP meetings have so far failed to limit the rise in average global temperature. *Rethinking Climate Policy* suggests that one of the most important reasons for this is that we are looking at the economics of climate change in the wrong way, arguing that we need to look at climate change as a problem of resource creation, not resource allocation. It identifies problems in current climate policymaking, breaking many taboos in standard economics, to offer a bold proposal for effective and achievable public policy to achieve a zero-carbon economy. Underpinned by both a sound economic and complex systems analysis, this book develops a groundbreaking metric of economic resilience to measure the capacity of economies to transform without breaking down, and accordingly, how to best design climate policies.

JEAN-FRANÇOIS MERCURE is Professor of Climate Policy at the University of Exeter's Business School, UK. He was Senior Climate Economist at the World Bank. He researches the economics of climate change and advises on policymaking. He has lectured at the University of Cambridge, Radboud University and the University of Exeter. He is an economist, innovation scholar and complexity scientist and works on varied topics from energy systems to quantitative finance to geopolitics. He has authored over eighty peer-reviewed articles and the textbook *Complexity Economics for Environmental Governance* (2022).

HECTOR POLLITT is Senior Climate Economist working at a major international organisation, focusing on climate policy solutions in East and South East Asia. He was previously the head of modelling and Chief Economist at Cambridge Econometrics, a consultancy based in the UK. He has twenty years of experience working with macroeconomic models and providing policy advice on climate policy to national governments and international organisations. He has co-edited two books on sustainability policy in East Asia and has co-authored more than forty peer-reviewed journal articles.

Rethinking Climate Policy

Innovation and the Economics of Resource Creation

JEAN-FRANÇOIS MERCURE

HECTOR POLLITT

CAMBRIDGE
UNIVERSITY PRESS

CAMBRIDGE
UNIVERSITY PRESS

Shaftesbury Road, Cambridge CB2 8EA, United Kingdom

One Liberty Plaza, 20th Floor, New York, NY 10006, USA

477 Williamstown Road, Port Melbourne, VIC 3207, Australia

314–321, 3rd Floor, Plot 3, Splendor Forum, Jasola District Centre, New Delhi – 110025, India

Cambridge University Press is part of Cambridge University Press & Assessment, a department of the University of Cambridge.

We share the University's mission to contribute to society through the pursuit of education, learning and research at the highest international levels of excellence.

www.cambridge.org
Information on this title: www.cambridge.org/9781009708371
DOI: 10.1017/9781009708395

When citing this work, please include a reference to the DOI 10.1017/9781009708395

First published 2026

Cover image: Anton Petrus/Moment/Getty Images

A catalogue record for this publication is available from the British Library

A Cataloging-in-Publication data record for this book is available from the Library of Congress

ISBN 978-1-009-70837-1 Hardback
ISBN 978-1-009-70840-1 Paperback

Contents

Figures and Table

FIGURES

TABLE

Foreword

Climate policy has long been shaped by economic models that prioritise market efficiency, yet the urgency of the climate crisis, together with the speed of technological transformation, demands a re-examination of these assumptions.

Rethinking Climate Policy by Mercure and Pollitt is a timely and necessary intervention, challenging conventional approaches and offering a more appropriate framework for designing and implementing climate policies. This is not just a critique of existing approaches; the book provides a constructive pathway forward, rooted in fundamental economics together with a deep understanding of system dynamics, technological change and policy realism.

Unlike some of the more evangelistic advocates of a clean transition, the authors do not sugarcoat the costs and disruption associated with rapid change. They dedicate one of the book's longest chapters to explaining, in great detail, why structural change on this scale will generate immense financial, social and political challenges.

The authors challenge traditional economic models and present alternative frameworks that emphasise real-world complexities. They show how conventional models often assume smooth adjustments, but structural and institutional constraints can lock economies into high-carbon pathways. Transitioning to low-carbon systems, therefore, requires proactive policies that disrupt existing development pathways, generating new feedback loops which enable new technological developments and new markets to grow.

A central concept is 'path dependence' in innovation. This process happens when, for example, scientists and engineers work in well-funded areas where other good scientists work. Deployment of innovation tends to leverage existing infrastructure and know-how.

This makes existing networks hard to disrupt, especially if the benefits of using a new product rise only with the number of others using it. Unilaterally switching to a radical alternative may be costly, risky and unattractive. Shifting the structure of the economy is painful, even if the end point is superior in terms of efficiency, productivity and wealth. Precipitating such a move, and generating private investment in new networks, therefore requires coordination and investment by government to overcome strong inertia.

However, there is a critical upside to all this. As technologies become cheaper, the incentive to deploy them increases. As the book explains, greater deployment is the main driver of learning by doing, discovery and economies of scale, in which the unit cost of a gadget produced in a massive fabrication facility falls. This generates a version of Wright's law, where every doubling in the deployment of solar PVs, wind turbines and batteries results in a roughly 20–40% reduction in cost per unit.

The authors show how even relatively uncoordinated, but nevertheless ambitious, policies across the globe have delivered staggering results at a pace few anticipated. The cost of key low-carbon technologies, such as solar photovoltaic electricity generation, has fallen by over 80% over the last decade.

Reinforcing feedbacks are rapid and unstable, as anyone who has held a microphone to a speaker can attest. Consequently, the transition to renewable energy and electric vehicles has caught most commentators and politicians on the hop, and the authors argue that this is just the beginning.

The book goes into detail examining what drives innovation. It describes how economic and technological transitions do not occur in a vacuum; they are shaped by existing infrastructures and institutional frameworks, as well as historical decisions made by governments and investors. Only purposefully directed innovation can generate structural change, as new networks and markets are created. The book carefully outlines the processes involved in past waves of innovation from waterpower and iron to the steam engine, railways through to electricity, cars and the World Wide Web.

By integrating these insights, the authors provide a more practical guide to policy-makers and investors, one that acknowledges real-world constraints while identifying leverage points for meaningful change. But they also have implications for economic analysis. Many of the features outlined in this book – increasing returns, multiple equilibria and non-marginal structural change – challenge the appropriateness of the core economic assumption of equilibrium. Yet Mercure and Pollitt carefully explain why, for all their shortcomings, economic models remain valuable. As the famous statistician George Box reportedly said, 'all models are wrong, but some are useful'. Models are simplifications of reality. By combining complexity with abstraction, they provide a consistent framework for analysis and comparison. They also impose a discipline on the modeller to articulate assumptions and parameters.

But economic models have not done a good job in supplying predictions of the structural change needed to drive the clean and resilient transformation. Virtually no analysis came close to predicting the rapid cost declines in solar photovoltaics (PV), electric vehicles (EVs) and battery storage. A large and persistent gap has emerged between projected and realised costs. Yet economists and policy-makers are finally recognising that a range of models with different strengths and weaknesses can help to identify tipping points and allow scenario analysis to articulate risks and opportunities. For example, simplified 'toy' models, which are unrealistic and 'wrong' in obvious ways, can provide very useful insights into the key behavioural characteristics which drive an economy. By the same token, models that offer useful insights into the future could be useless at replicating the past. It is the insights, not the numbers, that are most valuable.

A corollary of using models predicated on rational behaviour, optimal efficiency and a stable equilibrium is the reliance on carbon pricing as the cornerstone of climate action. The authors carefully explain why such 'market-based solutions', while theoretically sound, have failed in practice to deliver transformative change.

Political resistance, economic inertia and structural constraints often render these mechanisms ineffective.

For example, many of the leading climate economy models conclude that a universal global carbon price should start low and follow a slow but rising 'policy ramp', picking off increasingly expensive carbon abatement options with time. In his Nobel Prize speech, William Nordhaus, a globally renowned climate economist, described global temperatures of 3 or 4 degrees above preindustrial levels as 'optimal', given the high costs of adjustment in his models. Most climate scientists would regard such levels as potentially catastrophic. It is this sort of disconnect between conventional modelling and real-world imperatives, and the flawed policy choices they engender, that this book seeks to tackle.

In *Rethinking Climate Policy*, Mercure and Pollitt challenge traditional climate strategies. Many mainstream policies focus on resource allocation; carbon pricing, for example, makes pollution more expensive, nudging businesses and consumers to use existing clean options more efficiently. But the authors argue that this approach, while useful, isn't enough. They build on the economic theory of endogenous growth and emphasise resource creation – investing in new technologies, infrastructure and industries that expand what's possible, creating new markets and production possibilities. 'Creation economics' thereby describes economic growth as driven by disruptive technological effects that may have non-marginal and potentially irreversible impact. Artificial intelligence, mitigating climate change and genetic engineering are all examples of such irreversible shifts. Others will doubtless emerge.

Funding renewable energy, new transport networks and green industries increases the economy's ability to transition to sustainability while expanding long-run capacity. By unleashing new technologies, networks, institutions and behaviours, the economy can decouple from the systems and paradigms of the past and attain new levels of productivity and performance. Without such proactive policies, they argue, we risk bickering over a limited set of options, struggling to meet fiscal constraints and missing out on expanding our possibilities.

Ultimately, *Rethinking Climate Policy* tells us that while allocation matters, real progress happens when we create more sustainable resources to meet demand, rather than just rationing what we already have. It is why innovation creates new possibilities faster than economists can model them.

The book provides compelling evidence that driving new general-purpose technologies requires increased use of coordinated economic and industrial strategies to promote adoption and deployment. Economic and industrial policy requires choices. There is no 'technology neutral option'. In a path-dependent system, technology neutrality favours the incumbent sectors with fewer long-run growth opportunities but with the deepest pockets and access to the prevailing physical, institutional and knowledge infrastructure.

The authors propose a mix of policy instruments that best reflect real-world constraints. These include strategic economic ('industrial') policies that drive clean technology deployment; investments in core infrastructure as well as human and intangible capital that create enabling conditions for transition; support for innovation and research; regulations that phase out high-carbon options; financial policies that align capital flows with sustainability goals; management of the distributional consequences of socio-economic transitions for workers and industries; and public engagement and behavioural policies to build societal support and provide credible frameworks against which financiers can invest.

The latter should not be underestimated. Expectations about future returns drive investment and deployment, which in turn drive cost reductions. Expectations can thereby become self-fulfilling. Economists who overstate the costs of the transition will slow deployment and make the transition more expensive. In this sense, economists not only get the future wrong, they make the future wrong, to the extent that their flawed assessments are believed by policy-makers and investors alike. As the authors point out, some of the biggest progress made on climate has occurred despite, not because of, the recommendations by economists using conventional models.

As the window for effective climate action narrows, this book provides the intellectual tools necessary to design policies that are not only theoretically sound but also politically and practically viable. The timing of the book is apposite as policy-makers the world over grapple with where to commit limited public funds and how to induce private investment.

Rethinking Climate Policy provides a compelling critique of dominant climate policy models and offers a fresh perspective on designing effective interventions. By incorporating system dynamics, recognising the limits of market mechanisms and prioritising technology-driven transitions, the authors propose a more powerful and pragmatic approach to climate action. Their work highlights the necessity of government leadership, structural reforms and coordinated investments to achieve deep decarbonisation in a way that is socially, politically and economically feasible.

Mercure and Pollitt have made a vital contribution to the discourse on climate policy, urging us to rethink our strategies and adopt a dynamic, systems-based approach. For policy-makers, researchers and business leaders alike, *Rethinking Climate Policy* offers a compelling reassessment of how we manage the low-carbon transition at a time when technologies, institutions and markets are rapidly evolving. It challenges us to move beyond outdated models and embrace policies that align with the complexities of economic transitions and induce structural change.

Their insights serve as a crucial guide for those committed to addressing the climate crisis in a way that is both ambitious and grounded in reality. The world is running out of time, but this book provides a blueprint for those who are prepared to move forward with clarity, ambition and confidence.

Dimitri Zenghelis, University of Cambridge

Preface

Before we send the reader on a journey into a new climate policy, we thought we'd ask ourselves why we decided to write this book. We have been pouring our entire lives into analysing this topic for over fifteen years. That's a good reason to start with. But, more importantly, over this period we have engaged with lots of different types of users of knowledge on climate change, climate policy and climate economics, whether in companies, in government, in academia or in international organisations. We've come to understand what these people need and what makes climate policy work. It's fair to say, climate policy hasn't really worked up to now.

For a long time, we've been thinking that people are not asking the right questions. In particular, the way economics is used in climate policy is not right. We've written a lot about this in journals and reports. This book brings it all together.

Climate scholarship has come a long way since we started working together on this, back in the early 2010s. But the world has moved on faster still. Technology has changed, politics have changed and the economic context is radically different. For one thing, back then we could never have imagined that Donald Trump could become President of the United States – even less twice!

However, arguably the biggest problem is that climate economic theory remains stuck where it always was. So let's go back and see what things were like when we started, how things have changed since and how they need to change now.

CLIMATE ECONOMICS FIFTEEN YEARS AGO

We started working together on climate policy and economics back in 2011. One inspirational man brought us together, Dr Terry Barker.

He was a key leader when the Intergovernmental Panel on Climate Change (IPCC) won the Nobel Prize for Peace. His thinking was hugely important in developing our approach, but it was incomplete.

At the time, the UK's Climate Change Act still felt relatively fresh, and the Stern Review of climate change had a monumental influence. The European carbon market had been created, and we all had great hopes for it to produce great results.

Options for reducing greenhouse gas emissions all seemed expensive. Solar power was around $400/MWh, ten times more expensive than coal. Offshore wind was an experiment in the North Sea.

Electric vehicles were largely theoretical. Tesla wasn't yet mainstream. Some people were betting on hydrogen cars. In transport, we mostly talked about improving engine efficiency, plus the problem that rich people were buying cars with bigger engines that polluted more.

Carbon capture and storage (CCS) attracted much interest because it could avoid the unaffordable costs of renewable energy while reducing emissions. Most importantly, if we could attach CCS to existing coal plants and fuel them with wood chips, we could get 'negative' emissions.

And, of course, fossil fuel use was growing as fast as ever, even as oil prices jumped around. Natural gas was the bridging fuel if we wanted to replace coal. The Fukushima nuclear accident in Japan led to even more fossil fuels being consumed.

The cost challenge looked immense. A few people understood that technology costs come down as the technologies are used. But it was a niche topic. Climate change was also a niche topic, so the worlds rarely came together. No one could have imagined that zero-carbon technologies could become the norm within a generation.

Back then, the goal was to keep the costs as low as possible. People analysed scenarios using cost optimisation. 'Business as usual' scenarios, by convention, saw continued rapid growth in fossil fuels. We kept getting told that deviating from this would lead to huge economic costs.

We were the only economic researchers who claimed the opposite. We told whoever would listen that cutting emissions could accelerate economic growth, rather than impede it. Environmentalists listened to us. But other economists didn't believe us.

CLIMATE ECONOMICS TODAY

Over fifteen years, things have changed a lot, sometimes in ways we didn't predict. First, renewable energies are now cheaper than coal, and coal has not become more expensive. Solar energy is ten times cheaper than fifteen years ago. Offshore wind too. Onshore wind was already pretty good back then and, despite progress being slowed by planning permission and other regulation, is also now cheaper than coal.

In some ways, progress with batteries has been even more extraordinary. Electric vehicles that can travel useful ranges now exist at prices comparable to other ordinary vehicles. Electric vehicles are now seen everywhere. One of us even bought a *second-hand* one!

Put all this together and the game is completely changed. The two most polluting sectors have zero-carbon solutions at affordable prices. We no longer talk about efficiency improvements. We talk about eliminating carbon. We just need the infrastructure to get us there.

Some things haven't changed though. The European carbon market, although expanding, is much the same as it was back then. It was criticised for stagnating at low prices. It even had to be restarted when the price crashed to zero. Finally, prices have increased, getting near 100 EUR per tonne of carbon dioxide. But this was mainly because of the war in Ukraine and the closure of pipelines from Russia. A shortage of gas pushed electricity providers back to carbon-intensive coal, driving up CO_2 emission permit prices. Not what the carbon market was designed for.

Carbon capture and storage looks increasingly like a pipe dream. It was supported by the oil industry, and this should have given us a clue. Unlike renewables, its costs don't fall. We're still at the experimental stage, even though the technology has been used for decades for enhanced oil recovery. This tells us something about how motivated people are to make it work. Wind is now cheaper than wood chips, so negative emissions are now more unlikely than ever.

A really groundbreaking change is the new talk of 'peak oil demand'. We used to talk about peak oil as when supplies will run out. Now it is because we will want less of it. Like when climbing a hill, when near the summit, it's difficult to tell exactly where it is, but it will be soon. Our 'business as usual' scenarios will soon have declining oil demand. It's a huge shift, which oil companies do not seem to understand yet.

Either way, the idea that sectors will wither and die is focusing minds. It's already well advanced with coal in the US, EU and UK. China and India will soon go the same way. We've come a long way in those fifteen years.

If it happens to oil though, that's another story. The amount of money on the line is much, much bigger. Money invested in exploring and drilling for oil could be lost. All our pensions could be affected. A new kind of risk, called 'transition' risk, was highlighted by Mark Carney and the Bank of England.

And where does natural gas fit in? It's not clear that a zero carbon economy is needed. In Europe, the invasion of Ukraine was a wake-up call. Gas became six times more expensive and, because we never got off gas, so did electricity. We ended up with inflation, a cost of living crisis, lots of inequality and political backlash. Energy security has become a key consideration, even as concerns grow about China's dominance in solar panels.

Business as usual has changed. It's now difficult to say what will happen if we don't have any new climate policy. Surely coal is not going to come back.

More importantly, thinking is changing. The idea that climate policy might help economic development is increasingly accepted. In

2018, Nick Stern spearheaded a global report that said sustainability could be the growth story of the twenty-first century. Our computer modelling helped support the report but all of a sudden the message was getting out there. Climate policy doesn't have to be bad for the economy.

WHERE CLIMATE ECONOMICS NEEDS TO GO

The IPCC's sixth assessment report came as a disappointment. Not because it lacked cutting-edge analysis – anything but. But because it included a lot of economic modelling based on the old ideas. It published thousands of model simulations, all of which said that reducing emissions would have an economic cost. The axis on the chart only went in one direction!

As many people are now pointing out, models remain a major problem. Most people would take thousands of simulation results showing costs as a definitive answer. However, it's the same assumptions that determine the results, over and over again. Standard climate economics is the real problem.

Our experience confirms our earlier suspicions that climate economics starts from the wrong place. The 'polluter pays' principle is morally attractive. There would even be some logic to 'internalizing the externalities', if we had any idea what the economic cost of one tonne of carbon was.

The problem is that none of this solves the problem of finding zero-carbon ways to live our lives. The polluter pays and we might all feel better about ourselves. Emissions don't fall and we don't get cheap solar energy. Occasionally people say 'yes but the polluter has never *really* been made to pay'. But what would it take? A carbon tax rate of several thousand dollars?

The endless debates about carbon pricing seem to have been a costly distraction. Very little of the low-carbon technological progress we see today can be attributed to making the polluters pay. That was achieved with other policies, namely, feed-in tariffs, contracts for differences and investment programs. Luckily, policymakers did not put all their eggs in the 'polluter pays' basket, so all has not been lost.

In climate policy at least, it's time to bury the polluter pays principle once and for all. While carbon pricing may have some uses, making the polluter pay simply doesn't give us tomorrow's thriving economy.

The last fifteen years have shown us that investment in new technology works best when the risks are reduced, or if some revenue is guaranteed (along with careful progress monitoring). With this, renewables costs came down ten times! The large falls in battery costs also had nothing to do with making polluters pay. We now understand that 'the path is made by walking'; in other words, that investing in where we want to go makes it cheap to get there.

The two of us still believe that the transition will accelerate GDP growth, just as we did fifteen years ago. But we now understand something more: It will increase inequality too. There are three reasons. First, we need huge amounts of investment. That means more assets that generate income, which are usually owned by wealthy people. The rich 1% will own even more.

Second, we must also think about people losing their jobs through the transition. These jobs probably won't re-appear in a zero-carbon economy. Everyone involved in fossil fuel extraction, transformation and use will be looking for new employment. They may not be suited to the zero-carbon world.

But there is a third reason. Fossil fuel assets will at some point become worthless. Towns dependent on a single employer could be in trouble. If there is a financial crisis, as happened in 2008, the banker gets bailed out, but not the common worker.

The inequality comes from risk. And dealing with these risks will be necessary. What we've learnt in the past fifteen years is that we need to change focus, to look for *resilience instead of efficiency*.

Making the polluter pay is the old 'efficient' approach, where we try to minimise economic costs. But where we maximise efficiency, we minimise resilience. Without resilience, there is no chance in hell that we will succeed in transitioning to a completely different economy. Focusing on efficiency is the best way to fail. We hope this book makes it clear why.

The zero-carbon transition will stretch the economy close to breaking point. We need to improve our resilience, now more than ever. Although this book shows ways of measuring resilience, it is hard to show how much we will need. But there seems to be a constant trend that we are losing resilience just when we need it most. The financial sector has a lot to answer for.

How do we build resilience? Definitely not by pricing carbon. Investment in spare production capacity would help, as would creating buffers to cushion unexpected economic blows. This is a new profound insight. The same is true for all systems; resilience provides room to manoeuvre, which we need when we want to go around a sharp bend in the road. And we have a very sharp one ahead of us.

Maybe where this is most obvious is with political resilience. We have next to none at the moment, as many countries begin to sink into messy populism.

Policies that make poor people poorer and expose many to social and financial risks will make the political situation worse. We can expect more people to turn against climate action if it looks like the green economy is a rich man's dream paid for by everyone else.

The truth is we're all dreaming. We need to wake up. We need to rethink climate policy. That's what this book is about. It lays out a path forward. A path that is resilient and gives us our best chance of getting through what will be highly challenging times.

Acknowledgements

We decided to write this book to put down on a page a fifteen-year-long conversation figuring out the economics of climate change. But lots of people have also helped shape our understanding of how the economy works, from universities, governments, international organisations, companies, foundations and clients. We must thank everyone.

The story really starts with Terry Barker. We are both grateful to the University of Cambridge's Centre for Energy, Environment and Natural Resource Governance (C-EENRG), created by Professor Jorge Vinuales. We are grateful to Cambridge Econometrics and the University of Exeter.

J-F MERCURE

For me the story of this book starts when I was in charge of the large UK government-funded 'Economics of Energy Innovation and System Transition' project and came to consider an invitation to join the World Bank. This was about to turn my world upside down, and to question everything I knew about the world, politics, economics and finance. I remember deciding this with Hector late night at the White Swan pub in Cambridge. Then I took the jump. For this, I also have to thank Pablo Salas, and later Aileen Lam and Unnada Chewpreecha, for joining too. And of course, the man pulling all the strings, Dr Dirk Heine.

For my time at the World Bank and since, I am particularly thankful to Etienne Espagne, from whom I have learned a lot about how the financial system really works, and his tribe at Agence Française de Développement, the French development bank.

I thank the inspirational Simon Sharpe, whose own book also shaped my thinking. I will always remember him saying that even during the most unfavourable political times, there will always be civil servants willing to do the right thing as soon as they are given the chance to do so.

I thank Tim Lenton and the Exeter academic ecosystem at the Global Systems Institute for systems thinking and tipping points. Thanks also go to Gregor Semieniuk, William Oman, Romain Swartzman, Uli Volz and Emanuele Campiglio for contributing to writing our 'cross-border risks' paper, which for me has been an important milestone.

Thanks to Michael Grubb, Jorge Vinuales, Femke Nijsse, Cormac Lynch and the Future Technology Transformations (FTT) team, and Peter Cox. Thanks to Phil Summerton, Jon Stenning, Chris Thoung, Pim Vercoulen and the Cambridge Econometrics team. Thanks to Frank Geels and Dimitri Zenghelis, Marcelo Pereira, Joao Carlos Ferraz, Cadu Young and friends at Brazil's Ministry of Finance.

I owe my thinking to a bunch of old writers, including Schumpeter, Minsky, Phil Anderson, Brian Arthur and Stuart Kauffman.

Lastly but most importantly, thanks to my loving wife, Lori, my sister Catherine and my very clever little girl, Flora, to whom I dedicate this book. If for no other reason, we should save the planet for you, Flora. Otherwise, what would you think of your daddy?

HECTOR POLLITT

I will never forget the day that Terry Barker sat me down at Cambridge Econometrics and introduced me to the Energy-Economy-Environment Macro-Econometric model. So began my journey into post-Keynesian economics – starting with the application rather than the theory. This has probably shaped my mindset more than anything.

Our modelling already stood out from what everyone else was doing. I realised quickly that the standard approaches were deeply flawed and policy was going in the wrong direction. And that we needed to shout about it. I owe thanks to the modelling team at Cambridge Econometrics for helping to make this happen and, of course, especially to Unnada Chewpreecha.

Over time, we learnt that even our own modelling had important gaps. It was time to get into theory, for what eventually became my PhD – and for which I owe thanks to Jorge Vinuales. I was lucky to have the time to go back to Keynes and Schumpeter, and to read the more recent complexity literature. But it turns out that Veblen had already figured it all out at the start of the twentieth century!

Deciding to write a book while working full-time and undertaking a part-time PhD might seem like a strange decision, and it definitely wasn't easy at times. But it's urgent now. If we don't sort climate policy in the next few years, we could be in big trouble.

A lot of sacrifices were made along the way, and for this I owe the most thanks to my wife, Sanna, who has been more supportive than I could want or deserve. I hope that in ten years, time we can look at a world that's addressing climate change sensibly and say it was worthwhile.

The views expressed in this book are those of the authors and not their employers or any other institution.

1 What Is the Economic Challenge of Climate Action?

1.1 LET'S TALK ABOUT THE 'COSTS' OF SAVING OUR PLANET

This book is about policies to avoid the impacts of climate change. Before we get to that, though, let's make one thing clear. Climate change is real. The science is long past dispute and the effects are becoming visible across the world. Polling shows growing public concern about the climate.[1]

Pressure is therefore growing on governments to act on climate. We hear we must make sacrifices to do so. In rich countries like the US, campaigners say we can afford this sacrifice. However, we don't want to make poor countries prioritise climate over poverty reduction. Perhaps the rich countries could help the poor countries, even though that will cost the rich countries more.

All the discussion has been on how to get to 'net-zero' emissions. We hear that this will be critical if we care about the planet we leave for our children. Economists tell us it will be an expensive project, but we can minimise the costs by *getting the prices right*. Carbon pricing is the answer we seek, but we must still be prepared for sacrifice.

Another common story says that economic growth needs energy, and we cannot increase our energy use while cutting use of oil, coal and gas. To reduce carbon emissions, economic growth therefore *must* be curtailed – an even bigger sacrifice. Groups supporting 'de-growth' have duly appeared. They say we must atone for our carbon sins. They say that economic growth is a scourge and a cancer: If

[1] See, for instance, in recent news www.bbc.co.uk/news/science-environment-59067471.

someone supports growth, they presumably also support destruction of the planet for profit.

The politics is obvious. We quickly get to an 'us and them' story of 'good' and 'bad', or 'left' and 'right'.

But are these stories about sacrifice supported by the facts? Or do we use them only because it is convenient? There seems to be a contradiction between the 'costly but necessary' story and claims from the International Energy Agency (IEA) that solar power now offers the 'cheapest electricity in history'.[2] Furthermore, why couldn't growth be driven by green energy?

If the IEA is correct, surely addressing climate change could *save* us money and not be a cost? But if there are no costs, the ethical dilemmas would be turned on their heads. Decades of work in political and moral theorising would become irrelevant.[3] The problem of reducing emissions becomes quite different.

In this book we show that the IEA is indeed correct, and we see the same patterns in transport, heating and other things we use energy for. We also show that economic growth can be supported by green energy. We even suggest that the green transition will accelerate growth. The political theorising has misunderstood the nature of the problem.

The reality is that the transition to net-zero emissions is already happening – and, although perhaps not fast enough, it is certainly happening fast. The issue is the transition will destroy old ways of doing things and make many jobs and technologies obsolete.

Acts of charity, government action, subsidies and carbon taxes all help, but they are not driving the transition. The transition is happening because new technologies make people money.

Successful technological innovation does one of two things. It either introduces something new that people desire, or it offers

[2] See IEA (2020b).

[3] Economists sometimes discuss 'the tragedy of the commons' to describe exploitation of natural resources, and 'the prisoner's dilemma' on how to address such issues. These make no more sense if addressing the climate crisis is a win-win. See Aklin and Mildenberger (2020).

the same things at a lower cost. Zero-carbon technologies offer the prospect of lower costs because they skip expensive fossil fuel extraction, transportation and transformation. They may not already do that yet, but the potential is obvious and measurable.

In some cases, however, zero-carbon technologies are already cheaper than alternatives. This is where the transition is happening fastest (i.e. where it already pays for itself): Solar and wind power, electric vehicles (EVs) and, soon, electric heat pumps. These technologies are becoming affordable just as computers did forty years ago.

However, the battle to avoid dangerous climate change is not yet won. Other zero-carbon technologies are becoming cheaper but need further development. Even here, though, the story of costs and sacrifice for all of us is misleading; after all, one person's costs are always another person's revenues.

So are we already on a path towards net-zero emissions? Yes, we could be, although (and this cannot be stressed enough) not yet fast enough to meet our climate targets.[4]

The real question is why are governments not embracing the transition? Despite misleading guidance from economists and the fossil fuel industry, it is not because of a conspiracy. The transition threatens many ways of life. The result is political division; even if the transition happens anyway, politicians do not want to be seen as causing loss of livelihood.

Those who lose out will include oil and gas workers, vehicle engine manufacturers and coal miners. They have done nothing wrong, except maybe having made the wrong career choice up to forty years ago. Back then, their jobs were highly respected. Now, they have turned 'morally wrong', as many environmentalists would say.

However, their technological era is coming to an end, and probably their jobs too. Is there a plan for these workers? What will become of their communities? The closure of the UK's coal mines in the 1980s showed a glimpse of the possible hardship to come.

[4] As indeed can be observed in the recent historical data, see Mercure et al. (2025b).

Repeating this experiment at a global level across many different economic sectors could cause immense human suffering.

Furthermore, our finance-dominated economy introduces further risk. Oil and gas companies used to be reliable investments for pension funds. Now, not even our pensions are safe!

In fact, everything is at risk, just as it has been at the end of other technological eras throughout history. The risks include political, financial and economic instability, whether or not we prevent dangerous climate change. The risk is not that the transition is costly. The risk is it will make some people a lot of money, while leaving others facing poverty.

In this book, we will *justify* these claims with real-world data and revised economic thinking. The implications of it all for our society could not be more important. We need to understand properly what is about to happen.

1.1.1 Moral Philosophy and Cost-Benefit Analysis

There is no doubt that addressing climate change is a moral issue. The story that we have a responsibility to our children to limit the damages to the planet is surely correct, and we do not need to repeat the reasons why. The knowledge we have from climate science is clear, detailed and well established.[5] We simply don't know what will happen to humans if the world keeps warming.

Human society rests on fragile foundations that depend on available food, water, energy, shelter, lack of disease and many more things our planet provides. All of these foundations are threatened by climate change.

This fact alone should guide our decision-making. But for a long time it has not. Instead we relied on economists estimating how many dollars of 'damages' a changing climate would cause. Why?

[5] The best reference for the evidence on climate change is that assembled by the Intergovernmental Panel on Climate Change (IPCC), which involves hundreds of scientists, see IPCC (2021).

We come to one of the many problems outlined in this book: analysing climate action in terms of costs and benefits. Government economists are familiar with estimating the costs and benefits of policies. Many will do this, either consciously or unconsciously: add up all the costs minus all the benefits for the various possible courses of action, including doing nothing. Then choose the course of action with the biggest number.

To add things together, consistent units must be used. Because the method was invented by economists, everything is converted to money values, for example, dollars. There is the immediate problem that we don't know how to measure in monetary terms the costs of floods, heatwaves, hurricanes, and so on.

Worryingly, to do cost-benefit analysis (henceforth CBA), we must also put values on human lives lost due to climate change, for which we usually choose an arbitrary price. This is another moral question since, ultimately, there is no method to objectively measure people's values, let alone how much their life is worth.[6]

There is in fact a lot more moral philosophy hiding in CBA. The approach assumes we behave selfishly, producing and consuming as much as we can for our own benefit. Coincidentally, what is best for the individual is also best for society. Most importantly, we must decide how much we value having things now compared to having them in the future.

Even leaving aside all the moral issues, there is the challenge of adding up all the possible future costs of a changing climate. For the purpose of this book, we call this the fundamental 'knowability' problem of CBA. The uncertainty is so large that the exercise is hardly worth doing. The choice of numbers used by analysts has led to endless philosophical theories.

[6] This is a long and old debate, but to get a sense of the arguments, see Baram (1980) and Ackerman and Heinzerling (2002). For methods used to value the environment, see Hanley and Barbier (2009) and Bateman et al. (2002). Human lives are typically valued differently in different countries by these methods, which illustrates the moral unsoundness of the method.

How should one compare things that are completely unknown with things that we know already? The problem is that the benefits of climate policy are mostly unknown, whereas the immediate monetary costs are well known. This is not unusual; it is much easier to estimate the value of losing something you already have (like money in a bank account) than the possible value of something new or something hypothetical (like a new technology or averting disaster).

To be clear, two components of benefits in CBA suffer from the knowability problem. First, there is no way we can estimate the benefits of avoided climate change. It involves exploring too many possible complicated compounding cascades of disasters.

Second, the immediate benefits from climate policy may seem easier to predict, like the creation of employment, new skills, cost reductions, regional industries, new business models and so on. But how these impacts put the economy on a new long-term development track cannot be estimated with numbers very accurately. The level of complexity makes it impossible. As the poet Antonio Machado said, 'Traveler, there is no path; the path is made by walking'.

This asymmetry of known costs against uncertain benefits arises all the time in climate policymaking. It comes up whenever there are upfront financial costs with benefits appearing later.[7] It also applies to investments by business, especially, in innovation and the creation of new technologies. The asymmetry between the knowable and unknowable actually implies that a lot of the time, for people who decide this way, the 'do nothing' option wins almost all the time. If not, some cheap option with lack of commitment often wins.

However, business doesn't work this way. In these situations businessmen usually adopt a portfolio-based approach instead, experimenting with different options. In a good venture capital portfolio, many options risk failing, but some of them succeed and make all the money. Basic CBA misses this idea.

[7] See Mercure et al. (2021b).

We must also recognise that historically it has often been by solving problems that governments and businesses ended up creating the jobs of the future.[8] For example, how could policy-makers have valued the costs and benefits of investing in semiconductors back in the 1970s? They would have needed to value the contribution of computers and software to almost everything we do on the planet today! Good thing they didn't use CBA, or this might not have happened.

There is no doubt that addressing climate change requires system-level transformation. The economy must change fundamentally, in ways that we cannot predict. CBA has a fundamental challenge in assembling all the information it requires.

We thus propose something that some may see as blasphemous: that climate action is not CBA-able. CBA is simply not a good tool to guide climate policy decisions, because it will always have that status quo bias deeply embedded. It doesn't see the opportunities, nor does it see the risks. It leads to governments setting ever more ambitious emission reduction targets, but blocking all the initiatives to meet these targets, because none of them are economical. It leads to procrastination. And we've procrastinated for forty years at least.

1.1.2 *Using Models to Answer the Big Questions*

The cost-benefit analysis attempted to answer the 'big' question: How much effort should we devote to the climate problem? Two key economists have led the way: William Nordhaus in the US and Lord (Nick) Stern in the UK. As economists often do, they both turned to models to formalise their analysis.

Before getting to the models, it is worth noting that at the time, Nordhaus and Stern strongly disagreed with each other, not on the CBA method, but on the moral question of how much we value the future.[9]

[8] See Mazzucato (2013, 2018, 2021).

[9] Stern has since drastically changed his view of climate economics models (see Stern et al. 2022), but Nordhaus hasn't.

This question is extremely important for climate policy because the costs and risks (e.g. jobs lost in fossil fuels) happen now, whereas the benefits and avoided risks, notably a stabilised climate, happen many years into the future. However, the fact that two economists using the same method got such different answers should have already set alarm bells ringing.

Working for the UK government, Stern led possibly the most influential report on climate economics ever written.[10] The benefits of avoiding the effects of climate change (e.g. flooding, sea level rise, heatwaves and loss of human lives) overwhelmingly beat the costs of reducing emissions, assuming that we do value the future.

Both economists had to address all the questions posed in Section 1.1.1. They needed numbers to put in their models. William Nordhaus famously *made up* an economic 'damage function', essentially out of thin air. He plugged this into his model and found that the 'optimal' amount of climate change is 3°C.[11]

Nordhaus's model is based on solid CBA foundations. Humans should reduce climate change only up to the point where additional climate damages no longer exceed the policy costs of further action. The model puts a price on carbon emissions and finds the price that balances climate damages. Nordhaus found that the specific price should be \$49.87/tCO_2 in 2020, *with four significant figures*, despite knowing that the uncertainties should prohibit any confidence in his estimates. He called this the 'social cost of carbon'.

The model Stern used was almost identical in design but used different numbers and more credible uncertainty ranges. Stern's main conclusion was framed slightly differently though: that we needed to spend 1% of GDP to avoid dangerous climate change.

Many people in government and business welcomed the findings. The apparently rational message, against the irrational and

[10] See Stern (2007).

[11] Nordhaus published substantially on this, spanning decades (e.g. see Nordhaus, 1993, 2013, 2017), but the particular numbers discussed are from Nordhaus (2010).

emotional language used by environmentalists, was that it is not yet worth doing too much about climate change. We now know that powerful organisations were acting to ensure that climate policy be delayed as much as possible, for example, by financing some economists to say so.[12] Nordhaus's results still provide ammunition to these groups. Stern, however, has adopted a more critical message.

Fortunately, Nordhaus did not have an enormous impact on policy everywhere. For instance, the UK government recognises the impossible uncertainties in estimating the social cost of carbon. Its assessment system accepts that reducing emissions has a value that cannot be estimated, but instead must be decided as a government-wide policy.

Most importantly, the natural scientists in the Intergovernmental Panel on Climate Change (IPCC) refused to accept the results from the economists. In 2015, the world adopted the Paris Agreement, which aimed to limit climate change to well below 2°C, largely because we do not know what will happen if we exceed that.

The models used by Nordhaus and Stern lost their purpose. But the spirit of CBA lives on.

1.1.3 It Takes a Model to Beat a Model

With climate targets set by the Paris Agreement, the relevant question for policymakers became how to meet these targets. For example, Stern's analysis may have settled the question that the UK should act on climate change. However, it did not say how to do it, and this has been a problem ever since.

At the time, everything looked so costly it was not clear where to even start. Solar power cost between five and ten times as much as electricity coming from coal and gas. Could we imagine our electricity bills increasing this much? The economic sacrifice would be huge. And that was just our electricity bills. Everything else that was produced with electricity would cost more too.

12 See Franta (2021).

Minimising these costs became the priority. Once again, models were called in to help. Now computers were more powerful, so bigger models could be built. Two main types of models were brought into the climate change debate.

The first type was computable general equilibrium (CGE) models. These existed previously and in fact date back to the nineteenth century but were extended to include energy consumption and emissions. They answer economic questions.

The second type is integrated assessment models (IAMs),[13] which bring in a lot of detail about different technologies. They build a picture of what a future energy system might look like. The two modelling approaches are similar in design. They use the same basic assumptions.

With access to the right data, it is straightforward to build an economic model of energy consumption. The modeller must gather data on economic production in sectors (steelmaking, transport, power generation, etc.) and energy use in the same sectors (electricity, coal, oil, gas, etc.). Econometrics tells us the linkages between production levels, prices and different types of energy. Sometimes the modellers choose their own linkages.

Researchers have built large and detailed models. These models have almost developed a life of their own and have been used to develop future economic and climate scenarios. A big industry emerged that churned out endless numbers of scenarios for governments, for the IPCC, and now for central banks.

These models follow the economists' aims of 'getting the prices right'. According to economic theory, a carbon tax increases the cost of doing business in high-carbon industries, which should encourage innovating or bringing in green technologies. The consumption of high-carbon stuff falls, which is good for the climate,

[13] See www.iamcdocumentation.eu. These models bring together multiple tools, sometimes simple or sometimes complex, of global energy systems, the economy and the climate.

but costs increase for businesses who then charge higher prices to consumers. Ultimately, ordinary people pay for reducing emissions.

The oversimplified models only see a simple inverse relationship between prices and emissions: carbon emissions decrease when the carbon price increases. If the carbon price is later scrapped, the reverse happens, and energy consumption and emissions go back up again. We thus see a story of trade-offs and sacrifice since, at this rate, zero emissions becomes improbably expensive.

Of course, this is a gross simplification of how models work. But there is nevertheless something deeply problematic with this reasoning. It reduces human behaviour to a line on a graph: when prices go up, people use proportionally less fossil energy; when prices go down, people use more fossil energy.

In this imaginary world, a high energy price would not lead to permanent changes in fossil energy consumption. For example, high gasoline prices might encourage consumers to buy EVs, but only until gasoline prices go down again, at which point the models would suggest that consumers sell en masse their brand new electric cars and replace them with good old petrol cars again. In that worldview, fossil fuel use and economic growth go hand in hand – the equation is simple, less fossil fuel use means less growth.

To get to net-zero emissions, the carbon price would need to keep increasing, eventually getting extremely high.[14] It would also need to become permanent, so that fossil fuel use does not rebound. Humans have some deep but unexplained attachment to fossil energy. The last people emitting even small amounts of carbon could face an astronomical tax burden.

Unsurprisingly, these models fail to address, just as CBA does, the fundamental 'knowability' problem. It should be obvious that our social and technical system does not work like that and that humans

[14] For example, in the IPCC scenario database for the 1.5°C report (IPCC, 2018b), carbon prices required to decarbonise the economy in some scenarios/models rise up to values above \$50,000/tCO_2 in 2018 dollars.

do not have such a deep and special attachment to fossil fuels. After all, other technologies can provide the same services.

The models have at times been useful. However, they have deeply misled our thinking, giving an undeserved privileged position to fossil fuels and to fossil fuel prices. It is as if fossil fuels were fundamental to human existence. It is also as if modellers could not imagine society functioning differently, generating a bias towards the status quo.

Of course, in the current economic structure, getting rid of fossil energy very suddenly would be disastrous. But this says nothing about what the structure of a zero-carbon energy economy would be, say, in thirty years from now. And we know that human use of energy has evolved from using wood and water power to using coal, then oil, and more recently natural gas (and soon solar energy), and that at each stage, economic structures changed drastically, but humans did not all become poorer.

This succession has been driven by innovation. Humans find new ways to use resources. It is innovation, not economics, that must be central to the climate policy debate.

1.1.4 Let's Not Pretend We Know the Future

If Steve Jobs had known in the 1980s what the iPhone would eventually look like and do, he would not have so much to be credited for. If governments had known how the internet would change the world, they might have invested in it much earlier. But, of course, no one knew what the iPhone or the internet could do until they were invented. Even then, that was just the start of their stories.

The word 'technology' means different things to different people. So does the word 'innovation'. Some people think that future technology will solve all our problems, including climate change. They usually have less idea how to make the future technology happen. Technology doesn't happen by magic, it appears through hard work.

Let's be clear, technology must play a lead role in preventing dangerous climate change. Many of the necessary technologies exist already, but they must replace current alternatives. If they are to be used widely, more people must (a) know about them and (b) want to use them.

The only thing we know about future technology is that we don't know how it will develop. It is common knowledge that technology changes every day. Entrepreneurs, companies and R&D labs spend billions of man-hours developing new products and finding ways to make existing products cheaper.

This point is unfortunately lost on many of the world's economists. The models described in Sections 1.1.2 and 1.1.3 make brave predictions about future technology. Why do they do this? One reason is that making up stuff over the future makes the models simpler. However, economists also follow the official CBA guidelines, which of course were written by other economists. To do that, we need to pretend to know the future, so we need to make something up.

Does any of this matter? It turns out that it really does. For example, in 2007, when the UK Climate Change Act was passed, offshore wind power was very expensive (see Figure 1.1). Economists using CBA unsurprisingly advised the British government against investing in offshore wind. Planting trees in Indonesia to offset carbon emissions would have been much more cost-effective.

However, the government ignored the advice and invested in offshore wind anyway, because it had to prove to the EU that it was filling its quota of renewables. As a result, the cost of offshore wind fell by 80% and is now so cheap that the subsidy has at times turned into a source of profit for the government.[15] Moreover, other countries can now benefit from cheap, carbon-free electricity, and UK companies working in wind power have gained a competitive advantage.

[15] For the evidence, see Jennings et al. (2020) as well as Grubb et al. (2021a).

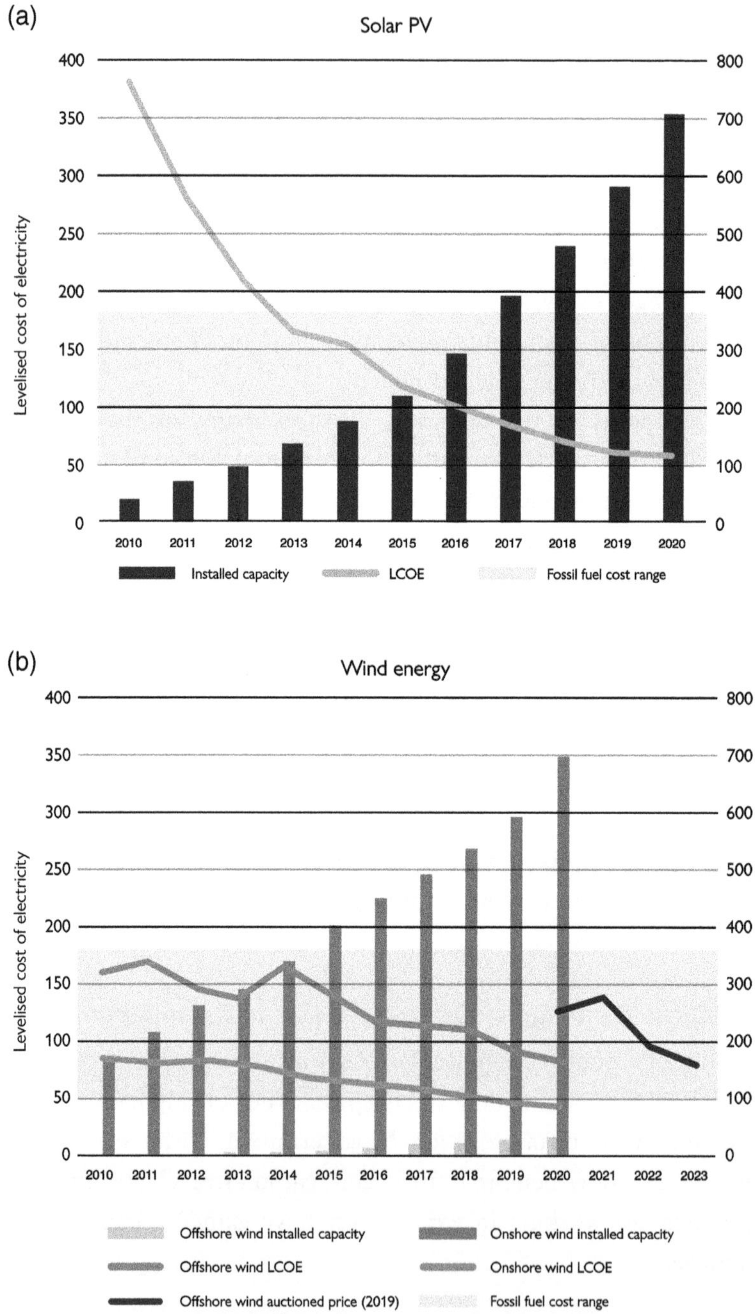

FIGURE 1.1 Diffusion and cost declines of renewables. (a) Solar PV; (b) Wind energy. Reproduced from Grubb et al. (2021a). Lines refer to the vertical axis to the left, while bars refer to the axis on the right.

If we had followed CBA (or any model based on it), none of this would have happened. And, if we want to, we still have the opportunity to plant trees in Indonesia, although planting trees cannot be made much cheaper and now looks expensive.

What went wrong here? The CBA was subject to the usual limitations, but the assumption that technology costs would not change by much was critical. In fact, the logic of the whole exercise was flawed. Offshore wind costs fell not just because time passed. It happened *because* the British government invested in it. The decision to go for it changed the CBA result!

This type of result is alien to most economists. They think in terms of the moral problem of allocating scarce resources between costly alternatives. In their world, as depicted in the models, everything involves trade-offs. If you want a better climate, you have to sacrifice something else. This story has been fed to governments all over the world. It is the reason that each year negotiators try to get other countries to reduce emissions while doing little themselves.

In reality, some choices create new resources, like really cheap wind-based electricity. And although predicting new technologies is impossible, trends in cost reductions can be estimated in advance.[16] We observed the same thing with cars, computers and many other products. For computers, this principle was famously called 'Moore's law', stating that the cost of computing power halves every eighteen months, but only if people keep wanting and buying better computers.

This is not the story our leaders hear though. To them, it is all about minimising sacrifice.

1.1.5 Why Delude Ourselves with Unrealistic Numbers?

The evidence against the resource allocation story created by economists is pretty strong. So, why do we still believe in this

[16] The literature on learning-by-doing for renewables is large, but see in particular Farmer and Lafond (2016); Way et al. (2022); Malhotra and Schmidt (2020).

problem of sacrifice? We have already noted how damaging it is to international negotiations. It is the same for domestic policy; it suggests we should only reduce climate change if the economic sacrifice can be limited.

And it is the same story in academia too. Many scholars criticised Nordhaus for his 'made up' estimates of the costs of climate change,[17] and also for his unrealistic costs of reducing emissions.[18] For all that criticism though, researchers kept using Nordhaus's model to publish more and more flawed papers. Scholars from a range of disciplines have discussed climate change as an ethical dilemma over how to allocate scarce economic resources, never considering if it could create resources.

The models continue to assume that we know absolutely everything: on future technology, on what will happen to the climate and on what that means for our economies. This is despite clear evidence otherwise. One sensible economist, Martin Weitzman, showed that the cost of climate change one should use in CBA is large or infinite and infinitely uncertain (e.g. the value of human extinction).[19] The climate scientist Tim Lenton demonstrated that the possible existence of 'tipping points' meant climate problems could unravel and get much worse very quickly if emissions are not rapidly reduced.[20] There are enormous risks with procrastinating because there is so much we do not yet know.

Do we have a deeper problem with our thinking? We seem to keep asking the wrong questions around climate change. The story

[17] For example, see Funtowicz and Ravetz (1994).

[18] For example, see Grubb et al. (1995), who discussed the idea that induced innovation should make costs change over time.

[19] See Weitzman (2009), who explains that the probability of future climate change damages is so 'heavy-tailed' that its average is infinity. Heavy-tailed probability distributions will be discussed later in this book, but in short, they are highly asymmetric distributions with a long tail on one side spanning very high values (in this case, for instance, the value of global GDP). In the case of climate change, it makes the expected damages (sum of probabilities times damages) equal very large and very uncertain numbers or infinity. Because of this, the 'knowability' of climate damages is limited, but it is just a reflection of a question that is ill-posed.

[20] Such as the Gulf Stream ocean current weakening or the Amazon forest dying off; see Lenton et al. (2008); Lenton et al. (2011).

of sacrifice predates modern economics and comes from the work of moral philosophers. Economists just added measures of money to it. And there is a certain moral appeal to the issue: we have damaged our planet and must now pay for it. Maybe we have come full circle back to moral philosophy.

Some people are asking for a new focus. Simon Sharpe is a highly respected climate policy expert who worked in the UK's Cabinet Office in the Glasgow climate conference unit. He says that the climate scientific community has always studied the wrong issues for policymakers. According to him, researchers have churned out endless scenarios and predictions with false precisions, while governments actually needed credible risk assessments.[21]

But perhaps we find doing this stuff is easier than addressing the real problem of identifying who will win and who will lose. Perhaps a model that tells us we must all atone for our carbon sins is more appealing than getting into the messy real world, full of social and economic divisions. Perhaps we are avoiding the more difficult problem.

1.2 IT'S THE TECHNOLOGY, STUPID!

1.2.1 The Quiet Progress We've Made Already

With all the doom and gloom about climate change, it is easy to forget that much progress has been made already. In fact, most of the technologies we need to meet net-zero targets already exist. They are getting cheaper all the time, because, despite the bad advice from economists, we invest in them.

And this has happened with only limited policy. While economists have kept calling for carbon prices, businesses have just got on with it. Solar power, wind power and LED light bulbs are now mainstream technologies. Batteries, EVs and heat pumps are heading in that direction.

[21] See Sharpe (2023).

Figure 1.1 shows the cost declines and rising investment in both solar and wind energy. Since 2010, the price of solar (photovoltaic, or PV) panels has declined spectacularly by a factor of almost 8, and by a staggering 99% since 1980. Wind energy, less costly to start with and declining less quickly but just as surely, has also reached the bottom of the fossil fuel range. Annual investment had meanwhile grown by a factor of 20 for solar and of 4 for wind. Wind and solar are now just about as cheap as coal and gas. Nothing so special about fossil fuels anymore.

But for more than twenty years, the standard economic models wrongly predicted that this trend would stop (Figure 1.2). You'd think learning would occur in models too, not just technologies!

The relationship between investment and costs exists because of the 'learning curve', as shown in Figure 1.3. These curves are measured over time, and they show a remarkable regularity. Every time the cumulative volume of technology production doubles, the cost goes down by a certain proportion, which is around 30% for solar power and 10% for wind power. Costs therefore typically decline rapidly in the early days of a technology because many doublings happen quickly, but of course the decline slows down over time as innovation and cost reductions become harder and harder to achieve.

In some ways, the story of EVs is even more dramatic. Tesla has grown from a niche player to a company that has been valued at over $1 trillion and at one point was worth as much as the traditional car companies added together. This value was despite the company not making many cars – in 2021 less than 1 million compared to the 5–10 million produced by other global firms. Investors understand the trends at play.

Figure 1.4 shows how the costs for EVs can be expected to fall if the technology continues along its learning curve, as solar and wind power have done for the last twenty years or more. Assuming people keep buying them, in most countries EVs will beat conventional vehicles on price early in the 2030s. EVs are already cheaper

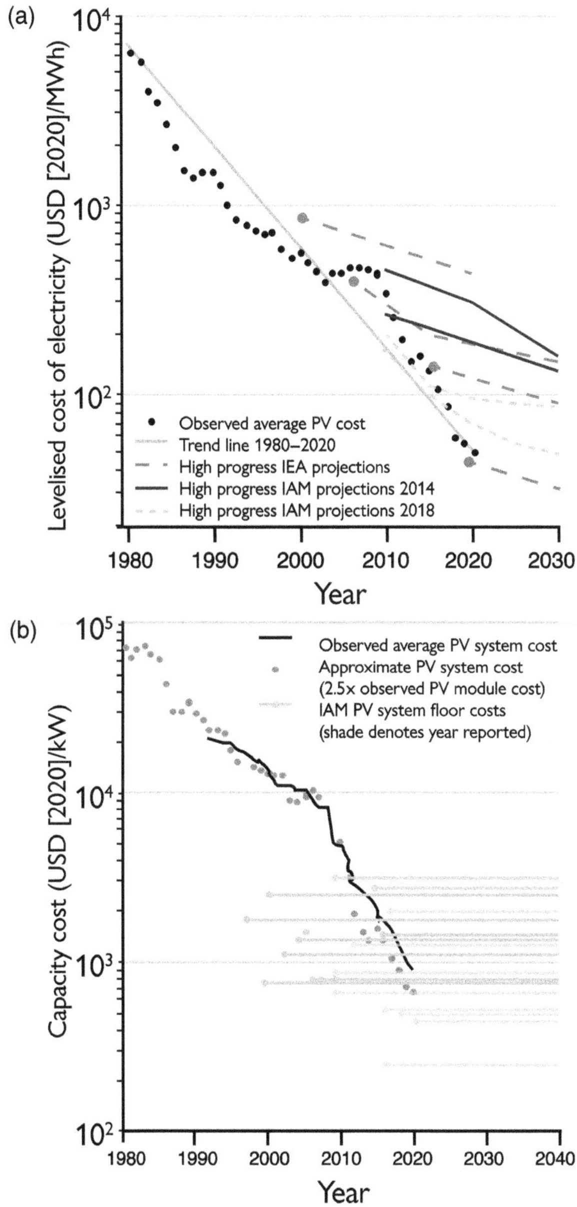

FIGURE 1.2 Cost reductions of solar energy superimposed with projections from the IEA (a) and IAMs (b). Model projections were consistently underestimating what happened. Reproduced from Grubb et al. (2021a).

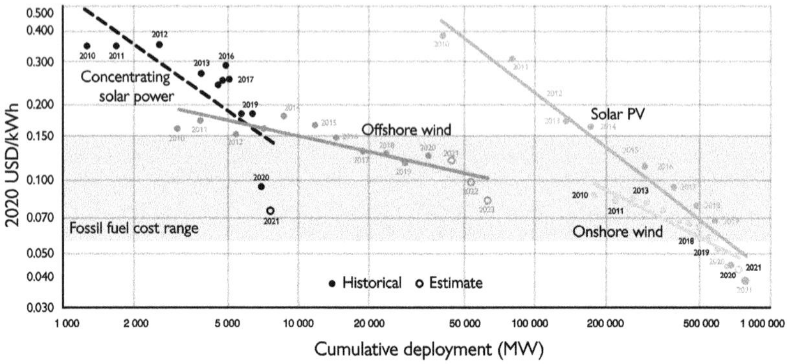

FIGURE 1.3 Learning curves for renewables. Reproduced from Grubb et al. (2021a).

in China.[22] In Brazil, however, unless import tariffs and taxes are changed, EVs may never become competitive, but this also means that transport will remain more costly than elsewhere, even if cars are powered by biofuels.

As more EVs are bought, costs decline further, so there is no reason to expect the trend to break, even without new subsidies. At some point, EVs will become the cheapest cars available to buy. Motorists could then benefit from both cheaper cars and lower running costs. We will all benefit from reduced climate change.

The story is similar for all the key technologies for emission reductions, including wind power, solar power, LED light bulbs and electric heat pumps. Compared to high-carbon equivalents, all these things are more expensive initially but have dramatically lower running costs.

1.2.2 *Getting Rid of Fuel Combustion*

As seen above, the costs of solar energy have come down to something below those for traditional coal- and gas-based electricity

[22] The comparison is challenging to make since it is ambiguous. Vehicle prices cover a distribution that has a standard deviation about as large as its median, which means that comparing like for like is not really possible: Which EV should we compare with which conventional vehicle? However, once every consumer becomes able to find a cheaper electric alternative to their standard vehicle of choice, it will be possible to say that EVs have become cheaper overall (Mercure et al. 2025b).

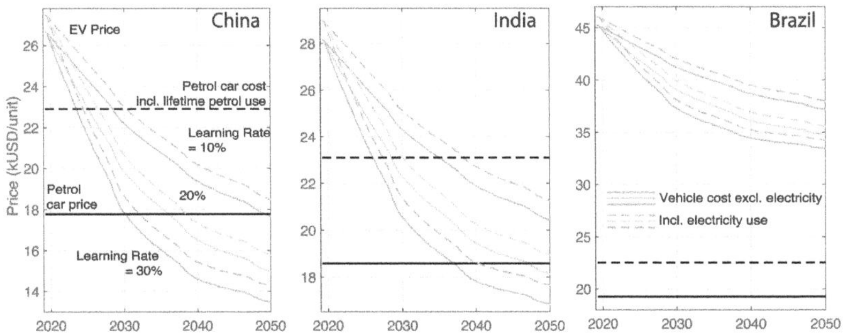

FIGURE 1.4 Rapidly declining projected ownership costs and prices of mid-range EVs against the stable costs of traditional vehicles in emerging economy markets, on the basis of historical trends of learning-by-doing, with variations applied to the learning rate used, assuming continued exponentially rising investment. Cost parity is likely to be reached in China and India within a decade.

generation. In many ways, this is understandable. Coal electricity requires a large boiler, a turbine and some cooling towers. People have known how to make these since the nineteenth century, and therefore, they are inexpensive, well made and difficult to improve further.

But coal electricity also requires a lot of mining, transport and milling of coal, all of which are very expensive, employing lots of people working in difficult conditions. Seen from a different angle, coal also supports the employment of many people. The costs of coal have not declined for over 100 years.[23]

In comparison, anyone can order from China a £200 solar panel, pay someone to install it and just wait for the sun to shine, nothing more to do. One coal power plant produces a lot of electricity, but that's just an illusion of scale, it also involves a lot of coal mining during the long lifetime of the power plant. It seems natural that solar electricity should one day beat coal, since mining coal does not get any cheaper. The same goes for wind power; once the windmill is up and running, it will give nearly free electricity for decades.

[23] See the data in Farmer and Lafond (2016); Lafond et al. (2018).

A very similar story explains the success of EVs. Conventional vehicles have a staggeringly bad energy efficiency (less than 25%) and, while they have improved over time, they do not improve quickly and do not get any cheaper.

Conventional vehicles waste most of the fuel they use, requiring a lot of it for what they do. That's a lot of drilling, pumping and refining oil. With EVs, we get rid of the combustion engine altogether, which makes them close to 90% efficient at converting energy into movement. Even if there is still combustion in generating the electricity, overall, the process is much more efficient than an internal combustion engine.

This makes replacing conventional vehicles by EVs, even when powered by coal electricity, a no-regret option for the climate in just about every case.[24] It also means much lower fuel costs because much less fuel is used, and petrol/diesel prices in most countries are generally high relative to electricity.

While running costs are drastically reduced when replacing coal plants with solar panels and conventional vehicles with EVs, eventually, the upfront costs will be lower too. Ultimately, a solar panel has much fewer components than a coal plant, per unit of capacity. The solar panel is just an infinite repetition of the same components over and over. An EV eliminates half of the components needed in a conventional vehicle and is therefore a lot simpler to make. No wonder they can become so cheap.

1.2.3 The Transition Raises Real Incomes

Once EVs reach ownership cost parity with conventional vehicles, the costs of mobility could begin to go down rapidly. It should be a no-regret option, a point of no return to combustion. Similarly, if solar powers electricity networks, electricity prices could in principle decline by a lot.

If solar powers EVs, there is no more wasteful combustion at all, which means no more heat loss, no drilling or mining and

[24] This was compared in great detail by Knobloch et al. (2020).

very little expenditures in anything other than making the solar panels and the EVs themselves. As these processes become increasingly standardised and automated, the cost of making all that keeps going down.

Lower electricity and transport costs will leave us all money to spend on other things. We will probably spend it on other things we want, which means the economy will grow as a result. This is what happens when innovation increases productivity: businesses initially cut production costs to sell at increased profit. However, if competition catches up, some of those profits can, in principle, become price reductions, in which case consumers benefit. In this book, we will explore this concept in detail, to try to understand what it means for the whole economy.

New ideas, especially profitable ones, are hard to contain. Companies follow what their competitors are doing because they cannot afford to be left behind. Take the example of IT and emails. It would be difficult to find a profitable company that does not use both of them and instead relies on staff with typewriters typing paper letters. These are things of the past. Most fossil fuel technologies soon will be as well.

When the transition starts, it is hard, perhaps impossible, to stop. It can also happen quickly; this is the reason for Tesla's high valuation. If we look at the current pace of diffusion of green technology, it would appear that the transition could happen much more quickly than decision-makers and analysts expect.[25]

For some technologies such as solar and wind, initial policies (e.g. subsidies) that were required to start the transition are no longer required. For other technologies such as green hydrogen and steel, we remain far from that. However, governments may also need to address new problems. There could be 'stranded assets' due to inadequate planning, including things like pipelines and tankers that never recover their investment cost. But, most importantly, people in the old industries will lose their jobs.

[25] See, for instance, Mercure et al. (2021a), Ives et al. (2021); Mercure et al. (2025b), where projections are made on the basis of existing trends.

This process is what the economist Joseph Schumpeter called 'creative destruction'.

The stories of EVs, solar power, wind power and all the rest are not that different. Products are simplified, efficiency improved and running costs vastly reduced. A virtuous circle is created of increased production and lower costs. The old technologies cannot compete and are phased out.

This is great for the environment. Indeed, it is probably the only way we will meet net-zero targets. It is great for motorists and users of electricity, for whom life gets cheaper. It is not so great, however, for workers in the coal and oil sectors or workers in large parts of the car industry. And while the transition could raise incomes, there is no guarantee that it will do so equitably. Some will win and some will lose, even if the average gains.

1.2.4 A Rapid Transition Causes Instability

So the transition to zero carbon could raise incomes, possibly equitably, but most likely inequitably. It will increase the profitability of some economic activities, while destroying it for others. It could make some of our investments worthless. In effect, it will create a complex entanglement of positives and negatives.

In this book, we make use of lots of knowledge from the sciences of complexity to make sense of this mess. Doing this is helpful, because we need a better method to analyse the problem than standard economics offers. Complexity economics[26] does not have any real political leaning; it mostly tries to make sense of complex problems, especially when everything changes really quickly and where the assumption of economic equilibrium really does not hold.

Complexity science will add a new layer to our understanding of the challenges in transitioning to zero-carbon. It will give us tools to study the stability of the economy. Why do we need this?

[26] See Arthur (2014); Mercure (2022).

The reason is simple. A rapid transition has lots of moving parts globally, and there is no real guarantee that all the parts cooperate. For example, reductions in oil demand could induce oil producers to grab larger shares of the declining market, and this could lead to conflict, unfair play (such as OPEC pushing other producers out) or boom–bust scenarios with great volatility. There are in fact very few incentives for oil producers to tolerate smooth decarbonisation.

Another example is with elections. Decarbonisation directly puts large numbers of people at risk of unemployment, which can fuel support for leaders who are against climate policy. We have seen some of this already.

And lastly, a rapid transition could cause an accumulation of toxic fossil fuel assets on the balance sheets of banks, pension funds and other financial institutions. A rapid devaluation could cause a 2008-style financial crisis. This could then paralyse the financial system with a credit crunch, which would stop decarbonisation in its track, at least for some time.

The tools of standard economics do not cover the stability of the social and economic system. They assume from the start that the system remains stable, by taking for granted that there exists an equilibrium in all situations. This is true, of course, except for all the times when it is not! Standard economic theory did not predict and still does not explain what happened with the financial system in 2008. It will not help us predict whether it could happen again and why.

After decades of moral philosophy and theory around climate change, we find ourselves with no way of assessing the risks that the upcoming transition could cause. However, as Simon Sharpe tells us, it is risks rather than hypothetical costs with false precision that matter to politicians, policy-makers and decision-makers in general. In this book, we plug this gap and develop a basic method to assess risks of financial, economic and political instability.

1.3 THE TRANSITION AND ECONOMIC GROWTH

1.3.1 What Does It Mean for Normal People?

The zero-carbon transition is necessary and probably now inevitable. But we don't yet know if it will happen fast enough to avoid dangerous climate change, and new climate policy-making could increase our chances.

We have so far been critical of economists, but there are some important questions we need their help on:

- How can we accelerate the transition?
- Can it be achieved without causing political, financial or economic instability?
- Who will be affected, both positively and negatively?
- How can the negative effects be reduced and instability avoided?

Section 1.2 hinted at some of the key issues. Tesla is not valued so highly because investors expect it to sell cheap cars. Investors instead think it will make large profits. At some point, however, other EV producers will push down prices. Even if Tesla keeps making large profits, there will be other cheap EVs for people that want them.

Many of these people would previously have spent a lot on conventional vehicles. What do they do with the money they've saved? And what happens to the people who made bits of conventional vehicles that we no longer require? And the people that did the drilling and the mining for fuel?

Although specific to the zero-carbon transition, these questions should be meat and drink to economists. We are simply describing the process of *economic growth*.

Surprisingly, many economists really struggle with these questions. Their models were simply not designed to answer them and instead *make assumptions* about the answers. Unfortunately, the assumptions are often not well chosen. For example, if you assume that companies cannot make large profits, why would they innovate in the first place?

In this book, we therefore explore the issue of economic growth during the transition in some depth. Although we consider GDP in our analysis, our focus is more on jobs and welfare, reflecting our experience of what matters to policy-makers.[27]

The first question is who benefits from the innovation. At least initially, companies may capture the benefits through higher profits. If competition catches up and prices are forced downward, households benefit too. Policy-makers need to ensure that happens.

The overall outcome for the economy depends on what happens next. Do companies use their profits for extra investment (usually they do not)? Do households spend their leftover cash (usually they do)?

We soon get to the fate of the workers who have lost their jobs. Can they instead work for companies that produce the new things that people want?

It gets complex very quickly, which is why we need help from economists. However, in general, the trend is towards economic growth *from innovation*, which maintains a steady employment level (with fluctuations). There is no reason why zero-carbon innovation should be any different.

So, what's holding us back?

1.3.2 The True Costs of Climate Policy

Change is difficult. Our economy has evolved towards being as efficient as possible in today's world. It is so near-perfect that it has become like a glass sculpture on the edge of a table with a cat staring at it. Changing the way we make things will disrupt that system, but it is already ready to come crashing down.

The economic system is defined by millions of companies that interact with each other and sell their products to households and

[27] Astonishingly, many of the current models used assume that people cannot be unemployed unless they want to be.

governments. Each product has a supply chain that collects all its various inputs at each stage of production.

These supply chains may be incredibly complex. Many of the things we buy include inputs from several different countries. Supply chains may also be brittle because attempts to minimise costs (e.g. in 'just-in-time' processes) mean there is little to no margin for error. The shortage of computer chips in 2021 that led to problems worldwide offers an example of this fragility. However, this is not just a feature of modern economies; supply chains have been more or less vulnerable since the first industrial revolution.

The shortage of computer chips in 2021 was caused by unexpected high demand in the recovery from the COVID-19 pandemic. The effects were widespread: for example, car production fell, and Apple reported slower iPhone production. There were also knock-on effects. For example, fewer new cars meant fewer new tyres, so demand for rubber fell.

With the diffusion of EVs, engines are not required anymore, nor are all the parts needed to make engines, but tyres will remain in use, and so will glass and steel. For coal plants, very few components will remain in use. Upstream, some parts will remain in production, others not, changes that crucially depend on the pace of success of green technologies downstream.

In turn, this generates an emergent political problem. German engine manufacturers will be left stranded. Contracts for building oil platforms in Northern Scotland will evaporate. Coal mining in India and China will peak and begin a painful decline. Drilling for oil worldwide will stop. In this book, we will call these occupations at risk in the old economy the 'sunset' industries.

The two key words in the previous paragraphs are 'complex' and 'unexpected'. When we make changes to our economy, surprising things can happen, sometimes referred to as 'unintended consequences'. Changing many things at once, as we need to do in the zero-carbon transition, will inevitably lead to mismatches between what we produce and what we need.

In addition, we must not forget that innovation will continue, since producers follow a moving target, and the pace of change is likely to be rapid. Businesses hate uncertainty, and they are going to get plenty of it. Job security will similarly fall in many sectors.

Workers in declining, 'sunset industries' will likely oppose the transition, public policy and a society that is leaving them behind. In the US and Europe, there are many examples of cases where deindustrialisation has destroyed local communities. The case of UK coal mines that we mentioned in Section 1.1 is particularly relevant for the zero-carbon transition. This means people may vote for leaders who propose to scrap the transition. But the transition is already moving fast, and even those leaders cannot stop it.

Unemployment, declining incomes and emergent poverty cause formerly prosperous communities to lose purpose, identity and respect. Areas of post-industrial decline in Europe have the most acute public health challenges and lowest life expectancy.[28] These areas are often the most opposed to climate policy,[29] which they may see as driving further decline.

There is no escaping that the zero-carbon transition means the end of several traditional manufacturing and extraction sectors. What is the plan for the workers in these sectors?

And then there is the question of the new jobs. Will they be in the same place and require the same skills as the jobs that were lost? Will new training be provided? Will senior staff in the old industries need to start again in junior positions? Or will they just take early retirement, stressing pension systems? These are critical questions to ask, but they are rarely heard in the debate. It is easy to understand why grievances and resistance towards climate policy may be rising.

Lastly, there is the financial value invested in fossil fuels and related equipment, which amounts to trillions of dollars, that could

[28] See Walsh et al. (2010).
[29] See Johnstone and Hielscher (2017).

be lost. Just like in 2007, when subprime mortgages became so toxic that they destabilised the entire global financial system, stranded fossil fuel assets could do the same all over again.

Designing effective climate policy and sorting all this out are one and the same problem. Contrary to the views of economists, climate policy is much, much more complex than just 'getting the prices right'. These things don't sort themselves out by magic.

In summary, a difficult political problem is brewing. In previous industrial revolutions, new political movements have grown. We now laugh at the Luddites who in the early nineteenth century smashed the textiles machinery that replaced their jobs.[30] The rise of fascism in Germany in the 1920s is not so funny. Allowing such grievances to grow unchecked is dangerous.[31]

Hence, the true cost of climate policy may be structural economic change and political instability, not simple sacrifice of GDP or transition 'costs'. Loss of income is one thing, but loss of livelihoods, purpose and meaning is another. We must learn from the ends of previous waves of innovation, which brought social, financial, economic and political instability.

1.4 WHAT NOW?

We, the authors of this book, are both economists who work with government officials and policy-makers. We believe that there is an urgent need to provide all decision-makers a better understanding of the climate challenge. Economics has an important role, but it must be grounded in the harsh reality of our messy political systems.

This book will unearth and substantiate several key facts about the upcoming zero-carbon transition:

(1) *The transition will happen anyway, but policy-makers can influence at what speed, whether it saves the climate and who wins and loses.*
(2) *Carbon pricing will not produce the zero-carbon innovation we need.*

[30] See Grübler (1998) and, most famously, Polanyi (1944).
[31] See Freeman and Louçã (2001). We will return to this in Chapter 4.

(3) *The transition will increase economy-wide productivity.*
(4) *The transition will transform our economic structures, creating and destroying entire industries.*
(5) *Large amounts of financial assets are at risk of devaluation.*
(6) *Many people risk finding that their skills are no longer required.*
(7) *We could end up with both labour shortages and unemployment.*
(8) *A disorderly transition could cause widespread global social, political, economic and financial instability.*
(9) *An orderly transition could be equitable and eliminate some conflicts but will require creating many guardrails.*

In Chapter 2, we explore the processes of knowledge production and innovation, showing how they 'build upon the shoulders of giants', that is, on the back of previous innovation. We find that the way our economies evolve depends on their previous development. We also find that our results are at odds with some of the key principles of standard economics.

Next, we review in Chapter 3 why useful resources are created in the economy, rather than allocated. Standard economic theory mostly ignores innovation, the source of resource creation. It is, therefore, not surprising that economic theory focuses on allocation problems. But when innovation is included, the resources to allocate grow as they are allocated, which changes the problem. Climate action indeed creates resources, and those resources are the sources of future growth. We also develop here our theory of economic resilience.

In Chapter 4, we look at economic history to see what happened in the past five industrial revolutions. We find lots of material relevant to the upcoming zero-carbon transition. Although there will be differences this time around, many of the risks and opportunities appear similar.

At this point, the book changes gear and introduces in Chapter 5 a new way to understand innovation and economic development. We use this theory to predict the rise and fall of industries, based on their activities and government intervention. This chapter is a core intellectual contribution of the book.

In Chapter 6, we consider the new 'sunrise' industries and the technologies that work together in driving the zero-carbon transition. This chapter is a story of how new, more productive technologies drive incumbents out of the market.

We then review in Chapter 7 the various ways that 'sunset' industrial sectors may decline and what this means for our economy, jobs and people. We assess what is really at risk: employment, incomes and social equality. We find that, naturally, the economies of countries that are exposed to high-carbon activities are most at risk and that this drives many of the distributional effects of the transition.

We then show in Chapter 8 that the transition will become the greatest societal transformation that this generation may see. We look at the changing nature of work and industry, the transformation of trade and investment and the deep rescaling of geopolitical power as oil, coal and gas stop generating the wealth they have done in the past.

In Chapter 9, we explore the true cost of the transition, which is that it risks causing widespread global economic, financial and political instability. We look at the risk of stranded assets and financial crises, the fragility of global supply chains and the risk of currency crises, all of which are drastically increased in the transition. We look at how 'pathways' proposed by economists have misled policy-makers for decades by ignoring these risks of instability.

Lastly, in Chapter 10, we conclude by proposing a policy strategy that embraces the zero-carbon transition but focuses on mitigating the risks of falling off-track or ending up with revolutions or financial crises. We shift the focus of climate policy from the notion that carbon markets solve everything to a paradigm in which policy for innovation and technological change underpin progress, but regulatory guardrails keep the transition on track. We highlight how the key risks that will arise can be managed by governments.

We acknowledge the level of our ambition in this book: to change completely the way we think about climate policy will not be an easy task. But what we present is the scientific view. It is based on history and on real-world data. It acknowledges the complexity of our natural and social systems – we know there are things that we will never fully understand.

We realise that we will probably upset a few people along the way. But the time for pleasantries has passed. We need to get on with the zero-carbon transition. We need to manage our way through it. That's what this book aims to help with.

2 Seeking Innovation, Not Optimality

2.1 INNOVATION IS THE BACKBONE OF GROWTH

2.1.1 Innovation Is the Economy

Decarbonisation is not entirely about innovation and technological change, but most of it is. We therefore dedicate a whole chapter to the topic.

It is widely accepted that innovation is critical in driving long-term economic growth. This popular narrative generally goes unquestioned. Governments are constantly looking for ways to spur innovation and increase the productivity and wealth of their citizens.[1]

The story is compelling. Inventors design new products, such as gadgets, technologies or software. Companies sell these new products and make profits. Managers find ways to improve efficiency, allowing the products to become cheaper. As productivity increases, the economy expands.

This economic growth lifts people out of poverty. Higher incomes trickle down to the poorest so everyone benefits. The process is continuous because it is human nature to tinker and experiment. Economic development is therefore continuous too.

[1] This idea became popular after Schumpeter (1934). Before then, economic growth was often explained by labour growth and capital accumulation. But the economy grows faster than either of these factors, and a paper by Solow (1957), which became iconic, suggested that 7/8th of growth was caused by 'productivity change' due to innovation. The effect measured was later shown to be an artefact of the capital accounting procedure by Shaikh (1974) and Felipe and McCombie (2014). Nevertheless, as this book discusses, innovation does accelerate growth. Although Solow's paper contributed early on to today's perception of the role of innovation and underpins the contemporary focus on labour productivity, it does not explain how innovation itself works, nor growth.

Is this story supported by the evidence? It almost is, but not quite. In reality, the standard proposition that innovation underpins economic growth is even more true than most people realise, including even economists, but for all the wrong reasons.[2] The study of economics could even be called innovation scholarship, but it is not. Innovation *is* the economy, but most economists do not see it. That's because they relegate it to one single unexplained parameter in their models, called 'total factor productivity'.

First, on some of the myths. Innovation is not generally driven by scientists in their garages. It does not automatically lift people out of poverty. It does not accelerate growth simply by increasing the productivity of all workers.

Furthermore, the development of ideas is not a stable and inoffensive process as the popular myth suggests. It is a story of revolutions, booms and busts. It includes financial crashes, inequality and painful transformation. Previous technological (or industrial) revolutions have created vast wealth for some but have left others behind. In each one, a *nouveau riche* class emerged, while the wealth of the previous elite stagnated or collapsed. The social impacts have each time been enormous.[3]

Nevertheless, as will be explained in this book, our current incomes and wealth accrue because of past innovation. If innovation somehow stopped, so would economic growth, eventually. Our incomes would then slowly decline, and the zero-carbon transition would slow down dramatically.

But innovation will not stop, because it really is in our nature to tinker and experiment. We therefore cannot stop all these things from happening. We can, however, learn how to manage the process better, for example, by looking at past industrial revolutions (more in Chapter 4).

We don't even need to look back too far. In 1947, a scientific revolution began when Bardeen, Brattain and Shockley invented

[2] A good narration of this popular myth is given by Mazzucato (2018).

[3] The classic narration of this is given by Polanyi (1944), and of course Schumpeter (1934); see Freeman and Louçã (2001).

the semiconductor transistor.[4] The transistor is like a water tap for electricity in a circuit. Engineers used it to develop logic operators and early computers.

Before semiconductors were invented, transistors used large glass lamps. These lamps generated large amounts of heat and took up a lot of space. The most advanced computer possible was a simple military device that filled an entire room with glass tubes.

It would clearly have been impossible to build a modern computer with millions of transistors from glass lamps. The semiconductor transistor changed all this. We now have computers that are both far more powerful and far smaller. Crucially, they are also much cheaper.

We now carry around computers in our phones. Cars and most household electrical devices contain computer chips based on semiconductor transistors.

This example shows how new innovation builds on previous innovation. Computers were built on logic operators, which themselves were built on clever arrangements of transistors. Software instructions were built on computers. Communication technologies including email were built on this software. Entire management systems were developed from the communication software.

It is now almost impossible to imagine what our lives would be like without the IT revolution. How would the COVID-19 pandemic have played out?

However, it is sometimes forgotten that many people were hurt along the way. The music industry has been severely 'disrupted' by online services. Shops on the High Street have lost out to online retail.

We used to have large rooms of typewriting staff that produced the messages people sent to each other. This entire profession has been wiped out.

There are knock-on impacts too, for example, on paper manufacturers. In fact, we would probably be unable to produce

[4] For which they got the Nobel prize in 1956.

enough paper to cover all our emails nowadays.[5] Without electronic communications, we would just have to communicate less.

In summary, we cannot separate the good and bad impacts of innovation. The process that allowed us to communicate more is the same one that forced all the typists out of their jobs. We cannot go back, and most of us would find it difficult to imagine what life would be like without modern inventions.

And the process goes on. Now the constraint on communications is not typewriting, but it is the time that people spend writing emails. 'Intelligent' software is being used to speed up communications. We don't even have to write emails ourselves. Further cost savings will be made.

In some ways, innovation is just the way that people get around problems that prevent them from doing more. These problems include climate change and also other things like population ageing. Economic history supports this argument. Either way, we cannot escape the fact that innovation is our economy.

2.1.2 *Innovation Is What People Do*

Let's return to the idea that innovating is part of human nature. Businesses innovate all the time – sometimes improving their products, but also finding ways to cut costs or improve their marketing. This is an everyday concern, from the smallest to the largest company.

For example, supermarkets invested in automated check-outs to reduce labour costs. This innovation led to lower prices and faster service for shoppers but at the expense of previous check-out staff. Once one supermarket introduced automated check-outs, the others followed so as to remain competitive. Automated check-outs are now standard in the industry.

[5] Since the economy is now so much larger than it was when typewriters and paper were still used, had we not transitioned to email, the volume of paper used now would be astronomical and clearly unsustainable. Innovation can solve some business sustainability issues.

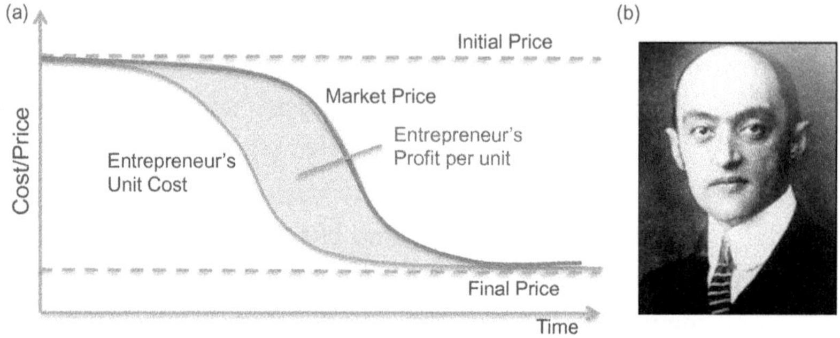

FIGURE 2.1 Schumpeter's entrepreneur and the origin of profit. Innovative activity decreases costs relative to competitors, generating (a) temporary monopoly power. However, competitors eventually catch up; therefore, profits (sales volume multiplied by the difference between costs and market price) are time-limited. (b) Photograph of Joseph Schumpeter.

Generating a continuous stream of cost-cutting innovation increases returns on investment. Investors expect growing returns and may even make speculative bets on expected innovation. Innovation is not a special unique rare event: it is so common and expected that it becomes priced into the value of assets.

Karl Marx wrote a lot about innovation, but the economist most associated with the topic is Joseph Schumpeter, notably in his 1911 book 'Theory of Economic Development' (1934 for the English translation).[6] Schumpeter is now best known for the term 'creative destruction', which is an important part of the story. However, there is much more to it than that.

The core of Schumpeter's idea (Figure 2.1), and the evolutionary economics school, is that innovation increases the 'purchasing power' of individuals over time. The story is powerfully simple, even if it glosses over many important things. It goes like this.

We imagine a simple steady-state economy. Companies produce all the goods, and households consume them, using the wages they receive from working for companies. There is a circular flow of money, and everything balances. Profits are zero.

[6] See Schumpeter (1934, 1939, 1942).

Then, an 'entrepreneur' appears. He/she is someone with an idea, usually for how to produce something more cheaply than it currently is. The entrepreneur persuades a bank to lend him/her money to implement the idea. If the idea is successful, the entrepreneur pays back the loan (plus interest) to the bank and keeps the remaining money as profit. If the idea fails, the entrepreneur goes bankrupt, and the bank loses its money.

But the entrepreneur's actions do not happen in a vacuum. To gain customers, they must offer lower prices than their competitors. They can do this because of their lower costs. However, competitors will at some point respond with their own ideas. The effect of all these ideas (or 'innovations') is to drive down prices.

Consumers benefit from the lower prices. They can buy the same products as before but still have some money left over to buy other things – this is what is meant by higher purchasing power. The entrepreneur may still profit if the reduction in costs exceeds the reduction in prices. Usually, this means they have reduced their costs more than their competitors. The competition to reduce costs by the most thus continues.

And what about the creative destruction? We have described the benefits of the creation of new ways of doing things. The destruction refers to what is replaced. Because someone's expenditure is always someone else's revenue, every time costs are reduced, someone somewhere will lose some of their income.

Sakichi Toyoda provides a great example of an entrepreneur.[7] Toyoda lived in nineteenth-century Japan and spent most of his life improving efficiency in the textiles industry. He first developed a wooden handloom, which enabled workers to use only one hand instead of two, and produced better textiles. This loom increased efficiency by 40–50%. Toyoda patented it in 1891.

[7] See Mass and Robertson (1996) for the entrepreneurial story of Toyoda. The son of Sakichi was also an entrepreneur and founded Toyota Corporation, the car manufacturer.

Toyoda did not stop there. He later introduced the continuously operating loom, improved spinning machines, the use of steam power, an automatic shuttle-changing mechanism and, most famously, the circular loom. Each new innovation increased the efficiency of textile production. In 45 years of work, overall efficiency increased by at least a factor of 10, and possibly a factor of 50.

If production becomes 50 times more efficient, prices could fall by 98%, with the producer still making a profit. Even today, a 98% fall in clothing prices would be a lot. But at the time, people spent a much larger share of their income on textiles, so the benefits would have been enormous.

The story of modern industrial competitiveness is of course more complicated. Globalisation has increased both the potential risks and rewards. Competition between companies in different countries depends on wage rates and other costs in these countries. It also depends on factors that are harder to measure like the availability of a skilled workforce.

Our purchasing power is also affected by other factors, including tax rates and the price of housing assets. It is difficult to separate all these effects, but the long-run effects of innovation cannot be denied. Everyday life constantly reminds most of us about our purchasing power. Just look at all the 'stuff' we accumulate in our houses.

2.1.3 *Innovation Is Driven by the Economy*

All economists agree that new technologies do not appear by magic. Beyond that, however, there is mostly disagreement. Many economists choose to ignore the topic altogether and lay responsibility to 'external forces'. Theoretically, this is indistinguishable from magic.

Schumpeter recognised that innovation is driven by the economy, specifically the desire for companies (his entrepreneurs) to make profits. To get finance, banks have to be convinced that there are profits to be made, and this is more likely when (a) there is an obvious market for the innovation and (b) wider economic conditions are favourable. Because higher bank lending itself boosts the economy (Chapter 5), we can already see an outline of the economic cycle, driven by innovation.

The role of banks destroys the myth that innovation arises from garages full of hermit scientists working for years inventing a machine to travel through time. Successful entrepreneurs like Elon Musk and Steve Jobs have had to demonstrate that people want their products. Otherwise, they would not have obtained the necessary finance for large-scale production.

The key point is that innovation happens when people in the economy ask for it. It does not happen when the economy is going wrong. Schumpeter famously suggested that innovation *clusters* in time, leading to business cycles.[8] His metaphor of 'gales' of creative destruction is appropriate: Lots of sharp bursts of wind, following longer periods of relative calm.

One of the reasons for the clustering of innovation is the way that innovations build on each other. A new idea provides the basis for other new ideas. The economic effects fuel this process. Lower prices boost product demand. More bank lending boosts product demand. More product demand leads to more innovation. We have a virtuous cycle.

It doesn't last forever of course. The ideas eventually dry up or turn out to be not as good as we thought. We suddenly realise we have created a lot of worthless things. The cycle goes into reverse, with even good ideas no longer receiving bank loans.

Eventually, new ideas are generated and confidence returns, and the cycle starts again. But there is no escaping the volatility and cyclical nature of the process. In Chapter 4, we tell the story of the past five great waves of innovation and in Chapter 6 we present the sixth one. We show the ups and downs that economies of those times went through. Innovation is never very gradual nor peaceful.

[8] That is, there are times when lots of innovation happens and times when there is very little; see Schumpeter (1939).

We are still missing an important part of the story. So far we have focused on *process innovation*, which may be described as producing the same things more efficiently. Process innovation results in higher profits for businesses and lower prices for consumers.

Economic growth happens when lower prices translate to higher demand. In nineteenth-century Japan, cheaper textiles would undoubtedly have led to higher demand. But it is unlikely that people bought 50 times as many items of clothing.

There were of course other things that people could spend their extra money on. At some point, however, they would have got their fill of these too. Contrary to economics 101, human wants are not infinite. We can only eat so much food and can only drive one car at a time. We only have 24 hours each day to fill with entertainment.

To answer the question of what happens next, we must turn to *product innovation*. Product innovation is the design of new products. Humans have evolved to crave novelty, and new products are perfect for absorbing any spare money that people might have. Crucially, new products also provide jobs for all the people who have been on the wrong end of efficiency gains.

Product innovation happens in the same way as process innovation. Businesses see opportunities and get bank loans to pursue these opportunities. Furthermore, the two types of innovation drive each other and therefore reinforce the cycle. We explain how it all fits together in Chapter 5.

2.2 EQUILIBRIUM IS AN ECONOMY WITHOUT GROWTH

2.2.1 *Standing on the Shoulders of Giants*

Science and innovation build upon themselves through a process that Schumpeter called 'novel combinations'. As the saying goes, we really are all 'standing on the shoulders of giants'. This is as true today as it has been throughout history.

Scientific papers make references to earlier scientific papers, and patents cite previous patents they build upon. In both cases, we can see what is called a 'small world' or 'scale-free' network.[9] In these networks, the most successful entries attract further attention. The same thing happens on Facebook, with the most popular people attracting more friends.

It is useful to think of humans as gradually creating a network of ideas. All new ideas will be added to this network. Naturally, new ideas will tend to attach to the more existing successful ideas. The network is constantly expanding.

Stuart Kauffman is an evolutionary biologist (and medical doctor) who has spent a lot of time considering the network of ideas. He describes the vast potential for new technologies that could be invented by combining the existing ones. He calls it the *adjacent possible.*

There are too many possible technologies in the adjacent possible for humans ever to fully explore them all. Past exploration led to life-changing inventions like cars, phones or television sets. Most of the possibilities, however, will be useless or will not work.

As our economy develops, inventors explore a very small subset of the adjacent possible. However, in choosing their focus, they also give up on a much larger subset of possible new technologies that they will never look at. Nobody will every know what could have been! And each time humans invent something, the adjacent possible becomes even bigger.

Digressing briefly, we could ask ourselves, if we were able to rewind the tape of history and try again, would the same story of science and innovation emerge? On the basis of the vastness of the adjacent possible, it seems unlikely. Even a small deviation early on could change the entire path of development.

Innovation decisions are made every second. Humans continuously explore the unknown. It is impossible to evaluate all possible innovation decisions and, without being able to predict the future, we cannot know which option is the best. For example, the

[9] See Katz (2016); Barabási and Bonabeau (2003); Barabási and Albert (1999).

COVID-19 pandemic placed a premium on innovations that led to teleworking.

We can illustrate this point with a simple calculation. There are over 10^7 (10 million) patents in the global register. All the possible innovations that combine just two existing patents with new ideas already make $(10^7 \times 10^7 - 10^7)/2 \simeq 5 \times 10^{13}$ (excluding combining patents with themselves and removing double-counting).

If we assume that there are (a hugely exaggerated) 1 billion (10^9) entrepreneurs in the world ready to patent new good ideas, each one would need to explore 10,000 new ideas to cover the whole adjacent possible.

It already looks impossible. Now, factor in that new technologies can cite any number of previous patents. The average number is 2–4, but some patents cite hundreds of others.[10] Our billion entrepreneurs now must search through between $10^{7\times2}$ and $10^{7\times4} = 10^{14}$ to 10^{21} possibilities. If they tried one every second, it would take them anything between three million and ten trillion years, longer than even the duration of human history!

This illustrates that exploring all possible inventions is hopeless, even without considering non-patented technologies.[11] But the key point is it gets much worse. Each time one of the entrepreneurs develops something new, more new combinations become available, so the numbers get even bigger. The size of the adjacent possible (the number of possible innovation directions) actually increases faster than we are able to explore it!

We must conclude that at any moment in time, there is a virtually unlimited number of future innovation and technology pathways and another unlimited number *being created*. Some of these pathways will have disruptive innovations that revolutionise certain

[10] The distribution is heavy-tailed with an exponent of −4; see Mercure (2022).

[11] Of course, entrepreneurs have better ways of sorting through the unknown than to try everything. But that doesn't change the fact that they will never be able to know the full range of what they are missing.

sectors. Others will not. We simply do not know what will happen or where we will decide to go next. All we know is that these pathways can generate more possible stories ahead of us than what they have left behind.

2.2.2 Back to the Future *and Its Contradictions*

Thinking of alternative pathways and storylines is reminiscent of film classics such as *Back to the Future* or *The Terminator*, in which characters travel through time to alter the past in order to change the present. The contradictions involved in *deterministic thinking*[12] become obvious in these films: even a small change in the past (e.g. preventing Marty's parents from meeting) should not merely have a small impact on the present (Marty not being born) while everything else remains the same.

It is not just a question of technology. Every event subsequent to the change in history should itself generate further changes of events upon which further changes of events would build. The result would be a radically different set of possible futures, including technologies we have not even heard of. These futures do not converge towards one single predictable outcome.

Therefore, in *Back to the Future*, when attempting to fix the past in order to remain alive in the future, Marty would have had to think through every possible future that his interference in the past could have put the system on. Not least, to see whether the time machine was still going to be invented by Doc. But that vast multitude of possibilities is certainly too much for anybody's mind to fathom. He should at that moment have had a brain meltdown as he gets lost in a maze of possible storylines as vast as the adjacent possible, never able to find the one that leads to where he wants to be.

It would be disingenuous to suggest that anyone could predict and sort through this vastness of futures. However, scenarios to 2050, or even to 2100, play an important role in climate policy-making.

[12] We will define here *deterministic thinking* as thinking that the future is predictable within known bounds or that the future is written somewhere waiting to happen.

Deterministic models play a key role in macroeconomic and financial analysis. There is a curious disconnect between the inventors, who sample a tiny section of the adjacent possible, and economists, who make future predictions.

Who could have predicted in 2018 that only two years later teleworking would become so widespread? The COVID-19 pandemic created a need for teleworking, which was filled by computer scientists and entrepreneurs. Once the pandemic ended, teleworking did not go away. Instead, it changed the global economy.

These trends influenced the financial values of Microsoft, Zoom and other companies and, more importantly, led to social and economic change. Once teleworking became possible and acceptable, people relocated and changed commuting habits. House prices duly adjusted, creating many further knock-on effects.

The truth is that the probabilities of positive returns on R&D investment cannot be quantified, because we don't know all the possibilities. We can make guesses about likely outcomes, but there is no limit on potential gains or losses.

Like for damages from climate change, calculating expected returns on innovation investment by multiplying outcomes and probabilities can generate any number or even an infinite value. This is because every possible scenario of the future must be included (plus all the scenarios that branch from those, and so on). Inevitably, some scenarios have extreme outcomes, such as financial crises.

The conclusion is that the return on investment in science and R&D is unquantifiable and that the risks and potential returns are generally high. The sensible approach for businesses is to spread these risks by using a venture capitalist approach.

2.2.3 *With Innovation, There Is No Optimality*

Economists and modellers are always looking for the 'optimal' outcome. This is also sometimes called the 'equilibrium' outcome and is described as the one that is better than all others. Logically, to find this best outcome, we must know with absolute certainty that nothing better exists. Can we do this?

Even with a narrow focus on today's technologies, it would be a stretch. But, as discussed above, when it comes to innovation, we only ever explore a very, very small subset of possible outcomes. We don't have all the time in the universe available to go any further.

We will therefore never know with any real confidence whether we could have done things differently to get a better outcome. We certainly cannot say whether current actions are optimal because we don't know what technologies will develop as a result. The multiple contradictions in *Back to the Future* tell us why the economy never finds its optimal equilibrium. It is the same reason that Marty should not be able to find his way back.

Many economists acknowledge the gaps in our knowledge. At least seven Nobel prizes have been awarded on the topic. However, standard theories and models (and especially the ones used in climate policy) still assume that we can accurately predict future events.

In these models, innovation is predictable (if it exists at all). People are also predictable, as are market prices. Companies can therefore produce exactly the right amount of goods to sell. Nothing goes to waste.

Although a world in which nothing is wasted seems surreal, it logically follows from the assumptions. After all, how can an outcome be optimal if things are being wasted?

This is not to say that nothing is predictable. For example, population growth can be predicted reasonably well. But there are many things that are just too difficult. Economists sometimes refer to these things as *market failures* because they prevent people from preparing properly for events. If these things went away, then we could return to a world where the economy is optimal as it fixes everything by itself.

Climate change is of course also seen as a market failure. No one seriously claims that it can be addressed by letting the economy carry on without intervention. And this points to the weakness with the idea of market failures. Market failures suggest that problems are clearly identifiable and easily fixable. Once we 'get the prices right', we can forget about the problem and let the economy go back to its pre-written optimal future.

Unsurprisingly, policy-makers generally like this framing. They can feel good about themselves in a world in which optimal policy can be identified. It makes them think they know everything. They can't do better than the optimal strategy recommended to them, and no one can blame them for not doing their very best. Problems get blamed on unpredictable external factors. When problems mount up, a lot of uncontrollable external factors have to be identified, to absolve blame.

Sadly, as we showed in Sections 2.2.1 and 2.2.2, none of it is true. The vastness of the adjacent possible makes identifying the optimal policy impossible. We can only get an optimal policy if we pretend the adjacent possible doesn't exist. That means ignoring innovation. It also means ignoring human behaviour, and not just our urge to innovate.

The truth is that an economy without innovation, and with a limited number of pathways forward, would not grow or develop. Incomes would stagnate, as a result of limited investment, profits, spending and productivity growth – all due to reduced expected returns on investment, due in turn to stunted innovation.

And this is not just abstract economics. Without healthcare innovation, life expectancy would gradually decline because of new diseases. In general, there would be little hope for life to improve.

The contradiction is impossible to miss. To get the 'optimal' outcome, we must forget about everything that to creates improvement of living standards. The optimal clearly is not so optimal after all.

Economists use the word 'equilibrium' to describe this state, which in reality is rather dismal. In many ways, the term is an appropriate metaphor. The equilibrium outcome is a steady state, one which does not change. This works well in a model, but such a state could only be achieved in the real world by stunting the human desire to improve our lives, the need of citizens for economic development, the want of consumers for novelty products and the creative spirit of people.

2.3 EQUILIBRIUM IDEAS HINDER CLIMATE POLICY-MAKING

2.3.1 Dangers in Equilibrium Thinking

Due to the contradictions embedded in the concept of equilibrium, it would appear that the perfect may be the enemy of the good when it comes to climate policy. Across all manners of government work, the concept of economic equilibrium is hindering sensible policy-making, of which innovation is an important part.

In equilibrium thinking, which has dominated climate policy-making for decades, it is recommended to use one (and only one) *pricing* policy instrument per market failure identified. The instrument will correct the problem, and we can let the market do the rest of the work. First, that's not what happens in practice, and second, this is a bad idea.

As we know from the economic historian Karl Polanyi[13], law-makers deliberately created economic markets for capital and labour during the first industrial revolution in the eighteenth century. Advocates of these 'free' markets at the time included the godfather of economics Adam Smith and the philosopher Jeremy Bentham. Both saw free markets as a way of sharing the wealth created by innovation.

The markets kept going wrong though. They couldn't find a stable equilibrium. There were periods of mass unemployment between other periods of frantic production. The poorest people in society

[13] Polanyi worked across economic history, political science and anthropology, In 'The Great Transformation', Polanyi tells the story of the creation of capitalism in seventeenth- and eighteenth-century England, exploring not only the thought of the great moral philosophers of the time but also what happened in practice in law, policy and economic development. The striking feature in Polanyi is the tension between seeking free markets to empower the industrial revolution and the havoc that free markets wrought upon the common people.

were stuck in poverty and did not gain any of the wealth. In fact, their plight may have gotten worse.

The stage was set for the revolutionary economist Karl Marx, who famously claimed that the market-based, capitalist system would collapse. The system has not collapsed, and this may partly be due to insights from another well-known economist, John Maynard Keynes, who established that rules were needed to save capitalism from its own instability.

In the modern economy, governments shape markets constantly for exactly this reason. Examples of rules that are used include competition and anti-trust laws, the minimum wage, unemployment relief, safety regulation and environmental law. Governments also provide the basic rules for markets to operate, for example, the need to honour contracts, maximum weekly working hours and financial regulation. In addition, governments can create markets where they do not naturally exist, like green hydrogen or energy storage.

Governments can also shape innovation by doing their own research. Typically, public research is carried out in areas that do not yet interest businesses but may do so in the future. These areas include new products that are useful but not yet profitable (e.g. certain medicines) and basic research that might one day in the distant future lead to profitable products.

Of particular interest here is how the government sets the direction of innovation and determines which bits of the adjacent possible are explored. There are some historical examples. One is Winston Churchill's decision to convert the British naval fleet from coal to oil, which kick-started the shift to internal combustion engines.[14]

As we discuss further in Chapter 4, this decision is the reason we now have plastics, cars, trucks, tarmac roads and aeroplanes. These are products that defined the twentieth century. However, at the time, Churchill could not have guessed where the adjacent

[14] See Dahl (2001).

possible would take us. His decision probably looked expensive to many people.

Governments can also invest in things that are too big for companies and other institutions, simply because they have the largest balance sheets and can stomach large losses. Governments may be the ultimate venture capitalists, because they already pool innovation risk, while still delivering social returns and spreading their investments.

Governments intervene in innovation all the time through funding universities and research institutions, supporting private sector innovation or forming partnerships with companies. In all cases, the government pushes us out into the adjacent possible, opening up new possibilities that could attract private funding. The state is the ultimate entrepreneur, who ensures that we avoid the dreaded steady state of economic equilibrium.[15]

Instead of aspiring to achieve optimality, what we should want is to continuously push the economy away from equilibrium using innovation, while using regulation to keep markets from going wrong.

It is clear that the concept of economic equilibrium contradicts government's desire to support economic development. Although some economists still talk of *laissez faire* economics (the notion that markets work better when left alone), we have centuries of evidence that this is not a good idea, including the 2008 financial crisis.

More importantly for this book, government withdrawal would deprive the economy of its ultimate entrepreneur. Eventually, innovation would dry up, and our economies would stop developing. No one, least of all economists, wants that. And, of course, if we want to direct our innovation towards addressing climate change, government action is required.[16]

[15] See Mazzucato (2013).
[16] See Mazzucato (2013) and Grubb et al. (2021a).

2.3.2 *Transition in Equilibrium: A Contradiction*

The zero-carbon transition is by definition an innovation problem. As Churchill's goal was to make the entire British naval fleet more powerful, we must now find ways to eliminate greenhouse gas emissions from every current source.

At this point, people usually ask why we need to talk about innovation when we already have solar panels, wind turbines and electric vehicles to address climate change. It is true that we need very few genuinely new technologies.

However, innovation is not just about new technologies. It is also about bringing down the costs of the ones we have, so that they become 'the new normal'. It is a circular relationship; once these products become cheap enough for people to buy, more companies see profit opportunities and join the innovation effort. More of the adjacent possible is explored.[17]

As discussed in Chapter 1, these effects are often missed from economists' predictions about the impacts of climate policy. It isn't really a question about prediction any more though. We can already see the costs of green technologies falling and becoming cheaper than the current alternatives. The story of brown being cheaper than green is becoming less and less true.

Even in a policy context that does not understand innovation, this is a game changer. The least-cost solution that economists always look for has just become something else, something greener. The costs of decarbonisation have just disappeared. And they have disappeared because we have worked hard to make them disappear. This is not surprising.

If the transition is going to accelerate innovation and break cost-parity with fossil fuels, it will probably accelerate economic growth. As we discuss in detail later, it first requires

[17] For example, during Second World War, a very successful US innovation and mass procurement policy allowed rapid scale-up of a wide range of new technologies at rapidly declining costs, driven by demand. See Lafond et al. (2020).

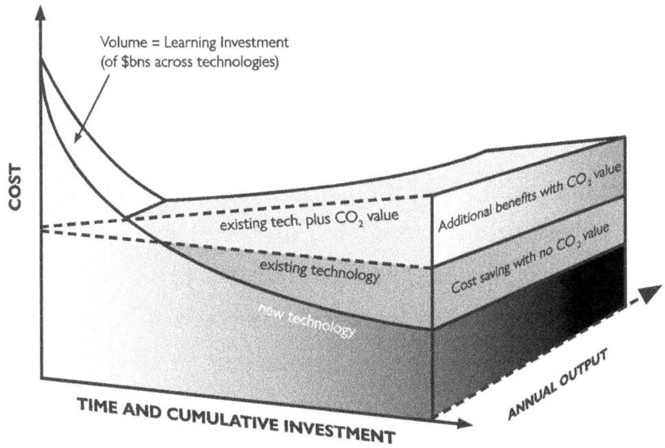

FIGURE 2.2 Costs and returns on investment in innovation. The vertical axis is the cost of investing in an innovation programme. The curved solid black line is the unit cost of a technology, which goes down with expanding roll-out following a learning curve. Cost parity with an incumbent technology (e.g. where solar PV beats coal-fired electricity) is where the solid curved line crosses the straight dashed line. Figure adapted from Grubb et al. (2021); all credits to Michael Grubb.

substantial upfront investment in innovation, R&D, construction and manufacturing, which will employ lots of people in the short to medium run. Second, in the medium to long run, this will reduce the costs of key energy services, leaving unspent income with households. If households spend this money on other things across the economy, it will lead to further economic growth.[18]

Figure 2.2 shows how it works. It illustrates the cost of a green technology, in relation to cumulative production (how much of it has been produced, ever) and time. As more of the green technology is produced, companies find cheaper ways to make it and its costs fall.

Costs are typically high at first, but with investment and production, often supported with public subsidies, they can fall below those of the corresponding fossil-fuel brown technology. The total cost of the investment programme necessary to bring costs down to parity is the volume of the upper left pointy wedge. But costs keep

[18] See Mercure et al. (2025).

going down thereafter: the return on innovation investment is the wedge between the solid and dotted lines.

In the figure, the block's volume is much larger than that of the pointy wedge. This represents either long-term profits or lower costs for the consumer (or a mix of both). Additional co-benefits, such as reduced air pollution and related diseases, are shown as the top wedge, generating additional non-monetary returns.

This illustration reflects what has often occurred. Solar and offshore wind power were both expensive at small production scale but are now cheaper than coal at large production scale. Soon, if not already, the savings compared to coal, with the large volume, will exceed the initial investment needed to bring costs down.

The story seems too good to be true. Innovation drives down the costs of our green technologies. Productivity increases, profits are made and incomes increase. So, why hasn't it happened already? Because this isn't the whole story. The innovation part is all fine. The problem is our capitalist system. As Polanyi warns us, this is not the story we've been told.

Entrepreneurs and businesses innovate to make profit. Successful ones drive innovation and make big returns. They may become fantastically wealthy. Most people will benefit, but we cannot forget about those that don't. We cannot forget about the typists losing their jobs.

In his book *The Affluent State*, the American institutional economist JK Galbraith asked the question why we always focus on the measure of national income, GDP. He concluded that it is important to monitor GDP because without growing GDP, we get increasing unemployment. However, GDP growth is not a goal in its own right and isn't of much help if it just increases inequality.

Our focus on GDP has got it all wrong. Higher GDP is great for people in jobs. It's even greater for people who get new jobs because of the transition. The twenty-first century typists will not be cheering though. We thus come to the real problem and why it hasn't all happened already: the transition will generate deep inequalities and cause social and economic instability. And the losers could include some very wealthy and powerful people.

The final problem with the equilibrium economic theory is that it leads us to think that a sufficiently high carbon price signal should move us from a high-carbon to a zero-carbon equilibrium. It changes the direction of investment, and that's all we need to do. However, as Nick Stern suggests, climate change involves more market failures than we can count.[19] Because the economy is never in equilibrium, pricing is far from enough to change direction.

The danger in following the equilibrium way of thinking is that we might blindly impose a carbon price and hope for the best. Then, one day, we will realise that we've wasted a lot of valuable time making the economy slightly more carbon-efficient. We might end up spending all our political capital managing the social and economic effects of high energy prices without seeing the deep degree of economic and technological transformation that we need.

As we describe in Chapters 6 and 10, it wasn't carbon prices that kick-started the diffusion of solar and wind power, EVs, etc. Other policies like targeted subsidies were much more effective. The carbon price has been useful in other ways, such as putting an end to coal-fired electricity in the UK, because there were already other technologies available.

The transition is as far from equilibrium as we are ever likely to be. Things will change in all parts of the economy, as we adapt current systems towards green alternatives, as we innovate to bring down energy and other production costs, as we phase out fossil fuel industries that used to be highly profitable and as we create new markets and change the rules of the game.

It is one thing to make polluters pay, but another to set in motion the innovation train that we need to meet our climate targets. We need an approach for climate policy that fundamentally

[19] Stern et al. (2022).

understands that the economy is not in equilibrium and that supports innovation processes in driving decarbonisation.

2.3.3 *De-growth Is Not an Out-of-Jail Card*

In this chapter, we have presented economic equilibrium as something best avoided, even if we could get there, as it would hinder growth and economic development. However, greenhouse gas emissions grow along with economic growth, the cause of the climate problem. How could more economic growth be part of the solution?

Many people think not, and interest in 'de-growth', or 'post-growth' has grown in recent years. Limiting population or economic growth has long been suggested as a way to cure social or environmental problems.[20] More recent studies have pointed the finger to 'capitalism' or 'consumerism' as pushing on environmental limits.[21] The arguments are morally sound; therefore, it is important to discuss them.

The de-growth movement is a broad church that promotes environmental sustainability, reducing inequality and rebuilding communities. These are worthy goals, but the question of this book is whether de-growth would make it easier to solve the climate problem or make it harder.

The general view in de-growth studies is that more economic production means more resource use and more environmental damage. It would naturally make it harder to solve environmental problems if we allow growth to continue without improving resource efficiency. We can only reduce environmental damage by producing and consuming less. Morally, this is what we must do. There is no free lunch.[22]

[20] Going back of course to Malthus (1872) and Meadows et al. (1972), but a more recent influential and accessible book is by Tim Jackson (2009), 'Prosperity without Growth'.

[21] Recent reviews include Cosme et al. (2017); Polewsky et al. (2024). Planetary boundaries' quantification is attributed to Rockström et al. (2009).

[22] See Jackson (2009).

Everyone will have their own opinion on consumerism and how we should live our lives. We generally try to avoid value judgements in this book but do agree that the economy must respect environmental limits. Our main critique of de-growth studies is that they do not explain how economic growth takes place to start with and hence cannot explain what the impact would be of de-growing the economy. It is actually quite difficult to really understand what a world without economic growth would look like. And crucially, we cannot even be sure this world would have less environmental damage. Here, we interpret de-growth as making the total production (or income) of a country peak and decline.[23]

Like us, de-growthers are critical of many aspects of mainstream economics. They can and should escape the restrictions of standard economic theory. Like these scholars, we do not see growth as a goal in itself, especially when it is rarely equitable. So far, however, the focus has been on sharing a pot of fixed resources, which is not much different to the mainstream. Innovation is usually ignored or appears in a confused way. And so is the banking sector and what drives credit creation for investment.

Because of this, we reach different conclusions. De-growth relies on three key assumptions. First, that we could reduce economic growth if we tried. Second, that this is the only way to stop using more and more natural resources. Third, that investment would remain in line with income in a de-growing economy.

We have already laid out in this chapter that stopping innovation seems impossible, and stopping innovation leading to growth also seems impossible (see Chapter 5). And, at least for climate change, the evidence suggests that we can reduce our environmental impact while growing the economy (see Chapter 1).

This makes de-growth a distraction from the real problem of managing the zero-carbon transition. But there is a more important

[23] Some of the de-growth literature focuses on reducing the natural resource use, and the need for this is self-evident; we do not discuss it here.

issue, which is that de-growth may actually slow the transition. Here is why.

To get to net-zero emissions, we must replace or adapt all our equipment that uses fossil fuels. This includes factories, trucks, power plants and much more. As we described above, much of it could be replaced already with zero-carbon alternatives, in some cases even cost-effectively. However, in nearly all cases, there are large *upfront investment costs*.

Upfront costs mean upfront revenues for construction firms and others that provide new equipment. And most of the investment will be financed by debt.[24] Reducing emissions requires to invest more in total than we would have otherwise. The investment implies more construction and manufacturing than would otherwise happen, which means more wages to be spent in the economy. This makes the economy grow, whether we like it or not.

This makes it difficult to invest and de-grow at the same time. But on the flipside, we also have to ask why businesses invest in the first place. If they see declining demand and few profitable opportunities, they cannot justify investing in new equipment and may not succeed in obtaining finance to do so.[25] It may be better just to run down existing equipment.

So, in a de-growth scenario, we would emit less greenhouse gas emissions because we produce less. However, without the ability to invest in zero-carbon technologies, it would be impossible to get to *zero* emissions, unless we de-grow to zero! We could end up stuck in a high-carbon de-growth trap with ageing polluting equipment.

Something like this happened in the former Soviet Union countries post-1989. The economies were left with a legacy of highly energy-inefficient, ageing and uncompetitive industrial equipment,

[24] See Pollitt and Mercure (2017); Mercure et al. (2019). For example, buying an EV instead of a diesel car replaces future diesel costs with a higher initial purchase price. When the bank advances the loan it creates purchasing power that boosts production demand; it similarly subtracts from production demand when the loan is repaid.

[25] See Van den Bergh (2011); Pollin (2019).

some of which can still be seen today.[26] This stemmed from a lack of incentive and capacity to invest in modernising over the economic transition period.

Some de-growthers argue that the solution is to overthrow capitalism altogether. What would replace capitalism, and, critically, how investment decisions would be made, is not yet clear.[27] The important point is that we will need all the resources we can get to build all the new zero-carbon stuff. Limiting our ability to produce things through de-growth will not help.

How did our de-growth colleagues arrive at the opposite conclusions from ours? Until the literature lays out a theory of economic growth, it is difficult to say. We say more on this in Chapter 5, in which we provide a compelling theory of growth. One plausible explanation is that the de-growth theories omit the fact that people need time to pay back the loans on their equipment and that real investors make allowance for this when investing (standard economics also omits this). De-growth theory supposes that investment works the same way in a growing or de-growing economy.

The problem is, we are talking about railroads, aeroplanes, steel mills, coal power plants, diesel trucks and so on. Buying or building them requires upfront investment and the money to pay for it is generated over up to 40 years.[28] With de-growth, we would end up with too many of them. No one would want to pay for even more (even if green), and some existing ones might even be scrapped. When scrapped, their value falls to zero and cannot be used for anything, including redistributing to reduce inequality.[29]

[26] See Grubb et al. (2014).

[27] Even in centrally planned economies, investment remains largely justified by profitability sector by sector, whether via decisions of financial institutions or through political debates within the administration in charge. Lack of progress in economic development leads to public resentment of administrations, whether democratic or not.

[28] See Chester et al. (2024a).

[29] As eloquently put by Schumpeter (1947).

The error in our view is this: in standard economic models, investment is usually assumed to be a fixed share of GDP, based on how much people save out of their income. In those models, under a de-growth scenario, investment would therefore de-grow just like production, but otherwise continue.

The real world does not work like that: with excessive productive capacity, investment in new productive capacity becomes *zero*, because no new factories are needed.[30] This means no more construction, whether green or brown. It might also come along with a financial crisis, if productive capital devalues wholesale.

The low-carbon transition will inevitably involve some assets becoming 'stranded' and scrapped. But maintaining overall industry profitability enables companies to transition to new efficient and zero-carbon production. The transition needs economic growth to work quickly enough. But this need not lead to more emissions, if the new productive structures emit zero carbon.

Our argument is specific to climate change, where renewable energy offers solutions with zero impact. But it also applies to other planetary boundaries, whenever reducing impact requires to investing in new clean capital. The argument may not apply, however, if the solution does not involve investment and construction to eliminate the extraction and consumption of other natural resources, such as when we change the way we use them. Further integration of degrowth and innovation research could in those cases be very useful for wider society.

That goes beyond the scope of this book, however, which focuses on climate change. We now turn our attention to the critical issue of climate economics.

[30] In standard economic theory, physical capital (factories, vehicles) is considered the same as financial capital (money in an account, or debt). Since, in standard economics, there is no time involved in creating productive structures, and since capital is allocated and re-allocated between economic activities each year, reducing production only means accumulating unused capital in one big bank account. Economists will then assume that this big bank account can be re-distributed between everyone to reduce inequality.

3 Economic Resources Are Created, Not Allocated

3.1 COULD WE IDENTIFY OPTIMAL GROWTH IF WE SAW IT?

3.1.1 Evidence on Full Employment

Chapter 2 described how an undue focus, and perhaps obsession, with finding optimal outcomes occupied economists' minds. As a result, the economists neglected the key question of innovation, as a driver of both economic development and transition. In this chapter, we show that seeking optimal outcomes is not good economics either: it's a road to disaster. It's time to dispel another popular myth.

We noted in Chapter 2 that economists often say the best way to run an economy is to leave it alone. People in the economy know what they want, better than the government does. Business owners know best how to run their businesses. Everyone does what is best for themselves because ... well, why would they not? They are rational after all.

The theory says that this approach also happens to produce what is best for society. Greed really is good!

This sounds a bit 1980s, and it's no coincidence that the economists' theories come from that period.[1] Free markets, as advocated by Thatcher in the UK and Reagan in the US, are still seen by most economists as essential to making things work. Prices in these free markets adjust so that limited supplies are made available to those who need them most.

[1] In reality, debates for and against free markets date at least back to the first industrial revolution in eighteenth-century Britain. Polanyi (1944) traces the origin and the evolution of the desire for free markets, notably for labour. It has come and gone at different times.

The same logic applies to workers. There is no unemployment in this system because prices (here wage rates) adjust automatically so that everyone gets a job. Unemployment only happens either if someone doesn't want a job or if someone interferes with the free markets. Examples of such interference include setting a minimum wage, restricting hiring/firing or allowing unions to influence wage rates.

It goes without saying that all factories are also run at full capacity. Otherwise, the outcome would not be optimal.

Special attention is paid to the limited supply of money. Each person makes a choice between using their money to buy things now or saving money to buy things later. The money that is saved is important, because it can be used to fund companies' borrowing to invest in capacity for future production.

Again, the market determines which companies get the money, this time through adjusting the interest rate. Only the companies with the best prospects get the chance to invest. The outcome is not just optimal for now but also for the future, according to our relative preference for consumption between now and later.

The point about how money is allocated for investment is important, because most of the ways of addressing climate change need lots of investment. The theory says, if we invest in green stuff, we need to invest less in the optimal stuff. By definition, we have just damaged our economy. As the economists tell us, we would be better off not interfering. The cost of interfering is the cost of addressing climate change.

This line of thinking underpins much of mainstream economics. True, many economists now take a much more nuanced approach. But surprisingly, little of the nuances find their way into the economic analysis of climate policy given to policy-makers.

More surprising still, and hugely problematic, is that there is little evidence to support the economists' story. In fact, much of the evidence contradicts it.

Let's start with the idea that everything is at full capacity. Remember, to be optimal, all available capacity must be used. Any unused capacity is expensive and, therefore, sub-optimal. But we have actual data showing that capacity is not fully used. Every country has unemployed workers. Statistical agencies in the US and the EU publish data showing that factories typically operate at around 80% of capacity. These figures are reported by the companies themselves!

But most importantly, there is no evidence that any economy has managed to operate 'optimally' at full capacity because there was no interference from public policy.

Would we even want an economy that's at full capacity? As we explore in Section 3.2, probably not. It would come at the expense of resilience. Our safety would probably be compromised. With the whole economy operating on a knife edge, prices would be high and volatile. Even tiny problems could become amplified into disasters.

The idea that business owners are not acting rationally by keeping spare capacity is silly. Chapter 2 explained why. Because of innovation, it is impossible for anyone to predict the future. Running at full capacity requires everyone to know perfectly the future and for only one pre-written future to exist. There are many uncertainties that business owners could in theory try to understand but in practice don't bother with. Keeping some spare capacity in reserve is much easier and cheaper. It is a prudent safety measure. It's a rule of thumb. It reduces the risk of not being able to cope with demand.

If all companies keep spare capacity, then the aggregate economy obviously does too. If production needs to increase, then it can do, within the limits of that spare capacity.

The same thing is true with money and the financial sector. In fact, the supply of money is technically not limited (Chapter 9), but, even if it was, banks would face the same uncertainty as other companies and keep some capacity back. If they operated by maximising the leverage of their borrowers, they would be at constant risk of insolvency!

Investment in green equipment, therefore, need not replace investment in other things. Again, there is plenty of evidence around. Banks charge different rates of interest to different people because risks differ between projects. The 2008 financial crisis and all previous financial bubbles show that it is not difficult to drift far from reasonable investment paths. Excessive borrowing happened at the expense of system resilience.

In summary, the economists' story is at best only half true. They warn that for climate change mitigation, green investment will displace investment in other critical parts of the economy, imposing on us a spending dilemma. In reality, there need not be at all a trade-off between green and brown investment. There is, however, an important trade-off between economic performance and economic stability, which we explore in the second half of this chapter.

It may all sound a bit abstract, and academic economics often is. But these issues are real. We have barely started the zero-carbon transition, but there is no evidence that action so far has slowed down economic growth. There is, however, already talk of a 'green bubble'. Volatile energy prices have been linked to investor uncertainty.

This chapter debunks the current story about the costs of climate policy. It then explores the trade-off between economic performance and stability. We write a new story about the economics of the transition. Our story is not one in which the outcome is a slightly lower global GDP with distributional dilemmas between rich and poor countries. It is one in which incomes may increase overall but with periods of rapid growth balanced by deeper recessions.

If the green transition accelerates in an uncontrolled way, it could destabilise the economy. Parts of the economy could grow too fast while creating inequality and risks of financial crash. But we need a rapid green transition, and in fact, because it will make big money, it's already pretty much unstoppable.

We find that the trade-off between growth and stability becomes more stark with a faster transition. The faster we go, the less time our economic and financial systems have to adapt and the more unstable everything becomes. And that's a problem, because we need to transition as fast as we can.

3.1.2 How People Invest and Why

We start our story with investment. An investment is something that has a cost today but will give a return in the future. Banks advertise investment products, and some people invest in the stock market to generate future income.

Economists mean something different when they talk about investment. They mean building new things like factories, cars or computer software (rather than changing ownership of something that exists already). It is this sort of investment we need to address climate change – unfortunately shuffling money between bank accounts will do little to help us.

Investments in new things embody the innovation described in Chapter 2. What we can build depends on both what we know (previous innovation) and what we have to build with (previous investments). Our previous investments don't last forever, and the economy's overall portfolio of investments is in a constant state of renewal.

Building new things is good for the economy. It adds to GDP. It creates jobs in manufacturing and construction. But investment does more still: it allows us to produce more in the future, so long as there is demand. People will have jobs building a factory, but others will later work in the factory too. Put this way, it is difficult to see how more investment can be a bad thing. Yet, when it comes to climate policy, investment is usually called a 'cost' in the story told by economists.

Whatever the definition of investment, there are limits to how much we can have. Investment only happens when a good payback can reasonably be expected. The word 'expected' is crucial here – in the same way that no one invests in a stock market they think will go down, a company will only build a new factory if it thinks it can sell the new production profitably. No one builds a factory that makes things we know for sure nobody will want.

But in truth, no one really understands how people come to decide what is expected. Our view of the future depends on what we see now, what the media tell us, what our friends think and many other things. As we have already discussed, no one can accurately predict the future, so the investor is always taking a risk.

Investors may use payback times to determine whether investments are worthwhile. The payback time is the length of time they think it should take to get their money back and start making a profit. The shorter the payback time, the better the investment. If the payback time is longer than the lifetime of the stuff being built, there is no point investing. But most investors will draw the line long before that.

Of course, when the investment decision is made, the payback time is a guess. The investor only finds out the real truth much later. There may be a long period before the investor gets their initial money back (if ever); while indebted, they may not be able to invest in anything else, if nobody will lend any more to them. In this way, high debt levels can slow investment and economic growth.

Here, we begin to see how zero-carbon investment could be called a 'cost'. Much of the equipment needed has a lifetime of thirty years or more. In the meantime, higher debt levels could reduce investment and growth in other things. But what is a 'high' level of debt? The catch is, it depends on context.

How serious is this concern? The speed of investment may be limited by other things, such as the amount of stuff that people can buy. The number of skilled workers (e.g. builders or carpenters) is also important – more skilled workers making zero-carbon stuff may mean fewer workers making other things.

The simple answer is it depends on where we start. If debt levels are low and there are skilled workers currently without jobs, then zero-carbon investment does not get in the way of other things.

As illustrated in the previous section, the story told by economists is based on the extreme opposite case. They suggest we are starting from a point where everything and everyone are already maxed out – because according to them the economy is always maxed out. There is no spare capacity to add anything, without taking something else out.

It doesn't seem to matter that there are no data to back up this idea. It must be true, otherwise it would not be optimal.

As bad as things may seem for the story told by economists, it's going to get worse when we look in more detail at the financial sector. But first, there's the important question of what happens if wrong investments are made.

3.1.3 *When Investments Go Bad*

Although constraints on the total amount of investment may slow long-term economic growth, policy-makers worry much more about sudden shocks like recessions or financial crises. Such shocks can occur if investments fail to generate an income. An obvious case is if the investment is destroyed, for example, due to war or natural disasters. Unfortunately, climate change may make both possibilities more likely, as the Bank of England told us in 2015.[2]

More commonly, an investor may just make a bad judgement. If no one wants the product they plan to make, or someone else starts making something similar but better (or cheaper), the investment can become obsolete, or 'stranded'.

Either way, there are losses that someone must bear. In some cases, it may be insurance companies. The investor will also be hit. Anyone that gave money to the investor will lose out too. These people may be unlikely to back the investor again.

None of this is specific to climate change. It is simply how a normal capitalist economy works. Innovation drives new investment and makes some old investments obsolete. If we speed up innovation, as we must to address climate change, we make it more difficult for investors to predict which investments will work. More mistakes will be made. More investments will go bad.

Imagine a company that built a coal-powered factory 40 years ago. The owners expected the factory to last 50–60 years, but climate policy will force it to close now. The factory has become a 'stranded

[2] See Bank of England (2015). On that topic, see also Bolton et al. (2020).

asset', and some of the owner's wealth has been wiped out. Is it right that the company should bear the losses? In some cases, maybe. In other cases, there may be a moral argument to help companies build new, cleaner factories and power plants. Moreover, their losses could be other people's losses too.[3]

While there may not be much sympathy for wealthy company owners, we must remember that we invest in people as well as factories. The time we spend in school and training is also an investment. These investments are also at risk in a technological transition, as we saw with the typists in Chapter 2.[4]

This story is thus all about risks, with no one wanting to be the one stuck with losses. Specifically relating to climate change, the Bank of England classified those risks in three classes: physical, liability and transition risks.

Physical risk is what everyone gets if no one does anything about climate change: more things will get destroyed by storms, floods and heatwaves. Liability risk arises if someone doesn't do their bit to address climate change: someone else that suffers damage from physical risks may try to make them pay for their losses in court.

In this book, we are more interested in transition risks, which arise when we do try to transition to zero carbon. This is the story of the investor trying to navigate changing technologies, policy rules and social attitudes, making what turns out to be the wrong investment.

Take EVs as an example. Every EV bought means that one less car's lifetime supply of petrol or diesel will be needed. Vehicles use over half of all oil produced. Predicting oil demand, therefore, requires predicting EV sales. If you are investing in an oilfield or a pipeline (lifetime 20+ years), you will have a problem if no one wants the oil in 10 years' time. But you might only find out when it's too

[3] That is, shareholders and creditors. See Battiston et al. (2017) and Semieniuk et al. (2022).

[4] See Chester et al. (2024b).

late. We will still need some oil, even if not that much, over the next 15–20 years. It's just hard to tell how much, whose oil will sell and whose will not.

The opposite problem is if the risk puts off too many investors. Here, we can end up with shortages, as we saw in oil and gas markets during the post-Covid recovery period.

The history of oil markets has shown times of both excess and tight supplies. As we said before, this is how a capitalist economy works, even in markets like oil where politics is involved. It is not peculiar to the zero-carbon transition, but, by increasing risk, the zero-carbon transition will make it worse.

Some people will be left with huge losses. Others will make a lot of money. It's going to be some ride, and the financial sector will be right in the middle of it.

3.1.4 The Financial Sector

Sometimes it seems like no one knows what the financial sector is doing in all of this. Campaigners often target banks, for example, for financing fossil fuel companies. Divestment campaigns and 'climate finance' initiatives focus on the role of the sector in developing the economy.

However, the models that economists use don't even include the financial sector. The economists simply don't see the sector as important enough to bother about.

Who is right? To answer this question, we must take a step back and look at how banks and the wider financial sector make our economy work.

Again, we must separate the 'investment' in existing (paper) assets that banks finance and the investment to build new things. Most objections that people hold against the financial sector (including the causes of the 2008 financial crisis) are about the investmentsin paper assets. However, for avoiding dangerous climate change (and also for economic growth), our story is focused on building new things.

It is just about possible that we could do the transition without help from the financial sector. Governments could lead the way. Companies could use their current profits to pay for new equipment. Households could reduce other spending to cover new costs.

The problem is it would just take way too long to save money in order to build everything we need to save the climate. It is much quicker to build new things using the money that is *'expected to be made'* in the future with the new investments, rather than from any money already made. And to be clear, this is how the economy normally works.

Of course, using our own savings also wouldn't work for the new green companies that don't yet have any profits. It would, therefore, be difficult for our economy to develop, and we would be a bit stuck.

So, we need banks and the financial system to help out. They provide money for investment now and get paid back later once profits have been made. This enables the economy to grow quickly and, we hope, reduce emissions quickly. This means a lot of borrowing and lending will need to happen.

In providing money upfront, the financial system is also taking on much of the risk that the investments might fail. For large investments (e.g. a new factory), the risk may be too great even for a bank. We come to the main function of the financial sector, which is pooling and managing risk.

Investment funds and banks can spread the risks across many people or companies. For example, if the cost of 100 investments is spread across 100 people, the failure of one investment has only a minor impact on each person. It's like insurance because, in theory, the risks are reduced for everyone. However, the 2008 financial crisis reminds us that we should not take this for granted.

To summarise, financial companies take savings from ordinary people, usually paying some interest in return. They use this as a cash base to underwrite the creation of new loans to entrepreneurs (investors) at a higher rate of interest. The entrepreneurs use the money to build new equipment and use this new equipment to make things that people want to buy. Financial companies expect those entrepreneurs to pay back their debts over time, to be able to give money back to depositors if demanded or to lend more money to more entrepreneurs.

From what we have described, there are still limits on how much investment can be made. For example, a pension fund can only provide the savings that are held in the fund. That's because they manage other people's money. If, for some reason, everyone kept their savings under the mattress instead of in the pension fund, there would be no new investment. But for banks, the story is quite different.

Is it? The popular wisdom is that the money lent by banks is just other people's savings. There is no free lunch, and money invested in one thing means that something else is not funded.

The popular wisdom is wrong! While it is correct that banks use people's savings for day-to-day liquidity, the money they lend out does not come from this pool of savings.

If you apply for a $100,000 mortgage, you do not need to wait for someone to deposit $100,000 at the same bank. Instead, if your application is successful, the bank gives you two things: $100,000 and an account with –$100,000 in it. For now at least, your net balance hasn't changed. The bank, however, has a new asset, which is your promise to repay $100,000, and remember, the same $100,000 of cash is still in the bank! When the $100,000 goes to the house seller, it might even come back to the same bank again. If not, other house sellers at the bank will receive similar amounts of money.

Where does the $100,000 come from? Well, obviously, both +$100,000 and –$100,000 are *created* by the bank when the mortgage is advanced. The bank puts them both in your account, the positive balance of which you give to the house seller. As you pay back the mortgage over the years, the money is gradually returned to the bank and the debt is gradually *destroyed*. Interest payments, however, are counted separately as bank profits.

If you fail to repay your mortgage, there could be problems for your bank. It needs your monthly payments to pay back its own debts or create new loans. Its asset (your mortgage) has just become worthless. If too many people fail to pay their mortgages all at the same time, your bank will go bust. However, normally, all the deposits are underwritten by the central bank.

The key point is that the limit on bank lending is not at all the deposits that banks have to begin with but how much risk they feel able to take from their lending. If all the banks lend a lot, there will be lots of money going around, but also very high risks that some of it is not paid back, like in 2008.

Why does this matter? Compare it to the story that economists tell us, based on their models. They say that banks lend other people's savings. They behave optimally, so lend everything they can. More lending for investment in zero-carbon equipment, therefore, *must* mean either less lending and investment in all the other things we want or people saving more, which means less consumption.

The story is completely wrong. Since there is no fixed limit on the amount of lending, and since borrowers don't wait for savers to deposit money before getting their loan, the 'crowding out' mechanism economists talk about doesn't actually exist. In fact, more investment in zero-carbon stuff is more likely to lead to more investment in other things too.

The whole story of climate policy having costs has been built on the back of these model results that misunderstand how banks really work, backed by no evidence at all. We're in front of the greatest challenge ever facing mankind, and we've delayed doing anything about it because of some false assumptions economists make so that they can solve their computer models. Let that sink in.

We must be clear, however, that there is not an unlimited stream of finance. Too many risky loans would put banks at risk, as we saw in 2008. But what do we define as 'risky'? How much is too much? As we showed in Chapter 2, no one can predict the future. Bank regulators have tried to set guidelines, but (again, as we saw in 2008) even professional risk rating agencies have difficulties assessing the real systemic risk. Nobody really knows.

There is some good news on zero-carbon investment. Banks can also spread risk across different parts of the economy. Although a huge amount of investment is needed in the zero-carbon transition, the amounts are not so large when compared to the size of the whole economy.

We must also recognise that without risk there would be no returns. If we could predict the future perfectly, it would be impossible to make worthwhile money by investing. Risk shouldn't be viewed as universally bad.

However, when things do go wrong, it can be spectacular. If a company is bankrupt and cannot pay its debts, other companies it owes money to lose out. These companies may go bankrupt too, starting a domino effect. As we saw in 2008, the whole process is super-charged when the financial sector is involved. No one knows the full level of risk at any one time.

What's clear is that governing the transition must involve some degree of financial sector management and regulation, to avoid the increased systemic risks that come with higher levels of lending.

In summary, we need the financial sector to be part of the solution to the climate problem. We need to avoid the financial sector becoming part of the problem. Unfortunately, the faster we try to force the transition to happen, the greater the risk of financial collapse. This is the subject of Section 3.2.

3.2 OPTIMAL ECONOMIC PERFORMANCE IS UNSTABLE

3.2.1 Performance–Stability Trade-off

There is always a trade-off between performance and stability. Academics have written about this trade-off[5], but we can also see it

[5] This has been established mathematically some time ago by Doyle and Carlson (2000) and Carlson and Doyle (2002), but the mathematics are difficult. In economics, more accessible papers are by Haldane and May (2011); Hynes et al. (2022). We review some

around us quite easily, as shown in this section. The trade-off is a key concept in this book.

The problem is what's called 'cascading failures'. These failures are the same as the domino effect that we described with company bankruptcies causing problems to other companies. In fact, this is one of the most important examples: companies can increase performance and growth by borrowing and investing more, but there is a higher chance of a domino effect if things go wrong.

It's the same idea at the economy level. The more debts there are, the more chance of economic crisis when something goes wrong. We need some debt so that we can have investment and innovation. But too much debt and things could unravel.

A simpler example to illustrate the performance–stability trade-off is the rail network. An optimal rail network is one that matches the demand for travel with as little resources as possible. It will have many trains running as close together as possible on as few tracks as feasible. A computer can work out how best to fit the different routes between stations together. It can also set times so that people making connections wait the least amount of time. Journey times are minimised for everyone.

When everything goes well, this is perfect. There are lots of trains, and people get from A to B as quickly as possible. The problem is when something goes wrong.

As any commuter knows, there are many reasons something could go wrong. Some are mechanical or electrical, some have to do with drivers not turning up and others relate to external factors such as sheep crossing the line. Some, like a passenger needing medical treatment, cannot be avoided. These events will cause delays that lead to missed connections or other trains waiting. Problems cause more problems, which cause more problems. This is a case of 'cascading failures'.

literature on this concept in Appendix A. See also Mercure et al. (2021b); Mercure (2022).

Commuters often hear something like 'train in front delayed'. Already we have a cascading failure. Things rapidly get worse; for example, fast trains may get stuck behind slow ones. Some trains must be held up to let others through. Before long, the whole network is affected, and the entire timetable becomes disrupted for the entire day.

It may get worse for the commuter. Quick connections become missed connections, and journey times become much longer rather than shorter. The risk of accident increases as train schedules are revised on the fly.

Having more capacity, for example, having more trains that are less full, and more tracks that can be used, releases those pressures greatly. It can make the difference between minor problem and disaster. But maintaining higher capacity is costly.

The more we try to tune the rail network to perfect timing at the lowest cost, the more spectacular the cascading failures become. There is a thin line between a highly optimised system and chaos. Sensible train operators of course understand this and build some leeway into their system (commuters may say not enough), for example, by allowing a few extra minutes for each journey or back up systems to correct for mechanical failure or human error.

All of this leeway comes at a cost and is by definition 'sub-optimal', because 'optimal', in the economists' sense, is in reality the point of zero resilience. Theoretical performance falls when adding leeway, but reliability is drastically improved since larger shocks can be dealt with before we get to chaos. The trade-off between performance and stability (or resilience) is clearly observable with rail networks.

There is a method in complexity science to study this. Figure 3.1 shows the real-life example of the delays in the London underground network over five years (Jan. 2020 until Feb. 2025). The x-axis on the figure is the duration of delays, and the y-axis shows how many times a delay that big occurred. Without compounding cascading failures, the frequency and magnitude of problems should

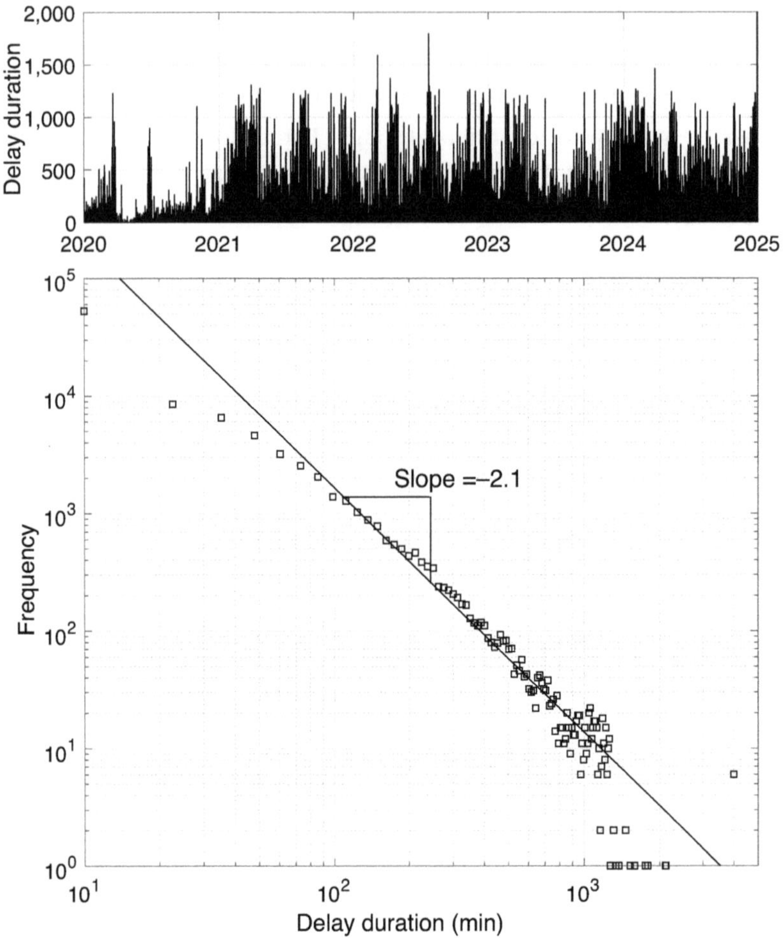

FIGURE 3.1 Frequency–duration diagram of delays in minutes on the London Tube between Jan 2020 and Feb. 2025 (available online from Transport for London, Freedom of information requests). The frequency distribution is 'heavy-tailed' (in fact 'scale-free'; see Chapter 9 and Mercure (2022) for details). Long delays are less frequent than short delays, but very long delays are much more frequent than they should be, because relatively small events can cascade into long delays. Delays are typically capped to 24 h.

show a narrow inverted U shape (the 'normal distribution'[6]), the maximum of which would show roughly the average delay. Large

[6] For those not well versed in probability theory, the bell-shaped 'normal' distribution is the observed probability distribution for the magnitude of random events or measurements when they are not connected with one another. For example, human height

problems would be extremely rare, and small problems would be the norm.

Figure 3.1 shows that reality is not like that. Cascading failures do arise all the time, and we see in the figure that disastrous delays arise much more frequently than any theory without cascading delays could predict. This lifts up the 'tail' of the distribution, the end of the curve on the right: long delays are more frequent. Complexity theory predicts that when there are cascading failures, the figure should show a straight line on the graph with log–log axes: it's a heavy tail.[7] This is precisely what we observe in the figure.

As we will explain in Chapter 9 (with mathematical detail in Appendix A), the slope of the line tells us something about how stable the tube system is. The slope measures the relative weight of probability between small and large delays. A slope close to –2 indicates an unstable network with disastrous delays. Above –2 and closer to –1, the system is in total self-destruction. A slope near –3 or below means the system is relatively stable, with disasters happening at acceptable frequencies.

Here, we measure a slope close to –2.[8] This indicates two things. First, that there is a lot of uncertainty and we cannot predict the duration of the next delay. Second, that the potential for large delays is real. This means that there is no 'average' delay, and delays of any duration can happen on any day.[9]

and weight are 'normally' distributed, and this indicates that someone growing to a certain size is not tied to someone else's growth. When events are connected to one another, the distribution deviates from the standard normal distribution. Scientists and economists tend to assume normal distributions for many things out of habit, but its validity can often be questioned.

[7] See Appendix A, as well as Bak (1996) and Mercure (2022).

[8] The various tube lines have heavy tails of between –1.4 and –2.1.

[9] For those interested in the technical reason why, calculating the standard deviation of such a power law involves taking the sum of the product of this probability (or frequency) function of delays, times the square of the duration of delays. It's easy to show mathematically that when the slope in the graph comes close to –3 (or past –3 towards –2), this becomes infinity. Measuring the average delay requires the sum of the product of this probability times the delay duration itself and gives infinity between –2 and –1. See Appendix A.

This is tricky, but see the data for this example. The average delay over these five years was 67 min, with an uncertainty of 137 min. This already looks odd, because the range of uncertainty (defined as the 'standard deviation') is greater than the average delay. This should ring alarm bells, because negative delays are not possible. Second, the longest of the 47,733 recorded delays was 6,562 min (four-and-a-half days, a rare case where the recorded delay was allowed to exceed a whole day). Long delays are not rare. There were 2,666 delays of more than 60 min during each year, about 7 per day, somewhere or other on the network. If you run into a delay, the 50/50 chance is 26 min, but 10% of delays last longer than 164 min, and 5% last longer than 271 min, or four-and-a-half hours.

Although quite long, this dataset is not long enough to measure the standard deviation properly. But because of the heavy tail, if we wait longer, and include more data, the standard deviation (the range of uncertainty) will slowly creep towards larger and larger values. The reason is that very large delays will start to appear, pushing the value up.

Because of this, it's more reliable to measure the 'tail heaviness' (the slope of the curve in Figure 3.1). The sad conclusion is that, if we use the London underground, we simply cannot know how long it will take to get to our destination.

Now, imagine having to catch a flight at Heathrow airport from, say, Cambridge, with a journey that takes about 2 hours, one of which is on creaking British railways and the other on the unpredictable Piccadilly tube line.[10] What optimal time allowance should one make not to miss the flight? The expected value from our data for the Piccadilly line says one could lose around 62 min per delay, and there are 3.5 delays per day (we would think, roughly a 1 hour delay with one in six chance). Leaving 4 hours ahead, we should get to Heathrow, with 1 hour left even if there is a delay, with virtual certainty.

Except that 10% of delays are longer than 2.3 hours (one in sixty chance), and 5% are longer than 2.7 hours (1 in 120 chance).

[10] Supposing that the Elizabeth line is unavailable, as we don't have data on that one.

The data is so skewed that we only have a 19 in 20 chance of catching the flight with a 4 hour allowance, and a 49 in 50 chance with a 5 hour allowance. The truth is there is no optimal answer to the question, it's all about our tolerance of risk. Because the uncertainty is so big, we just don't know how long it will take.

Performance on the London underground is relatively unstable, but it is still able to run. Its problems are that much of the network is very old, demand to use it is very high, it runs near full capacity all the time, and therefore things often go wrong.

The system could be improved to reduce chaos. Increasing resilience, for example, by increasing the numbers of spare trains or drivers available, could rotate the line in Figure 3.1 clockwise, so that long delays are much less frequent (say maybe a slope of –3 instead).

This would require train operators to invest and increase capacity in the system, which has costs. But if we let the current system continue without more investment, the situation could get worse. Older and older trains will run more often and be more crowded. There will be more frequent breakdowns and too few drivers. We can expect spectacular delays.

There are plenty of examples of performance–stability or performance–resilience trade-offs. Racing cars have high-performance engines designed to maximise acceleration under very specific conditions but with a high failure rate. Ships have engines that are inefficient but ultra-reliable on a range of different fuels and conditions.

Economic supply chains face the same issue. Disruptions from COVID-19 and (in the UK) Brexit led to shortages of household goods that depended on 'just-in-time' supply chains. The shortage of computer chips in the COVID-19 recovery was caused by factories operating at capacity leading to price instability.

And our energy systems are no different either. Wild swings in oil prices (including a negative price during COVID-19) show a system with limited flexibility in the face of wildly changing demand and supply. As oil demand becomes harder to predict during the transition, we can expect more volatility. We explore this more in Chapter 9.

There are actually very few quantities in economics that are not heavy-tailed like the London underground network. Rather than the exception, heavy-tailed probabilities are the norm, and the appropriate response is all about risk tolerance.

We return to this in Chapter 9. But suffice to say that, whereas economists spend most of their time solving optimisation problems and assuming normal distributions, the real world is rarely like that. Usually, these problems do not even have solutions, because the uncertainties are much larger than the economists are willing to admit.

We really need to change this way of thinking.

3.2.2 *A New Economic Principle of Stability*

The trade-off between performance and stability is a defining feature of our economy. Running everything at full capacity leaves no space for dealing with the unexpected. It is the opposite of optimal, and it is an unsustainable way to run an economy. No economy ever operates at full capacity. Most countries try to set interest rates so as to keep some economic capacity available, aiming at a certain level of unemployment to limit inflation. Most of us do understand the performance–stability trade-off, but we won't admit it.

Since the economy grows, some investments must be made just to keep up and avoid running into full capacity. For example, if road and rail networks do not expand as demand grows, we can expect them to suffer an ever-growing number of delays and other problems.

For factories, a lack of spare capacity leads to unstable prices when product demand increases and consumers start to bid up prices for what is available. In financial networks, crises occur if uncontrolled lending leads to high debt levels that are not justified by the investment returns. This is commonly called a bubble, which leads to a crash.

Thus, it is clear that any story that says the economy operates optimally at full capacity is untenable and more like a myth. It would be great if it were true, but at full capacity, there is no space to accommodate anything unexpected. Complex systems cannot operate at their capacity limit, largely because the future cannot be predicted with any certainty. Because we don't know the future, we keep spare capacity to prepare for the unexpected. How much spare capacity we maintain determines the stability of our economy.

And, as we have noted throughout this chapter, governments and business owners do not aim to use 100% of available capacity. Consciously or not, they recognise the trade-off between performance and stability. They recognise the uncertainty they have to deal with every day.

Capacity use must lie within a reasonable range, maybe somewhere above 50% and below 95%, to make a reasonable business case. Economic data suggests it generally lies near 80%. The lower the capacity use rate is, the less profitable the industry is. The higher the capacity use rate is, the more risky the business becomes. Full capacity is often difficult to define clearly, because it is tangled up with issues of efficiency of resource use. But the trade-offs businesses face are the same as those for the whole economy.

This is all super important for climate policy. The story that climate policy automatically leads to economic costs is not true. It depends on everyone optimising everything, which only happens in models. If we have spare capacity, then we can realise economic benefits by using it.

Given the need for zero-carbon investment that can draw on this spare capacity, economic benefits may be quite likely. However, these benefits could come at the expense of economic resilience, if demand is pushed towards capacity limits. There are still trade-offs but not the ones we have been led to believe.

We illustrate this in Figure 3.2.[11] The figure has three 'regimes' that determine how strained the economy is. In the regime in which the economic system has plenty of capacity, the system is stable, and

[11] The concept the of 'edge of chaos', illustrated in this figure, has been developed by the Danish physicist Per Bak (Bak et al., 1987; Bak, 1996). This theory originally applied to natural science systems such as piles of sand collapsing, traffic jams, earthquakes and neural networks. He also applied the concept to the evolution of species (Bak and Sneppen, 1993) and economic networks (Bak et al., 1993). See Mercure (2022) for more information.

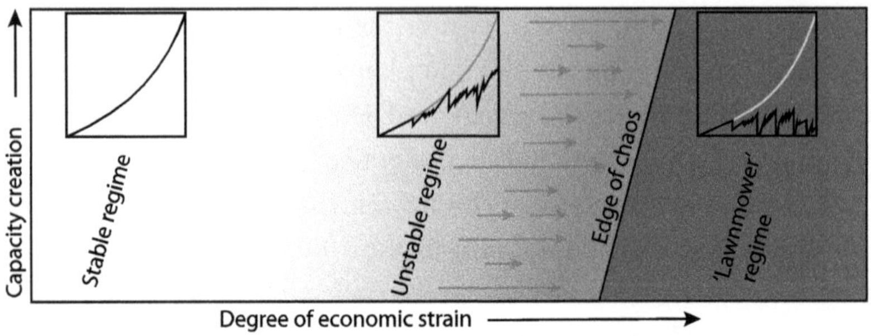

FIGURE 3.2 Efficiency–resilience trade-off in economics, dependent on the degree of strain on the system (i.e. capacity used), against investments in system improvements. The edge of chaos is a state of repeated cascading failures of all magnitudes that occurs when the economy reaches full capacity. The 'lawnmower' (or chaotic) regime is where damage from instability occurs more frequently than the rate of repair. Economic systems tend to lie somewhere between the stable and unstable regimes but naturally creep towards the edge of chaos. Investing in expanding capacity can pull the economy back.

there is continuous moderate growth. When strain increases (moving rightwards in the figure), growth is much faster, but we begin to see occasional failures and disasters. The more strain, the more frequent and intense the cascading failures are, and the more growth becomes hindered by the damage.

At some high degree of strain, we reach what is called the 'edge of chaos', where the system is completely unstable. At this limit, the system is on the edge of self-destruction, in a steady state of repeated 'earthquakes', where as much construction as destruction occurs. Beyond this line is what we will call the 'lawnmower state', the chaotic situation where destruction occurs more rapidly than the system can repair itself. Growth cannot occur at all. We don't want to go there, but this could be where climate-related damages lead us. In fact, we don't want to go anywhere near the edge of chaos and should stay a safe distance from it, as when walking along a cliff-edge.

On their own, because of slow demand growth towards fixed supply constraints, systems gradually creep naturally towards the edge of chaos and into increasing instability. In the figure, the system is attracted slowly towards the right. However, investments in capacity improvement and expansion relieve this pressure and can drive the system away from the edge of chaos. The system moves upwards in the picture, and as we can see, since the edge of chaos lies at an angle, moving upwards drives the system away from the edge.

Thus, in short demand, growth brings the system towards instability, while investment drives the system away from instability. We consider that this ought to suggest this should become established as a basic principle of economics.

In standard economics, students are taught that capital is allocated optimally to match demand for every good at every time and that production generates its own demand. This is the equilibrium solution, and any deviations from the equilibrium would lead to losses that would have been foreseen by investors and, therefore, cannot occur.

Here, we are saying that such a situation would lie right on the edge of chaos and could not be stable nor sustain itself for long. We say that investment occurs to relieve pressure gradually building up with demand growth. Without sufficient investment, the economy becomes unstable and breaks down.

3.2.3 A New Definition for Economic Resilience

What does 'economic breakdown' mean? It is when the economic system stops working the way we want it to. We can imagine various ways the economy could go wrong. We had a global financial crisis that started in 2007, where for a little while, the financial system was dysfunctional. There was the breakdown of health systems in some countries at the height of the COVID-19 pandemic. We had rapid inflation after COVID. The Venezuelan currency value crashed between 2019 and 2023 (reviewed in Chapter 9) and never functioned properly again. These are examples of breakdowns.

In Sections 3.2.1 and 3.2.2, we explained a mechanism for economic breakdown. The system comes towards the edge of its capacity to absorb shocks. It becomes more and more unstable, until it reaches the cliff edge, which we called the 'edge of chaos'. Past the edge of chaos, the system breaks down, because the shocks and domino effects break the system more quickly than it is able to repair itself.

We all know the expression 'the straw that breaks the camel's back'. When we analyse the possibilities of system breakdown, the natural question that comes to mind is, how big is the last straw needed to break the system? How far are we from breakdown? For effective policy-making, we would like to analyse a system and be able to say, this is how much 'resilience' it has, how much more strain it can take.

Definitions for 'resilience' in economics are a bit all over the place, and none are widely recognised, in part because resilience is not really a thing in economics.[12] But we need one here, and with what we've said in this chapter, we are able to be a bit more precise. Resilience for us is simply the distance we are from the edge of the cliff in Figure 3.2. It is a measure of how big the last straw that breaks the camel's back has to be. If we are far from the edge, it takes a really heavy straw, or maybe no straw can break the camel's back. We are resilient. When we are just on the edge, any small thing, or indeed maybe even just the wind, can push us over the edge. At this point, we have zero resilience.

Resilience in this book will simply be measured as the slope in graphs like Figure 3.1. We will discuss this again in Chapter 9: this slope can tell us how far from the edge of the cliff we are. What is sometimes also needed is to translate this number back to some measure of risk. An example could be how big a financial loss it takes to trigger a global financial crisis when there is a lot of barely sustainable debt around. That's how big the straw needs to be to break the camel's back.

We note that this is never going to be an exact science. But we think it is hugely useful in risk assessment and sensible policymaking.

In standard economics, people assume that the economy operates at full capacity, which means it always has zero resilience.

[12] See Holling et al. (1973); Hynes et al. (2022); Kemp and Cline (2022); Hallegatte (2014).

Or they say that it is preferable if it does so, because it is then considered 'efficient'. In practice, this is never true. But this means that the 'performance–stability' trade-off can also be called the 'efficiency–resilience' trade-off. The economy is most 'efficient' when it has zero resilience.[13]

3.3 ECONOMIC RESOURCES ARE CREATED, NOT ALLOCATED

3.3.1 How Much to Invest in Innovation?

We now come to the title of the chapter. Standard economics is concerned only with the allocation of productive resources. This is important in some situations. For example, the most profitable retailers usually end up with the best shop locations.

But, as we argued earlier, the more interesting problem in economics is how to create more resources to better address needs. It is difficult to understand why standard economic theory awkwardly avoids this topic. And it is simple. Alongside regular investment, we create resources using innovation, although we can never predict exactly what innovation will produce.

Research and development (R&D) is a special type of investment for companies. It is an investment in the development of new capabilities, usually to make better use of resources, or new things we could do with existing resources. As discussed in Chapter 2, it is hard for the investor to predict exactly the economic outcomes of R&D. They may not know at the time of investment what the resulting product will be, let alone whether anyone will want it.

It would be great for business if entrepreneurs could identify the optimal level of investment in R&D. But, once again, this is asking for too much from the available information; there are just too many possibilities. However, it is possible to develop a sensible strategy for R&D.

[13] See Hynes et al. (2022).

In 2014, some researchers carried out a large survey of innovation in European companies.[14] The researchers found that success depended on a combination of trying out different ideas, strong commitment to promising projects and willingness to terminate unpromising projects. It was also important to try out both low- and high-risk projects.

It is a bit like taking over the care of a garden that is not doing very well. Our strategy could be to keep growing the same plants, which have shown they can at least survive in the garden. This is very cheap, but creates little new. Another strategy would be to dig out the entire garden to start afresh, with new better plants that in theory are well-suited to conditions. Their chance of survival could be increased by using fertilisers and employing a gardener to care for them. This could be very productive but is probably expensive as well as risky.

A third strategy would be to dig out only some of the less productive plants and experiment with a few new varieties in different parts of the garden before spending too much money. Over time, we can buy more of the plants that thrive and abandon those that don't to try something else. This strategy is much more productive than the first and far cheaper than the second. This is what any sensible gardener would do.

While fine as a strategy, the approach doesn't tell us exactly how much a company should spend on R&D, compared to other things such as simply expanding existing activities. Too little R&D means less innovation and falling behind competitors. Too much R&D increases the company's costs and may lead to wasteful spending.

There is no easy answer, because we cannot optimise this, given that we cannot predict the outcomes of innovation. It partly depends on how old the sector is, how easy it is to innovate and how much innovation competitors are doing. Remember that innovation

[14] See Klingebiel and Rammer (2014).

builds on past innovation, so the chances of success are much higher where products are new and in full development. In older sectors, there is less scope for improvement, so we see less R&D spending by companies (see later in Chapter 4).

The same principles apply to public investment in R&D. Again, we cannot identify for sure the optimal amount. However, we know that having no public R&D will not work because economic development requires high-risk basic research that companies will not be willing to carry out. Too much public R&D will carry a cost that must be borne by the rest of society.

There are, however, countries with thriving knowledge economies that are generally very dynamic, resilient and productive. A happy middle ground thus exists. But as with companies, no one really knows where it is, and it may vary between countries and over time.

The final point worth noting is that R&D is rarely completely wasted. All knowledge that is created is useful, and there are many examples where past innovation has become useful only decades later (think about solar power). All innovation expands our future possible steps into the adjacent possible.

3.3.2 *The Creation of Economic Resources*

We get to the core message of this chapter. Resource creation activities take place all the time. Economists that ignore them are only telling a small part of the story. It's the part that leads to very depressing debates about scarcity, sacrifice and difficult decisions.

As discussed above, we don't generally use the economy's entire capacity, because that would be unstable. The key point is that what we do in the present determines how much resources may be used in the future and how.

You could think of knowledge as an economic resource itself. It is different from other resources though. We can use our existing knowledge an unlimited number of times. We can develop new knowledge from our existing knowledge.

In this sense, R&D and innovation create economic resources, because they create better ways to use resources. For example, if we find a more efficient way of making cars, we may have more metals in the economy to use for other things. If we invent a new IT technology, we create a new economy-improving skill that wasn't there before. But we cannot count our chickens before they hatch: we cannot allocate our creation (or saving) of resources until we try and innovate successfully.

As we saw in Chapter 2, addressing dangerous climate change is all about getting the right technologies in the right places. We need to scale up the production of solar panels, batteries, EVs, etc., but also of many technologies yet to be invented or made commercial such as green hydrogen. As revenues grow, the companies involved will invest in larger production scale and more R&D. As we said, R&D and learning economies have a higher impact in young sectors. More knowledge will be created.

Critically, this knowledge will not just be useful for finding ways to reduce greenhouse gas emissions. The knowledge can be applied for many other things, across the entire economy, including things that make big money. It can be used for further innovation and job creation in other sectors. It's amazing how many of our current technologies can be traced back to the space race.

In short, all of this knowledge resource created today will shape tomorrow's economic growth. Investing now in knowledge and know-how creates the actual resources upon which the future economy will sit. In other words, growth and development economics is not really about allocating our scarce resources. It is about creating those resources.

In practice, GDP is not a pie of income that we must divide equally between guests at a party. GDP growth is something we all create and is just a metric measuring how fast we are learning how to make more and better pies out of what we have.

We are not presenting anything really new here. We are just describing how an economy develops. Promoting any new sector will lead to innovation, knowledge creation and further development. In rich countries, this is sometimes called industrial policy, although the topic is taboo in standard economics. In poor countries, this is simply called economic development.

Resource creation does not get any quicker if we 'leave the economy' to its own devices, as standard economics and its models recommend. It goes quicker if we support it, and reducing emissions is a great excuse to do so.

Thus, the story the economists tell us about the economic impacts of dealing with climate change is badly wrong. We need a new story, a story that replaces 'optimal' outcomes with discussions about risks and opportunities, including in the financial sector; a story that focuses on the creation of economic resources and how we can use this to improve our lives and economy as well as avoid climate change, while keeping the economy resilient.

Many economists won't like this new story. Fossil fuel companies probably won't like it much either. So let's conclude with something for them to think about.

We used to think of solar panels as a cost, but they now produce the cheapest electricity in history.[15] They are a resource we have created. They are now appearing in all sorts of gadgets and cheap devices. Some people and companies are benefitting from this already, but many have not yet had the chance. There is so much more we can do with solar panels!

What will people do with this super-cheap power? It won't just be used for EVs. Operating machinery will become cheaper. It could be used for robots, artificial intelligence or 3D printing and many things we have not yet thought of. We will then see further innovation.

Switching to solar power will not lead to a small decrease in GDP, as the economists have repeatedly suggested. It will be part of a technological revolution that's going to transform our lives in ways

[15] See IEA (2020b).

we cannot yet imagine. It will boost GDP. It will be a core part of economic development in the twenty-first century, as we describe in Chapter 4.

That is, if the strain it creates doesn't make our economy go unstable. As we will see later, there is a fair chance that it might. But there are solutions to prevent that too, and they must be included in our strategy.

4 The Transition in Context: The Six Great Waves of Innovation

4.1 WHAT IS A TECHNOLOGICAL REVOLUTION?

4.1.1 Constellations of Innovations

We know that we need a lot of innovation to avoid dangerous climate change. We need a technological revolution, nothing less. The good news is that it looks like we are about to have one. According to Schumpeter, industrial revolutions happen every 50–60 years. Since he wrote 'Business Cycles', two more have occurred following this pattern and a third is beginning. Each time, the economy is completely transformed with new possibilities and new ways to live and to make a living. In this chapter, we look at what industrial revolutions have been like, so that we can compare them with what's happening right now.[1]

Innovations tend to cluster in big waves of related stuff. There are times of great innovation, with lots of new inventions that transform the world and create upheaval. There are other times when it seems difficult to create new ideas.

Innovations also cluster in economic sectors.[2] We see this now, for example in the current rapid advances in biomedical technology. Meanwhile, other sectors like chemical engineering and cement production continue working the same way they have for more than a hundred years.

[1] For theoretical and empirical evidence, this chapter relies primarily on Schumpeter (1934, 1939), Freeman and Louçã (2001); Perez (2001) and Mercure (2022); but it goes back to Kondratieff (1928). A more recent strand of literature on socio-technical transitions can be found in Geels (2002); Geels and Schot (2007).

[2] See Brian Arthur on technology and industrial clustering (Arthur et al., 1994).

Finally, innovations cluster in space. Again, we can see examples in the world around us. Silicon Valley in California has led the development of computer software systems since the 1980s. Meanwhile, a previous cluster of innovation in Detroit turned to decline as new ideas in the conventional (oil-based) car industry dried up.

This last point may seem an exaggeration. Doesn't the conventional car industry still innovate? It does, but the pace of innovation is now much slower than before. The basic capabilities of conventional cars have not changed. In fact, much of the innovation in the US since the 1980s has been focused on catching up with Japanese competitors.[3]

What we are seeing is the tail end of a great transformation that first created the car and oil industries. In the early twentieth century, local economies in Michigan and Texas grew rapidly because new innovations found ways to enable mass ownership of cars and mass consumption of gasoline. The ideas started to run out in the 1980s, and Michigan's economy suffered. Global demand has held up the oil industry, but it too will soon go into decline.[4]

As oil and cars came to their golden age, the information age took off. Economic power has moved to California, all driven by a new great wave of innovation.

In these great waves, we see 'constellations' of related and co-dependent systems.[5] An obvious example is the car and the oil industry. To be useful, cars needed a fuel supply. To have purpose, oil needed cars. One would not have existed without the other.[6]

As we know from Chapter 2, innovation does not stop there. Cars required all sorts of inventions, such as specialised glass and steel, rubber for tyres and new standardised mechanical systems. The

[3] See Miyoshi and Kii (2011) on the Japanese car industry.

[4] For example, oil demand may already have peaked in China because of the exponential rise in electric vehicles (Mercure et al. 2025b).

[5] Freeman and Perez (1988); Dosi et al. (1988); Dosi (1982).

[6] In the early twentieth century, a competition actually existed between battery-powered and liquid fuel-powered cars. For reasons related, among others, to performance and distance, oil-based vehicles took the market (Geels, 2005).

fuels required developments in cracking hydrocarbons and refining, as well as new ways of transporting and drilling for oil. The industry also saw a revolution in production chain management, with Henry Ford's new mass production principles, which later were applied in other industries.

Entire industries were built. Some people became extremely rich. And it didn't end there. Oil provided the fuel for the new air travel industry. Shipping became more effective. Over time, people found other ways of using oil, including the invention of plastics. Our whole way of life is built upon these innovations. It was a technological revolution.

4.1.2 The Life Cycle of Industrial Revolutions

People say all good things come to an end. Technological revolutions certainly do, as we show in Section 4.1.3. In fact, we can identify a 'life cycle' in these revolutions, involving a birth phase, a frenzy of investment, a golden age and a decline phase (Figure 4.1). We discuss life cycles more generally in Chapter 5.

Technological revolutions start with a big idea. This big idea forms the platform for a new 'system' (way of doing things), as cars

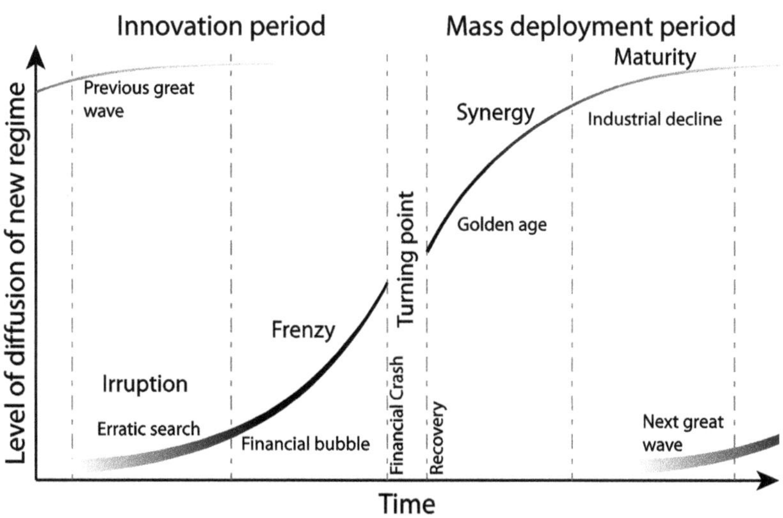

FIGURE 4.1 The life-cycle of technological revolutions. See Perez (2001).

and oil did together for transport. A wave of innovations built on this platform takes off. But remember that innovators only gradually discover the great potential of the great wave, as they build it. They also only discover gradually the point when they run out of ideas in the current revolution.

The birth phase is full of risk. This is the moment when visions must become reality. To do so, the big ideas must reach the mass market. That means they must also become affordable. As they do so, a frenzy of investment happens.

Famously, Henry Ford had a vision that his workers could afford to buy the cars they were making. He raised wages in his factories to make it possible. His plan worked. Sales of cars increased and production costs went down as mass production became possible. Each car sold made less profit, but total profits vastly increased because far more cars were sold.

We always remember the success stories. But many technologies fail at this stage, including ones that could have been revolutionary. They fail to cross the 'technology valley of death'.[7] This is the real test: are the technologies good enough to make it in the market?

The frenzy phase is one where great profits are made. Once the new products reach mass markets, they really take off. Companies innovate to keep costs going down faster than prices. This is where people can make a lot of money and business empires can be built. Past examples include Andrew Carnegie's steel empire and John D Rockefeller's Standard Oil: these are names still known today. Our current technology companies have followed a similar path.

Production costs continue to fall as volumes increase. People become accustomed to the new technology and cannot imagine everyday life without it. They may become dependent on it (think cars or smart phones). Investment piles in.

At some point though, the innovation will slow. We become familiar with the technology and know what we want from it.

[7] See Grubb et al. (2014).

The technology stops changing, and there will be a dominant design.[8] We also begin to see the things that don't work. Sometimes this means discovering that investment has gone to those unworkable innovations. There has often been a financial crash at this point.

With less innovation, companies start to compete on price, meaning that profits fall. We move into a period of consolidation, with a focus on cost reduction and larger volumes. We know what the technology is, and we want to make it cheap in order to sell lots of it.

Eventually, the technology becomes outdated. It may be replaced or merged into something else. For example, cars replaced the use of horses for transport. In the coming decades (Chapter 6), cars will probably not disappear, but they will be merged into electrical technologies. In contrast, the internal combustion engine will slowly die.

This is how we, as humans, pick out the things that work well and replace the things that are not needed anymore. As we show in Section 4.1.3, it has happened throughout history. It will happen again, many times.

The final point to note is that companies do not manage declining markets and sales well. As production falls, costs per unit increase. Investment is cut to limit costs, and workers are gradually made redundant. Skills are forgotten, and eventually the company collapses. Companies are made for growing, not shrinking. This means that the maturity phase is usually economically painful.

4.1.3 Why Industrial Revolutions Happen

Industrial revolutions cannot be prevented from happening, even if we wanted to. Inventors cannot be stopped from having ideas. The societies we have built cannot stop them from using these ideas. And policy-makers often want technological progress too.

[8] See Abernathy and Utterback (1978); Geels (2002); Dosi (1982).

The problem is that the effects can be explosive because of the way new ideas generate more new ideas. Once the internal combustion engine was proven to work, first in ships, and later in cars, tarmac had to be invented. The petrochemicals industry developed alongside rubber. We got a new kind of personal transport.

New types of companies emerged, for example, in the delivery of goods by road. New work and life patterns emerged in which people could commute long distances to work in cities. Housing markets were transformed. So was much of our society.

Once it happened, there was no going back. Most people wanted the change, and those that didn't were swept along anyway. No one could stop people from buying cars; no one could stop Henry Ford from selling cars; and no one could stop Rockefeller drilling for oil. All this was caused by someone inventing a modified steam engine.

Importantly, industrial revolutions create new resources that can be used later to make other new things. Examples include iron, coal, steel, textiles, oil, engines and computer chips. In each case, they were expensive to begin with but became cheaper over time, allowing ordinary people to use them.

We saw in Chapter 1 that new technologies follow a 'learning curve' with costs falling in line with total production over time. Once products reach mass markets, lots of people using them make costs go down ever more.

The range of products that can be used to make new products at affordable prices can be called the 'design space'.[9] The design space changes all the time, because new things are invented and prices of materials and components come down, continuously expanding the range of the possible for inventors and entrepreneurs.

Industrial revolutions transform society every time they happen, with no return because they rapidly change the design space. They have generated most of the economic growth observed

[9] See Stankiewicz (2000).

throughout history. They find ways to get around the things that prevent us from making, and consuming, more stuff.

4.1.4 *Are We Witnessing an Industrial Revolution?*

Schumpeter taught us about industrial revolutions. Our understanding of the role of innovation in economic development can mostly be traced to him. He explained the entrepreneur as part of the economic process, including how entrepreneurs access finance and compete with other entrepreneurs (see Chapter 2).

There have been five past industrial revolutions and a sixth one based on artificial intelligence, bio-tech and related technologies is now happening. Section 4.2 explores what we can learn from the previous revolutions (summarised in Table 4.1). Chapter 6 discusses what's coming.

Can we call the zero-carbon transition an industrial revolution? Looking at the data shown in Chapter 1, the answer is almost certainly yes. Electrification, energy efficiency and 'getting rid of combustion' are driving productivity change alongside automation, artificial intelligence and big data.[10] As we saw in Chapter 1, we will soon have cheaper energy without the need for fuel combustion.

No fuel combustion means no need to drill and refine oil, or dig coal. We will no longer need people to do this, which in the short term will mean job losses but in the longer term opportunities to do other things instead. We will also avoid the enormously inefficient process of burning fuels to extract energy. Money will be saved and profits made.

Tesla's astronomical valuation reflects this. Investors expect lots of profits. Either they have all got it wrong, or electro-mobility is positioned to make a lot of money. But first, let's look at how technological revolutions have happened over history.

[10] See our modelling of productivity growth due to decarbonisation in the UK, in Mercure et al. (2025).

Table 4.1 *The great waves of innovation in world history*

Constellation of technical and organisational innovations	Examples of visible, successful, profitable innovations	'Carrier' branches or sectors	Core and key inputs	Transport and communication infrastructure	Managerial and organisational changes	Timings of upswings/ downswings
1. Water-powered mechanisation of industry	Arkright's Cromford mill (1771) Henry Cort's 'puddling' process (1784)	Cotton spinning, iron products, water wheels, bleach	Iron Raw cotton Coal	Canals Turnpike roads Sailing ships	Factory systems Entrepreneurs Partnerships	1780s–1815 1815–1848
2. Steam-powered mechanisation of industry and transport	Liverpool-Manchester railway (1831) Brunel's 'Great Western' steamship (1838)	Railways and railway equipment, steam engines, machine tools, alkali industry	Iron Coal	Railways Telegraphs Steam ships	Joint stock companies Subcontracting to responsible craft workers	1848–1873 1873–1895
3. Electrification of industry, transport and the home	Carnegie Bessemer steel plant (1875) Edison's New York Electric Power station (1882)	Electrical equipment, heavy engineering, heavy chemicals, steel products	Steel Copper Metal alloys	Steel railways Steel ships Telephone	Specialised professional management systems 'Taylorism' Giant firms	1895–1918 1918–1940

4. Motorisation of transport, civil economy and war	Ford's Highland Park assembly line (1913) Burton process for cracking heavy oil (1913)	Automobiles, trucks, tractors, tanks, diesel/petrol engines, aircraft, refineries	Oil Gas Synthetic materials	Radio Motorways Airports Airlines	Mass production and consumption 'Fordism' Hierarchies	1941–1973 1973–1980
5. Computerisation of entire economy	IBM 1401 and 360 series computers (1960s) Intel microprocessor (1972)	Computers, software, telecommuni-cation equipment, biotechnology	Integrated circuits Recording magnetic media	Internet email wireless telecom	Networks Email systems digitisation of archives	1980s–2001 2001–2020
6. Machine learning, artificial intelligence and genetics	IBM/Google artificial go/chess players (90s–2010s) Google self-driving electric car (2010s)	Intelligent machines, social media, cancer treatment, renewable energy	Artificial intelligence, 'Big' data, Photovoltaics, Energy tech.	Social media 'Smart' devices, Intelligent electric vehicles	Big data, targeted advertising, firm automation electrification	2020–??

Reproduced from Freeman and Louçã (2001), with authors' additions reproduced from Mercure (2022).

4.2 FIVE PAST GREAT WAVES OF INNOVATION

4.2.1 *Iron, Water Power and Textiles*

Iron and textiles were not the first industrial revolution, but they were the first one worth discussing here.[11] Coal and water power were also key to this revolution.

The revolution was started with the discovery that coal could be used to turn iron ore (rocks from the ground) into useful iron that could be used to make tools. First, the coal is turned into 'coke' by heating it, and then it is mixed with iron. The chemical reaction when lit in a furnace produces liquid iron.

Humans had previously made iron since the iron age, but using charcoal instead of coal. Charcoal required large amounts of wood and cutting down whole forests. Using coal made the process much easier. It also meant effectively limitless energy resources, at a time when many forests had been almost completely cut down. Iron prices fell rapidly (Figure 4.2), and production increased.

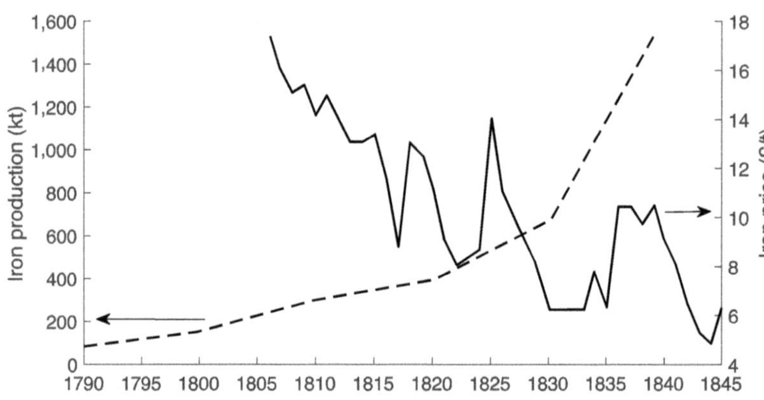

FIGURE 4.2 The volume and price of iron during the first industrial revolution. Data obtained from Freeman and Louçã (2001).

[11] For instance, the Stone, Bronze and Iron ages refer directly to innovation and revolutions in how humans used materials and tools. The seventeenth century also saw mechanisation of agriculture. However, they are not typically labelled 'industrial' revolutions, perhaps in reference to the fact that work had not become organised along industrial principles. This whole section draws largely from Freeman and Louçã (2001); Perez (2001); Schumpeter (1939).

The availability of low-cost iron coincided with the development of new methods for spinning and weaving cotton, which itself was a new product from plantations in the New World (what is now the Caribbean and the US). Prior to that, British wool was used, spun in small-scale water mills and in cottage industries. The new methods led to productivity increases and cost reductions of a factor of more than 10 between the 1740s and the 1760s. These cost reductions naturally spurred increases in demand, leading to the virtuous cycle between demand rises and cost reductions with further innovation.

The textile machines were built from wood and iron and, therefore, drove part of the other virtuous cycle happening with the volumes and cost of iron produced. The more textiles made, the cheaper textiles *and* iron became.

The third factor was water power, which came from water wheels set in rivers. The mechanical power was used, among other things, for driving the textile equipment and helping bellows to increase temperatures in iron furnaces.

The demand for coal and the mismatch between its locations for mining and use led to the building of large-scale transport networks, roads, turnpikes, canals and bridges, across the British Isles. Easier transport meant that production costs fell by even more.

Lastly, the 'factory' came to exist, by which we mean a new way of organising increasingly specialised work. The factory was an amalgamation of major social and managerial innovations, which included defining hours of work, wages and work discipline. Factories relied on pools of unemployed workers. Earlier mechanisation of agriculture provided these workers.

The result was the development of a new industrial economy that relied on organised work to produce all kinds of iron products. Iron was now used to produce machinery, water wheels, textile equipment, ships and weapons, as well as coal and the textiles that started it all off. The rapid cost reductions coincided with rapidly rising demand and exports of those products.

4.2.2 *The Steam Engine*

Eighteenth-century Britain was still largely made up of agricultural communities tied to local regions, with little mobility between regions. However, with the large-scale availability of both iron and coal, building upon the first industrial revolution, this was going to change rapidly.

Water power is a resource that is not widely distributed geographically. For a wider expansion of industrial activity, alternative sources of mechanical power were needed. In the late eighteenth century, James Watt and other industrialists developed the coal-powered steam engine as a solution, going through multiple improvements and modifications. The steam engine was originally developed to pump water out of coal mines more efficiently. However, through the first half of the nineteenth century, it was used to replace water power for many, if not most, industrial applications.

Crucially, the steam engine found its use for mobility, through the development of railways (Figure 4.3). Railways enabled the rapid transport of people and goods, allowing new types of economic activities and business to be formed. The demand for mobility and

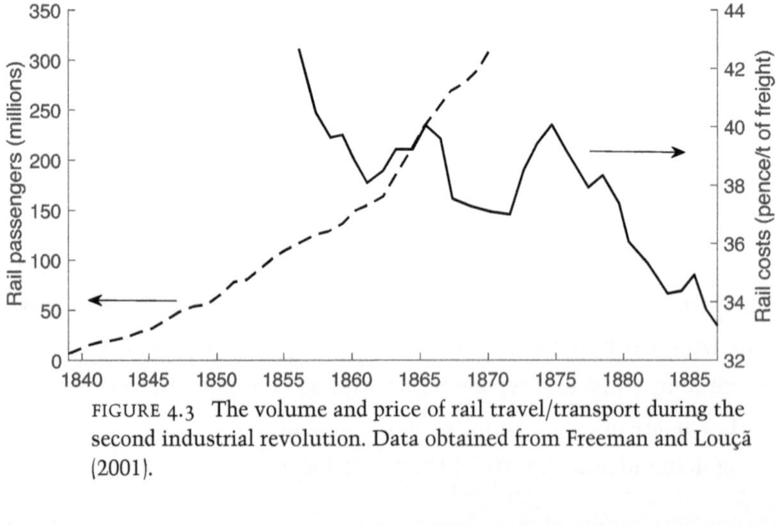

FIGURE 4.3 The volume and price of rail travel/transport during the second industrial revolution. Data obtained from Freeman and Louçã (2001).

freight henceforth climbed exponentially, with prices declining along a learning curve.

Another important innovation was the steamship, which rapidly replaced the sailboat and the clippers of the time for more effective transatlantic and international trade. The expansion of trade also rapidly increased British exports.

Britain was soon covered with railways. The expansion generated its own demand. With rapidly expanding investment and further declining prices, expansions in coal mining, iron smelting, the building of steam engines, machinery and ships quickly accelerated. The railway revolution expanded across Europe and later across the US and Canada. The telegraph was also developed and deployed along railway lines, offering a new mode of communication.

The variety of goods sold to the emerging middle classes exploded. The rapid growth of industry made early management systems untenable and required further innovations in factory management and hierarchy.

The end of the second industrial revolution towards the second half of the nineteenth century was, however, riddled with economic instabilities and depressions. Stagnation in investment led to widespread unemployment in factories and with railway workers. The economy saw major structural changes, many of which were due to innovation in steelmaking and industry belonging to the next industrial revolution.

4.2.3 Electricity and Heavy Industry

During the late part of the nineteenth century, key innovations were made to improve the production of steel and other metals. The Bessemer process, famously commercialised by Andrew Carnegie, allowed companies to produce large amounts of cheap steel. The cost of steel fell by nearly 70% between the 1870s and 1930s, as steel gradually replaced iron in all applications (Figure 4.4).

As a result, the cost of building materials declined substantially. Steel is much stronger and consistent than iron, so could

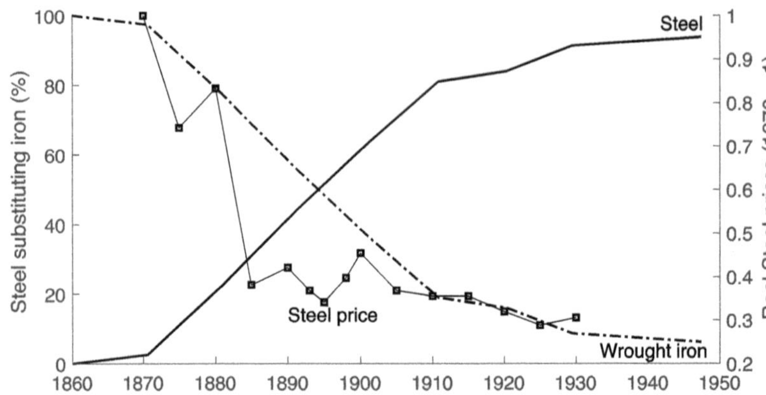

FIGURE 4.4 The volume and real price of steel during the third industrial revolution. Data obtained from Freeman and Louçã (2001).

be used for many more purposes. It improved the precision and reliability of engineering.

However, innovations of the third great wave also included methods to produce other metals like copper, widely used in the nascent electrical industry. Key electrical innovations included the dynamo, the electric steam turbine, the electric motor, the lamp bulb, and, eventually, the telephone. The steam turbine produced the electricity needed by all of these new devices.

The electric motor replaced bulky steam engines with much smaller and more versatile sources of mechanical power. Factories no longer required central spinning shafts and belts to carry mechanical power from a centralised steam engine to individual work stations. Instead, electric motors with just simple wiring would power each work station, allowing much better space management and flexibility. Energy efficiency rose considerably, reducing input fuel costs.

Electricity was also used for mobility. The London Underground system was built without needing to worry about the pollution generated by steam locomotives. Electric lighting was used to improve and expand working hours in factories and other working environments. Iconic companies such as GE, AEG and Siemens designed and sold the products.

Substantial further management innovations were made, notably following 'Taylorism', to optimise plant management, use of materials and management of waste. The organisation of ever larger companies and emergent bureaucracies was an important challenge of the period.

4.2.4 *Oil and the Internal Combustion Engine*

The twentieth century started off in the midst of recurrent economic, financial and political instability. The financial crises of the late nineteenth and early twentieth centuries gave way to the rapid rise of new technology during the so-called roaring twenties, but not before the First World War (WWI) had taken place.

The core input for the fourth great wave of innovation was oil. Mineral oil had been used during the nineteenth century, to gradually replace whale oil used for lighting and lubrication. John D. Rockefeller made his business initially on the basis of demand for lighting and heating.

Then people found new ways to make petrol and diesel a lot cheaper, through the development of a whole chain of petrochemical innovations. The internal combustion engine, petrol and diesel engines, were developed during the late nineteenth century by Nikolaus Otto in 1861. While Rockefeller was looking for oil in the American Mid-West during the 1870s, William Burton figured out how to crack all the components of oil to produce refined liquid fuels in sufficient quantities that could be conveniently used in engines. This meant that Rockefeller's oil could all of a sudden be used to power transport, not just lamps. An explosion of investment and growth in car making and petrochemicals followed.

Diesel engines first found applications in ships and heavy machinery. Lighter petrol engines were used for cars. These innovations hugely disrupted the US economy as they took off between 1910 and 1925 (Figure 4.5). Horse-drawn carriages were quickly abandoned, sometimes literally.[12]

[12] See Grübler et al. (1999) and the original work by Nakicenovic (1986).

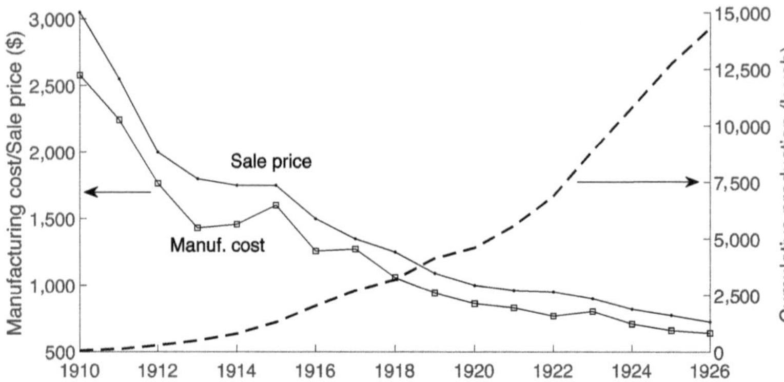

FIGURE 4.5 The volume, nominal price and manufacturing cost of Ford Model T cars during the fourth industrial revolution. Data from Yelle (1983).

And that was just the beginning. The technology opened many possibilities like replacing coal steamers by faster fuel oil ships, aeroplanes, new war machinery and oil-fired electricity. Petrochemicals also had their use in heating, lubricating and paving roads that all the new cars and trucks needed. Plastics came later. This explosion of innovation kept economic growth going for more than 50 years. It lasted through two world wars and began to slow down earnestly only in the 1970s.

The early twentieth century, however, was not peaceful. The outcome of WWI and the reparations rule imposed onto Germany led to fiscal problems and hyperinflation. The great depression happened as a result of a financial crash following an investment bubble in the late 1920s, very similar to what we saw in 2007–2008.[13] The ensuing unemployment fuelled resentment and grievances, which in turn fuelled populist politics and the rise of fascism in Germany and elsewhere.

Discontent partly emerged from a lack of work in the traditional industries of the third great wave. For example, steelmaking suffered from overcapacity and reduced its need for workers and

[13] See Perez (2001). A great account of the 1929 crash and great depression is from Fisher (1932).

machinery. Process innovation led to less and less being needed, and the depression led to stagnating demand for everything. The war effort 'solved' many of these problems by creating a state-driven demand for weapons. Going to war was a quick fix for an ailing global economy.

Naturally, widespread war generated a strong motivation to accelerate technological innovation. After the war, good or bad, the economy was left with a legacy of new knowledge and technological knowhow, which found countless applications in civilian applications, including nuclear energy. The war produced a pretext for the massive and rapid expansion of production scale which made costs decline as well.[14] Technological innovation can be a side effect of conflict.

For example, developments in aviation during WWI created the technologies used in the 1920s. Similar developments during WWII led the way to improving aeroplanes during the 1940s and 1950s. Notably, the jet engine was invented during WWII.

Other great innovations were developed in the run up to, and during, the great wars. These included faster oil-powered ships, machinery, tanks, rockets and plastics, but also new things like the radar and basic electronics. Most of these innovations were the outcomes of the oil-based focus of the fourth great wave. Oil giants consolidated their power worldwide. However, the early electronics also set the stage for the next great wave on information technology.

The fourth great wave also saw key innovations in management and industrial organisation. Many of these are credited to Henry Ford with his development of the assembly line and mass production principles. This higher level of worker specialisation pushed yet further the boundaries of worker productivity in the factory, enabling vast declines in production cost. All of a sudden, people could afford their own cars, and personal mobility took off.

[14] See the analysis of US war production data from Lafond et al. (2020). We do not view war as 'good'; however it did have those effects.

The rise of the car industry continued well into the 1970s, the point at which the oil industry saw its turning point and start of a slowdown in growth. The formation of OPEC and the oil embargo signalled a new oil market regime, in which it became more profitable to rely on high prices than growing volumes. King Hubbert famously warned the US Congress that a peak and decline of the American oil industry was imminent. This never happened, and it is only today that we may be witnessing the true start of a decline of oil markets. It is likely to start with peak oil demand in China, followed by Europe and then the US.[15]

4.2.5 Information Technology

During the second half of the twentieth century, many information-related technologies already existed, whether for computing, recording, detection or communication. Examples included the telephone, the calculator, the microphone, the radio, the radar and disk and magnetic recording. There were also Turing's and others' early computing machines. Many of these devices emerged during WWII. Turing famously invented an early computer to decrypt German coded messages, while the radar was developed in Britain for the early detection of oncoming German war planes.

What arguably made the information technology (IT) revolution distinctive was that its core input was data-digitised and encoded into discrete numbers. Earlier, data recording, management and transmission had been on the basis of 'analogue' systems. 'Digital' systems greatly improved the effectiveness and efficiency of data management, whether for sound, images, text or computed values.[16]

[15] Decline turned out to happen much later than Hubbert's prediction. With increasing oil prices, ever more oil was discovered, and it is now unlikely that oil will ever be exhausted. The picture got reversed when discussion turned, in recent years, towards 'peak demand'. See Meinshausen et al. (2009); McGlade and Ekins (2015); Mercure et al. (2018b, 2021a).

[16] 'Analogue' systems operate directly with electrical signals as measured, for example, by amplifying and transmitting the electric voltage generated in a microphone. 'Digital' systems convert the electrical signals into numbers. This means that only numbers

The development of digital data management systems started with Bardeen, Brattain and Shockley's invention of the transistor using semiconductor materials. With the following innovations that combined transistors and other electronic components to create various logic operators, digital information management and computation became possible. This was the first step.

The second step was miniaturisation of electronic circuits. Managing useful amounts of data implied using extremely large numbers of logic operators, so miniaturisation was needed to keep costs manageable. Transistors were made of semiconductors already. The strategy used was to carve and integrate whole circuits into the same piece of continuous semiconductor material and to make the circuits smaller and smaller.[17]

As the circuits became smaller, they could be operated at faster and faster speeds. More and more computations could be made per second per chip. The trend that emerged from the industry was that chips became twice as powerful roughly every eighteen months. This process became known as Moore's law, after Gordon Moore, co-founder of Intel. With a relatively stable price per chip, computing power expanded rapidly. Concurrently, computer sales took off (Figure 4.6).

Computers rapidly became a general purpose technology that could replace and simplify tasks in an extremely wide scope.

are required to be recorded and transmitted, making operations, recording and transmission much more effective, efficient and versatile. Compression algorithms allow us to reduce drastically the amount of information required to transmit text, sound and images.

[17] These are the so-called single crystals of semiconducting materials, most of the time silicon. Silicon is 'grown' into very large crystals, where the rows and layers of alignment of atoms are perfectly parallel and regular, in the shape of cylinders of about 10 cm in diameter or more. Slices are taken and polished like mirrors. Electronic circuits are etched into the surface using chemicals or plasmas, using photosensitive resins to 'draw' the circuits, very much like the etching of copper plates for printing has been done since the 1600s. Metals are deposited at the right locations to create electrical contacts. Increasing the precision of etching lets us make chips with ever larger numbers of components. We now have chips that contain billions of transistors and other components.

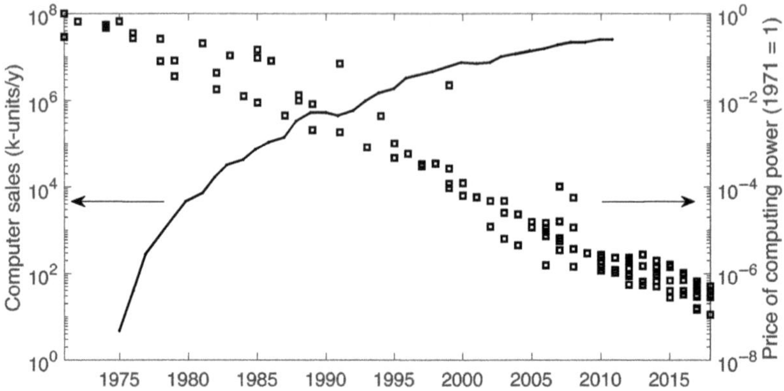

FIGURE 4.6 The volume of computer sales and the price of computing power during the fifth great wave. The computing power price indicator was assumed to be inversely proportional to the computing power per chip at constant chip prices, the inverse of Moore's law. Data obtained online from Intel and Gartner.

They simplified administration, eliminated paper use, stored large amounts of information efficiently and automated previously labour-intensive calculations. What justified Moore's law was that users kept finding new needs for these machines as they became more powerful.

Digitalisation was also applied to telecommunications, going beyond computations on individual machines. The first wide digital telecom network was developed by the US military as a decentralised system to ensure operation in the event of nuclear war. This technology eventually became available to civilian society as the basis for the internet. Since then, data transmission also followed its own version of Moore's law. Telephone networks were also digitalised with the development of the wireless mobile phone and network.

On the back of the combined digitalisation of telecoms and the development of personal computers, new ways of communicating like email, online chat rooms, forums and later social media were developed. These have revolutionised how people communicate. The technologies have also enabled a radical revolution in business management and organisation. Typists lost their jobs, but so did filing managers, printing staff and many others.

New markets like Amazon and eBay developed online, starting the revolutionary practice of shopping from a computer screen, rather than from a physical shop. Not having a physical shop meant big cost reductions, and the economics of the high street changed. Products could be shipped from far away, giving consumers a much larger choice.

Many products, like music, cinema and culture, became sold on a material-free basis. Records, cassette tapes and CDs were replaced by streams of ones and zeros. We don't need to make things to store music on any more.

Computers and telecoms also revolutionised manufacturing. Robots have begun to replace large numbers of manual workers. They are 'capital-intensive', which means that through upfront investment they replace future staff wages. They may last a long time but often pay for themselves in just a few years. We will return to the typical capital-intensive character of technological revolutions in Chapter 5.

For all that, the digital revolution is now reaching its limits, and progress is slowing. Moore's law began to be questioned in the 2000s, as the limits of miniaturisation became increasingly visible. As transistors reached dimensions in nanometers, they got nearer and nearer to the size of the silicon atoms themselves. Components made up of just a handful of atoms are not stable nor reliable. Furthermore, the increasing heat and high temperature generated by ultrafast computations in nanoscale semiconductor structures also became a problem. Moore's law is running into the brick wall that is the fundamental laws of physics.

What happened instead was that the computer changed and became something else. The 'smart' phone was commercialised, a combination of a computer, internet terminal, television and mobile phone. Sales of the traditional desktop computer with keyboard and mouse peaked and began to decline, replaced by the smart phone, the 'tablet' and all sorts of other devices that became smart (cars, TVs, home heating systems, etc). Microprocessors became so cheap that they could be incorporated into every home appliance.

In this way, the brick wall that is the end of Moore's law could be avoided by decentralising the work of computers. Online servers gather lots of processors to offer high-level computing, sold by computing power units. Personal computers do not need to do all the work any more.

In that sense, the IT revolution has begun to consolidate itself in the last decade. There are few additional surprises to expect with the internet and computers. We appear to have seen most of it. We are looking back on the golden age of the IT revolution, and its end may be in sight. A new great wave is brewing or even taking off now.

What is coming, seems to be something different: automation and artificial intelligence, where robots really begin to replace humans on a very large scale. We discuss the new wave of innovation in Chapter 6, including how it could affect the zero-carbon transition. But before that, we look at the common threads across the great waves to see what matters most.

4.3 COMMON THREADS ACROSS THE GREAT WAVES

4.3.1 *The Signs of a Revolution*

There are many common threads in the past five industrial revolutions (Figure 4.7). Identifying them may help us to determine where

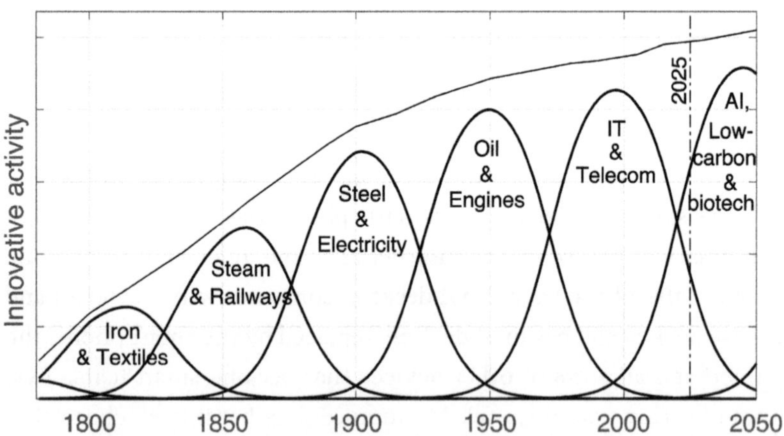

FIGURE 4.7 Sketch of the great waves and clustering of innovation, according to when they started and ended. The curves are only illustrative. IT = Information Technology; AI = Artificial Intelligence.

we are in terms of a new great wave of innovation and in which phase. They are as follows:

(1) *A cycle of roughly 50 years in duration;*
(2) *The spread of a cluster of innovations that revolutionise the economy;*
(3) *Profound changes in the structure of the economy;*
(4) *The creation of a whole range of new industries;*
(5) *The decline of another range of outdated industries;*
(6) *Radical change in economic productivity in many sectors;*
(7) *Economic, financial, political and social instability at the end of the cycle.*

In each of the revolutions described in Section 4.2, there was a big increase in the rate of innovation and new products during the upswing. For example, towards the beginning of the twentieth century, as the steel age drew to an end, there was not as much innovative activity. That changed in the 1920s when the car and oil frenzy started.

The lull between waves has usually been a difficult time of instability. Most recently, the period since 2000 has seen growing instability, including the 2007 financial crisis. In the 2020s, there is no sign yet that we are through this period.

The most important feature of the upswing period is that, without fail, use of key products has increased quickly as prices have fallen. The result is that the cost reduction of key new elements in terms of cumulative production follows the classical learning curve. The bigger the scale, the cheaper it gets. Almost by definition, its price beats the incumbent obsolete version, which has a stable price.

The upswing usually leads to a period of financial sector frenzy around the new technologies and, according to the technology historian Carlota Perez, to a financial bubble and crash. The frenzy reflects the high profit rates possible from the new technologies because of radically declining costs. But it is also because investors lack knowledge about technical limits and when to stop investing. Exaggerated expectations eventually lead to a financial bubble that bursts. A prime example is the dotcom crash in 2001 when many IT companies were grossly overvalued.

The golden age of technologies is generally more peaceful and characterised by moderate profits and expectations. But it is during that period when the next wave begins to brew in the background, setting the stage for the decline and new upswing.

Although each great wave involves lots of 'creative destruction', it need not be the outcomes from the previous wave that are destroyed. The IT revolution did not destroy petrochemicals. But it has helped to make petrochemical plants more efficient, reducing the need to employ people.

And this is usually what happens. Each great wave solves a key productivity bottleneck in the economy. The productivity gains obtained from cutting out obsolete technologies can affect anyone, including those that grew wealthy in previous waves.

The golden age and decline of a technological era happens when it discovers its own limitations. Investors start to turn their attention elsewhere as they seek better returns. They are willing to take on more risk, including on untested products. The next wave is set in motion.

4.3.2 The Evidence for Great Waves

Quantitative evidence supporting unambiguously the great waves in terms of production, employment or investment is scarce. However, the historical evidence corroborating them is plentiful, as described in this chapter. One indirect way to find some evidence is to look at present-day R&D activities by sector, which is indicative of where productivity gains, cost reductions and profits currently come from.

Michael Grubb discusses R&D investment trends in his landmark book.[18] Figure 4.8 shows R&D expenditures of the top 2,000 companies worldwide as a fraction of sales income. A company that has little to gain from R&D, for example, one that sits in an old industry, will usually invest a low share of its revenue. Companies in new sectors in full development will in contrast invest a large share of

[18] See Planetary Economics (Grubb et al., 2014).

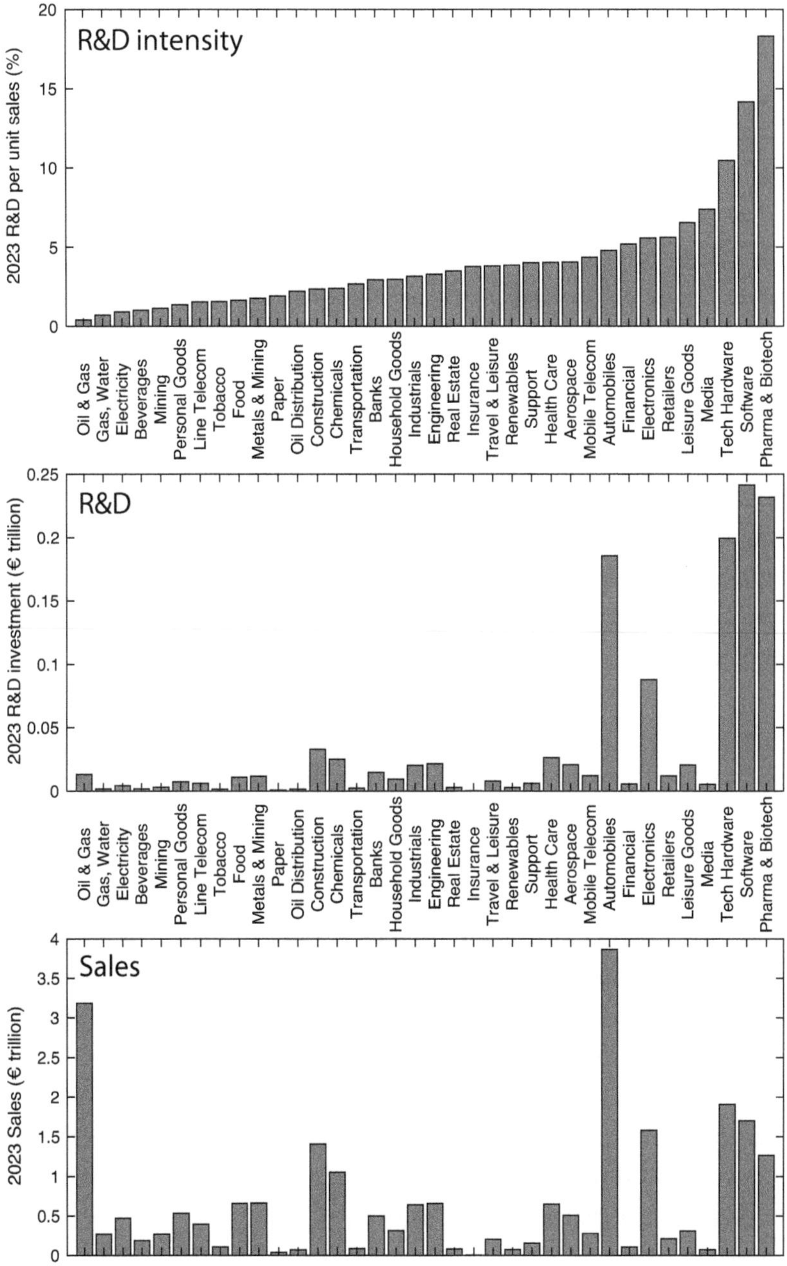

FIGURE 4.8 R&D investment by the top 2000 companies worldwide, in 2024 EUR. Data from the European Commission's 2024 EU Indus- trial R&D Investment Scoreboard, at https://iri.jrc.ec.europa.eu/scoreboard/2024-eu-industrial-rd-investment-scoreboard.

their revenues. They have many opportunities for discovering new products or efficiencies and cannot fall behind their competitors.

The data show that IT and software, these sectors can be identified with the new industries from the latest great wave in its golden age, and the new great wave in development. Automobiles are still going strong too. However, chemicals, oil & gas, metals and mining, the heavy industries, transport and electricity see little R&D investment. These sectors can clearly be identified with older technological paradigms, where much less can be gained from R&D activities.

A new great wave could trigger lots of R&D by rejuvenating many old sectors including, notably, power generation (renewables) and automobiles. The classification of data is therefore tricky. Higher disaggregation between high- and low-carbon activities could improve the analysis. But, nevertheless, the connection between Figures 4.7 and 4.8 is obvious. The sectoral distribution of present-day investment in innovation is reflective of economic and technological history.

4.3.3 The End of Technological Eras

In this book, we are interested in both the rise and decline of technological eras. It is certainly interesting to try to foresee what the new age of technology will bring us. However, the new age has not been fully invented yet, and there are therefore clear limits to the knowable. We explore this in Chapter 6.

Where the study of technological change has most relevance to social and economic analysis, well-being, politics and stability is with the end of technological eras. The study of the end phase helps us understand structural change in the economy and the painful 'crises of structural adjustment'.[19] This is where many older technologies and skills become obsolete. This usually leaves deep marks in economic, social and urban landscapes.

[19] Freeman and Louçã (2001).

For example, travelling across Northern English, Scottish and Northern Irish cities shows landscapes and cityscapes scarred by the first two industrial revolutions, with disused textile mills, warehouses, coal pits, canals and harbours. Some of the buildings have been redeveloped into trendy, red-brick flats and habitable urban environments. This is notable in Manchester, Leeds, Birmingham, Newcastle, Glasgow and Belfast. Little of the work in textiles, coal transport on barges, steelmaking and shipbuilding remains nowadays, but many of the structures remind us of the history.

Post-industrial decline has been severe in these areas following the gradual decline of the industries of past technological eras. The last few spots of coal mining and steelmaking died during the Thatcher years. Deep marks have been left in the spirit and culture of British working class communities. We review this in Chapter 7.

4.3.4 Are We in a Sixth Technological Revolution?

Because we cannot predict the future, there is no scientific justification to think that every wave should last for 50 years as Kondratiev and Schumpeter suggested back in the 1920s. The fact that it was like this in the past does not determine the future. However, that there have been five full 50-year cycles gives good evidence that it works this way. Will the future look the same? If we want to argue that we are about to see the upswing of a new technological revolution, we need to find evidence.

The signs are there, as discussed in Chapter 1, and some evidence can be seen in Figure 4.8. The trick is that, to see the future, you must look at research at universities. In the last two decades, it's all been about medical research, biotechnology, artificial intelligence, robotics and green innovation. Research in chemistry and physics had its heyday in the post-war years and is now taking the backstage.

Artificial intelligence and automation are already causing severe structural change in the economy. A great deal of money is spent on innovation in biotechnology and pharmaceuticals. We need to piece this puzzle together. What is the next great wave really about? Nobody has the overview, but, nonetheless, research continues.

AI and biotech may yet still give us an incomplete map of the new constellation of innovations, since we are now also seeing that 'getting rid of combustion' in the energy sector might solve another productivity bottleneck. The costs of solar panels, wind turbines, batteries and heat pumps are declining rapidly, soon to cross parity with the older ways of doing things. By definition, these technologies must therefore be part of the next great wave. These are the key building blocks for a combustion-free economy.

The combustion-free revolution may have been kick-started by climate policy aimed at reducing emissions. But no technological change happens without innovation driving cost reductions in search of profits, as otherwise the movement would die in the womb. Climate policy may have given industry the grounds to create part of a technological revolution that will, among other things, solve the combustion-based productivity bottleneck. We review this in the next chapters.

5 The Life Cycle of Products and Sectors

5.1 THE NEED FOR A NEW THEORY OF ECONOMIC GROWTH

5.1.1 No Theory of Economic Growth in Economics

Growing up in Canada, J-F, used to frequently hear that the paper industry, a pride of the nation, was endlessly in financial difficulties. He couldn't understand why. We use plenty of paper, and we are not running out of trees. So what is the problem?

Maybe we should not expect children to answer this question. More surprisingly, after learning economics, J-F realised he still had no answer.

Let's start from the beginning. Most economists now agree that economic growth comes from building things, accumulating them and improving what we build through innovation.

The big names of mainstream economics have it all figured out. Philippe Aghion tells us that the more innovative countries grow faster, provided they have competitive markets. Daron Acemoglu insists that we direct growth if we tell scientists which way to orient their innovation. Paul Romer told us that accumulating knowledge and human skills together are a source of growth.[1]

But in the end, this seems a bit thin. Is this all that economic theory can tell us about what growth is and where it comes from? Economics is good at keeping track of how many machines we have but not how they get better as we build more.

Economists from outside mainstream economics can say a bit more. Thorstein Veblen (in the late nineteenth century) and

[1] See Aghion et al. (2021); Acemoglu et al. (2012); Romer (1986).

Joseph Schumpeter (in the 1930s) described 'cumulative causation' (of knowledge accumulation) and 'novel combinations' (of inputs to production) to describe technology development. However, the link between new technology and economic growth has still not been properly explained.

There have been other insights too. An economist called Petrus Johannes Verdoorn told us in 1949 that growth came from scale effects – producing higher volumes means more efficiency. In the 1950s, Nicholas Kaldor linked technological change to falling costs that generate consumer demand and lead to economic growth. Tony Thirlwall expanded on this theory to identify competitiveness increases as a result of higher output, generating increasing returns.[2]

Economic historians, including Schumpeter, Chris Freeman and Carlota Perez told us that economic growth comes from great waves of innovation, as we saw in Chapter 4. Giovanni Dosi pointed out that technological change is deeply path-dependent and clusters along particular trajectories with occasional discontinuities.[3]

All this is better, but it still doesn't predict or explain growth in any practical way. We haven't really progressed that much from Veblen's original insights in the nineteenth century.

It is astonishing that there isn't a more sophisticated theory of growth in economics. After all, economists predict economic growth rates all the time. Highly respected organisations, like the World Bank, the IMF and the OECD, make economic forecasts quarterly.

Mainstream economics must take some of the blame. Technology development is not really covered in most economics degrees. It is instead assumed to happen autonomously 'outside the system'. But technology development is also incompatible with the theories of equilibrium that underpin mainstream economics. We can't have both at the same time, so the economists choose equilibrium.

[2] See Kaldor (1957); Thirlwall (1979).

[3] See Freeman and Louçã (2001); Perez (2001); Dosi (1982).

This is rather depressing for people who want to know the impacts of a zero-carbon transition (or any transition) on economic growth – including policy-makers. Most economists seem to have a view on the matter but cannot give a good explanation. It becomes some kind of obscure fortune telling.

Most economic models do not even try. Instead of predicting what happens to technology and economic growth, they assume that technology doesn't change, but improves 'productivity' at a certain rate, without explaining what that means. The models leave out the single most important factor that determines how wealthy we are.

Instead, the models tell us what might happen if technology doesn't change but we rearrange our economies a bit differently. Reallocation. Even this they don't do well. They assume that we can't arrange the economy better than we do already. Trying to prevent climate change can therefore only make things worse.

So the models say there is no free lunch for saving the planet. There are costs. Always costs. The job for policy-makers is to minimise these costs and protect the economic growth that was entered in the model by assumption. The easiest way is to do nothing while other countries reduce emissions. Unsurprisingly, with this sort of advice, nothing happens quickly.

As should now be clear to the reader, this view misconstrues the fact that transitions are fundamentally about technological change. They are about innovation. Innovation that leads to economic growth.

And there is a paradox that even the economists cannot explain. If you ask them, they will say that innovation leads to economic growth. But they also say that the zero-carbon transition does not. Why is it that any kind of grey or brown innovation is *good* for economic growth, but green innovation, very specifically, is *bad*? Surely, it doesn't depend on the colour!

This is what happens when there is no proper description of how economic growth happens. A book like this one should not need to get into these issues, but the gaps in current economic theory make it necessary. This chapter covers the basics. We make no distinction regarding the colour of the innovation.

5.1.2 *The Role of Innovation in Growth*

Nearly all economists recognise that innovation is key to economic growth. Innovation means inventing. It could be inventing entirely new things (product innovation) or inventing better ways to make existing things (process innovation).

These 'things' may be physical goods that we buy in shops. They could also be less tangible, like services we buy or even business models.

Let's now put innovation into a basic theory of growth.[4] There is no point beating a dead horse: they get better but we cannot reinvent the car or the computer multiple times. To generate economic growth, we need genuine product or process innovation.

Many things in our lives cannot be improved anymore. They are as good as they can be. Think about basic commodities that have existed for centuries. They will not drive economic growth.

We could therefore run out of sources of economic growth if we run out of ideas and things to improve. Fortunately, this seems never to happen. We always seem able to keep inventing new things or improving existing things. Doing this gives us even more new ideas. We have this virtuous cycle between having new ideas, creating new things and improving existing things.

The closest we have for an innovation theory of growth comes from a journal article that was published in 1975 by James Utterback and William Abernethy.[5] Tellingly, the journal that published the article focused on industrial innovation, sitting outside traditional economics.

[4] Let's define growth as that of purchasing power in an economy, and innovation as any change in production processes or products made that increases profit, whether by developing new knowledge or using knowledge from elsewhere.

[5] See Utterback and Abernathy (1975).

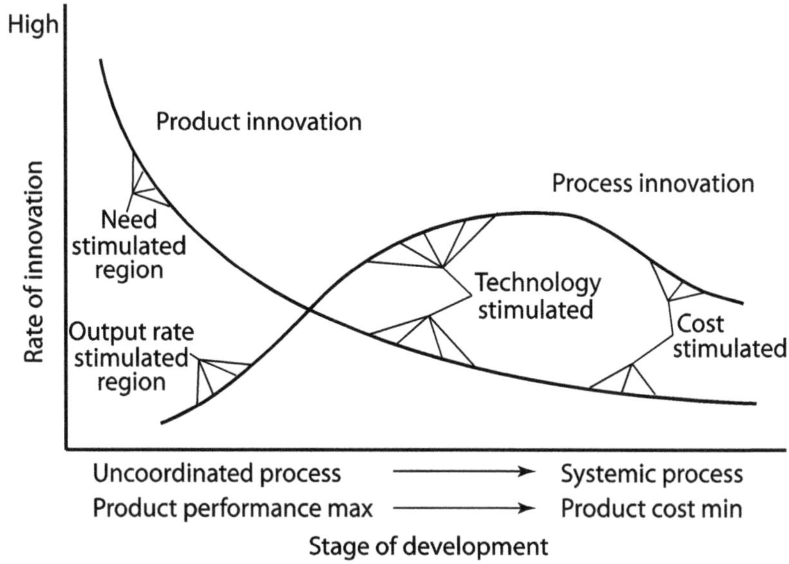

FIGURE 5.1 The innovation life cycle, according to Utterback and Abernathy (1975).

The two authors showed, with plenty of real-world evidence, how products are invented and are improved later (Figure 5.1). A product is first invented and then developed to become sellable. It is brought to market, focusing on performance. As the product takes off, the focus turns to cost-cutting. The product becomes cheap and can be sold to mass markets.

How does all this relate to economic growth? We could think of the economy as a fire in a stove. To start with, there is a small flame to which we add fuel, maybe newspaper. The fire is very slow at first, because it must build heat around itself and heat up the surrounding fuel.

If it takes off, the fire burns brightly for a short period but dies down when the paper runs out. Even if there is wood in the stove, it may be too cold to catch fire. Adding more paper allows more heat to be generated. Eventually, the wood burns too.

As the fire grows, we regularly add larger logs of solid wood. Not too quickly, because new logs are damp and cool the fire down.

Not too slowly, because the fire could run out and lose heat. If the fire dies, it may be difficult to restart.

The fire creates its own fuel by drying the incoming logs. Each log keeps the fire going and grows it a little. The fire cannot burn just paper, because it would last no time at all. It also cannot burn the same log twice. The heat generated by old logs helps start the flame on new ones.

The important point is that fuel for economic growth is like lumpy logs of interrelated ideas and investment fed to the economic fire. The fire creates its own fuel with the help of the people that benefit from it. The same happens with innovation.

As we know from Chapter 4, great waves of innovation are like big logs that come in big clusters of related things. We can't burn ideas one at a time. They come in groups. Putting new logs in is mostly about *product innovation*, whereas drying off the logs is more like *process innovation*. The flame is the flow of economic value, and the smoke in the flue is the waste product.

To grow the economy, we must endlessly burn off ideas to find new ones.

For example, in the early 1900s, the economy was unstable and sluggish. As we saw in Chapter 4, the internal combustion engine had already been invented (by Nikolaus Otto in 1861), but, although new, it was still a bit niche and expensive. Meanwhile, the existing economic fire wasn't doing well because electricity and steel production seemed to have gone as far as they could.

Then, a very large log in the fire caught light. Oil extraction was commercialised, and oil refining developed the fuels that the internal combustion engine needed. The possibilities for new ideas suddenly seemed endless.

The results included car making, petrochemicals, airplanes, paved roads and plastics. All of this kept the economic fire going until the 1970s.

The next log on the economic fire was completely different. It included semiconductors, transistors and microchips. It brought in the age of information and changed how people communicate.

This particular log is still burning, although it may now be dying. We are all now looking to the next log. As we saw, several are getting hot, including making people live longer, 'smartification' and 'getting rid of combustion'. They may have already been lit.

5.1.3 Designing an Economic Model of Growth

Computer models are as close to a laboratory as we can get in macroeconomics. They can help us to understand how the economy works. They can also be used to make predictions, as economists frequently do. We develop and modify our models until the outcomes really describe well the reality that we see around us. However, models always remain flawed to some degree; they are just models.

And we have to be careful. Economic forecasts are notoriously bad already. Lots of unexpected things can affect the economic fire in the short term, such as Vladimir Putin going to war in Ukraine or central banks increasing interest rates.

Here, we are more interested in longer-term effects. This does not mean we can ignore the short term, however. We have just discussed how apparently small developments can change the course of history. And of course, the long term is just the outcome of a series of short-term periods. But often, short-term surprises either delay or accelerate what would have happened anyway. If so, we can make some predictions.

Our focus is on explaining the gradual addition of logs to the economic fire. We start with the idea that logs must be added regularly to the fire and that the fire maintains itself by heating the new logs until they can be burnt too. There are lots of small logs and occasional big ones.

An account of economic history is helpful, as we did in Chapter 4. This tells us about the logs already in the fire and how much of them remain. We call these logs economic sectors. They include agriculture, mining, coal, oil, gas, chemicals, cars, electricity, distribution, IT, health care and so on. We have data on all of that.

The sectors are often closely related. Cars need petrol that is refined by the chemical sector. The chemical sector gets its inputs from the oil sector. The distribution sector links the sectors together, which may be in different geographical locations. We have tables that account for transactions between sectors that help us link the sectors to one another. We have tables of trade of goods that help us link countries to one another.

But these numbers don't explain growth still; they just explain what flows of economic value we see today. The fire will stop growing and die if it runs out of logs that are ready to burn. It needs logs added. It needs to be able to heat these logs. That's our innovation system.

This is the difficult part to put in a model, because nobody can predict exactly what the new innovative ideas will be. Therefore, we have to make assumptions about what new ideas we will have and how much investment these ideas will motivate. That is, how much heat is to be released by the new logs of fuel that we assume will be added to the fire. We can make good guesses about that. But we can't be sure.

Is it possible that the fire could run out of fuel and die? Yes. There was a long period when the economy was mainly agriculture and was too cold to light other logs. Since the industrial revolution, however, new logs have kept coming. For the time being at least, human problem-solving and our constant desire for new things seem likely to keep the fire going.

More of a risk may be that someone, or perhaps everyone collectively, pours water on the fire. Wars, or unchecked climate change, could indeed do this.

It should be clear from the analogy in this section that the future path of innovation has not already been written; therefore, economic growth is not yet determined. No two fires burn exactly the same. Some may not catch light. We do not know what will be invented in the future, if anything at all! Our theory should expect many different future stories of innovation and economic evolution.

5.2 THE LIFE CYCLE THEORY OF GROWTH

We sort of take it for granted that some sectors in the economy grow quickly and others do not. The growing ones include IT and internet services, smart phones and similar high-value electronic products. Some of them, including EVs and renewable energy equipment, may struggle to grow fast enough to produce all that people want.

The ones that always seem to be in some kind of decline (in the west) include car manufacturing, steelmaking, textiles and coal mining. As young J-F realised, paper also falls into this category.

As we discuss in Chapter 7, oil and gas extraction, transformation and distribution may be about to move from the growing quickly group to the always in decline group.

We rarely ask why this sort of thing happens. It is obvious that the sectors doing well are new and the sectors in decline are old. That seems to answer the question. But agriculture is old. Food production is old. Although not high-growth sectors, in developed countries at least, we don't generally think of these sectors as being in decline.

We saw in Chapter 4 that the maturity of sectors comes mainly from the timing of the great waves of innovation. The IT revolution was the last great wave. Oil and cars came before that. Some basic logic tells us that sectors from old revolutions see less prosperity today because all the innovation that could be done in them has mostly been done by now.

That is only part of the story though. The innovation in the new sectors steadily chips away at previous growth. We still need as much food as before, but tractors and automation have drastically reduced the numbers of workers we need to produce it. We use plenty of paper, but computers and the internet have gradually limited our use enough for growth in the paper industry to stagnate. Finally, an answer to young J-F's question starts to appear.

As our analogy with logs on the fire suggests, there is a *life cycle* in innovation and economic growth. Each log is a discrete sector. It's added to the fire. It burns, brightly at first, then produces

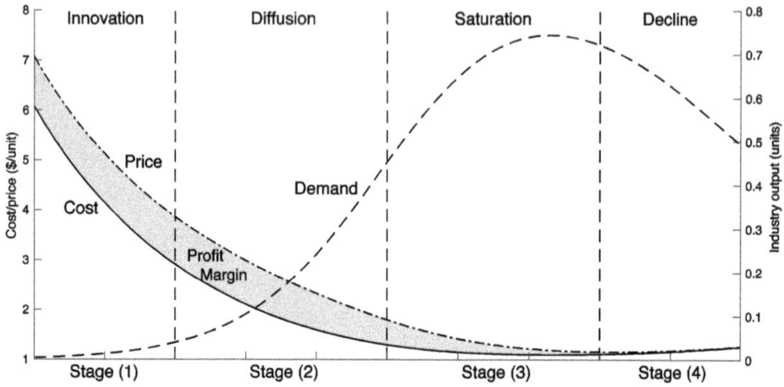

FIGURE 5.2 The life cycle of products and sectors (Mercure, 2022).

heat, but declines over time. Eventually, it is turned to ash. Figure 5.2 illustrates the life cycle.

We did not invent this life cycle theory of economic change. Plenty of scholars have worked on it before, but they were mostly based in geography departments, rather than in economics.[6] They mainly tried to explain why and how cities develop around specific sectors, rather than the growth of the entire economy.

In the new sectors, companies like being close together because they can learn from each other and come up with new ideas. In the old sectors, companies often with financial difficulties see only problems in their location, because it maintains old ways of doing things. This makes them uncompetitive and unable to move on.[7]

This type of research forms a critical part of understanding the wider effects of rise and decline in the sunrise and sunset industries.

5.2.1 *Stage 1: The Birth of a Sector*

Tech companies sometimes talk about building *platforms*. Amazon is a platform that allows other companies to sell things online. On a much bigger scale, platforms are the basis of the great waves. The combination of oil extraction and refining provided the platform for cars, plastics and much more.

[6] See, for instance, Klepper (1997); Krugman (1991).
[7] See, in particular, Potter and Watts (2011).

New sectors are established. At first, only small amounts are produced, maybe serving niche uses. Costs are high because it is expensive to produce in small volumes. There is a lot of investment, which initially adds further to costs.

For example, a printing company will monitor its average cost per page printed. A new printer is expensive, but paper and ink are not. So, the average cost of each page falls quickly as more pages are printed.

It is not just scale effects though. Over time, the printing company will find cheaper ways of printing, for example, using only black ink for some purposes. At this early stage, they have not yet had a chance to explore these options.

High costs are reflected in high prices, and the companies may still make losses. The focus is on building a future market. Here, we must think about the whole constellation of innovations. As we already saw with fuel and cars, the parts of the constellation work together, with falling prices driving demand for multiple new products.

The sunrise period begins. Everyone looks to the future. Companies in the new sector are full of ideas. They want to be near each other and work together.

5.2.2 *Stage 2: Rapid Growth and Returns*

Great fortunes are made in the second stage. Innovation turns increasingly towards cost reduction and streamlining. Sales increase rapidly as prices fall. Profit margins may decline, but this is more than offset by rising volumes. Large profits result.

This is how John D Rockefeller, who owned most of the US oil industry in the late nineteenth century, became the richest man in the world. Oil started to change the whole economy. Oil-powered engines were used, directly or indirectly, in almost everything people did. And everything started to fit around all the new things oil could do: cars, airplanes, machinery, plastics, paved roads and war machines.

Here, companies make money out of rapidly rising volumes and high profit margins.

Over time, new companies start to take advantage of the opportunities. Competition grows and prices may be forced down further. Competition drives further innovation, especially in ways to reduce costs. Companies that cannot reduce costs sometimes go bankrupt. Consumers win with cheaper products. Demand continues to grow.

5.2.3 *Stage 3: Volume and Profit Squeeze*

There is a point, however, at which innovation bites back. At this point, companies making the product start to run out ways to cut costs. Buyers of the new products start innovating themselves. They find ways to reduce their own costs, by using less of the product.

For example, companies have strong cost incentives to improve fuel efficiency. They innovate to do so. The outcome is good for them but less good for the fuel companies. The rapid growth from Stage 2 slows.

Innovation can also bite back if natural limits are reached. Sales volumes may remain high, but growth slows. Prices may increase, or continue to decline, but finding further cost reductions becomes difficult. Profit margins come under pressure.

Stage 3 is the golden age, when companies still make profits out of large volumes and low profit margins, and consumers benefit from both more products and lower prices.

5.2.4 *Stage 4: Decline and Decreasing Returns*

Companies are usually good at handling rapid growth. They are less good at managing stagnation or decline.

Finance may be a problem. If no one expects profits to grow, it will be difficult to attract finance to repair existing equipment. Banks rarely lend to companies in stagnation or decline, unless a turnaround is expected. This can make it difficult to manage cashflow.

Staffing may also become a problem. If income stagnates, companies cannot hire. If income falls faster than natural staff turnover (i.e., people retiring or moving jobs), then redundancies become necessary. These bring further costs to the company (and of course the people). Even without laying off staff, career opportunities will be limited.

Usually, companies do not gradually wind down operations. They instead go through a series of painful reorganisations. They may go bankrupt. The human cost can be substantial.

Take the example of Kodak, once digital cameras took over. Kodak knew about chemistry and old film photos. It was not an electronics company. When demand for Kodak products fell, the company faced financial problems. It was broken up.

Kodak found what many other companies in similar positions did. People still use film for photography and video, but as production falls with demand, scale economies go into reverse, and the average cost of each production unit increases. But raising prices pushes more customers towards digital. It's a doom loop that often ends in bankruptcy.

In addition to rising average costs, equipment and machinery start to degrade. With no expectation of future profit, companies cut investment, even if finance is available. Product quality may deteriorate, pushing more customers away.

As long as there is some product demand, the sector will still exist. But it is a tough life both for the companies left and their workers. There is a constant threat of plant closure and unemployment.

In many countries, the paper industry is in Stage 4. Yes, we still use paper, but not as much as we used to. The sector could supply much more paper than we need. Remaining companies must scrap equipment to stay alive and supply the remaining demand. They are under constant pressure.

Worryingly, in a de-growth scenario (see Chapter 2), most of the economy would be in Stage 4. We have only just begun to explore the challenges that would pose.

5.3 GROWTH FROM PROCESS AND PRODUCT INNOVATION

The story of the life cycle of products and sectors is easy to understand. It can explain a lot of what we see today, including the rising economic power of Silicon Valley in California and the declining car industry in the Great Lakes region of the US and Canada.

It is a good story, but it is less good at predicting future trends. For that, we would need to predict future inventions. We cannot know about something that has not yet been invented.

It is possible to make some predictions, however. Economic growth is very regular, and so are the life cycles of products and sectors. History tells us that each great wave of innovation lasts about 50 years.[8]

In the life cycle, Stage 1 may be impossible to predict, but we may have a pretty good idea about Stages 2, 3 and 4. We can make informed guesses about how young and old sectors age.

We can build a simple model to illustrate the growth process. The model simulates innovative activity and investment without knowing in detail what the nature of the innovation is – thereby avoiding the problem of not knowing what will be invented.

The model includes a basic macroeconomic framework that covers expenditure in investment and operations (we call these CAPEX and OPEX[9]). It is split into sectors and shows how the sectors interact. We build the process of creative destruction into this framework. The model shows the growth and decline of sectors. We can use it to examine how all this affects economic growth.

Utterback and Abernethy tell us that we need to understand how process and product innovation work together. To do this, we

[8] See Kondratieff (1928); Schumpeter (1934, 1939); Freeman and Louçã (2001); Perez (2001); Mercure (2022).

[9] We classify expenditure into two categories, depending on whether or not the spender expects the spending to generate future income. If they do, we call it CAPital EXpenditure (CAPEX, e.g. a taxi driver investing in a vehicle). If they do not, we call it OPerational EXpenditure (OPEX, e.g. someone buying a train ticket for immediate travel).

break down process innovation into basic building blocks. In each building block, a company makes investment to reduce operational costs or increase income.

Each building block looks at the life cycle *over time* of the investment (either in innovation or new equipment). The model looks at how many life cycles occur and how they overlap. Many investment life cycles (e.g. each lasting ten years) will make up the entire sector's life cycle (lasting over fifty years).

Each time investment is made, it contributes to economic growth. Conversely, when investment stops, it contributes to economic decline. We develop a prediction for overall economic growth by adding lots of overlapping building blocks together. We start the model simple and gradually add real-world features.

5.3.1 Process Innovation

We start off with a simple model of process innovation. For now, the model does not look too far ahead or to the point where we run out of ideas for improving existing products.

The model uses Schumpeter's teaching device,[10] an ordinary circular flow of purchases in the economy, representing money and goods changing hands at a regular pace. To begin with, we make the (very unrealistic) assumption that profits are zero and that companies are hugely competitive. Companies can produce a fixed amount of goods. They pay to maintain their equipment but do not enhance it. Their capacity to produce things, therefore, starts off constant. We will improve this model gradually in this section and Sections 5.3.2 and 5.3.3.

We add to this simple zero-profit economy a company that disrupts the circular flow, by doing the following project:

1. Developing a new method that reduces average production costs for a particular product;

[10] Schumpeter used this approach to explain economic growth in his *Theory of Economic Development* (Schumpeter, 1934).

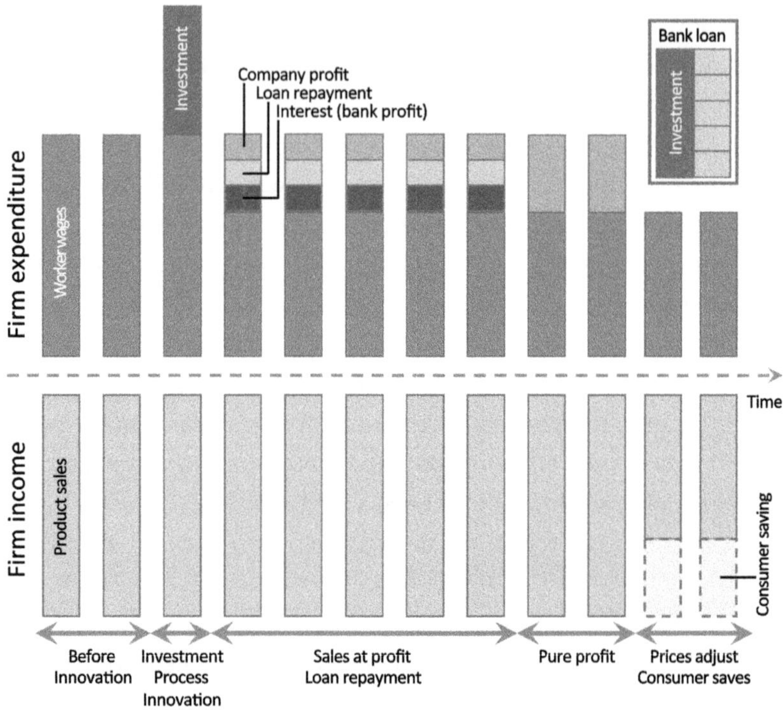

FIGURE 5.3 The income flows through time for one firm's process of investment in expansion and improving production capacity, following Schumpeter.

2. Convincing a financial institution to lend it money (or invest in equity) to apply this idea;
3. Investing the money and changing its production method;
4. Making a profit by producing at a lower cost while selling at the prevailing price;
5. Repaying the loan with interest (or paying out dividends to shareholders).

Investment in process innovation does not always work out. If the new production method does not work, the company may be unable to repay the loan. It could go bankrupt.

The full process for a company is illustrated in Figure 5.3. The figure looks at economic flows over time for one project in a company that sells one product. The normal circular flow is shown in the first two bars. The product initially sells at a price equal to production costs. There is, therefore, no profit.

In the third bar, someone lends money to the company. The company invests in improving its equipment. It can now produce at a lower cost.

The fourth bar shows the period when costs are lower but the product is still sold at the same price. Some of the leftover income goes to paying off the loan, including interest (the bank's profit). The rest is the company's profit. Once the loan is fully paid off, all the difference is profit.

As long as the company is not a monopoly, eventually, other companies can make similar investments and catch-up in competitiveness. They can then also produce at a lower cost and could set prices to undercut the first company (though it does not always happen). Market prices can be forced down until once again they match costs and there is no more profit (although they could also collude to keep the prices high). Consumers benefit because the product is now cheaper (or that's what ideally happens).

We should keep in mind that a zero-profit circular flow, if it ever exists, lasts only for a moment. That's because companies, in reality, when in a highly competitive market, continuously invest to cut cost, in a race for dominance, and the zero-profit outcome is never reached. But we use Schumpeter's teaching device for clarity.

As we will also see, this is an idealisation. Things don't always turn out this way, as numerous monopolies are created that don't benefit consumers. But nonetheless, we assume for now that process innovation plays out like this regularly and repetitively. Companies do it on a continuous basis so that their profits don't decline to zero – as long as banks will keep lending them money to keep improving the productive equipment.

In the model, we therefore repeat the investment process displayed in Figure 5.3 over and over in an overlapping manner. People lend at every time step, and companies endlessly invest. Companies are, therefore, always in debt, even though they pay back their loans. Costs and prices in the economy are always falling.

This all sounds realistic, until we get to the last point. Prices tend to go up, not down. Is this how things really work?

Figure 5.4 shows that the costs of lots of consumer goods have fallen over time, as more of them have been made and sold. However, we must not deceive ourselves: innovating gets harder the more we do it.

Tellingly, the figure uses logarithmic scales. This means that over time we must put more and more effort into innovation to maintain the same rate of cost reduction. Another way of looking at it is we can only invent what has not been invented already, and we typically invent the easier things first, leaving harder and harder things to do later.

The best known example is Moore's law, which says that computing power doubled every eighteen months during the IT revolution. The prices of computers stayed about the same though; it's the computers that could do ever more stuff. These benefits were maintained by ever-increasing investment, funded by increased sales of computers (see Chapter 4).

The finance sector gets involved too. With the expectations of future growth, banks are willing to lend more. Borrowing costs may also fall. Share prices may rise. The available money to invest, can grow *exponentially* ... for a period.

Innovation theory tells us that every innovation opens the door for more future innovation. This is critical for understanding product innovation (see below) but is also important in process innovation. As products become cheaper, businesses find new ways to use them.

For example, cheap computer chips are now used well beyond computers. Many are used in cars. Whereas once the chips would have cost more than the entire car, now they add little if anything to the car's price. And consumers like what they get.

If we add lots of instances of Figure 5.3 in a sector, plus some random variation, we get something like Figure 5.5 (to see mathematically how we generated these graphs, see Appendix B). As the reputation of various companies grow with successful innovation, so

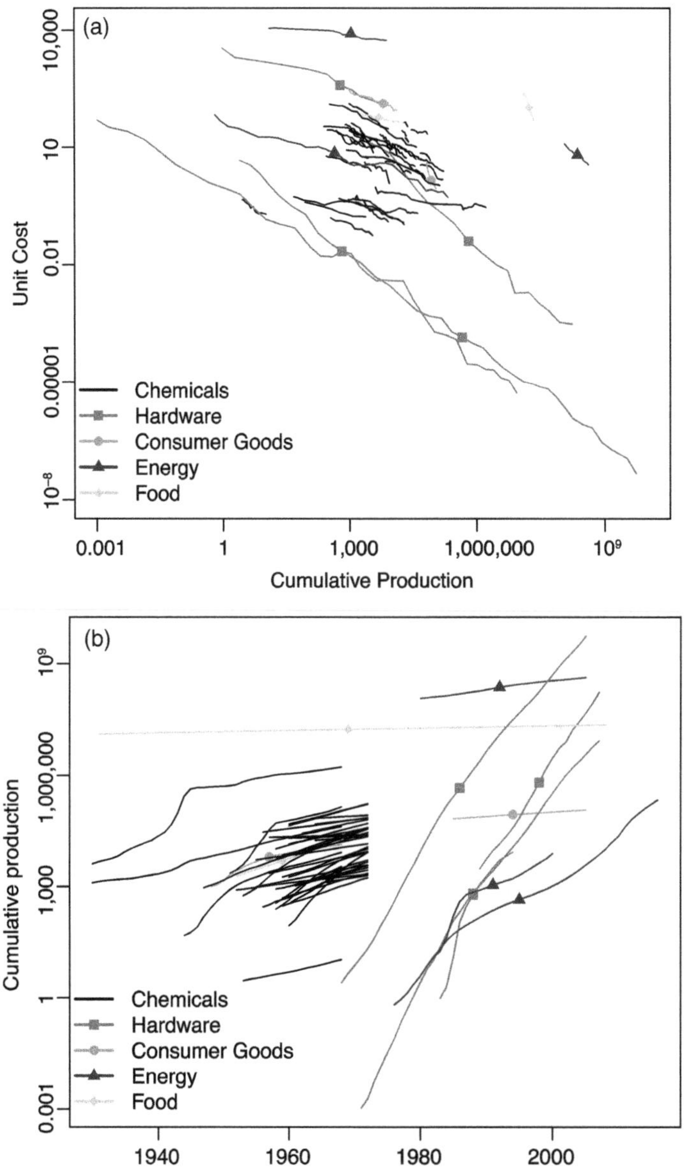

FIGURE 5.4 The experience curve, where (a) costs come down by a constant factor with each doubling of cumulative production (experience) and (b) cumulative production rises exponentially over time (Lafond et al., 2018).

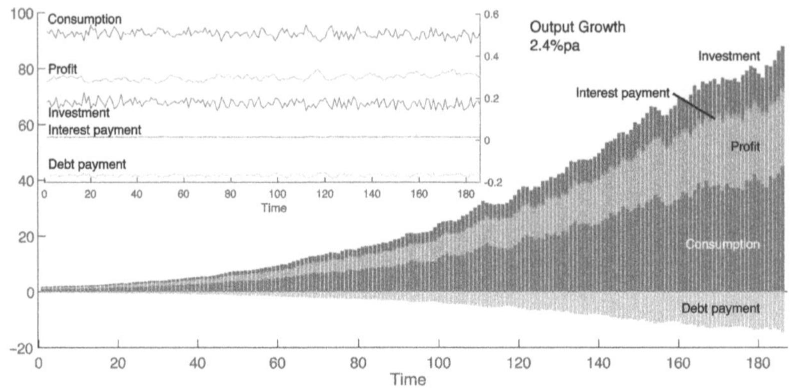

FIGURE 5.5 The mechanism of process innovation applied over and over with exponentially rising investment.

does the amount of finance available to them. People invest in companies with a proven track record. The more they lend, the more confident they become, which allows investment to grow.

This helps both the firm and the wider economy, because the sectors that provide the investment goods (e.g. construction and manufacturing) benefit too. As long as the investment keeps increasing, we get economic growth. That is until the sector (or the economy) gradually runs out of ideas or innovation becomes too hard.

The figure shows quite a stable growth (see the inset of Figure 5.5). It suggests that process innovation can drive economic growth, until we run out of ideas for improving efficiency, for as long as it motivates investment.

What is critical to understand is what makes purchasing power grow like that. For each project, by definition, more profit is generated than what it costs in terms of investment to produce that profit. Otherwise, the investment is not worth doing. Therefore, one might think that if the profits are not fully spent again in the economy, money would gradually drain away into companies' bank accounts in the form of profits.

Indeed, during his PhD, HP demonstrated that just to maintain current employment levels, 100% of the extra profits that a company makes from process innovation must be put back into circulation in the economy. This means one of three things: companies spending the profits on goods and services (and not financial assets), companies giving profits to shareholders who then spend them on goods and services, or immediately reducing prices so that there are no extra profits. It means that none should be accumulated in obscure bank accounts.

First, profits. The whole reason companies innovate is to make profits, so we cannot expect them to cut prices straight away. And the zero-carbon transition will be no different.

We are already seeing it. J-F bought an EV because it would be cheap to run. In theory, the energy cost should be 4p per kilometre, compared to 10–25p per kilometre for a conventional car (depending on the size and fuel prices). So far, it has not turned out that way.

The reason is that public charging points set prices that cost 15–20p per kilometre, rather than the 4 p people pay at home. People that cannot charge vehicles at home (especially poorer people) rely on public charging points. The electricity in the public charging points is the same as the electricity that goes to people's homes. It just costs more.

The public charging points do not cost much to build or maintain either. So, someone is making a big profit, by taking advantage of drivers who cannot charge their cars elsewhere.[11] They have captured the benefits of the new technology for themselves.

More competition and maybe regulation too will eventually come. But for now, a few, rich people will get most of the money. The same will no doubt happen in other sectors.

[11] Public fast chargers in the UK cost £100k–200k, and a quick estimate suggests a payback time of less than two years if they are used six times per day or more (generating £100k/y at 80 p/kWh, removing VAT), and less than a year if used twelve times or more (generating £200k/y). Given it takes about 45 min to charge a standard 62 kW battery, the max number of charges daily would be about sixteen, roughly one per daytime hour. At these prices, after a year, fast chargers generate pure profit of £100k–200k per unit per year until the end of their lifetime of 10–15 years. For reference, petrol and diesel retail make a profit of about 5p per litre sold, of which less than 1 p goes to the petrol station operator.

The problem is, rich people can only buy so many fast cars, homes, phones and computer games. They usually run out of things to spend their vast fortunes on. They frequently end up creating large endowments.

Mainstream economists have no issue with this. They simply *assume* that 100% of profits are always spent in the economy, because to them, savings mean investment. But the data are clear it does not. If we are lucky, at most half of those profits is used for the production of other goods. The rest is absorbed in wealth piles that do not return into circulation, which makes the economy smaller.

However, this is only what would happen in a steady-state economy. Profit can attract substantial investment, to the extent that if the lending and investment growth rate is sufficiently high, it can cause overall economic growth even if profits are not spent entirely in the real economy. This is what is shown in Figure 5.5.

We are assuming, as happens in many countries, that every time step, more debt is created, for financing investments, than is repaid or kept in wealth piles. That's because paying back takes time, and by the time debts have been repaid, the economy has grown quite a bit. Like water in a basin, if the tap runs faster than the water can escape via the drain, it will accumulate and remain in the basin for a period before escaping.[12]

The issue is that, for each product, entrepreneurs eventually run out of ideas. Therefore, for a set number of products, growth cannot be maintained forever as it would become more and more costly to maintain the rate of profit. The economy needs new products to improve and make a profit with when old products have run out of potential.

[12] The economy has been growing on the basis of debt creation since at least the Mesopotamians 5,000 years ago. This has been remarkably documented by the late David Graeber (2014). It follows from this fact that economic growth, innovation and development functioned fundamentally on the basis of creating more debt than is being repaid, simply because investment occurs at a moment in time while profit occurs over varied but longer periods (years, decades) of time afterwards.

5.3.2 *Product Innovation*

As humans, we have a constant craving for new things. We probably evolved this way. We like to experience new things, like different food or places to visit. We don't usually watch the same films or sports events repeatedly.

As we saw in Chapter 4, the great waves of innovation always start with something new. This new thing takes off, and new industries are formed. Other new things connected to it then appear too.

The great waves have occurred roughly every fifty years. The reason they occur so regularly is not fully known. It is remarkable though. One possibility is that it takes people and companies fifty years to make the most of previous inventions. Only then do they turn to the more difficult challenge of starting a new wave.

We return to the simple model from above and allow new products to appear. We use the famous '*S-curve*' of technology adoption to demonstrate the process.[13]

First, we create random new products produced by new sectors. Few people use the new products (or even know about them) at first, except some early adopters. Then, the new products suddenly take off as they reach the majority. Eventually, nearly everyone is using them, so growth slows again. This has happened with more or less every mature product and system we see, such as cars, televisions, power plants and so on.

The innovations succeed each other, as shown in Figure 5.6a (see Appendix B for technical details). They may or may not compete. For example, mobile phones have largely replaced landlines, but steel did not replace food.

Figures 5.6b and c shows what might happen. We create a new sector every 25 time steps, with its own learning curve, using random learning rates between 10% and 40%. The figure shows results from

[13] The seminal work on this is from Grübler (1998). See also, for instance, the Rocky Mountain institute description of the S-curve process at https://rmi.org/insight/harnessing-the-power-of-s-curves/.

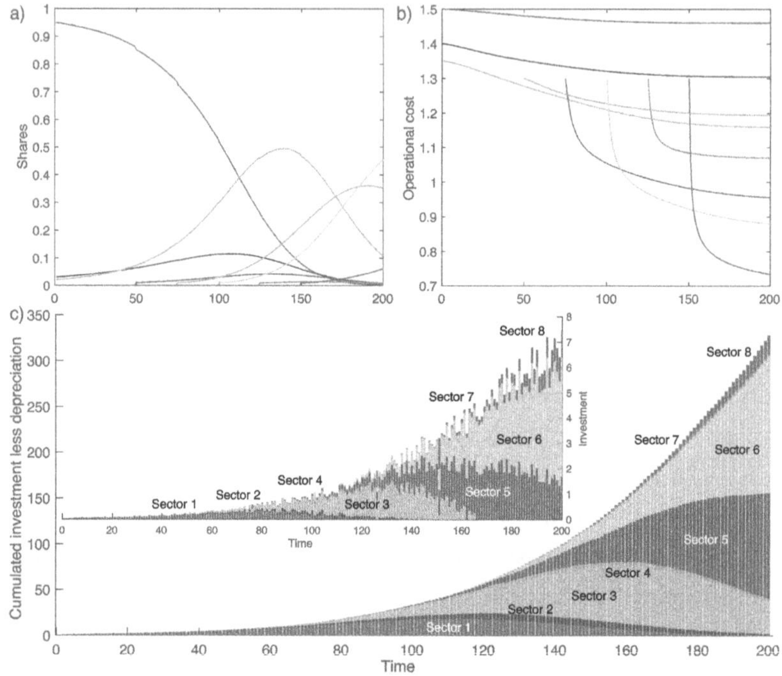

FIGURE 5.6 The process of succession of S-curves of creative destruction.

one simulation. We see new sectors coming and going. It *looks* like a story of great waves.

When a new product replaces an old product, the story may be the same as for process innovation. Some people win but others lose out. Growing profits may be harmful to the economy.

However, when the new product doesn't replace an old product, the economics changes. Spending, ultimately coming from consumers, increases. Think about the queues to buy new gadgets. This extra spending creates additional production and jobs. The circular flow of income increases.

The investment may be super-charged too. The returns could potentially be huge, so companies are willing to spend large sums. The tech companies' 'moonshots' in driverless cars and other artificial intelligence are good examples. Again, this spending creates production and jobs.

So, if product innovation creates jobs but process innovation kills jobs, why do we not just focus on product innovation? The problem is we will eventually run out of people to do the jobs. Product innovation alone will lead to a boom, as we often see at the start of the great waves.[14] The bust soon follows.

Fortunately, product innovation encourages process innovation, and vice versa. From this, a realistic story of economic growth starts to emerge.

5.3.3 Product with Process Innovation

It seems simple. Product innovation creates the demand for all the new things. Process innovation allows us to make the new things by freeing up resources from the old things. Put it all together, and we get an economy that grows indefinitely. All we need is a constant flow of ideas.

Since the industrial revolution, human nature has provided the ideas. As soon as a new product is invented, people find ways to make it cheaper. When the product gets cheaper, people find new ways to use it. When it eventually runs out of steam, we move to the next new thing and start another great wave.

It's a good thing. Product and process innovation have worked together to build our economy for over 200 years. Overall, it has made us wealthy and shaped the world today. It has come at an environmental cost, which is why some people want to stop it (see next Section 5.4). And as described in Chapters 1 and 2, it has created losers as well as winners.

It should be clear by now that we need to look beneath the surface. Understanding the links between products and sectors is key

[14] Carlota Perez (2001) covers innovation and technological history, including the history of the great waves, with a focus on the financial sector. In her narrative and typology, a financial crisis happens at roughly the same point in each great wave of innovation. Whether this is the case or not, it is clear that bubbles occur every so often because of exaggerated collective expectations about the financial returns on innovation.

to identifying who will win and who will lose. The final bit of theory in this chapter builds a simple model to show how.

Economists link sectors using something called 'input–output (IO) tables'. The IO table is a matrix that tells us what each sector buys from every other sector. It's an accounting way of showing supply chains.

For example, the sector that makes smartphones will buy its inputs from the sectors that make computer chips, plastic casings, wires, connectors and packaging. It will need to pay transport companies to deliver these goods. It will probably also buy services from insurance, accounting and consultancy firms. The IO table shows us how much.

Companies in other industries will in turn buy smartphones for their staff. Again, the IO table shows us how much. Companies may also buy products from their own industry, such as the car industry buying cars for its own workers.

The IO table provides a snapshot in time. The amounts of course change over time. An IO table for 1900 would look very different to an IO table for today.

The most obvious difference is that some of the things that are bought and sold today didn't exist back in 1900, such as computers. There would be no entry for smartphones. These sectors have appeared, and the table has become bigger over time.

The other difference is that efficiency improves. Clothing companies use much less material to make each garment than they did before. They also need far fewer workers. The numbers in the IO table are adjusted over time to reflect this and other process innovation.

The process is evolutionary. When a new product is created, it builds on the products from older sectors. These older sectors will buy more and more of the new product, following the S-shaped curve. However, the new sector will gradually buy less and less of the old products, as it cuts costs. This follows a learning curve.

We now create a new model version that starts as simple as possible with just one sector (e.g. agriculture). As product innovation

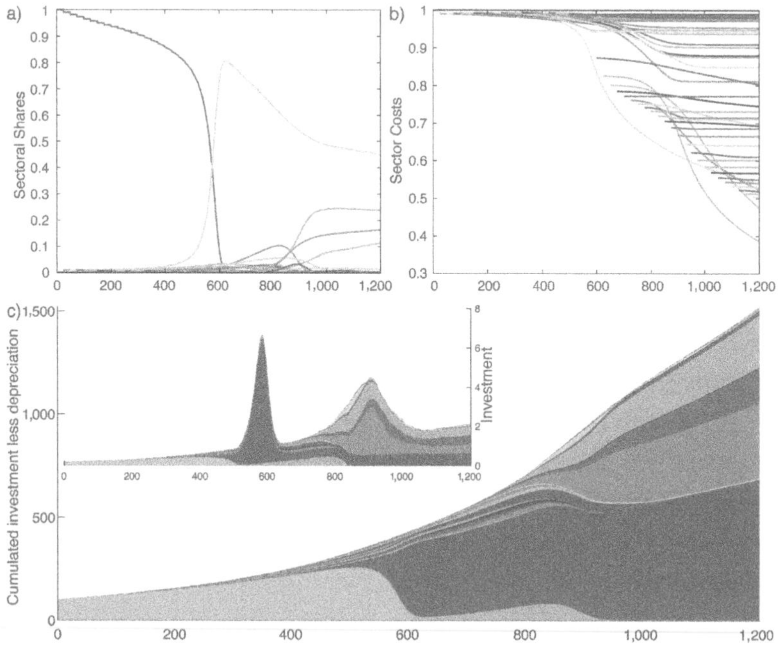

FIGURE 5.7 The process of growth through the creation and diffusion of new technologies and sectors.

occurs, new sectors are added, and the IO table expands. Meanwhile, the older sectors become more productive and cut costs. More new products start being added, some of which replace old products. The economy becomes more complex. Each sector and its product battle to make as much profit as possible.

As each new sector is added, the economy becomes more and more complex. Longer and longer supply chains develop. If we let the model increase in size to millions of sectors, it could become like the modern economy.[15]

Figure 5.7 shows one possible storyline (see Appendix B for technical details). A new sector is added every 25 time steps. What it looks like, and how quickly it improves efficiency, is random.

[15] In reality, statistical offices group together products (e.g. 'food') to make the data manageable.

In the figure, the first sector is entirely replaced by the second one. The second one never disappears but goes on to coexist with many more sectors. In the cost graphs, we see that most sectors go nowhere and disappear, but a few sectors progress with both rapidly declining costs and rapidly increasing sales.

The inset shows investment, which is clearly cyclical. The periods of great transformation see huge investment, boosting income and jobs. Consumption will also rise fastest at this time. In between, there are slumps. This reflects what we have seen in the previous great waves.

This will not come as comfort to people tied to the sectors that disappear. We have already talked about them in Chapters 1 and 2 and will again in Chapter 7. The model may be very simple, but it is trying to tell us the story about the winners and losers. The story of the transition.

5.4 WHAT DOES THIS MEAN FOR THE ZERO-CARBON TRANSITION?

The theory is nice for academics to debate, but what does it mean for the zero-carbon transition? Two critical questions arise. The first question relates to whether the zero-carbon transition is a great wave, or whether it is part of something else. The second question is whether we would be better off not having growth at all.

5.4.1 Is the Zero-Carbon Transition Another Great Wave?

As seen in Chapter 1, and will see in more detail in Chapter 6, the zero-carbon transition is attracting a lot of investment already. New innovations are affecting companies in other economic sectors too.

In Chapter 6, we will link 'getting rid of combustion' to solving population ageing, artificial intelligence and 'smartification'. At least initially, getting rid of combustion using low-carbon technology improves efficiency and is process innovation. But people are already finding ways to use solar technology in new products.

All these things together are definitely changing our lives. Will they keep the economic fire burning for fifty years like previous great waves? This remains to be seen. We argue in Chapter 6 that the data suggest the answer may be yes.

If true, we can say we are at the start of a new great wave. We could start to tune economic models like the one in Section 5.3 to show paths of future growth.

However, we need to be sure that we have finished the previous great wave first. Researchers say that the end of each previous great wave involved lots of financial and political instability and polarisation. As we see this exactly happening all round the world, it is possible that we are not out of the woods just yet.

5.4.2 *Green Growth versus De-growth*

Regardless of where we are with great waves, there are people saying we need to bring economic growth to an end. The idea of de-growth is becoming increasingly popular as a way to solve environmental problems, including climate change.

The reason is simple: innovation and economic growth created the problems. What else than suppressing those could solve the problem?

But as we saw in Chapter 2, de-growth is not an out-of-jail card. It would put the entire economy in a terminal Stage 4 of the life cycle of sectors. It would paralyse investment and, with that, our ability to replace the old polluting capital stock with new clean production methods. We would get stuck in an economy that doesn't grow but that remains polluting.

The counter-argument is called green growth. With green growth, people argue that we can keep becoming wealthier, but new technologies and improvements to efficiency can limit or eliminate environmental harm while continuing to cause the growth of national income.

Looking back to Section 5.3, it might seem that the green growth story has to be based on process innovation only. We would need to avoid any product innovation, as it would create new demand for non-renewable resources. The focus, one might think, should be on making things more efficiently.

But as we showed above, the problem with this approach is that it would not lead to economic growth. The people that made the resources we no longer need would find themselves unemployed, we would run out of ideas, growth would stop, there would be significant unemployment and investment would stop, trapping us there too.

There are fierce arguments between people who believe in de-growth and people who believe in green growth. But our analysis shows that policies for green growth, if they are based on supporting process innovation while eliminating product innovation, would actually lead to de-growth!

Therefore, instead, green growth will have to be based on the same interplay between process and product innovation but on the basis of products that involve zero environmental harm. This, in a few words, is the challenge. And to be realistic, it's not really possible to stop product innovation anyway.

From a climate perspective, de-growth is counterproductive. It is true that if we produced less, then it might seem easier to meet carbon targets. But the lack of growth bites back, because it stymies investment. However, renewable energy, built using previous renewable energy, allows us to produce as much as we want without increasing emissions. A growing economy provides the investment for new zero-carbon energy sources.

From a broader environmental perspective beyond climate change, the issue is less clear-cut, for instance, in what regards chemical pollution, land degradation, freshwater use and so on. What is clear is that much more research is needed, covering many different fields. A deeper understanding of innovation, as laid out in this chapter, could help a lot. But allocation economics, in general, does not.

6 The Sunrise: A New Technological Constellation

6.1 HOW INNOVATION WORKS

6.1.1 The Missing Branch in Economics

Chapter 4 described how innovation, development and economic growth have evolved together since the first industrial revolution. In Chapter 5, we showed the mechanisms that underpin this type of economic change. We also suggested that a new great wave of innovation is already beginning to unfold. We discussed how the zero-carbon transition is part of a broader transformation that will make many people richer, although probably others poorer.

To repeat, the zero-carbon transition is going to accelerate economic growth, not slow it down. With AI and digitalisation, zero-carbon is a component of a new industrial revolution, which will transform how industry works and what employment means.

This is obviously controversial and needs some explanation. We must look at the broader landscape of innovation and technological change currently happening. Zero-carbon technologies do not just address the climate crisis, the main reason why we *think* we are doing it. Zero-carbon, along with digitalisation of the economy, also means a much smarter use of resources.

In this chapter, we describe in more detail some evidence on this new digitalised, smart and low-carbon great wave of innovation. However, first, we shall discuss the standard intellectual framework for how innovation works, including what we call '*induced innovation*'.[1] By that, we mean innovation that comes from within the economy, without policy-makers having asked for it. Chapter 5

[1] See Grubb et al. (2021b, 2014).

described more formally how this innovation can lead to economic growth.

As we discussed in Chapter 2, there is nothing peculiar about induced innovation. It is part of human nature and how we have all found ways to improve our lives. We bring this nature into the companies we work for, leading to new and cheaper products. Over time, these products become the new normal.

Also, as discussed in Chapter 2, *innovation is the economy.* The current state of innovation determines what we can produce. New innovations lead to economic growth. Chapter 2 showed that an economy in equilibrium is one that does not have new innovations. But, in reality, we see new innovations all the time, and therefore, the economy cannot be in equilibrium.

For similar reasons, the economy does not optimise nor operate at full employment. Even if one person controlled the entire economy, there are simply too many possible futures to work out which one is best. Operating at full employment makes the economy unstable because it cannot cope with any additional strain.

Unfortunately, most theories we have for describing economic growth are based on equilibrium. University economics departments do not teach innovation. Economists do not see innovation as part of their subject. Instead, they use the equilibrium tools they are familiar with. They assume that innovation only merely changes the productivity of workers and capital. The sole role of economics is to describe the distribution of resources, not the creation of resources. The results can be confusing and unrealistic.

Innovation does not merely change productivity: it constantly revolutionises what the economy is. It is a vibrant area of research and scholarship. However, it is usually only taught in schools of business and management, not economics. Students learn to manage companies and create new products, ideas and intellectual property. It makes no sense at all that students of economics should ignore scholarship over what drives business and what it means for wider society.

Economists cannot address climate change and many other important issues without understanding innovation. We really need innovation to be made part of the economics curriculum. We need innovation theory to replace equilibrium theory in the models that economists use.

6.1.2 *The Innovation Chain*

We come back to the question what does innovation look like? Many people picture Doc Brown in his garage in '*Back to the Future*' making a time machine. Some Silicon Valley companies were started in garages. But many of us will also think of scientists at universities and research labs with all sorts of tubes, lasers and reactors. Some will imagine white-bearded Cambridge professors in front of blackboards covered in equations. Fewer people will imagine people in suits shaking hands with investors.

In fact, innovation is a little bit of all of the above. It does not happen entirely in the garage, the lab or the classroom. It also happens at banks, in the market, at conferences and on social media. All these elements have their own way of turning knowledge and discovery into something people will pay for.

The different stages of innovation are shown in Figure 6.1. This is called the *innovation chain*.[2] We go from ideas towards finished mass-produced usable products from left to right.

Basic ideas usually come from *fundamental research* and general knowledge creation that students, researchers and professors do every day at universities. Examples include astronomy, quantum physics, cell biology, genetics or social science. It is a mixture of observation and theoretical explanations of what we see.

Typically, these basic ideas are very abstract. The researchers may only vaguely understand how they work, if they work at all. They will not understand how much products based on these ideas could possibly cost to make.

[2] For textbook energy-related innovation theory, see Grubb et al. (2014) and Grübler and Wilson (2013).

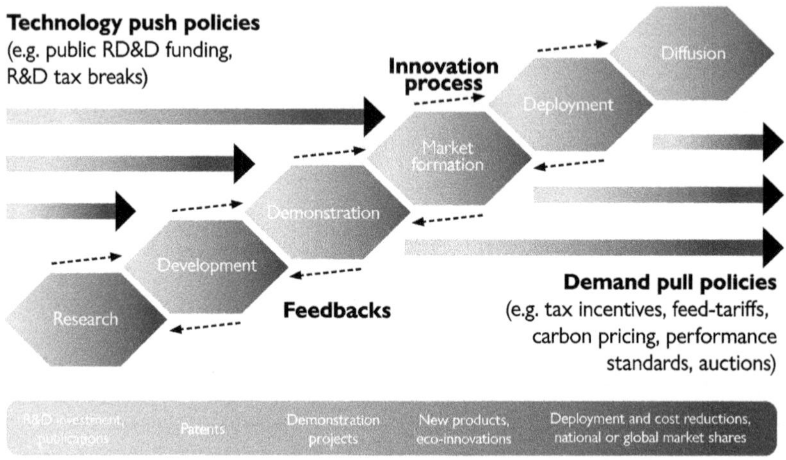

FIGURE 6.1 The innovation chain, after Grubb et al. (2021a).

Engineers and more practical researchers may try to make these ideas work in practice at the *development* stage. They focus on technical development. They still have no idea whether the outcome would be something they could sell. It can take a long time to go from fundamental research to something working, with no guarantee of success. This work can take place at universities or in specially created start-up companies.

Take, for example, the CCD and CMOS arrays that are the main elements of digital photography and mobile phone cameras.[3] These were first invented for high-end imaging, part-funded by the US military. While still being produced in university labs, they were used in telescopes for astronomy, where the high cost (tens of thousands of dollars) could be justified. After a long and complex path of R&D, the devices were miniaturised and became so cheap that they could be incorporated into phones for everyday use. Billions are now produced and they cost just a few dollars each.

Innovation and creating products involve so much more than just making a technical idea work. Huge upfront investment is required. Businesses patent their ideas to protect this investment.

[3] CCD stands for Charge-Coupled Device. CMOS stands for Complementary Metal–Oxide–Semiconductor. See Wikipedia https://en.wikipedia.org/wiki/Charge-coupled_device.

They must also find ways to reduce costs from the first very expensive prototype, so that they end up with a product that is sellable. That's because the prototype is usually the most expensive unit the company ever makes; it has all sorts of flaws and errors that the innovators later find ways to fix.

Most crucially, however, there must be people wanting the product. Consumers must understand how the product improves their lives. Business owners may need to *demonstrate* the product's purpose. Investors pour finance into demonstration prototypes to show the world that they work. This process builds trust in the new ideas. If it fails, the product may need to go back to the development stage.

Products can move on from the demonstration stage only after successful *market formation*. The new market can be a niche, for example, where no alternatives exist and customers are willing to pay high costs. Like the CCD and CMOS arrays, many products take off in niche markets. The revenues, even if small, are critical for start-up companies to continue developing the product.

It is this continued development that brings down costs. Solar panels provide another example. Costs initially were so high that they could only be justified for space satellites. Gradually, costs fell, and new niche markets opened (e.g., energy in remote areas, weather stations, road signs).[4] Costs continued to fall, eventually allowing the mainstream uses of the products.

We now see solar cells used in cheap products like garden lamps. But more importantly, they are a key part of the zero-carbon transition. The initial sales supported further activities that led to later developments and cost reductions. Solar panels are now at (and arguably past) the *deployment* stage.

Development and cost reductions continue, and the product starts to grab market shares from competitors. Technical development slows but mass production means lower costs still. The product is now in the *diffusion* stage.

[4] See Nemet (2019) for a detailed history of solar energy.

The innovation chain is also dangerous! Many products reach a dead end and go no further. Products can die in the technology valley of death, when start-up companies run out of funds before they have enough customers to support further development.[5] However, experience is rarely forgotten, and failed products often come back with a vengeance.

6.1.3 Innovation Policy and Finance

Although expensive and risky, innovation can be very profitable. In total, innovation pays off, and the economy grows. However, even great ideas often fail, and, as noted in Section 6.1.2, failure can occur at any stage of the innovation chain. Potential reasons for failure include finance not materialising, unsuitable staff or limitations in business management.

For that reason, the venture capitalists who finance innovation search carefully for companies that will make them big money. They often finance lots of start-ups and see how they perform. They cull without regret companies that do not deliver but not before giving them a good chance. Venture capitalists lose money on most of their companies but make a lot of money from the few that succeed.

Venture capitalists hover around universities and innovation hubs to find the companies that will make money (Figure 6.2). They offer investment in exchange for stock in the companies. Some of them offer guidance to the business owners, increasing their chance of success. Venture capitalists are therefore important in the early phases of the innovation chain.

However, venture capitalists do not finance basic research. Partly, this is because returns are too uncertain and too far into the future. It may also be difficult for private companies to capture the returns. Basic research instead relies on government funding.

For example, government funding supported basic research into semiconductors. Using this research, companies developed transistors and, later, computer chips. The long-term returns on the

[5] See Grubb et al. (2014).

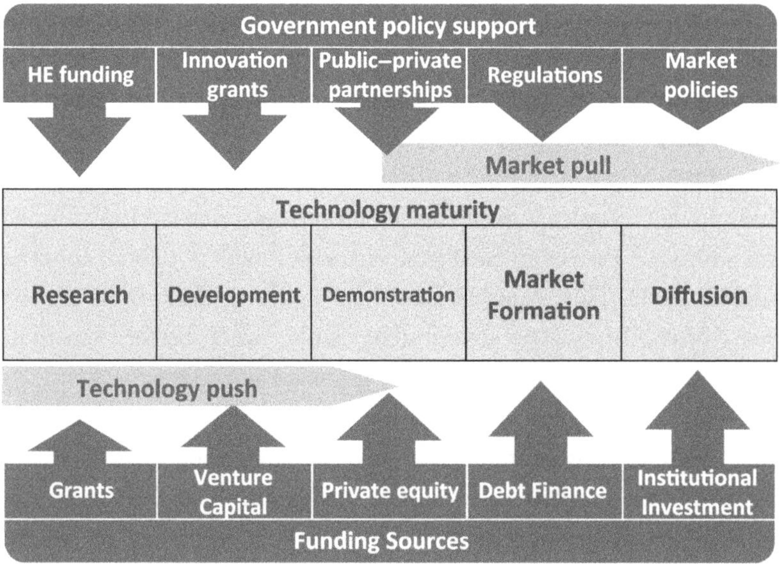

FIGURE 6.2 Who finances the innovation chain? After (Mercure et al., 2016). HE funding stands for higher-education research funding.

original basic research have been enormous, but they took 30–50 years to materialise. No bank or venture capitalist would invest with that time horizon.

Because government funding does not seek private profits, governments often let universities decide what they research. However, some research efforts are directed towards military benefits. More recently, governments have directed research to areas that could boost exports and create jobs. The research may also play a role in creating a skilled labour force.

Once a product becomes big enough and moves to mass production, it requires more finance than what venture capitalists can provide. Companies must then turn to banks, debt and equity markets and other large financial organisations. These institutions cannot monitor performance in small businesses and do not have the specialised knowledge to determine which companies might succeed. They therefore usually only provide affordable rates for low-risk loans, so the company must be well established. However, these organisations operate at scale and can provide finance at a lower cost.

Often, large companies with access to reliable financing from banks will buy start-up companies to scale up production. In doing so, they acquire the staff and the intellectual property, taking on the risk themselves.

Innovation is limited without the government getting heavily involved. Not least, basic research takes place at publicly funded universities.[6] However, good innovation policy is *not* about funding random R&D. This would be like shooting in the dark; there are too many possibilities. The government can do much better than that, by coordinating the direction of the innovation it funds.

The government also guides innovation indirectly through its other policies. For example, the government regulates, subsidises, taxes, creates markets, sets import duties and promotes domestic industries and products abroad. These polices influence the entire innovation chain. As noted in Chapter 3, economists have long criticised such industrial policy. But it is not possible in practice for governments not to make choices over the vastness of innovation possibilities, and addressing climate change implies an industrial policy.

In standard economics, government is often portrayed as obstructing innovation rather than enabling it. In that perspective, it takes a market failure to justify funding anything and, at best, the outcome will be general R&D subsidies. But this is a fairy tale from the academic ivory tower. It would amount to shooting randomly in the dark, and no government does that.

The Silicon Valley myth claims that, without government interference, innovation from new companies supported by venture capitalists would be much more effective. But it is just a myth because, even where Apple, Microsoft, IBM and Google are concerned, much of the product development underpinning their businesses was publicly funded and directed. The early achievements of these companies was in business management, product design and marketing, rather than scientific or technical development.

[6] See Mazzucato (2013, 2018).

In great contrast to the standard economic myth on innovation, governments have always played a key role in guiding the direction of innovation and not just for military purposes. For example, before it abandoned its 2017 industrial strategy,[7] the UK government organised its research funding around a set of 'grand challenges' that it deemed UK society must solve. But in practice, whether it has an official industrial strategy or not, UK research funding agencies continue to make deliberate choices on what to fund.

Government innovation policies can be classified into two broad groups, *technology push* and *demand pull*. Technology push policies apply to the early stages of the innovation chain. Here, governments support the creation of ideas and technologies, for example, with research funding, subsidies and R&D tax breaks. Demand pull policies apply to the later stages of the innovation chain. Here, governments get involved in creating markets for products, for example, with taxes, subsidies, carbon markets, regulations and standards.

6.2 THE SUNRISE SECTORS AND WHAT THEY DISPLACE

6.2.1 *The Grand Challenges of Our Time*

As we saw in Chapter 4, each great wave of innovation has *addressed restrictions that held back economic productivity and profits*. Even though Adam Smith's invisible hand is not real, and nothing coordinates entrepreneurs, over history entrepreneurs have together generated the great waves. Each of the great waves seen in Chapter 4 solved a critical economic problem, whether it was mobility (e.g. railways, cars), materials (iron, steel), communication (telephone, IT), mechanical power (oil combustion, electricity) or industrial organisation (e.g. Taylorism, Fordism).

[7] See BEIS (2017). The policy survived approximately two years, after which it was officially abandoned. This could be due to the Conservative leadership being shy with the use of the loaded term 'industrial strategy', deeply at odds with standard economics. It is hard to tell whether the funded R&D really changed at all as a result, however, because the grand challenges facing British society haven't gone away, and government agencies continue to fund the same research and investment as they did before the abolition.

It is as if the innovation system can see the next problems coming and organise its research around solving these problems. Entrepreneurs do not do this altruistically, because solving productivity bottlenecks is loaded with profit opportunities. We should thus ask ourselves: what are the *current restrictions on productivity*, and what will the next great wave of innovation seek to solve?

Remember where R&D investment is going (look back at Figure 4.8): pharma and biotech and IT and software together take over 50% of spending. Automobiles take 15%. Innovators are trying to reduce disease and disability burdens and develop the role of information further in society. They are trying to link all this to transport services, notably driverless cars. In comparison, oil, gas and electricity take just 1% of R&D investment. Green energy R&D will not be the driver of the next wave. Nor will heavy industry or even the service sectors.

One key restriction that most advanced economies face is the combination of reduced birth rates and increased lifespans. An ageing population will not just provide fewer workers but will rely on the workers that are left to provide care. Older people also tend to spend less in the economy and have fewer ideas that drive economic growth.

As the share of retired citizens grows, total spending in the economy falls. Profits fall, and companies have no incentive to invest. Incomes decline, especially in construction and engineering companies that provide investment services. Prices may also fall, as has happened in Japan.

Changes in population have been accompanied by technological advances. In earlier eras, when the populations of advanced economies were growing rapidly, companies benefited from an inexhaustible supply of young (mostly male) workers who would operate machinery in factories and spend their wages back into the economy. The skill requirements were low, and young men could work in factories straight from school.

These days, factories need much smaller numbers of mostly highly skilled workers (male and female). There are major benefits for companies that keep their workers for longer. Raising retirement ages and working later in life is beneficial not only for keeping pension funds solvent but also for companies to maintain profitability.

But to work later in life, workers must be healthy. Since everybody dies in the end, reducing the burden of disease is needed to extend people's working lives. Hence, one of the key restrictions on future economic productivity is disease burden. Less disease means higher life expectancy, longer working lives and higher returns on training.[8] The current burden falls on health systems, which are now struggling to cope. How could innovation help them?

Another way for companies to solve this problem is to replace the workers altogether. Since the early days of agriculture, replacing people with tools or machines has increased production. Intelligent machines are replacing many of the jobs in factories. Increasingly, they are replacing other occupations too.

There are still limits. It is difficult for machines to replace humans where creativity or traditional crafts are involved. ChatGPT may be 'creating' art and literature but only based on what already is available. Machines will not any time soon repair the old churches of Europe or the old thatched cottages of England. But, machines are now encroaching upon the formerly safe haven jobs that involve management and decisions.[9]

Computers can drive cars and trucks, recommend holidays, run hotels, identify travel itineraries and buy and sell shares on the stock

[8] We are not suggesting that the health system reduces health burdens *to make people work for longer*. The aim of curing diseases is to improve people's lives. But doing so enables them to work for longer and increase economic productivity. We are furthermore not suggesting that raising the retirement age is 'good' or 'bad', as such a value judgement is not for us to make – for example, raising the retirement age may benefit companies rather than workers.

[9] Artificial intelligence is beginning to produce realistic images and music. However, whether this is something people will spend money on remains to be seen, given that art is all about communication between humans. The traditional crafts, such as carpentry, stone masonry and thatching, can hardly become automated, since the work is bespoke in each job and involves tacit or traditional knowledge.

market. This has the potential to save companies enormous costs by automating decision-making across a wide range of economic sectors.

Intelligent machines can also help productivity by improving companies' use of resources. Whether material, energy, logistical or information inputs, computers can optimise if data is available. Hence, an important focus of the new great wave will be gathering *'big data'* and building the *'Internet of Things'* where every device is connected.

Energy is an input, so how does the energy transition fit in the new great wave? As discussed earlier, combustion is probably the energy sector's current limit on productivity. Combustion science and engineering, from another era, have long reached the end of their potential. The innovation will be in new types of energy transformation, likely using new automated production. Looking at R&D in energy extraction is, therefore, the wrong place to understand this.

The next great wave will thus be led by efforts to improve health and replace human work with machines. Side effects of this innovation will include efficiency gains in resource use and energy transformation. Sections 6.2.2–6.2.6 review the potential developments in each case.

6.2.2 *Genetic Engineering to 'Solve Ageing'*

Over the last century, medical science and pharmaceuticals have been hugely successful in addressing (and sometimes eliminating) disease burdens that originate from infections. Viral infections are prevented by vaccines. Bacterial infections are cured using antibiotics. Severe diseases, such as smallpox, rubella, mumps, measles, tuberculosis, polio, leprosy, cholera, typhoid, rabies, diphtheria and many more, have become scourges of the past for most advanced nations.[10]

What characterises these diseases, and the methods for curing them, is that a *'one-size-fits-all'* approach worked for everyone. The

[10] These diseases have not all been eliminated in developing countries, where national health systems are often underfunded or face challenges of unaffordable medicines and equipment made in developed countries.

target is the disease, not the person, and the fact that every person differs does not much reduce the effectiveness of the solutions developed. Everyone gets the same vaccines and antibiotics, each of which target a specific disease.

New diseases are emerging naturally all the time, and humans face a perpetual arms race with bacteria and viruses. Since 2020, the new COVID disease has been mutating faster than scientists could update vaccines, sometimes reducing the vaccines' effectiveness. However, the impact of the disease has weakened as our immune systems 'learned' the virus, either by surviving the disease or with the COVID vaccines.

Substantial R&D funding goes into developing the traditional one-size-fits-all approach towards curing new illnesses. Substantial funding also goes towards fighting the growing resistance of known diseases towards existing cures, a related problem. Under stress, diseases mutate.

The next advance in medicine is where diseases are person-dependent, meaning where they work differently in different people. The two main examples are genetic disorders and all types of cancer. For those diseases, one-size-fits-all methods are not very effective. Genetic disorders are, almost by definition, only cured with solutions personalised for each patient. The standard therapies for cancer (chemotherapy, radiation therapy) are blunt methods that sometimes work only marginally if at all. They impose enormous stresses on the body and mind of patients.

Now that most common infections can be neutralised by vaccines and antibiotics, what's left are diseases that depend on individuals' genetics. For people in advanced economies, it is now cancer that 'gets you in the end'. The great challenge is personalised medicine, where a cure is tailor-made for each patient.

Cornerstone innovations for this are as follows:

(1) Genetic sequencing, *the Human Genome Project that first decoded the human genome;*
(2) CRISPR, *a tool that lets us edit the human genome;*

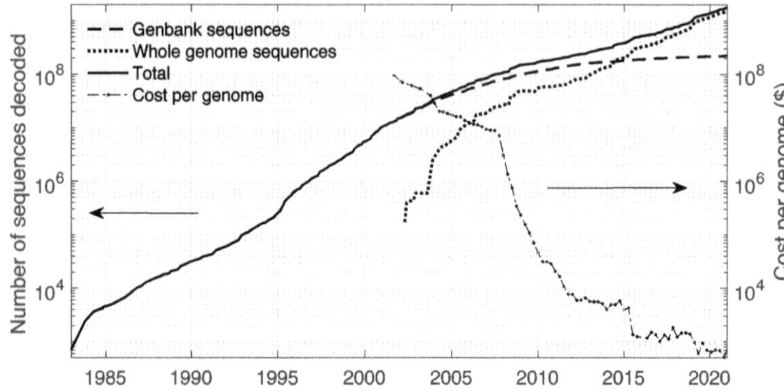

FIGURE 6.3 Cost for decoding genomes and cumulative volume decoded.

(3) Mapping genetic functions at the single-cell level, *e.g. in brain or kidney cells;*

(4) Stem cell reprogramming, *which lets us grow human tissue or impose the function of new human cells.*

Together, these methods could enable personalised medicine to help '*solve ageing*' and cure cancer. The first two are already becoming affordable, transforming radically the medical design space. The human genome project cost $3bn, starting in 1990 and taking thirteen years to complete. Now, doctors can decode someone's genetic code in one week for less than $600.

As costs have come down, the numbers of genomes decoded have increased exponentially (Figures 6.3 and 6.4).[11] Similarly, CRISPR is now applied worldwide with similarly declining costs. Costs are becoming low enough for them to be deployed widely in hospitals, a real game-changer.

6.2.3 *Automation and Artificial Intelligence*

Replacing people with machines has, over human history, very often made a lot of sense for businesses in agriculture and repetitive factory work. The question is whether a one-off payment for a machine is

[11] Costs are from www.genome.gov/about-genomics/fact-sheets/DNA-Sequencing-Costs-Data while volumes are from www.ncbi.nlm.nih.gov/genbank/statistics/.

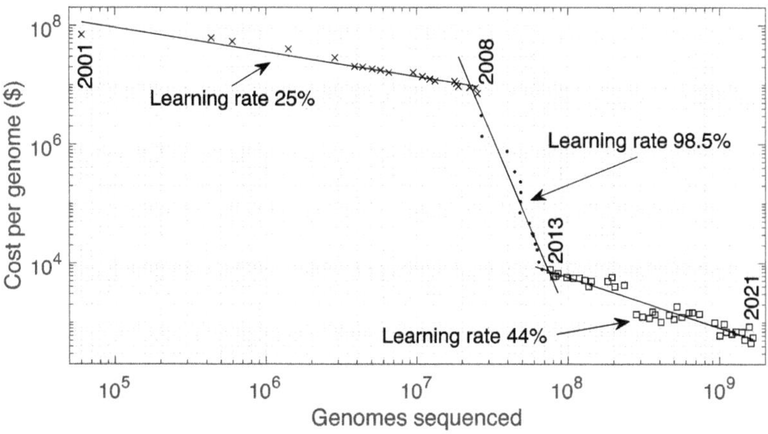

FIGURE 6.4 Learning rates for genomics. Three rates are observed, but the abrupt price drop between 2008 and 2013 is due to scientific discoveries. The calculation uses cumulative whole genome sequences against their cost. Using instead cumulative total sequences, as shown in Figure 6.3, generates learning rates of 57%, 99.8% and 57%, but may be inexact since Genbank sequences are not all whole genomes.

better than paying wages indefinitely. Usually, as an economy grows, wage rates increase, but the costs of machines come down. Over time, machines become preferred.

In advanced economies, most repetitive factory tasks have already been replaced by machines. Developing countries, with lower wage rates, still maintain factory jobs. But even there, machines are becoming more common.

Machines are being used more widely too. For example, work by accountants and lawyers on record-keeping, filing and searching is now automated, leaving only the more ambiguous and judgement-based tasks to be done by professionals. In these occupations too, there are now fewer jobs per unit of production.[12]

The ultimate substitution of human labour for machines is where ambiguous decisions and judgement also become replaced by 'intelligent' machines. Artificial intelligence (AI) works by making machines learn using large amounts of existing data (see 'big data'

[12] See for instance Acemoglu and Restrepo (2018); Arntz et al. (2017); Autor (2015).

below) in order to discover patterns and become able to reply to questions. 'Trained' software can then be used to operate in a wide variety of settings, such as parsing and finding information based on incomplete or ambiguous inputs. AI can generate plausible answers to unclear questions, as opposed to traditional automation, which replaces very specific tasks.

We now see AI being deployed at scale worldwide in unexpected domains, such as publicity and marketing, design, art and audio–video production. Of course, AI remains for now constrained to operate within the constraints imposed by the training datasets. But the datasets keep increasing in size, and machine learning methods keep improving, while the area where it applies keeps expanding.

6.2.4 *Smartification of Industry*

Non-labour resources can be used more efficiently too. The *'fourth industrial revolution'*[13] or 'Industry 4.0' describes part of the great wave that will be based on intelligent manufacturing. Automation and new management techniques will minimise downtime, waste and idleness of equipment.

Optimising complex manufacturing systems requires data and some sort of automated intelligence and self-awareness. Thirty years ago, it was unthinkable that machines in a factory could develop any degree of self-awareness. However, already some know when they need repairs or how to reconfigure themselves to change production.

A combination of *AI*, *Digitalisation*, the *Internet of Things*, *Big Data* and *Cloud Services* makes all this work. Digitalisation puts a computer inside all machines and makes them monitor their own activities. The internet of things connects the machines, allowing

[13] See Kagerman et al. (2013), as well as Castelo-Branco et al. (2019); Lasi et al. (2014). Following Chapter 4 and the original works on great waves by Kondratieff (1928); Schumpeter (1939) and later Freeman and Perez (1988); Freeman and Louçã (2001); Mercure (2022), we should be at a *sixth* industrial revolution, rather than a fourth. Different strands of scholarship account for this differently.

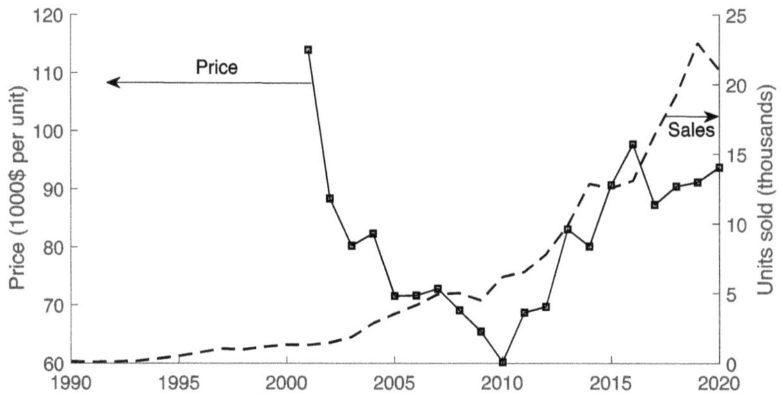

FIGURE 6.5 The rise of additive manufacturing (3D printing) and its price trends. Sales include only industrial systems costing more than $5,000 and grow exponentially. Prices declined until 2010, after which the rise of desktop 3D printers below $5,000 has exploded. This led to industrial systems sharpening their application towards higher end products and new applications. Industrial systems continue a downwards cost trajectory within their own domains of application. Cost data on desktop 3D printers does not appear available. Data from Wohlers (2021).

centralised monitoring and (automated) coordination. The internet of things produces big data that can be used to improve performance in 'smart' factories. Cloud services allow data storage and analysis to be outsourced.

The result is a factory that self-regulates, automatically repairs itself, responds exactly to product demands and produces no waste. Producing small batches of goods may become as cheap as current mass production, because reconfiguring production lines becomes costless.

Figure 6.5 shows the rapidly declining costs of 3D printing (also called additive manufacturing).[14] In the same way that a computer printer can easily print two different documents, 3D printing can easily make two different products. The approach eliminates the need to create moulds, drill bits, tools for assembling and, of course, workers.

[14] See Benson et al. (2018), and the industry report of Wohlers (2021).

It can be used anywhere, so also reduces shipping costs. People can even design objects at home and then order the physical item by mail.

Going beyond Industry 4.0, the concept of 'smart' resource use is now becoming broader. For example, digitalisation in hospitals allows staff to do more with their limited time. Doctors and nurses use smart devices and tablets instead of paper records. In theory, fewer administrators are needed.

The COVID-19 pandemic gave a taste of what could be possible. Teleworking became not just possible but necessary. It allowed companies to reduce office space, lowering total costs. It also allowed employees to cut commute times. The long-term effects on labour productivity are not yet clear, but studies have shown that employees are working longer hours, covering some of the time what would otherwise have been spent commuting.[15]

Teleworking was forced onto many of us, but it is now here to stay. Many companies have struggled to get their workforce to come back to the office. The productivity restriction that teleworking overcomes is commuting distance and, in some cases, family responsibilities.

The retail industry is also being transformed. Long before the pandemic, high-street shops struggled to compete with online-only retailers. For many customers, seeing a picture on a screen has replaced seeing the product in a shop. The customer saves time not going to the shop, and the company saves the cost of maintaining the shop. Gradually, even the process of buying the goods may soon be done by machines.

The fate of shops seems tied to that of workers. If never-ending rent payments can be replaced with the one-off cost of building a website, companies will do it. Businesses now encourage people to use online services, so that they do not need to pay for a physical presence. The new shopping infrastructure is immaterial, ephemeral, but effective and lucrative.

[15] See Criscuolo et al. (2021).

Again, the long-term effects of eliminating human interaction are not yet known. For centuries, the shop has been a location not just for buying things but also for socialising and participating in community life (protecting mental wellbeing). The online retailers effectively link anonymous customers with equally anonymous producers and cannot replace this interaction. Sometimes, the online retailers are not themselves even aware what they are selling, as Amazon found out with the sales of counterfeit goods.

However, the big data generated in the process has allowed online retailers to predict accurately what people will buy. With no physical limits on shelf space, they can 'stock' infinitely larger and broader ranges of products than old-fashioned shops could ever achieve.

The nature of how we buy and sell things is changing. Buying is done from our sofas. Minutes after the order is made, somewhere in the world, machines start to prepare the order. The only bit not yet changed is the shipping. But Industry 4.0 could change that too, if 3D printing allows products to be made locally.

These changes are happening already. Despite some protests about big companies abusing their power, the profound changes have largely been accepted. Retail and transport services employ many more people than the energy sector. But the important point is that these changes will all happen at once and will impact each other. The energy sector will get pulled along, but it will be going through its own changes too.

6.2.5 Getting Rid of Fuel Combustion

Energy is a resource, and so Industry 4.0 is expected to improve energy efficiency. However, although improving energy efficiency is a critical part of climate policy, it will not on its own reach climate goals.

Renewable energy technologies offer another solution. Renewables have been spurred by climate policy. The recent spectacular declines in costs for solar and wind energy (Figure 1.1) have resulted from this technology and not from Industry 4.0. However, nothing happens in isolation, so what happens when low-cost renewables meet Industry 4.0?

One thing is clear: further innovation is unstoppable. Industry 4.0 will become a key part of the zero-carbon transition, and AI will become embedded in the production and operation of zero-carbon systems. Digitalisation and '*smartification*' will cut costs further. Economists, who tend to look at issues in isolation, have mostly missed this insight.

In the midst of international debates about energy use and greenhouse gas emissions, a landmark study introduced digitalisation into the discussion. Arnulf Grübler is recognised as a veteran innovation scholar. Writing with colleagues, he claimed that the digitalisation, notably through using smartphones, could drastically decrease energy intensity (energy use per unit of economic activity).[16]

Grübler's scenario was completely different to the ones produced by economists. The economists all expected energy use to rise substantially, whether or not climate targets are met.[17] Their models said that higher energy use would be compensated by 'negative emissions', using unproven systems that remove CO_2 from the atmosphere. The models thus told a story that we needed untested technologies to meet climate targets. But they implicitly assumed that Industry 4.0 would not happen.

The economists did not believe Grübler's results. They perceived his scenario as highly utopian and aspirational (P1 in Figure 6.6). In their models, energy use growth is hard to control. Zero-carbon energy is expensive, while fossil fuel use promotes economic growth.

[16] Grubler et al. (2018). Grübler authored many celebrated works on technological change; see Grübler (1998); Grübler (1990); Grübler and Wilson (2013); Grübler et al. (1999).

[17] In the run up to the 2018 Special Report on 1.5°C by the Intergovernmental Panel on Climate Change (IPCC, 2018a), which was marked by intense debates over how to achieve the Paris Agreement.

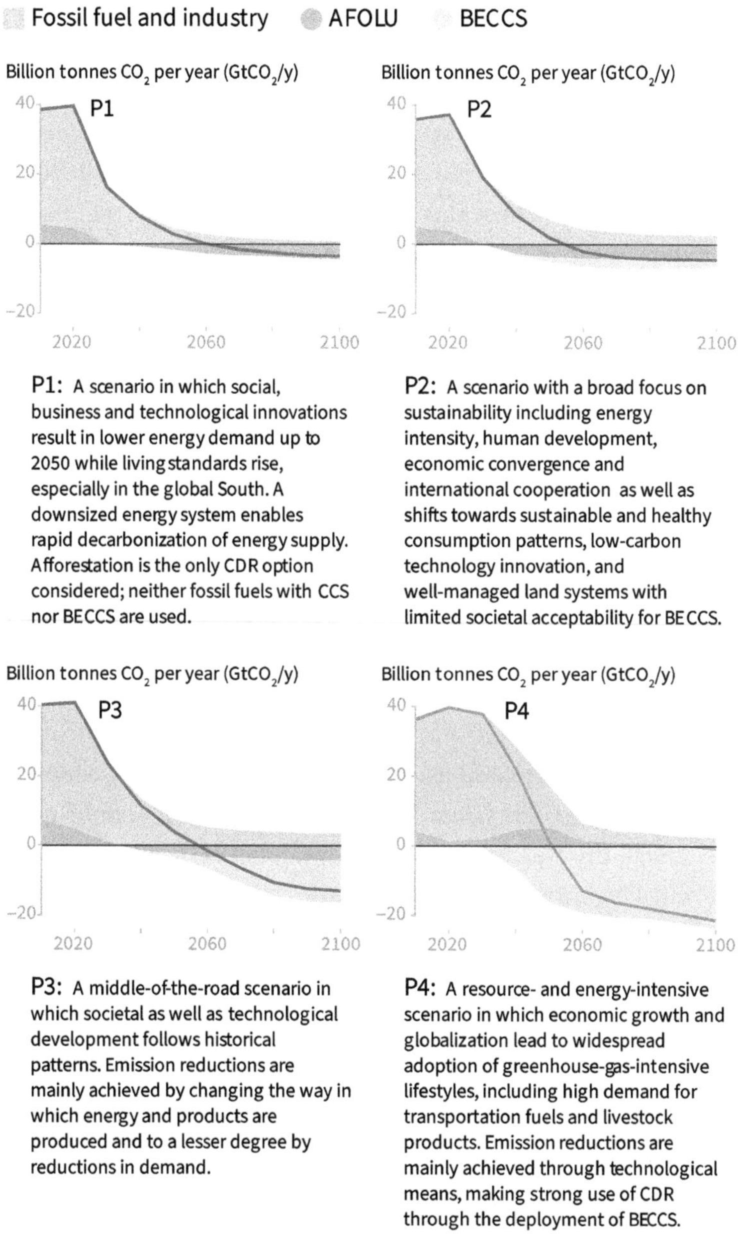

FIGURE 6.6 Global emission scenarios of the IPCC (2018a) report. P1 reproduces Grübler's scenario. CDR = Carbon Dioxide Removal technology; CCS = Carbon Capture and Storage; BECCS = Bio-Energy CCS; AFOLU = Agriculture, Forestry and Other Land Use.

Everyone agreed, however, that negative emissions would be expensive. Planting trees would use huge amounts of land, and costs will likely increase, rather than decrease, over time.[18] Industrial methods are still at early stages of development. The models suggested that large-scale deployment would be needed after 2050. But who could guarantee that this would happen, given that there will be no product at the end to sell, and hence no profits?

Looking at this question from the Great Waves perspective puts the problem on its head. Grübler's scenario is the only one that makes real business sense. In his scenario, use of energy services still increases: heating, mobility, communication and so on. However, delivery of these things is revolutionised by electrification, renewables *and* digitalisation. Industry 4.0 provides the basis for its low cost.

Smartphones and tablet computers have already replaced some of the devices that people used to buy separately, like cameras, radios, televisions, GPS systems, stereos and game consoles. Fewer materials are needed to build a single device, and energy is saved in production and use.

'Getting rid of combustion' is the contribution of decades of climate policy to the Great Wave. Its significance should not be understated; fire was important in developing early civilisation. We have relied on burning things ever since.

Combustion lacks the precision needed for Industry 4.0, however. Burning things cannot compete with moving around individual electrons. The process just cannot be controlled closely enough.

The process of combustion is also incredibly wasteful. Only half of the potential energy at best is captured and used for the things we need. It is true that wind and solar power also do not capture all

[18] For obvious reasons, little innovation can be done in planting trees, no matter how many we plant. Regarding carbon capture systems, it may seem like a cheap solution to retrofit existing coal plants to capture the carbon in the flue. But in reality, each of these projects are different, which prevents standardisation and replication of the technology. Bespoke installations will see little cost reduction with cumulative investment. See Malhotra and Schmidt (2020).

the energy from the wind and the sun; however, this matters less when the inputs are provided for free.

The coming Great Wave will even change the way we measure energy. Energy is traditionally measured by how much heat can be generated from combustion. When nothing is burnt, this will no longer be relevant!

As it turns out, getting rid of combustion means that in the statistics less energy is 'consumed', because we no longer count the energy lost while burning. So, energy use does apparently fall. Importantly though, we can still do all the same things as before.[19]

Leaving aside the measurement issues, the share of energy lost while burning expensive fuel is a clear opportunity for improving efficiency. Eliminating it makes obvious business sense in the long run. In fact, the technology is already going even further: heat pumps draw on ambient air to provide three to four more heat energy than they consume in electricity.

The alarmist discussion about 'Energy Return On energy Investment' (also known as EROI) falls into the same measurement trap. The EROI is the ratio of energy outputs to energy inputs. It has been falling over time because the fossil fuel reserves that are easiest to access have become exhausted. EROI alarmists say that renewables have dramatically lower ratios and therefore will lead to very high energy costs.

The EROI still uses the old measurement system.[20] The comparison should instead be in terms of the services that we get (or don't get) from the energy systems. For example, if we build a wind turbine

[19] Take, for example, the electric Renault Zoe car compared to the near-equivalent petrol-based Renault Clio. The Zoe uses 0.49 GJ of electricity per kilometre (239 miles on a 53 kWh battery). The Clio uses 1.49 GJ of petrol (at 54 mpg). If the electricity is generated by burning oil in a 45% efficient generator, then 1.09 GJ/km of oil is used, and switching to the Zoe increases efficiency by 27%. A car's engine is usually less efficient than electricity generators. But if the 0.49 GJ of electricity is generated using solar panels, no oil or heat is involved. Can the two cars still be compared using thermal units? All the energy numbers become three times lower. A similar story holds for solar-powered household heating using heat pumps.

[20] See Hall et al. (2014); Lambert et al. (2014); Diesendorf and Wiedmann (2020).

from steel that is made using coal, the energy lost while burning the coal is counted in the calculation. And we cannot get the energy from the coal without losing a substantial share during combustion. But the wind turbine could also be made using wind energy, which gives a more correct input for the energy invested. Given that the electricity generated by the wind turbine can be used without much loss, the input could be as much as two times lower.

The EROI comparison would be better expressed in terms of, for example, equivalent kilometres driven versus 'invested', for a petrol-based car against an EV. This would produce a balanced estimate. But, crucially, the comparison would be made in terms of future highly efficient electrical systems, rather than previous highly inefficient fossil-based ones.

Solar panels and wind turbines are already inexpensive, operate largely unsupervised and have almost no maintenance costs. Electric vehicles have recently gone past cost parity with conventional vehicles (but have much reduced fuel and maintenance costs). These are going to become the dominant technologies because of their higher efficiency.[21] The services they provide should become much cheaper for everyone.

And, as discussed above, other things are going on too. Medical advances will change the way we think about the long term. Automation will rip up labour markets. Teleworking will change commuting patterns. More and more electrical devices will be integrated, reducing material demands. Grübler's scenario was the only one that saw all this coming.

6.2.6 *Genomics and Smart Agriculture*

Another vast area of potential for innovation, higher efficiency resource use and cost reduction lies with agriculture and all food-related industries. The issue here lies largely around establishing more efficient uses of land areas, increasing agricultural yields and

[21] See Nijsse et al. (2023); Mercure et al. (2025).

reducing food waste. We need to feed more people while reducing environmental harm.

Scientific publishing makes it clear that agriculture is pushing the planet's chemical cycles far off-balance.[22] In simple language, we use way too much fertilisers for the environment, but we do this to maintain a certain level of agricultural productivity. Without fertilisers, we'd run out of good soil to grow food. But fertilisers not only generate pollution in production, they also damage ecosystems around agricultural areas when spread in large quantities. Overabundance of nutrients is as bad as not having any. It is choking off life.

Reducing fertiliser use is inevitable, but the reduction in crop production that comes with it could make the food system unsustainable. This is covered in the debate on 'yield gaps' between organic and conventional agriculture.[23] The yield gap is the ratio between the maximum theoretically possible production and the observed production levels. Other measures must be used to maintain yields (i.e. production) as they are or increase them while reducing the fertiliser input.

Yields are not optimised around the world in any way. They can be increased in many places. But it is not clear that they can be increased enough to feed the increasing global population with increasing purchasing power. Food shortages can lead to food price increases, which ultimately price out poorer countries and people from food markets.

The traditional ways that yield gaps can be increased include improving agricultural machinery, land management systems and plant varieties. Plants are traditionally improved through selection. The problem with this is that it takes a long time, and it is not clear that much more improvements in yields can be obtained. Another issue is that this approach increasingly leads to monocultures with

[22] See, for instance, Rockström et al. (2009); Steffen et al. (2015); Richardson et al. (2023) and the references therein.

[23] See, for instance, De Ponti et al. (2012).

very low genomic diversity. When this happens, crops are vulnerable to disease.

Genomics is a potential solution, which edits genes to produce better crop varieties. It is sometimes called Genetic Modification, or GM for short.

Genomics could revolutionise agriculture.[24] First, genome editing makes searching for and creating better plants much, much faster. Second, it does not rely on what already exists in the pool of genes but, instead, directly rewrites genes. It allows us quickly to create new versions of existing plants that have better resistance to droughts and pests and generate higher yields. It also allows us to avoid the trap of creating monocultures.

There is, however, a lot of reluctance towards GM crops and their use as food. Here, we take no position on this matter. But genetic modification is already happening. Genome editing has been improving not only human health directly but also plants and increasing yields for some time. Used for the right purposes, it could help solve issues of food insecurity.

The other obvious way to reduce yield gaps is with intelligent agriculture management. AI could allow us to farm more 'precisely' by combining automation technologies (e.g. for agriculture machinery), digitalisation and big data (including satellite measurements) and the Internet of Things to manage growth conditions (notably in greenhouses).[25]

6.2.7 *Smart Energy, Industry and Products*

'*Smartification*' may be the word that describes best the new great wave of innovation. Smartification reduces costs for companies and ordinary people. It is already progressing rapidly, working its way through the world's energy and industrial systems.

[24] See, for instance, Varshney et al. (2021); Gao (2021).

[25] So-called precision farming; see for instance Pathan et al. (2020).

As described above, smartification is the combination of digitalisation, electrification (getting rid of combustion), AI, the Internet of Things, big data and cloud computing. It also includes the new management principle of Industry 4.0: self-aware production systems, intelligent systems management and high-efficiency resource use.

Meanwhile, the quest for ever-extended human lifespans relies increasingly on genetics and personalised medicine, which also uses big data and artificial intelligence. Longer working lives will incentivise more training for workers in an economy with little need for low-skilled and manual labour.

Will the great wave of innovation be a good thing or a bad thing? This may be the wrong question to ask, because it is impossible to stop. However, the chances of producing good outcomes are much better if we understand the underlying processes.

6.3 THE MACROECONOMICS OF '*SMARTIFICATION*'

6.3.1 Resources Saved Are Profits

Before ending this chapter, we reflect on the possible economic consequences of the new sunrise industries. This is not easy; it is impossible to predict fully the effects of new technologies.

Most obviously, the new industry signals hope and good news. It involves new jobs, new opportunities, new technologies and new markets. These are all things policy-makers strive for.

However, even leaving aside the jobs that will be lost (see Chapter 7), there are other possible outcomes perhaps best avoided. During each previous great wave, wealth accumulated to a few rich individuals. We are already seeing this happen in the current great wave. Why?

Great waves of innovation are characterised by new products and price cuts. In both cases, there is the opportunity to make large profits, unless other companies can undercut prices. The degree of competition between companies is therefore important.

According to Schumpeter, profits made by business owners are short-lived. Other companies imitate innovations, and the opportunity for excess profits disappears when they work out how to do so. Before long, prices adjust downwards, and the chance to make large profits has gone.

However, in reality, other companies cannot always catch up. Prices may not adjust, and the chance to make large profits may last for a long time. Instead of wider society benefitting from lower prices, the business owner captures the value. The outcome may be extreme inequality.

6.3.2 *Wealth Concentration by Large Corporations*

The macroeconomic outcomes depend on what happens to the money. The more that gets spent back into the economy, the more jobs are created and the better the outcome (Chapter 5). Here, extreme inequality is a bad thing: rich people spend a much lower share of their incomes than poor people.

For example, imagine a large international company with millions of workers. The company buys AI software and lays off half its workforce. It reduces its costs but not its prices, meaning it makes gigantic profits. Eventually, these profits are returned to shareholders.

Wealthy shareholders gain, and regular workers lose out. The rich get richer, while everyone else has to make do. It sort of sounds familiar.

Obviously, this can lead to extreme inequality. But it affects the general economy too. The laid off workers will cut back on spending. These effects will not be offset by more spending by the wealthy shareholders. They already have most of the things they need. They will probably 'invest' this money into financial assets and real estate.

Once again, standard economics fails us. Standard theory *assumes* that all income is spent one way or another, so inequality does not matter. Some economists even say that more inequality is *better* for economic growth, because it incentivises risk-taking.

Even leaving aside the social problems of inequality, however, high inequality can be a drag on economic growth. Money that ends up in bank accounts does not create opportunities for others to profit. Economists' claims that banks need this money to lend to other companies are based on a complete misunderstanding of the financial system (Chapter 3).

The extreme wealth accumulation and concentration that we are seeing in the current great wave indicate that things may not be going well. We all know about some of those who own the wealth: Silicon valley CEOs and executives. We all also know or suspect that substantial wealth is being accumulated by anonymous industrialists in China. We can see the big houses, yachts and trips into space. And, despite all the new technologies, global economic growth is slowing.

So far, many of the systems developed for '*smartification*' have natural monopolies, meaning that competition is limited. Companies like Meta, Google, Amazon, AirBnB, Microsoft and TikTok have few competitors and operate in many countries. The result, unsurprisingly, is astronomical profits.

Remember that large corporations do not work towards global economic growth. They work towards their own profits, and the best way to ensure profits for the long term is to establish monopolies.[26]

What is true for wealthy shareholders is even more true for the super-rich. The wealthiest of all will not spend the money simply because they have nothing to spend it on. For example, Mark Zuckerberg won't spend all his income on 1,000 luxury cars, or buy 100 expensive homes to live in. His money will be used to buy ever more paper financial assets.

Already there is a backlash to tech billionaires. Increasing inequality will backfire for them one day. But we are still only starting on the great wave. Inequality continues to rise, and more monopolies with gargantuan profits will probably come.

[26] See Zenghelis et al. (2018).

The coming great wave will be so large that it could harm the entire economy. If robots lead to mass unemployment, no one will be able to afford the things the robots produce. Such extreme inequality would surely lead to system breakdown. Even the super-rich would then suffer.

In summary, the sunrise industries offer a lot of promise, but there are dangers too. Chapter 7 explores the more obvious dangers of what happens in the declining sunset industries. Again, workers, financial markets and wider society are all put at risk by rapid innovation.

7 The Sunset: Deindustrialisation and Post-Industrial Decline

7.1 CREATIVE DESTRUCTION IN THE SUNSET

7.1.1 *The Process of Industrial Decline*

Chapter 6 described how extending the working lives of workers, making industry intelligent and getting rid of combustion will make our economies grow in the next thirty years. Huge profits will probably be made. But one person's profit could be another person's loss. For example, improving our energy efficiency is great for us if we end up with lower energy bills. It is not so great for the energy companies and their workers.

What matters is how we use the money we saved. If we spend it on real things and not paper assets, then everyone might benefit. However, if we save it or buy paper financial assets, the result could be inequality, financial bubbles and economic crashes. This choice is played out across all the people and companies that make efficiency gains.

Either way, there will be disruption. In this chapter, we look at the flip side of the coin. Someone gains from every expenditure, and, therefore, every cost cut described as 'efficiency' or 'productivity' gains means someone, somewhere losing income. Job losses soon result.

Economists call this process creative destruction. Getting rid of combustion is a great example. There will be massive efficiency gains, and we will pay less for energy. But this will support fewer jobs. We will not need people to get fuel out of the ground, refine it or transport it.

The process of industrial decline is the reverse of what we described in Chapter 6. As things we currently use become obsolete, companies and jobs will disappear.

Some effects will be less obvious. If less fuel is transported, then we will need fewer ships, trucks and pipelines. That means fewer people to build engines and other specialised equipment parts. Anyone that contributes anything to building an oil rig will find less money coming their way.

Some of the less obvious effects may even come first. Companies will stop building oil rigs long before they stop selling oil. The first workers to lose their jobs may not have much to do with producing oil. They may be factory workers making parts used to make oil rigs. And they won't be able to do anything about it.

This is the story of investment, and it is one that can change quickly. As soon as oil companies see no future in selling oil, they will stop investing in new equipment. Even a *risk* of not being able to sell oil could be enough to put them off. This has already happened with coal companies in many countries, even though some coal production still goes on in existing mines.

The job losses in the obsolete products (including also things like non-electric cars and gas boilers) come later, as people switch to cheaper alternatives. At this point, though, it is too late to do anything to stop it.

7.1.2 The Sectors and Regions Affected

Creative destruction happens all the time, but AI and the smartification of industry could super-charge it in the next thirty years. In reality, it is impossible to separate the upcoming mega-trends (hence the descriptions in Chapter 6). Zero-carbon technologies will link with AI systems, and new technologies will be invented. Robots will increasingly build and operate our energy system. But to avoid drifting out of scope, this chapter focuses only on the zero-carbon transition and getting rid of combustion.

Which economic sectors will be affected? Some we can say for sure will be, like mining fossil fuels or building combustion engines and heating systems. Others we can make a good guess about, like those that build and supply oil rigs. However, all sectors could be affected, possibly in ways we do not yet know, because we can't predict everything that will change.

There is another important question: where will the jobs be lost? Fossil fuels account for just 2.2% of global wages and 1.0% of jobs. But many of these jobs are concentrated in particular industrial towns and cities. If fossil fuel jobs are lost, these towns could be devastated – at the same time as other towns thrive. Extreme inequality would result.

The same is true for making cars. Vehicle manufacturing accounts for 1.5% of wages and 0.7% of jobs. Most of these jobs are in large factories. If these factories close, then their workers suddenly have no money to spend in local shops. Again, the local economy collapses, and inequality rises.

We have seen this before. Detroit and the Great Lakes cities once produced cars for all of America. They were hugely prosperous – until people stopped buying so many cars. The factories also became more efficient. Now the cities suffer from unemployment, poverty, declining infrastructure, poor health, substance abuse and other social ills. Only recently have they started to rebuild.

It's happened before in the UK too. When the coal mines were closed in the 1980s, entire towns in the North of England were devastated.[1] The inequality and deprivation created can still be seen today.

So who is in the firing line? Some of the world's great cities currently make a lot of money from oil production and refining. They include Houston, Singapore, Rotterdam, Antwerp and Ulsan in Korea. All of Mid-West Canada is at risk.

And remember, it is not just fossil fuel production that will be affected. Cities with large chemical plants could be impacted. The death of the petrol and diesel cars will affect areas such as the South of Germany and parts of Japan and Korea.

[1] See, for instance, Mah (2009).

Places in poorer countries will be affected too. The Mpumalanga coal mining region in South Africa will face decline. Jamnagar in India hosts the world's biggest oil refineries. Other oil-dependent places include parts of Nigeria, Angola, the Persian Gulf, North Africa, the Gulf of Mexico, Brazil, Venezuela and Colombia.

Some of these places may benefit from new, green jobs. However, there is no obvious reason for the new jobs to be in the same place as the old ones. In many cases, they may not even be in the same country. Countries that export lots of oil look vulnerable, including several Middle Eastern countries, Venezuela, Australia, Canada, the US and Russia.

Finally, there is a time dimension. In the next fifteen years, the zero-carbon transition will create lots of construction and manufacturing jobs as new capacity is built. After that, though, the boom will peter out. Some green jobs will remain, but likely far fewer than before.

Ultimately, we cannot escape the fact that the zero-carbon transition will reduce energy costs and therefore jobs in the energy sector. More jobs earlier in the transition must mean fewer jobs later. As Chapter 6 described, new opportunities will be created, but they will be doing different things, in different places and at different times.

7.1.3 Stranded Assets, Labour and Skills

Industrial decline is a process in which things that were once highly valuable become disused and worthless. In the economic jargon, these things are called 'stranded assets'. Examples include factories and machinery (physical assets), which may be torn down or thrown away. But people may also find that their skills are much less useful than before – and we cannot simply discard people.

Standard economic theory is not of much use here. It actually denies that stranded assets can exist. Many macroeconomic models group all physical assets together and assume that they can be used by any sector to produce any product. Oil rigs can transform into wind turbines, if that's what the model wants.

Schumpeter warned us, 79 years ago, of the dangers in making such assumptions:

> That the theorist's teaching, according to which capital 'migrates' from declining to rising industries, is unrealistic is obvious: the capital 'invested' in railroads does not migrate into trucking and air transportation but will perish in and with the railroads.[2]

As Schumpeter said, it is obvious there is a problem. We shouldn't need to say that an oil rig cannot become a wind turbine.

The value of the asset is not how much it costs to make but the value of what it is expected to produce. If no one wants what it produces, the asset's value falls to zero. Companies write off assets that are no longer useful. Sometimes, the company itself may be written off. It is rarely possible for the assets to be recycled into something else, beyond scrap metal.

Stranded assets happen all the time in the economy, and this should not be alarming. Investors frequently make bets that later turn out to be mistakes. That's because they don't know the future. However, there could be situations in which lots of assets get stranded at once. That's more worrying.

For example, a company that makes gas boilers could be caught out by a sudden change in policy – or simply a sudden realisation that it has produced more boilers than anyone wants. It may be unable to absorb losses without going bankrupt. It may be unable to pay for the new equipment needed for the transition. The result could be immediate job losses in factories and on building sites of half-finished factories.

People can become stranded assets too. Once people are trained, they often rely on their skills until either they retire or their skills are no longer required. Their skill levels determine what they get paid. If their skills suddenly become useless, their incomes fall,

[2] Schumpeter (1947).

and they may not find work at all, especially if lots of other similar workers also find themselves out of work.

Likely examples include coal miners, chemical engineers, steel plant workers and workers in car factories. We will still need things like cars and steel, but they may be made in different places. For example, steel factories used to be found near coal mines, but in future, they will more likely be located near reliable electricity supply.

As famously shown in the hilarious British comedy 'The Full Monty', it may be impossible for redundant workers to find any job in their local community, unless they become 'creative' in the work they are willing to do. The workers can suffer a loss of pride and identity, again making finding new work difficult. These people may also be attracted to extreme or populist politicians who claim the ability to bring back the old jobs.[3]

Again, people may be affected in unexpected ways. If a town loses a large employer, everyone can suffer. Local shops will see fewer visitors and may cut further jobs. Local tax receipts may fall, leading to yet more spending cuts and job losses. Take, for example, the small towns around tar sands extraction in Mid-West Canada: nearly all jobs there either directly or indirectly rely on income from oil sales.

To add to the problems, industries can leave behind scarred landscapes, with contaminated land, pollution, disused mine shafts and factories. None of these encourages new companies to choose these places for setting up. Workers are left with a loss of livelihood, purpose and little sense of hope.

Much research has been carried out on industrial decline during transition in the coal, chemical and textile sectors in the UK and US in the 1970s up to the late 1990s.[4] We explore Section 7.1.4 what lessons we can learn.

[3] See Thorleifsson (2016). For example, Donald Trump promised to bring back coal jobs in the US, although he never did.

[4] See, for instance, Thorleifsson (2016); Martin et al. (2016); Johnstone and Hielscher (2017); Gherhes et al. (2020); Mah (2009); Dennis et al. (1956).

As with physical capital, standard economic theory does not help much. Usually, economic models assume that any worker can fill any job – so problems of skills and location do not exist. In reality, however, it is difficult for workers to move.

Take one well-known example. It would be difficult for car factory workers in Detroit to move to California and work in the new EV industry or the IT industry.[5] Even if they can find a job that matches their skills, property prices may be unaffordable, and the culture is different. Even the weather is different. It is a long way to move from current friends and family. There are many reasons the workers may not want to move. Thus, often, the workers instead become trapped and *may have little choice* but to file for unemployment benefits and wait for retirement.

It can get worse. If many people try to leave at once, house prices fall. The workers who lost their incomes now also lose their wealth. They may be unable to afford to move or do much at all.

As workers become trapped and their lives lose purpose and meaning, their health suffers. Medical analysis finds that all the regions of Europe with the greatest health challenges (and shortest life expectancies) are areas that experienced deindustrialisation in the 1950s to 1990s. The challenges are greatest in the former coal and steel-making regions.[6]

As with physical capital, stranding of skills is part of creative destruction and happens all the time. It is part of innovation and constant improvements to efficiency. We wouldn't have economic growth without it, and workers must always retrain. The problem is when entire towns lose their production. Then, there is nothing left to retrain for.

[5] This is reminiscent of Steinbeck's classic novel 'The Grapes of Wrath' (Steinbeck, 1939), in which agricultural workers leave the US midwest and migrate to find employment in California, only to find poor jobs and suffer from exploitation.

[6] See, for instance, Walsh et al. (2010).

7.1.4 A Precedent: Coal Transitions in the 1970–1990s

The previous great waves can give us some idea of what might happen. In his novels 'Shuggie Bain' and 'Young Mungo', the Scottish author Douglas Stuart tells a story about growing up in 1990s Glasgow. The stories are set shortly after the closure of the last coal mines, downsizing of shipbuilding and the decline of other heavy industries. They are stories of poverty, division, loss of status and hope, alcohol abuse and all the social issues around all of that. Most of all, they are stories of the people left behind. Glasgow workers had given their lives to those industries, but those industries left them with nothing.

What happened in Glasgow also happened in other parts of the UK. In the first half of the twentieth century, large sections of British society worked directly or indirectly around coal mining. Coal powered the first and second industrial revolutions, which started in Britain. It was used in transport, industry and in homes.

Coal miners often lived in towns situated on top of the coal seams, where no other industries existed. All young men in these towns expected to work in coal mining, making their way up the hierarchy from support workers up to miners working on the coalface, which was the most prestigious role. Their entire way of life was shaped by the structure of work and pay in mining, something that contributed to the development of trade unions in the UK and to the general attitude towards life in industrial communities.[7]

Coal's fate may have been sealed as far back as 1912, when Churchill converted Britain's naval fleet from coal to oil. This decision kick-started the oil-based technological avalanche.[8] It created a competitor to coal.

The subsequent decline of coal had a huge impact on British society, especially over 1950–2000. Most people remember Margaret Thatcher closing 150 coal mines in the 1980s. However, coal mining

[7] See the celebrated sociological study of coal mining in Dennis et al. (1956).

[8] See Dahl (2001).

was already in a long and slow decline – not for political reasons but because of competition from oil and because of new technologies that improved fuel efficiency.[9]

At the time Thatcher became Prime Minister, many coal mines were loss-making. She shut them down (and privatised some other parts of the industry). But what's important is what Thatcher did *not* do, which was to outline an economic plan for the people left behind.

This was deliberate, of course, because Thatcher strongly believed in the power of the market to deliver better welfare outcomes. She believed in the principles of what later became mainstream economics, that markets are best left undisturbed.

The outcome was immense human suffering and inequality. Countless local communities around Britain suffered a downgrade in income and status. Their economies stagnated, while London moved on. During the late nineteenth century, Tyne and Wear miners and shipyard workers were amongst the most highly paid manual workers in the world (outside the US). Their plunge into oblivion started from a great height.[10]

The decline of coal caused a loss of identity and purpose for those communities. Businesses would not invest in stagnant economies, so construction and manufacturing also declined. Everyone was affected.

The impact of this terrible decline can still be seen today in industrial towns in the North of England and central Scotland. Disused and decaying infrastructure provides a constant reminder of what once was. These areas are still recovering, fifty years later, from the impacts of deindustrialisation[11] : the time when the industry left and never came back. They are still waiting for something to come back. The free market did its job – which was to move development elsewhere.

[9] See Turner (1985).
[10] See Byrne (2002), although not all pitmen were well paid (Dennis et al., 1956).
[11] See Martin et al. (2016).

It is important to reflect on why these communities were unable to move on for an entire generation. There is no simple explanation, but a few elements are clear. The communities were organised around employed manual labour in big companies. They formed particular industrial cultures, identities and ways of making a living. They expected this way of life to continue.

The people could not become entrepreneurs or service sector workers because it would require a complete change of identity.[12] Specialisation and a lack of diversification can also make progress difficult; if everyone is a coal miner in a town that no longer needs coal miners, opportunities will be limited.

The same thing happened in North America's Rust Belt. Towards the end of the twentieth century, there were declines in coal and iron mining, steelmaking, car production, chemicals and other heavy industry. Cities between the Appalachian range and the Great Lakes, including Detroit, Pittsburgh, Buffalo, Cleveland and Chicago, went into decline from great heights. They lost population, and investment collapsed. The people left behind suffered from poor health and a range of social problems.

Why this matters for this book should be clear: decarbonisation could cause the same problems in a new set of towns and cities. Most obviously, towns built around remaining coal mines (notably in Asia) face similar fates to the ones described above.

It's going to be the same for oil and gas towns. They are now where coal towns were in the mid twentieth century: affluent, with high wages, but on the edge of the precipice. They can look at former coal communities and see the future, and it is bleak. Nobody rescued coal communities, so why would someone rescue them? The same story will unfold again, from great heights down to oblivion.

Margaret Thatcher only ever closed loss-making mines and a few loss-making heavy industries. But the criticism she receives is

[12] See, for instance, Gherhes et al. (2020).

relevant, and here is why. It is possible to wind down an industry less brutally than she did. It is possible to re-orient communities towards new futures without letting everyone down. We take an example from Germany.

The Ruhr region is similar to the North of England. It had a core industrial complex around a number of cities (including Duisburg, Essen, Dortmund and Düsseldorf), focused on coal mining and steelmaking. The region took quite a different path, however, because the decline of its heavy industry was carefully managed.[13]

At the start of coal's decline in the 1960s, the government's response was to help the existing system through public investment. By the 1970s, however, it became clear that the steel industry was non-viable in its current form. The government helped local economies to diversify. Training programmes were set up to give workers new opportunities. A 'Thatcher' fate was averted.

7.2 THE END OF WORK IN FOSSIL FUELS

7.2.1 *The Coal Sector in Terminal Decline*

As described above, coal transitions happened in the UK, the US and Europe from the 1950s to the 1990s. However, at least until recently, coal use has been still growing elsewhere, notably in India and Indonesia. China may be about to move from growth to decline. Figure 7.1 shows the history of energy use globally. The global *share* of coal in energy use peaked before 1925 and followed a volatile decline. The *absolute* amount of coal used has continued to grow. Absolute global peak coal use may be occurring around now.

We have one story in the developed world and another in developing countries. In the developed world, coal no longer fuels economic progress. The original uses for coal, powering engines (including railways) and heating homes are mostly gone. Steel production now demands less coal. Electricity generation from coal is in rapid decline.

[13] See Galgóczi (2014).

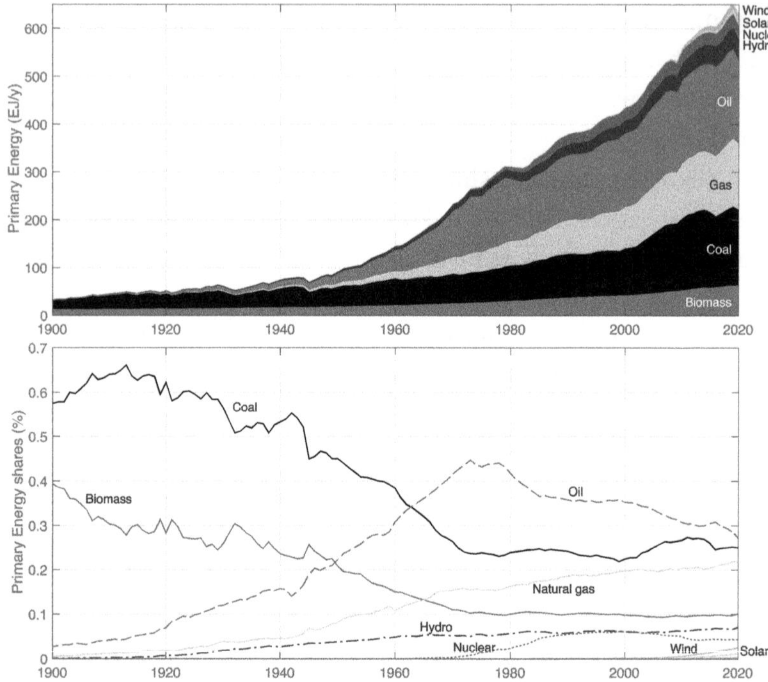

FIGURE 7.1 History of use of primary fuels (data from De Stercke, 2014; IEA, 2023b).

Although technology and the use of alternative fuels have mostly been responsible for coal's decline, environmental policy has helped too. Climate concerns are important, but worries about air quality have also led to policies like the EU's Large Combustion Plant Directive, which place strong restrictions on coal use.

In the developing world, coal consumption has risen because economic growth has increased demands for electricity and steel. However, here as well, peak coal may be in sight. China is the most advanced country, with consumption likely to fall in coming years. Consumption in South Africa is already flat. The transition away from coal will come to all these countries at some point, whether they bring in climate policies or not. It is a matter of when.

The global end of coal would conclude a long story of deindustrialisation that started in the early twentieth century. Much of the developed world has told this story already, with some places having a happier ending. The developing world, led by China, will soon have its own stories to tell.[14]

7.2.2 *Oil and Gas: High Value Destruction*

Oil and gas are not exactly in decline, at least not yet. They may be where coal was in 1950. Oil consumption is falling as a share of energy demand and may peak in absolute terms in the next few years. Gas consumption is growing, albeit slowly.

Oil is used mostly for transport. By far the largest share is pumped into cars and trucks. Aeroplanes and ships use it too, and it is also used to make plastics. Oil can be used to generate electricity, but it is very expensive to do so.

Gas is used for electricity generation, making chemicals and fertilisers and for heating buildings. It competes with coal for electricity generation and in some manufacturing. It is more expensive than coal but more efficient and less polluting.

The phrase 'peak oil' was once used to describe when the world would start to run out of oil. Peak oil will come soon, not because of oil shortages but because of lack of demand.[15] More efficient cars and, increasingly, use of EVs are reducing oil consumption.

As discussed in Chapter 1, EVs may now become standard even without new climate policies. New cars in Norway are already nearly 100% electric. More importantly, in China 50% of new cars are now electric; oil companies previously saw China as their main source of growth. Despite growth slowing recently, EVs are taking over in Europe and China. The big unknown is how quickly they will take off in other countries.

Gas consumption has increased because it has replaced coal. Climate policies have helped because gas produces one-third of the greenhouse gas emissions of coal. Gas also does not pollute local air in the same way coal does. However, it is now cheaper to generate

[14] See Clark and Zhang (2022).

[15] See Mercure et al. (2025b) and news in 2024 reported by Bloomberg www.bloomberg.com/news/articles/2024-03-28/electric-cars-pass-adoption-tipping-point-in-31-countries.

electricity with solar and wind power than it is with gas. Gas's advantage will soon be limited to times when the sun doesn't shine and the wind doesn't blow.

Oil and gas prices have always been volatile, but especially so since 2003.[16] Oil prices rose from $30 per barrel in 2003 to $130 just before the financial crisis. They then crashed to $45 per barrel, before increasing again to over $100 per barrel in 2014.

An OPEC decision to increase production in 2015 caused another crash, followed by recovery in 2018. The pandemic then caused an even larger crash in 2020, with prices even going negative briefly. They have since recovered to $80 per barrel, with a further spike after Russia invaded Ukraine.

The war in Ukraine caused gas prices in Europe to increase by a factor of 6. But restrictions on Russian exports also led to changes in trade patterns. Many oil and gas companies made huge profits. Regular people paid the cost.

We don't know if the zero-carbon transition is already increasing oil and gas price volatility. It surely will do in future though. Decline will not occur peacefully; it will involve volatility, conflict and instability (see Chapter 9). Political, economic and technological forces will not always align.

However, we must remember that it's how we use oil that matters. People with EVs will no longer pay attention to petrol prices. If trucks don't use oil, freight costs will not depend on oil prices. The oil industry can't change this. No one can force people to buy oil if they don't want to.[17]

The same is true for gas. Europe found itself dependent on Russian gas and took immediate measures to reduce gas use. 'Energy

16 See, for instance, Van de Graaf and Bradshaw (2018).

17 Many people will argue the reverse, that oil companies use their political power to protect their interests. There is certainly some truth to this. For example, Shell has often been caricatured as an extra ministry of the Dutch government. However, increasing shares of EVs changes the situation because the availability of EVs empowers consumers (consciously or unconsciously), who can escape the power of the oil industry.

independence' is a big issue for other countries too. Some of them have invested in liquefied natural gas (LNG) terminals to allow them to import gas from different places.[18]

LNG terminals may keep gas going for a while, but they are expensive and will struggle to compete in electricity generation with renewable technologies. Gradually, electricity is replacing gas for other uses, like heating buildings. The trends are the same for oil, just less advanced.

In short, our trillion dollar oil and gas industry faces decline. It could be sudden, and it will not be pretty. Growing use of EVs means that oil is in the firing line first. An oil transition could look just like the coal transitions of the 1960s–1990s. That would imply a spectacular fall from great heights into the depth of oblivion.

7.2.3 *The Internal Combustion Engine*

Electric vehicles will not only disrupt the oil industry. The car industry is in the firing line too. People will still buy cars, but the new cars they buy are already different and could become more so.

Making and maintaining EVs require a different industrial structure to what we have today. The electric motors in EVs are much simpler than the internal combustion engines in petrol and diesel cars. Electric vehicles do not need many (in some cases any) parts to manage fuel, coolants, air flows, exhausts and lubricants.

As well as the engine, many of the tubes, tanks, belts, alternators, carburetors, filters and silencers seen in current cars will thus soon be gone. These make up much of the cost of petrol and diesel cars – and therefore pay for the jobs producing and maintaining them.

What is left? Wheels, a metal frame, a plastic body and windows. Electric vehicles add a battery, electric motors and, increasingly, various computer chips and video screens connected by wires. None of these additions take up much space, so the design of cars could be reinvented. Cars may not even look like cars anymore.

[18] See Kemfert et al. (2022).

The trade-off is that EVs need powerful batteries, and these are expensive. The battery is where most of the cost of the vehicle is. But as we already know from Chapter 1, battery costs are falling rapidly. If costs keep falling, EVs will soon become much cheaper than petrol and diesel cars.[19]

The story of Detroit already tells us what could happen if a car industry disappears. It is probably not large car companies like Ford or VW that are under threat, because they can sell EVs. Smaller companies that make parts only used in petrol and diesel cars are the ones in big trouble.

There are lots of these companies in Germany, Korea, Japan and China. Many have little to no expertise relevant for EVs, and in any case, EVs will require fewer parts. These companies tend to be located near each other, so specific areas could suffer serious decline.

One unknown is who will make the batteries. Currently, it looks like a few large factories in China will supply the whole world. Countries with these factories may save some jobs, but the process is highly automated and the skill requirements are quite different to those in current car industry jobs. It won't be a saviour even for the countries that get the factories.

7.2.4 *Heating Buildings*

In cold countries, people need heating to survive. In the UK, the Netherlands and much of Europe, most homes are heated by burning gas. Some of this gas used to come from the UK's side of the North Sea, but now it is mostly provided by Norway and Russia.

Using gas to heat homes is the outcome of a previous transition away from coal. Burning coal in simple fireplaces was highly inefficient but also led to toxic smog in cities. The transition to gas cleaned up the air.

The laws of physics mean that combustion cannot generate more heat than the energy embodied in the fuel. There will always be

[19] See Mercure et al. (2025b); Ziegler and Trancik (2021).

some waste going out of the chimney or flue. Engineers have done a good job to minimise this waste – a modern gas combi boiler converts over 90% of the energy into usable heat.

Electric heating does better because electricity can easily be converted to heat with virtually 100% efficiency. However, if the electricity is generated using combustion, the waste appears instead at the power plant. This is one reason why electricity is more expensive.

Heat pumps have changed the rules. Heat pumps do not use electricity to generate heat directly but instead move existing heat from outside to inside. This works like a fridge in reverse and can achieve efficiency rates of 300–500%. It means they use three to five times less electricity to give the same heat. Even if gas is used to produce the electricity, they use less gas than a standard boiler would.[20]

Heat pumps are, therefore, cheaper to run, but the catch is they are expensive to buy and install. Even now, most people go with the cheaper and easier option to replace one gas boiler with another.

This has left households vulnerable to increases in gas prices. When Russia invaded Ukraine, the sharp increase in gas prices caused a cost-of-living crisis. The UK government had to subsidise gas prices.

Heat pumps would not have completely spared households from higher energy prices in 2022, because electricity prices also increased. The reason is that gas was still used in most countries to generate electricity. As renewable electricity generation takes over, though, electricity prices need not increase with gas prices. The economics changes.

If the cost of heat pumps falls, then how we heat our homes could really change. And this is slowly happening. For the same reason as EVs and solar panels, the technology is being improved and mass-produced. Even leaving aside climate benefits, heat pumps

[20] See Knobloch et al. (2020).

will eventually take over. People will be spared from volatile gas prices.

The decline of the gas boiler industry will not be as drastic as that of the car industry. Heat pumps can be made in most countries. As long as they are more expensive than gas boilers, they will support more jobs, especially in installation. Training workers to do these jobs should be a priority for governments.

7.2.5 *Heavy Industry*

Heavy industry includes petrochemicals, fertilisers and the wider chemical industry, steelmaking, coke production for steelmaking, cement production and various other industries that require heating inputs to high temperatures. The story across such a wide range of companies is less clear, but it is clear that change will happen.

The change will be driven by two factors: first, the direct effects of policies to reduce emissions; second, by the new technologies and material inputs that become available (and cheaper) during the wider transition.

While the zero-carbon transition is now advanced in electricity generation, and well underway in cars, it has barely started in heavy industry. In some cases, the technologies to move away from fossil fuels either do not yet exist or remain very expensive.

One particular issue is that heavy industry does not just use fossil fuels for combustion. Fossil fuels are also used in chemical reactions, for example, in making fertilisers, plastics or reducing metal ores into pure metals (notably for iron). Replacement technologies would not automatically have the efficiency benefits of eliminating combustion.

Even for combustion, there may not be low-cost clean alternatives. Heat pumps are great for houses because they generate low-temperature heat (<100°C) very efficiently. But they do not generate the high-temperature heat that heavy industry needs (e.g. >200°C). Using electricity directly to get to these temperatures would be expensive.

Nevertheless, green innovation will probably eventually reduce costs in heavy industry. Hydrogen or ammonia could be produced using renewable electricity and used for making fertilisers and iron. If this happens, these sectors will develop their own industry.

Other uses for hydrogen and ammonia would soon follow as the industry develops. One potential use would be to store electricity and provide power at times when the sun is not shining and the wind is not blowing. This could eventually be the final nail in the coffin for the gas industry.

Whether hydrogen and ammonia take off depends on two factors: cost and volume. The two go together because lower costs will bring higher volumes, and vice versa. Getting started is the difficult bit.

Hydrogen and ammonia can be used for combustion and may be needed to get high temperatures. They will not get round the efficiency losses associated with combustion, however. The use of hydrogen in long-distance transport, including aviation, shipping and road freight, could increase volume. All of these could help the technologies become established.

Creative destruction in heavy industry from the zero-carbon transition thus depends a bit upon setting up a successful market for green hydrogen or ammonia. What this means for jobs is hard to say.

However, the effects will almost certainly be much less than those from automation and artificial intelligence. Manual jobs are already being replaced, and the same cost/volume dynamics is at work. This transition could be as painful as previous coal transitions, regardless of its cause. Many of the same lessons and potential solutions will apply.

7.3 DEINDUSTRIALISATION ALL OVER AGAIN

7.3.1 *Will It Be Really Bad?*

We should think carefully how bad zero-carbon-related deindustrialisation could be. As we said in Chapter 1, what policy-makers need most is a risk assessment; they need to know 'who', 'how', 'where' and 'how bad'. And not just policy-makers, everyone else too.

The main issue is the mismatch in location, sector and time between the loss of high-carbon activity and the new zero-carbon investment. It would be easy if they matched up, but they will not.

We must, therefore, be especially wary of economists and their simplistic models that assume that physical assets (like factories and machinery) and labour flow freely from where they currently exist to where they will be needed. There is no evidence for this, but plenty against it. And what can move goes to where growth is happening, and flees areas of decline, making worse what's already happening.[21]

This chapter mostly looked at direct job effects, but the point about indirect effects is worth repeating. When a community loses lots of jobs, everyone suffers. If the local corner shop loses its customers, it will close too.

It is these broader indirect effects that prevent towns from bouncing back. The cycle is vicious. As communities lose income and spending and go into post-industrial decline, shops close, buildings become run down, alcohol and substance abuse creeps in and homelessness appears.

It becomes difficult to reverse. It becomes hard to attract newcomers who could bring in fresh ideas and needed skills. New investment is no longer enough, because numerous other issues must be dealt with. The longer we wait, the harder it gets.

Local and national tax systems provide further indirect effects. For example, royalties from oil and gas extraction will be difficult to replace. Governments face a choice of cutting spending or increasing taxes, both of which could accelerate the decline.

Finally, decline may be super-charged by a loss of investment. If there is no expectation of growth and future profits, no companies will invest. If governments lose tax revenues, they may not

[21] See, for instance, Arthur et al. (1987) and Potter and Watts (2011) on industry clustering. The geographical structure of industry readily shows clustering, which is the antithesis of freely flowing capital.

invest either. Construction workers quickly find themselves with little to do.

As soon as demand for oil, gas and high-carbon manufacturing peaks, investment will stop. The descent to oblivion will begin. Job losses will quickly start to appear.

While some regions will pull ahead, those tied to fossil fuels will suffer. Loss of livelihood, identity and purpose will follow. There will be no hope. Numerous social issues will result.

A sense of injustice in the regions that bear the burden of the transition could fuel resentment and political polarisation (see Chapter 9). We have seen it already in previous transitions. It could create a backlash against climate policies.

The worrying thing is this could all happen soon. Peak oil could happen by the end of the 2020s or early 2030s. We are not prepared for what is coming.

7.3.2 *Can Post-Industrial Decline Be Averted?*

For communities already in post-industrial decline, like former coal towns, there are no short-term solutions. Jobs are already gone, infrastructure is ageing, and people have lost their sense of purpose.

For most of the zero-carbon transition, we are not there yet, but time is running out. For communities depending on oil, gas, high-carbon manufacturing and traditional chemical industries, we must act now.

Selling inevitable doom will not help. Communities do not want to hear stories like 'your future misery is the cost that must be paid for saving the planet from climate change', or, 'we have to move on with the times' or 'the market will sort it'.

We must offer these communities a stake in the transition.[22] We must find a positive story to tell them.

This story could start with the wider benefits to society. Most countries will gain wealth from the zero-carbon transition. Some

[22] See Markkanen and Anger-Kraavi (2019).

may gain a lot. The question is how this wealth can be used to improve the lives of everyone, including those that may be left behind.

There are lessons from past cases where deindustrialisation has been managed. The case of the Ruhr region in Germany is insightful.[23] But it is not easy to apply in practice. The German government engaged for fifteen years. It created universities, invested in the local economy and developed training and re-training programs.

All this is expensive. And some people would say that governments should not pay for the mess left behind by companies that were once highly profitable. But these companies will be gone. And they will have left behind legacies, both good and bad.

Public money can be used to sustain the good things they left and clean up the bad. We can use some of the wealth created by the new companies. Someone has to do it.

[23] See Galgóczi (2014).

8 The Great Transformation of Our Time

8.1 TRANSFORMATION OF INDUSTRY, WORK AND LIFE

The new great wave of innovation will radically change our lives, in some ways we cannot yet imagine. Almost all aspects of work, rest and play will be affected. As we saw in Chapter 6, the great wave will drive economic growth and prosperity. Some changes will benefit everyone. Others will benefit only a few people at the expense of others.

All this has already started, but it will become more deeply embedded as the new technology becomes part of everyday life. It cannot be stopped.

Getting rid of combustion will be a core part of the transformation. It will save us large amounts of money and time that we currently spend on energy. We can spend this money instead on other things that we want. Artificial intelligence, automation and 3D-printing will make these things cheaper. They will also widen the selection of available products.

And as we saw in Chapter 7, there will be people left behind. The people that used to power entire nations will struggle to find a place in society. We have already seen it with coal miners in Europe and America. The same will happen to oil and gas workers. Resentment will result.[1]

It will be no consolation to oil and gas workers that they won't be the only ones. Again, we have seen it before, where deindustrialisation has led to large-scale loss of manufacturing jobs.[2] This

[1] See Thorleifsson (2016); Johnstone and Hielscher (2017).

[2] See our overview of this in Chapter 7 and Byrne (2002); Galgóczi (2014).

time though, it will be much wider. Accounting, clerical, customer, hospitality and many other services are in the firing line. And, again, it's already happening; ask a translator how business is going.

The change will be so big it could redefine how we see work. It could even redefine what it means to be rich. Relationships between people and between countries will change permanently.

In *The Great Transformation*, the anthropologist Karl Polanyi tells us how society changed in the run-up to the Second World War, leading to the emergence of polarisation, facism and conflict.[3] Changes from the coming great wave could be just as deep. Chapters 6 and 7 discussed about individual winners and losers. Now, we take a step back and look at the potential rise and fall of nations.

8.1.1 The Changing Nature of Work

People take pride from hard work. Humans have probably evolved to do so. Even if the work is low-paid, people in agriculture, factories, mines and mills, on ships, in office buildings or in government take pride in what they do. As discussed in Chapter 7, it gives them an identity and a sense of purpose.[4]

Chapter 7 also described how people cannot just move from one occupation to another, as most economic models assume. It is not just a problem of retraining or physically moving people to the right place. It is most definitely not just a question of setting wage rates to encourage people to change jobs.

Many of us dedicate our entire lives to our jobs and do not want to do anything else at all. Think of school teachers, nurses and carers. These occupations are often not highly paid, but the people are motivated by other things, including their positive impact on the lives of others. They don't want to give that up. They don't want to do something else.

According to Polanyi, the idea that people can easily move between occupations emerged with the industrialisation of Britain

[3] See Polanyi (1944).
[4] See Dennis et al. (1956); Graeber (2018).

in the eighteenth and nineteenth centuries. This is what business owners *wanted* labour to be like. Machines were replacing people on farms, so there was an excess of workers. Businessmen building mines and factories wanted to use those workers.

It was a political choice to push the 'inefficient' worker from the land and create a liberalised labour market for the new industries to pick from. It was convenient if the workers did not have any say or preference. Polanyi suggests that the industrial revolution made workers' living conditions much worse than they were on farms.

Economists happily accept the choice. It promotes ideas of efficiency. More importantly, it makes their models easier to solve.

We, therefore, need to go beyond standard economics. Schumpeter discussed at length how the great waves of innovation generate social upheaval. Old money goes into decline, and new money rises. With money comes influence. Look at how much the technology companies are paying to lobbyists. But one thing we know for sure is that those that stand to lose power and influence will not be happy.

We hope it is by now clear to the reader that the reality of social and economic changes in technology transitions is much more difficult than economists would like us to believe. Our focus in this book is on 'getting rid of combustion' and the zero-carbon transition. The impacts of this alone will be big enough. Adding in all the other bits of the great wave will make the impacts bigger still.

We saw in Chapter 7 that we stand to lose entire supply chains. The oil and gas supply chain includes drilling, exploration, making equipment and machinery, transporting fuels, refining and distribution. There is a whole range of other industries that support these activities. All stand to disappear, sooner or later.

We also saw that some cities and towns stand to be devastated. We will lose oil exploration and extraction hubs in the Middle East, Northern Canada and Aberdeen in the UK. We will also lose large hubs for refining and distribution, such as Rotterdam, Taipei and Houston.

Can we imagine Rotterdam or Houston going through a steep industrial decline like what happened in Detroit? It is hard to picture now, but it could happen quickly if people abandon oil-powered cars. Fifty-two per cent of global oil production is used just by vehicles on roads. How much of that will be left in twenty years depends on how many EVs are sold between now and then. Electric vehicles in China already have a 50% market share and are expanding rapidly, while China uses 18% of global oil.[5] Other countries will catch up too, with Europe leading the way.

Trucks and ships will also gradually move away from oil. Rotterdam and Houston could easily lose over half their trade volumes or even more if Saudi Arabia decides to capture the remaining market. Just as importantly, prices will fall too. The effects in these cities will extend well beyond oil and gas companies. The path to oblivion could begin.

8.1.2 Evolving Supply Chains across Countries

What affects people and cities will affect countries too. Many of us know already that most of the products we buy are not made in our own country. We may be less aware that within products, for example, computers, phones and cars, even the parts are made in different countries. These products, their components and the components in those components already cross many borders before they get to us.

Making these products is like a train line with many stations. At each station, a little bit of work is added. To make a smartphone, a battery may be made in Korea, a chip and circuit in Taiwan, an encasing in China and the assembly in Viet Nam or Thailand. The design may be made in the US or Finland.

Many supply chains are highly globalised. When one of them disappears, it creates challenges that cross borders. A policy in one country could, therefore, affect many other countries. For example, a policy to get rid of oil-powered cars in Europe will affect workers in all the countries that produce components for these cars. Even countries with no climate policy will be affected.

[5] According to IEA energy tables (IEA, 2024). Vehicles in China alone use 33% of its oil supply, which makes 6% of global oil.

Technologies quickly cross borders too. Car companies must produce large numbers of vehicles to be profitable, so they may stop producing oil-powered cars altogether. A country with no climate policy may find that it has to manage the transition to EVs anyway.

It is not difficult to identify the biggest losers from all this. Countries that are heavily focused on fuel exports are most at risk. Saudi Arabia and Kuwait are two prominent examples. Norway and the US may have large oil industries, but they also produce lots of other things. They have economies that are *diversified*. In diversified economies, a global transition to EVs could cause some measurable loss of production and exports. In undiversified countries focusing on oil production, the transition could obliterate the entire economy and public finances.

How do fuel-exporting countries diversify their production? If it has not happened already, it will require *industrial strategy*. This is controversial. Most economists, and organisations like the IMF, have for decades advised against countries having industrial strategies. They claim it is inefficient because it favours some industries over others. It is better to let the free market 'discover' alternatives on its own.

Of course, the free market does not do it. Instead, large oil exporters suffer from what's called the 'resource curse', according to which resource-exporting countries tend to neglect their other sectors and do the opposite to diversification.[6]

Furthermore, it is not possible for a government to be completely neutral towards industries, technologies or sectors. Sectors or technologies are never equal themselves. Some are already well developed, while others are in their early stages. Some may need more support now but deliver more in the long run. Sticking to free-market ideologies mostly means abandoning the development of new technologies and leaving it to other countries.

[6] See Ross (1999); Savoia and Sen (2021).

Simon Sharpe makes this point convincingly in his book 'Five Times Faster'.[7] Since making industrial choices is inevitable, he suggests that government should make them deliberately rather than accidentally.

Standard economics is of limited use here because it ignores the stages of progress in technology. The more technology changes, the further from reality these assumptions become. And the whole point of the great wave is that a lot of technology is going to change quickly. Some economists are now recognising this. Some are even suggesting that industrial strategy might be a good thing after all.

An industrial strategy attempts to guide the economy deliberately rather than hope for the right thing to occur accidentally. It also helps to cope with economic changes imposed by other countries, like in the car industry. Even so, successful and resilient industries (and their supply chains) are not easy to build. They take a long time to become stable. Unfortunately, like a house of cards or a game of Jenga, they can be shattered in no time at all.

Having no industrial strategy means having nothing to fall back on if things go wrong. In contrast to what economic models say, new industries do not automatically appear. It takes a lot of work, involving both government and businesses. The whole discussion about coal mines in Chapter 7 described the 'Thatcher fate', of what happens when there is no plan.

8.1.3 We Need Economic Resilience

Investors care about two things: expected returns and risks. They go to great length to maximise returns and minimise risks. Financial advisors build 'risk profiles' to understand how much risk their clients are willing to take.

Most of the discussion about the zero-carbon transition focuses on expected returns. But the zero-carbon transition will also increase the levels of risk. More risk means less resilience. This could have important consequences.

[7] Sharpe (2023).

In Chapter 3, we established the performance–stability trade-off for economies and policy strategies. The faster growth is, the less stable it is likely to be, marred by booms and busts. The more optimised a policy tries to be, the higher the likelihood that it fails spectacularly.

A Faster transition would mean faster economic growth with more investment. Does it also mean more risk and less resilience? The answer is likely to be yes. For example, there could be a financial bubble leading to a crash. According to Carlota Perez, this has happened once before in every great wave.[8]

In the face of the greatest economic transformation of our times, it is worth asking whether we care more about economic performance or resilience. What is our collective risk profile? Does a collective risk profile even make sense? Some people will care more about returns. Some people will care more about resilience.

Intuitively, you would expect people who are wealthy already to care more about resilience. They would accumulate less wealth over time but would not be risking the wealth they already have. The Nobel Prize-winning work of Daniel Kahneman, Amos Tversky and Richard Thaler in behavioural economics[9] shows exactly this. Psychology experiments show that people value avoiding losing $100 more highly than the benefits of gaining $100.

Other experiments by Kahneman, dating back from the 1970s, look at risk more explicitly. When asked to choose between getting $500 or a 50% chance of getting $1,000, 84% of respondents preferred the $500. If respondents who already had $2,000 were asked whether it was worse losing $500 or having a 50% chance of losing $1,000, two-thirds of people took the gamble. People are risk-averse, but losing seems to affect us more than winning. We can probably all relate to this.

It seems reasonable that people would also be risk-averse at the whole-economy level. They would be happy with slower growth

[8] Perez (2001).

[9] See Kahneman and Tversky (1979); Thaler (2016).

if it meant less risk of things falling apart. They would prefer economic resilience so that they could maintain their current standards of living.

8.2 TRANSFORMATION OF TRADE AND INVESTMENT

8.2.1 The Fundamental Quest for Foreign Currency

Risk and resilience mean different things in different countries. One thing rich countries don't have to worry about so much is currency. The story is much different for the developing world.

The authors had the chance to debate with Brazilian economics professors and policy-makers about the choices developing countries can make for promoting economic growth. Professor Marcelo Pereira argued that developing sources of foreign currency is the holy grail for economic resilience in developing countries. The quest is to accumulate lots of US dollars.

Currency is a gaping blind spot for standard economics. In standard models, currency does not really exist, and certainly does not cause financial instability. The theory doesn't have anything to say about these problems. But Professor Pereira argued that, by exchanging oil, minerals and agricultural commodities for dollars, Brazil enjoyed rapid growth. Before then, it suffered from repeated currency crises that prevented economic development.

The reality of currency shortages is painful because of debt. Debt is created in currencies and other assets that are not interchangeable. A \$100 loan cannot be repaid in euros. A central bank can create new money in its own currency but not in any other currency. Therefore, most of the time, a government cannot run out of its own currency. But running out of foreign exchange is a serious matter.

As we saw in Chapter 5, countries and businesses take on debt all the time. They use debt for building the infrastructure, knowledge, equipment, methods and resources that they use for production. The use of debt boosts economic growth.

If someone both borrows and earns income in their domestic currency, then usually we can ignore currency effects. Investment happens through the creation of ordinary credit at local banks. However, if someone borrows abroad in foreign currency, but their income is in local currency, they must buy foreign currency to repay the loan. If foreign currency becomes expensive because of exchange rate movements, they may be unable to repay the debt. They would then face defaulting on foreign debt payments.

If exchange rates did not change, there would be no problem. However, usually, exchange rates do change. They can sometimes change by a lot in a short period of time, even if officially they are not supposed to. International trade in financial assets (sometimes called 'hot money') has a strong effect on exchange rates – but is itself often unstable. For example, if the US central bank (the 'Fed') increases its base interest rate, US dollars usually drain away from developing countries because returns are higher in the US.

The obvious question is why should any country borrow in foreign currency?[10] The obvious answer is that they may have to do so if they have to import goods that can't be found at home and lack the dollars to buy, for example, solar panels. In most countries, a large share of imports is fossil fuels. Another large share is paying interest on existing foreign loans. However, countries also need to import essential things whatever the cost, for example, computers, military and medical supplies. Without these things, they could quickly collapse, but to get them, they need US dollars.

Brazil gets its dollars from exporting fuel and food. Although commodity prices can swing, fuel and food provide reliable sources of US dollars. Brazil should be able to avoid currency crises. It has a good stock of US dollars to prevent that. But what could happen in other countries?

[10] See Reinhart and Rogoff (2010) for the standard economics view and Eichengreen and Hausmann (1999) for the developing country perspective.

When a country imports more than it exports, its reserves of foreign currency decrease. The country's currency will lose value because fewer people want it. The exchange rate declines. All imports become more expensive.

Standard economics says that this feedback should be sufficient to balance exports and imports. However, as we noted above, many countries must import fuels and other essential goods. Even when these goods become more expensive, they still import them, and to do so, they may have to borrow in foreign currency.

When foreign currency reserves run out completely, there is nothing to catch the falling exchange rate. A vicious cycle emerges where the country creates new domestic money to buy foreign currency and pay foreign debt. This lowers the value of the domestic currency, pushing the exchange rate down further.

Debts become harder and harder to repay. The vicious cycle quickly becomes a death spiral. A 'lender of last resort', usually the IMF, bails the country out, with a big affordable loan, but not without conditions. Those conditions may require privatisation of state assets or reductions in public spending on welfare.

It's a tragic story, and the links to the low-carbon transition should be obvious. To reduce emissions, countries must invest in zero-carbon solutions, many of which come from abroad, and this requires finance in foreign currency. But many countries may not have the capacity to repay those loans in foreign currency, because it all depends on their income from exports, even if they an borrow sustainably the same amount in domestic currency. Many developing countries are currently at the limit of their capacity to borrow in foreign currency, due to a debt hangover from the Covid crisis.

Lots of countries would actually end up better off, including many in Africa and Asia, in a zero-carbon economy. If they did not need to import fossil fuels, then they would need to find fewer sources of US dollars and have a lot more economic freedom. Their economies could keep working even when fossil fuel prices become unaffordable. They could use their dollars to buy other things to help development.

The problem is how to get there; the transition period requires investing using US dollars, when they're already indebted. Raising domestic funds using taxes (e.g. carbon taxes) doesn't really help, because that's still in domestic currency. Using carbon tax revenues to buy dollars would not help the exchange rate.

The problem is particularly difficult for countries that use fossil fuels to get the US dollars they use to import the rest of what they need. Brazil could see a large part of its 'reliable' source of earnings disappear. And keep in mind that as global oil demand falls, so will oil prices. That means fewer US dollars for each barrel of oil sold, even for countries that keep exporting.

Currently, fossil fuels account for a staggering 16–20% of the total value of all international trade worldwide.[11] Getting rid of combustion will reduce this trade drastically. Only a few countries normally get most of their US dollars from the trade of fuels. If these countries cannot get US dollars from somewhere else, they could find themselves in a death spiral. Such an outcome already happened in Venezuela (see Chapter 9) and could happen to many African countries.

It gets worse. Fossil fuel prices will become more volatile too. The reliable earnings from exporting fuels will become more unstable at the same time as they are getting smaller.

In the quest for US dollars, getting rid of combustion will thus create winners and losers. It could be on a spectacular scale. Some countries will end up in crisis because they cannot pay for necessary imports. Others will find new economic freedom. The balance of economic power will change.

Many people believe that countries will escape paying for fuel only to instead pay for importing solar panels and other equipment and end up worse off. Some people say that getting rid of combustion

[11] See the WTO statistics portal.

could imply *higher* imports for most developing countries. This is likely not true for two reasons.

The first reason is that key low-carbon technologies are already cheaper on a lifetime basis, so total spending on energy should fall (Figure 8.1).[12] For example, the cost of an EV plus its lifetime use of electricity is less than the cost of a new petrol car plus its petrol. Imports cannot really increase in this situation, at least in the long run. Having said that, we must recognise the short-term need to get US dollars to pay for upfront investment costs.

The second reason applies to renewable electricity and energy efficiency measures. As well as becoming cheaper overall, a big share of their costs is in installation, which must be done locally. This does not require US dollars.

It seems undeniable. Global trade patterns will change, and there will be casualties.

8.2.2 *Redefining What We Trade*

One country's actions affect other countries, but the effects will not be felt just through trade in fuels. Figure 8.2 shows the range of impacts that countries can have on each other through decarbonisation. We will probably largely stop trading energy across borders. Electricity is expensive to trade because it requires long-distance high-voltage power lines. But trading electricity will also be mostly unnecessary, because all countries have sunlight and wind.

Instead, we will see increased technology exports to harvest the sunlight and wind. Mass-producing zero-carbon technologies will require developing brand new global supply chains. Along the way, companies will develop new technologies and intermediate components. Demand for certain materials will increase.

[12] The cost calculation in Figure 8.1 makes use of a 10%–20% discount rate to value future expenditures against present ones, assuming that future expenditures (fuel) are less valuable than present ones (upfront capital). At zero discount rate, most zero-carbon consumer technologies (electric cars, heat pumps, solar panels) are already competitive, simply because fuel is so expensive. However, this assumes that consumers can finance high upfront investments at a low cost.

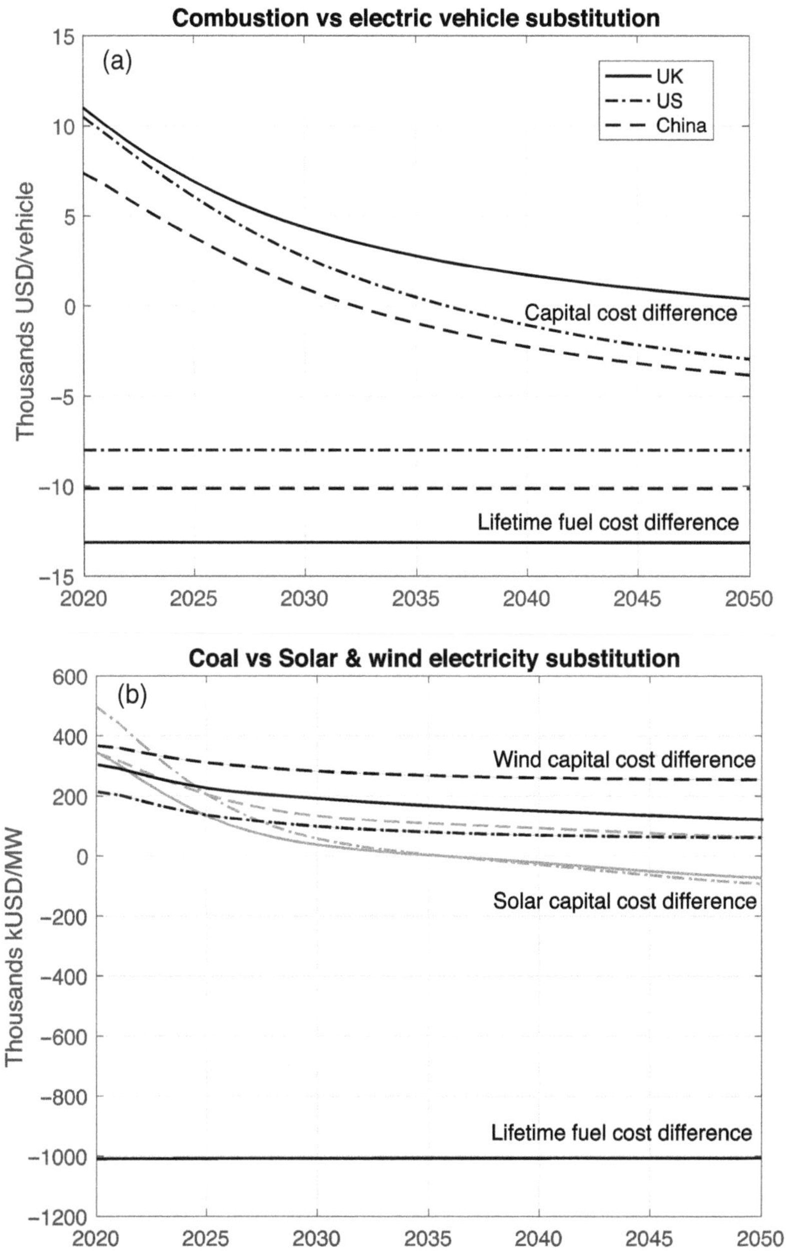

FIGURE 8.1 Total cost difference over time between green and brown technologies, namely cars and power generators. Projections were made using the FTT model.

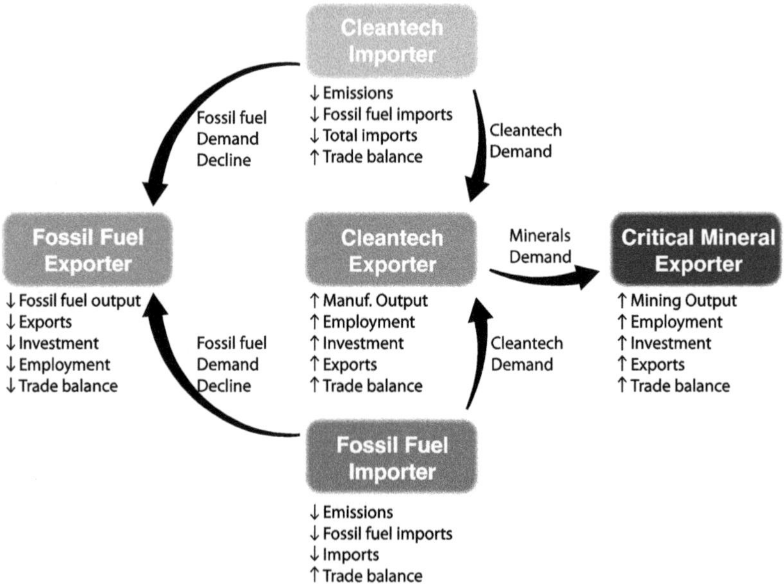

FIGURE 8.2 Different types of countries affect others in different ways in the transition (Espagne et al., 2023).

There will be plenty of opportunities for countries to develop new types of exports and secure US dollars. Particularly promising opportunities may attract foreign investment and more dollars. In most cases, it could be any country that benefits, so probably not the few that currently export fossil fuels.

The one bit where we can confidently predict who will benefit is in minerals, because we know where the minerals are. New 'critical minerals' are used in lots of zero-carbon technologies, particularly in batteries. Examples include lithium, cobalt, copper and nickel. Much more of them will be used in a zero-carbon future.[13]

Supplies of these materials are constrained. This is not so much because they are scarce on planet Earth but because the global economy lacks capacity to process raw ore into useful forms. Building capacity takes time, but we will keep on demanding more and more zero-carbon equipment.

[13] See the International Energy Agency on critical minerals (IEA, 2021).

The mismatch between supply and demand is worst with raw materials. Manufacturing companies can usually expand production quickly, if they know people want their products. Mining and ore processing require huge investments though. A guaranteed large demand is needed to justify this investment. By the time they see this, however, demand is already growing quickly. There is already a mismatch problem.

Critical minerals exports will never be as valuable as current fossil fuel exports. This is necessarily the case given that getting rid of combustion is profitable. We save money by replacing fuel-guzzling equipment with zero-carbon technology. If it's profitable, the new technology can't use more critical minerals than the old technology for which most of the cost is fuel. And if we spend less money, we send less money to other countries.

Zero-carbon technologies also incorporate costs from other things. Critical minerals may make up most of the cost of batteries, but the cost of assembling cars or installing solar panels does not depend on minerals. So, even as we spend less, a smaller share of what we spend goes on imported minerals.

Still, countries will compete to supply the world's energy needs. Giant factories can produce solar panels much cheaper than smaller ones. If we only have a few giant factories round the world (for now mainly in China), most countries will need to import their solar panels. The same is already happening for batteries. High transport costs change the logic for wind turbines, but we still have important manufacturing centres in Europe, the US, China and Brazil.

The story of the quest for dollars changes. Ending the need to import fossil fuels may be the easy part. Being able to build and maybe even export zero-carbon technologies will be much more difficult. Many countries are trying.

Brazil is one of these countries. Brazil's national development bank has provided low-cost loans for building wind farms for more than ten years. Critically, to qualify for the loans, some of the turbine components must be made in Brazil. Developers thus had to work with Brazilian companies. Over time, these companies became competitive globally.

China does it on a much larger scale. Although demand for solar power came from European subsidies, China created a solar industry that could supply the whole world.[14] China is doing the same with EVs. The opportunities are huge: China could both slash its expensive oil imports while supplying the rest of the world with technology.

It is worth pointing out again the benefits. If countries stop spending their hard-earned US dollars on fuel, they can import other things they cannot make themselves. Examples include medical and IT equipment. Both could improve the lives of their citizens.

8.2.3 A New Geography for Foreign Investment

Foreign investment can be the most important source of US dollars of all. Not only does it provide currency, it may also support debt sustainability or build new things that can support jobs. Countries compete fiercely for foreign investment.

If we made a map showing where foreign investment comes from and where it goes to, it would show that much of it starts in two places. The first is countries with highly developed financial systems, like the US, the UK and the EU. The second is countries with large trade surpluses, like China, Russia and Saudi Arabia.[15]

Most foreign investment has little to do with fossil fuels or the zero-carbon transition. It could fund property purchases, new infrastructure, IT, healthcare or biotechnology. However, a chunk of the money comes from countries that sell oil. Oil exporters need places to invest the vast profits that they are still making.

For example, Norway and Saudi Arabia get huge amounts of US dollars from exporting oil. They put the money in 'sovereign wealth

[14] Both case studies are described by Grubb et al. (2021a).

[15] However, it is challenging to draw such a map with numbers, because data on foreign investment and international capital flows are generally incomplete or missing.

funds' that invest all over the world to generate future incomes. People who have made fortunes from oil also look for places to invest.

Much of this investment finds its way to the US, the UK or the EU, because there are lots of investable opportunities in these countries. However, some of it also finds its way to developing countries that use it to get access to US dollars.

We don't know exactly how much money poor countries receive, because there are no clear data. But we do know that selling oil makes a lot of money, so the amounts are probably large. We also know that an end to the oil trade will make these petrodollars disappear.

Even rich countries will be affected. Countries like the US and the UK can import more than they export because they get foreign investment from other countries. Think Treasury bonds and London property. When the oil money stops flowing, they will lose this investment. It won't be catastrophic because they get investment from other sources too, but it could have a noticeable impact.[16]

We don't yet know what the new map of foreign investment will look like. But it will be very different. And this will change who has power worldwide.

8.3 TRANSFORMATION OF (GEO)POLITICAL POWER

8.3.1 New Economic Strategies

As discussed in Chapter 4, the age of oil started when the internal combustion engine took off. The petrochemicals industry followed, and a huge money-making constellation of industries developed. These industries were thriving until recently.

Until the 2007–2008 financial crisis, most of these companies believed we would keep using more and more oil for the foreseeable future. Concerns about running out of oil were mostly gone, because

[16] However, the decline of oil could change how much countries use the US dollar for international trade. They may begin to trade more frequently in euros, Chinese yuan or another major currency.

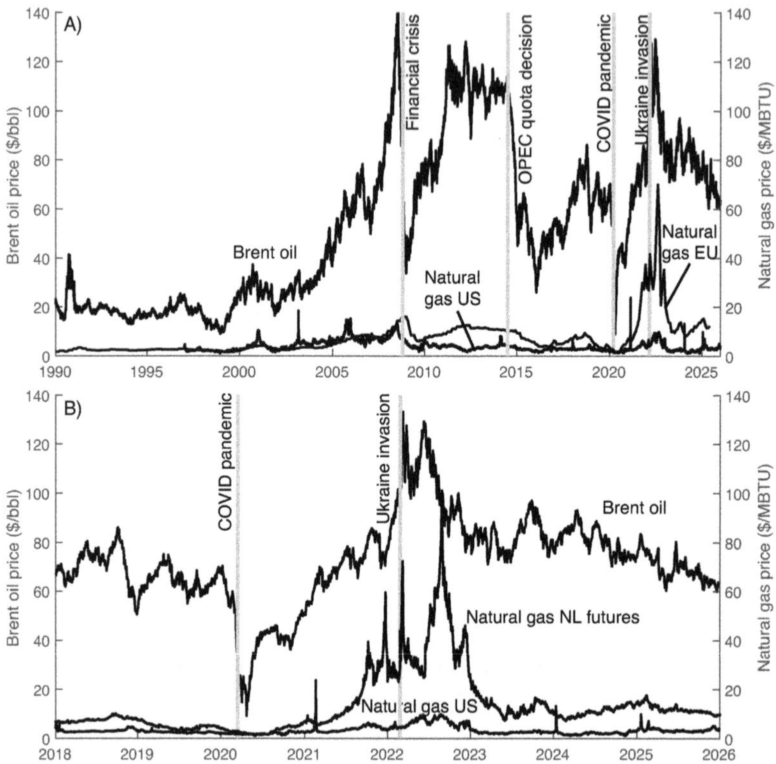

FIGURE 8.3 (a) Price of Brent oil (daily) and US (daily) and EU (monthly) natural gas prices since 1990. (b) Price of Brent oil, US gas and Netherlands gas futures (all daily). Gas prices have been more volatile in Europe and the US since the run up to the war in Ukraine.

oil prices were high, and we kept finding new sources of oil. Since the financial crisis, however, oil markets have been constantly disrupted (see Figure 8.3).[17] Most importantly, fuel efficiency standards for cars have limited the amount of oil we need.

Much of the policy came from Europe and Japan, but the whole world was affected. European regulations made car companies find

[17] The end of the age of oil may have started with the 2007–2008 financial crisis and ensuing recession. Since then, oil markets have been highly unstable (Van de Graaf and Bradshaw, 2018; Mercure et al., 2021a). There have been chaotic output decisions by OPEC, unstable demand and stocks of oil (especially since the COVID pandemic) and steeply rising geopolitical tensions. Russia's invasion of Ukraine caused even more upheaval in oil and gas markets.

ways to make more efficient engines. The car companies then put these engines in cars sold in other countries too. The reason they did this is because it is cheaper to sell the same cars in different countries.[18]

The result is that the amount of oil we are using in our cars doesn't grow as fast anymore, even though the amount of driving keeps growing. Global oil production is still gradually increasing but mainly because of other uses (e.g. in planes or to make plastics). But a wider use of EVs will probably soon send oil into the start of a slow decline.

The oil industry has so far struggled to adapt. With growth no longer guaranteed, companies do not know when to invest in new production. There have been times with little investment and times with far too much investment.

US shale oil and Canadian tar sands provide a good example. Both of them have operated in a hectic stop–start mode since the financial crisis. Although they have found ways to reduce costs, both are still expensive (over $50 per barrel) and can be undercut by OPEC countries increasing supplies (less than $10 per barrel). The result has been economic volatility and unstable prices.

The balance of power in oil is changing. Traditionally, Saudi Arabia's national oil company Aramco has called the shots on global oil prices. Linking with other OPEC countries, and more recently with Russia, gives Aramco more power. However, volatility since 2007–2008 shows that controlling prices has become more difficult. Underlying this, the politics of oil have also become more difficult, for example, with disagreements between OPEC member countries and Russia, US shale oil and US–Russia relations.[19] More recently,

[18] Three regulators effectively cover three quarters of the world's vehicles: the EU, California (the US) and China (Sharpe, 2023). These regulators have forced car companies to develop low- and zero-carbon vehicles. The companies then sell the same cars in other countries. This has also led to global adoption of vehicle safety measures. For example, airbags were invented in Japan but appeared in North American cars even though safety regulations did not require them (Miyoshi and Kii, 2011).

[19] See Van de Graaf and Bradshaw (2018); Van de Graaf and Sovacool (2020).

COVID and Russia's invasion of Ukraine have complicated things further.

Why countries make certain decisions will always remain mysterious. We can make some educated guesses based on the available data though. Russia's economy depends heavily on exports of oil, gas, fertilisers, food and several other basic commodities. It has a lot of oil and gas, but it is expensive to extract and sell. Typically, it costs Russia $20–60 to produce a barrel of oil, compared to $5–20 per barrel in OPEC countries.

People therefore only buy oil from Russia because OPEC doesn't produce enough for everyone. When OPEC produces more oil, Russia gets to sell less oil. In many ways, this basic fact helps to explain Russia's fierce and defensive stance in global energy markets.[20]

The story nowadays is the same for North America. The oil industry really took off in the US, so North America has the longest history in the oil business. King Hubbert famously warned the US government in the 1960s that oil resources might run out.[21] But it never happened, because there always seems to be more oil available, whether mixed with sand, trapped in hard rock, deep underwater or in the Arctic.

The catch is that this oil is expensive to get to. Technology has helped to reduce costs, but it still takes $60–90 to extract each barrel.[22] No one is going to buy this oil if they can get much cheaper barrels from OPEC or Russia. Companies in North America thus rely on OPEC and Russia, limiting their production. Even so, they make little profit and are unable to tolerate any tax, regulation or environmental standards that would increase their costs.

As we explored above, the story is vastly different for the EU, China, Japan, Korea, India and other countries that import oil. These countries want two things: oil to be as cheap as possible and to use

[20] For the numbers and costs in this section, see Mercure et al. (2021a), especially Fig. 3.
[21] Hubbert (1962).
[22] See Ansari and Kaufmann (2019).

as little of it as they can. They can then use their dollars for other things. It is not surprising that policies to reduce oil use started in these countries. Japan led the way in the 1970s. In 2013, European cars were twice as efficient as their American counterparts. Cars sold in Japan were the most efficient of all.[23]

We shouldn't forget coal, but here it is less important. Coal is difficult to transport and has lower economic value. Fewer countries rely on trading coal, and for those that do, volumes tend to be smaller. The same principles apply though – countries that import coal could use their dollars for other things.

Economists have noticed the relationship between energy costs and energy use. Igor Bashmakov first noted that countries tend to spend 8–10% of their GDP on energy resources and services.[24] When energy prices rise, they find ways to use less energy. Conversely, when energy costs fall, wasteful energy use increases. The changes come about because of innovation, replacing old machines, changing behaviour and government policy. This can take time, but it explains why oil-importing countries focus much more on energy efficiency.

To summarise, we can partly explain why countries do what they do by looking at their economic structure and natural resources. But this will all be upended during the transition.

8.3.2 *Playing the Climate Policy Game*

In earlier work, we asked ourselves the question how countries would behave in the zero-carbon transition, based on how the transition affects GDP and jobs.[25] Of course, countries care about other things, but GDP levels are connected to geopolitical power.

In that exercise, we grouped countries into three types, depending on whether they are oil and gas importers (EU, China, Japan, Korea, India), low-cost oil and gas producers (OPEC) or high-cost oil

[23] See, for example, Mercure and Lam (2015).

[24] See Michael Grubb's book *Planetary Economics* (Grubb et al., 2014), Chapter 6. Data originally by Igor Bashmakov; see Grubb et al. (2018).

[25] In Mercure et al. (2021a) and Espagne et al. (2023).

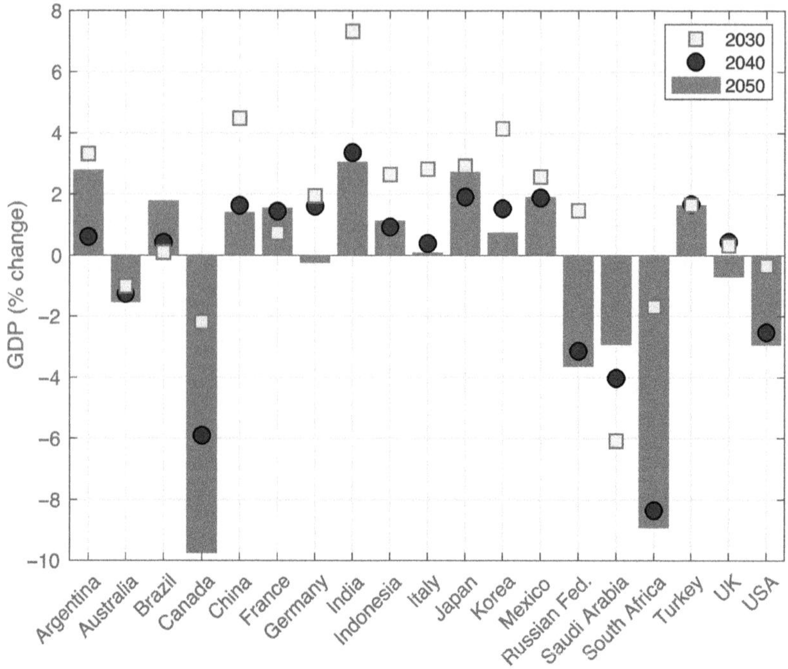

FIGURE 8.4 Changes in GDP relative to baseline in a rapid transition for G20 countries.

and gas producers (US, Canada, Russia). We estimated what might happen to GDP and jobs in seventy countries up to 2060, using a combined economy – technology model.[26]

We created scenarios in which the three country groups may or may not adopt policies to get rid of combustion to achieve emission reduction targets. Figure 8.4 shows the estimated GDP impacts in 2050 if everyone moves towards net-zero emissions.

From this exercise, we could make a mental map of possible behaviour. For example, countries that import oil and gas could see net-zero emissions as a win–win because they no longer need to import fuel. Instead, they can boost their domestic economies and create additional jobs. Jobs in fuel production are lost, but these are

[26] The authors co-developed the E3ME-FTT model over the last decade; see Mercure et al. (2018a).

mostly in other countries. These countries effectively export job losses.

Moreover, the oil and gas exporters cannot stop the importing countries from cutting fuel consumption. Remember that India, China, the EU, Japan, the UK and Korea account for 3.5 billion people. If all these people stop using oil and gas, everyone will notice. And, not by coincidence, these countries are trying to reduce oil and gas consumption.

When oil and gas consumption falls, so do prices. This hits all countries that export oil. Even countries that can produce a barrel of oil for $5 would rather sell it for $90 than for $60. But if forced to sell at lower prices, low-cost producers can still make the same profit, if they sell more of it. OPEC countries can do exactly this if they want to because they have spare capacity available. As the world consumes less fuel, they could soon find themselves meeting the entire global demand and push all other countries out of the market altogether.

If fuel importers cut back and low-cost producers increase production, high-cost producers like Russia, the US and Canada become double losers. They become powerless, unable to produce fuel at a price that anyone would buy. Their own climate policies may even make things worse, by further harming their oil and gas industries.

These simulations, to some extent, explain why implementing climate policies in Russia, Canada and the US is difficult. Most people understand that these countries could lose a lot. Fewer people realise, however, that it will mostly be other countries that decide how much they lose. Researchers presented these results at a US Senate hearing in 2023.[27] People that understood the message realised the urgency, but it was clearly not commonly accepted.

The other uncomfortable message is that high-cost fuel exporters have a strong interest in stopping other countries from

[27] S.Hrg. 118-72 – Left holding the bag: the cost of oil dependence in a low-carbon world. www.congress.gov/event/118th-congress/senate-event/LC70832/text?q=%7B%22search%22%3A%22semieniuk%22%7D&s=2&r=2

decarbonising. When we look back over the decades, we see this is broadly what has been happening.

Based on this research, in 2021, we predicted that oil and gas importers would reduce emissions quickly, and OPEC would increase quotas to sell oil and gas while people still wanted it. Oil and gas prices would fall as a result. We also said that other oil and gas producers would avoid climate policy and would perhaps even try to stop other countries from reducing their emissions.[28]

Just three months after our research article was published, Russia invaded Ukraine. Oil and gas prices, which had been moderate for some time, suddenly shot through the roof. Supply restrictions in a tight market meant higher prices. We were wrong!

In the past wars have been fought over resources like fossil fuels. And this time, fossil fuels were very much tangled up with the war. Russia has previously used energy as a weapon, for example, in its threats to continental Europe. Although the war caused Russia to lose much of its oil and gas exports to Europe, Asian countries continued to buy Russian oil. The war changed the oil map.

The Ukraine war has become an economic war as well as a conventional one. A side effect of it was an inflation crisis worldwide, particularly in European countries that needed to find alternative energy supplies. Oil prices doubled and gas prices went up by a factor of 6–10 times (depending which times we compare (see Figure 8.3), with knock-on impacts on interest rates, bank lending, investment and economic growth. Oil and gas exporters asserted that they still have global power. Oil and gas importers learnt that they need to protect themselves by reducing their fuel needs.

Oil and gas markets have entered an age of extreme volatility and unpredictability. We face a new age of global political, economic and financial instability. Getting rid of combustion is just one factor amongst many. But we know that declining fuel use and consumption is not something that large oil and gas exporters will easily accept. These countries are awash with cash now, but may

[28] In Mercure et al. (2021a).

not be in the future. It may seem to them in their interest to intervene while they still hold that wealth and power. This gives a bleak prospect for global cooperation.

8.3.3 The Rising Geopolitics of Technology

For all the noise around oil and gas production, geopolitics is increasingly about technology. We only need to pick up a newspaper (or read one online) to see that. Tensions have stiffened between China and the US. International trade of technology has become an area of concern for security.

China has long exported more to the US than the US has exported to China. The US's deficit has been counterbalanced by foreign investment, as we discussed earlier in this chapter. But Chinese imports were accused of replacing things produced in the US and costing people their jobs.

Although this caused tension, it was manageable. The two countries were partners and needed to find ways to define their relationship. More recently, things have changed. China has ventured into sophisticated high-tech, IT and telecommunication devices. Not only do these devices challenge high-value industries in the US, but they also find military use.

The technology originates in the US. The IT revolution was born in California, and silicon-based devices were originally made there entirely. Making the chips that power these devices is not easy. It requires lots of investment, as well as knowledge of semiconductors and related technology.

Over time, the needs for designing and building the chips were separated. Design stayed in the US, but, in the 1980s, the Taiwanese government helped to create the Taiwan Semiconductor Manufacturing Company (TSMC). This company became highly successful at making the chips, and Samsung in Korea developed a similar business model.

TSMC and Samsung have been astonishingly successful. Computer chips are now used in almost every household technology we see. Things like fridges and washing machines now rely on chips.

As artificial intelligence becomes established, they will be used even more. And the same companies still dominate the market. We rely on Taiwan and Korea to produce the chips.

China has tried to get in on the act but remains behind Taiwan and Korea. Much of the chip-making in China has been set up by foreign companies. However, Chinese companies, with substantial help of the government, are beginning to advance. This is the threat that the US perceives.

In some ways, computer chips is the new oil. After finally getting away from OPEC's power to set oil prices, are countries now getting to the same situation with chips? We saw in 2021 that a chip shortage could severely disrupt the car industry. The fact that Taiwan is in the middle of a stand-off between China and the US only adds heat to the fire.

It is beyond the scope of this book to review IT revolution-related geopolitics. But getting rid of combustion will add to current tension. We will need computer chips for everything, as we used to need oil for everything. Technology geopolitics may well replace fossil geopolitics. In 2022, China comprised 80% of solar photovoltaics production and a large share of wind power and battery manufacturing. It is rapidly expanding in EVs.[29]

Then we throw in the security risk. Many American people will welcome cheap zero-carbon technologies from China, but reliance on a geopolitical rival for such a wide range of daily activities will inevitably draw attention. Zero-carbon activities and chips were mixed up in the US's 'Inflation Reduction Act'. More recently, tariffs and restrictions on trade have been implemented as security measures.

All this is contributing to the fragmentation of global trade. Along with Europe, the US used to support harmonisation of regulatory standards and free trade between countries. This led to lower production costs but also a concentration of production in a

[29] See Mercure et al. (2025b); IEA (2022).

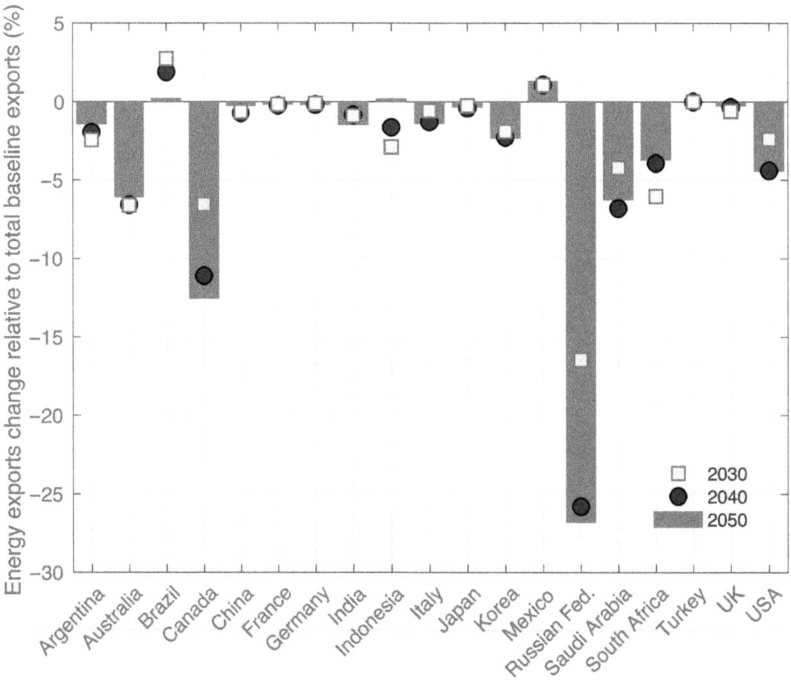

FIGURE 8.5 Losses of fossil fuel exports relative to baseline exports in a rapid transition for G20 countries.

few countries – including China. As the focus shifts from efficiency to resilience, it looks like the previous trend is reversing.

8.3.4 The Purchasing Power of Countries

The international purchasing power of countries is their ability to get foreign currency. It is a measure of success in the quest for US dollars and allows the country to buy imports. Exports increase purchasing power. Getting rid of combustion will transform the purchasing power of all countries, because fossil fuels make up 16–20% of all global trade.

Coming back to the model simulations we discussed earlier, Figure 8.5 shows the potential loss of fuel exports for major countries in the zero-carbon transition.[30] For Russia, more than

[30] Reproduced from Espagne et al. (2023).

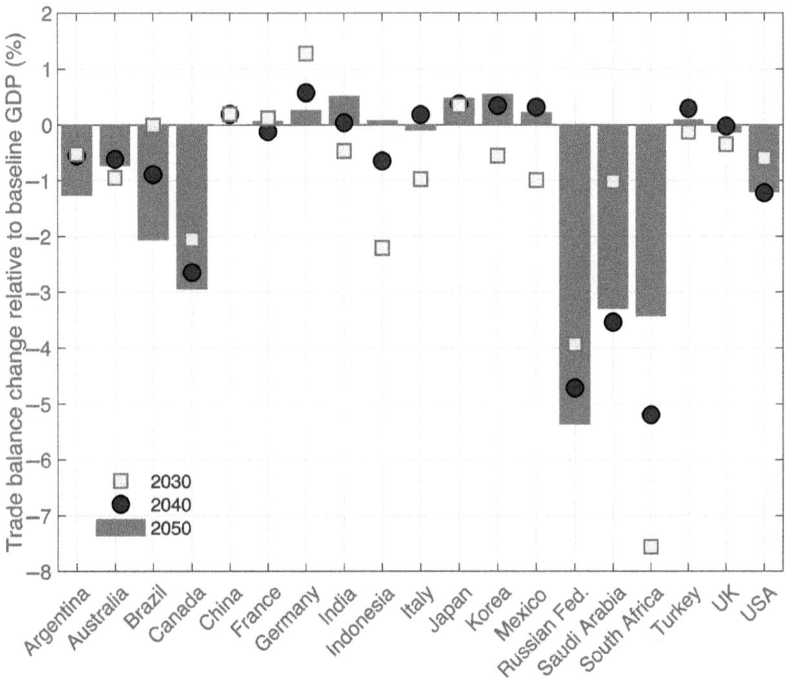

FIGURE 8.6 Changes in trade balances relative to GDP in a rapid transition for G20 countries. Generated by the authors using the E3ME-FTT model and reproduced from Espagne et al. (2023).

25% of exports could be lost. This is enormous. It would drastically reduce the country's international purchasing power and, therefore, its economic and even military power.

It doesn't really matter how we do the transition. Any mix of policies to reduce oil and gas use will have the same effect. And, although some fuel exporters may prolong their industry, in the end, only the cheapest producers will survive.[31]

[31] We must remember that fossil fuels are not just used for combustion. They are also used as inputs to various materials and chemical industries, notably plastics. This is particularly important for oil (16% of oil used in 2022 was for purposes other than combustion). Even if the world manages net-zero emissions, we can still make plastics if we do it without emitting greenhouse gases. However, with a much smaller oil market, it may no longer make economic sense to make plastics from oil.

Figure 8.6 shows how trade balances change for the same countries. Some changes are small, but others are large. It depends critically on countries' economic structures. What is clear though is that oil and gas exporters all have declining trade balances. Eventually, these countries will also reduce imports because they lose international purchasing power.

In contrast, fuel importers could see big improvements in their trade balances. For emerging economies like India, this could be critical for economic development. India could receive a staggering boost to its international purchasing power, exceeding \$100bn by 2035, by getting rid of oil.

8.4 A BRAVE NEW GEOPOLITICAL WORLD

There is much we don't yet know. The modelling described above is limited. The model is trained on recent data, but all kinds of things could change in the zero-carbon transition. It seems clear, however, that a huge economic transformation may be about to happen. The economic power of all countries is going to be impacted.

This could have deep consequences. Several oil and gas exporters are already involved in conflicts around the world. Loss of economic power would lead to loss of military power. The global map of political power could become redrawn entirely.

The control of various seas and navigation channels could also change hands. The direction and intensity of global trade will likely change drastically, being less bound by infrastructure around fossil fuels. For example, large ports around petrochemical hubs may attract less traffic. Some entire towns could sink into deindustrialisation and decline.

Meanwhile, the other geopolitical tensions around IT and smart technology will become entwined with our requirement for chips to supply our energy needs. Existing tensions may just be the tip of the iceberg. Since energy is vital for all countries, the trade of zero-carbon technology, and its materials and intermediate components, is certain to generate its own new range of geopolitical issues.

9 Instability Is the True Cost of Transition

9.1 ARE TRANSITION 'PATHWAYS' MISLEADING?

9.1.1 The Mid-Transition Period

Lots of people say we should do something about climate change. For some people, it is a moral question – we should preserve our planet for future generations. For others, it is a simple question of economic logic – the costs of climate change will outweigh the costs of doing something about it. A third group argues, as we have in this book, that getting rid of combustion is something we want to do anyway.

All these people (including us!) make great points. But we are all saying different things – and that's just on climate. There are plenty more people warning about other environmental limits. There is no clear political message. Maybe, this is why we still are so far behind on climate policy.

The fact is to avoid dangerous outcomes, we have to reduce emissions to zero by around 2050. Academic economists say that if we don't do this, we will lose a few percentage points of GDP. We will lose some resources that are useful for producing stuff, but not much will change.[1]

This misses the key issue. As global temperatures rise, extreme weather events will become more common. More stuff will get destroyed. Things that are important to us will become constantly at risk: our roads, our public services, our water supplies. Even our homes.[2]

[1] See, for example, Nordhaus (2017); Tol (2024).
[2] See Bank of England (2015); Bolton et al. (2020).

Losing our homes is something many of us cannot even imagine. Even so, we install smoke detectors and security systems to stop it from happening. We have insurance against the very worst-case outcome. A payout by an insurance company is little consolation for losing everything. But it can be a lifeline. And let's not forget about people in countries where insurance is a luxury at best.

Businesses sometimes say 'hope for the best, prepare for the worst'. We are definitely doing the first part right. Maybe if we talked more about risk, we could also do the second part. But this is harder to communicate. People understand certainty better.

Doing something about climate change also carries risk. We've discussed it already in previous chapters. Whenever things change, uncertainty grows. That means more risk for companies and households. Risks of economic, political and financial vulnerability are generated by *both* climate change *and* the zero-carbon transition.

Banks refer to the threat of climate change as 'physical risk' and effects from reducing emissions as 'transition risk'. The name 'transition risk' is not very clear (all transitions mean change, uncertainty and more risk), and it could equally be used for artificial intelligence or any other major technology. However, this name does focus our thinking on the process of change.

To help further, we define a new term, the *'mid-transition'* period. This is when things change the fastest (see Figure 9.1).[3] It is when the risk of something going wrong is highest. This is when we risk pushing our economies to the edge of chaos that we described in Chapter 3.

Laurence Tubiana was one of the main people behind the Paris Agreement on climate change. She has been a professor of economics and sustainable development at Sciences Po in Paris and founded the 'Institut du développement durable et des relations internationales' (IDDRI). She later became the head of the European Climate Foundation and advised the French government in various capacities.

[3] See Grubert and Hastings-Simon (2022); figure published by the authors earlier in Espagne et al. (2023).

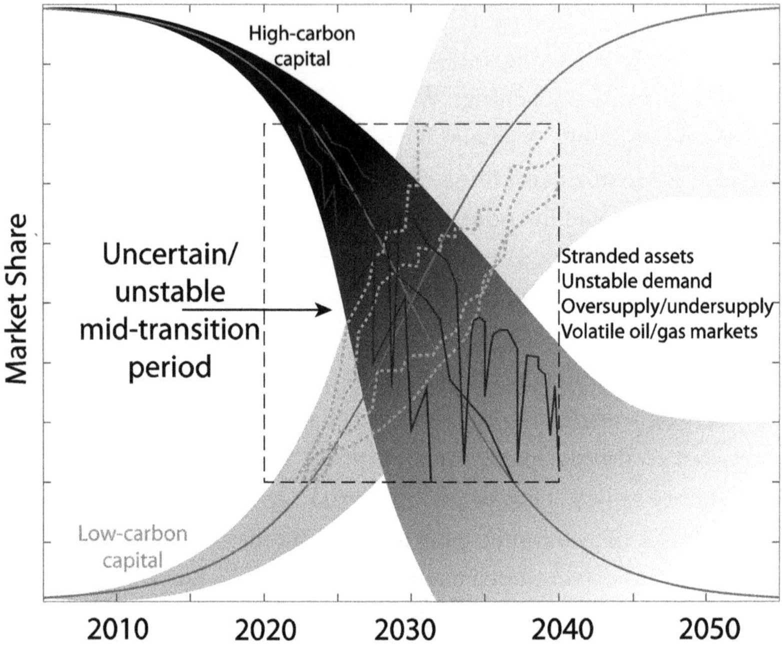

FIGURE 9.1 Illustration of the mid-transition period and the instability that could occur.

At a meeting at COP26 in Glasgow, she asked top economists to change their thinking from allocating resources to risk management. Government officials already often think this way about other things, out of practical need, while the academics lag behind. The aim is not to estimate in detail what will happen to GDP. It is to think about who might face a crisis. This way of thinking should incorporate both risks and opportunities.[4]

The Bank of England adopted this way of thinking in 2015. It had to because it is responsible for financial stability, and research was showing that climate change is a threat to financial stability. The financial crisis of 2007–2008 was still fresh in people's minds, so the debate took off. This is when we got the terms physical and transition risks.[5]

[4] See Mercure et al. (2021a).

[5] See Bank of England (2015); BoE (2018); Bolton et al. (2020). The Bank of England also defined the term 'liability risk', which worries that past environmental damage bears the risk of lawsuits.

The mid-transition period is critical because it is when society is most vulnerable to rapid change. Government institutions and social organisations may not be prepared for rapid social change. Social groups may not tolerate the lifestyle changes that the new technologies demand. As we saw previously, jobs and livelihoods will be upended. Migration is likely.

Worse, this will also be the point when climate impacts will be becoming more common. Most likely, we will not be ready in time – very few places are properly prepared for the effects of climate change. So, at the same time as some of the old stuff stops being useful, some of the new stuff will get destroyed. Put it all together, and everyone could be affected.

When will we reach 'mid-transition'? We know the transition has started, and there is already no way back to the old fossil fuel technologies. We cannot stop technological progress getting rid of combustion. Too much has already been discovered, invented, committed and invested. People are already reaping the rewards while other risks are building up.

In this chapter, we build on our theory of economic stability from Chapter 3 and, especially, our picture of the 'edge of chaos' (Figure 3.2). The transition will push the economy to the limit. We will see more common and more severe impacts, including severe weather events, financial crashes, protests and riots, price instabilities, inflation, deflation and currency crises. Worryingly, also more armed conflict.

Things could become *really* messy. Therefore, the right question to ask is not how much it costs to save the planet but how we can do it without spreading chaos. If we don't get it right, we risk shooting the transition in the foot. Chaos would paralyse our ability to move forward. And of course, the resulting delays to reducing emissions could become a matter of life or death for much of what lives on the planet.

How do we know where we stand in terms of economic, financial and political stability, and how much additional strain we can take? Are we already at breaking point?

We need to figure out how close to the edge of chaos we already are and then understand how much additional strain the zero-carbon transition will add. This chapter looks at how to do this. Chapter 10 will look at ways we could reduce the risks.

9.1.2 *Are Transition Pathways on a Knife Edge?*

Thanks to the Bank of England, the risk to financial stability is well known. In contrast, the conversation about economic and political stability has yet to start. For all the years of climate research and six IPCC reports, are we sleepwalking into an era of instability? Have we been telling ourselves fairytales about scenarios of emission reductions that don't have risks?

We introduced Simon Sharpe in Chapter 3. He argues that scientists and economists have been giving policy-makers the wrong type of information for years. He says that they have offered fairytale scenarios of transition pathways when instead we needed risk assessments.[6]

We certainly have plenty of these scenarios, including ones produced by the authors. They aim to explain the 'choices' that policy-makers face on climate policy. We can't legally have new climate policy in the UK and Europe without producing these scenarios.

However, a lot gets lost in building these scenarios. They ask the question what *will* happen rather than what *might* happen. Policy-makers should be asking whether the scenarios are realistic or whether something would break before we get there.

The problems run deep. They relate to the scientific method that dates back to the times of Francis Bacon and Isaac Newton. The scenario is like a laboratory experiment. Everything remains the same except the one thing we want to examine, reducing emissions. The scenario then shows the effects of reducing emissions and nothing else. Policy-makers can see the effects of their choice: to reduce emissions or not.

[6] See Sharpe (2023).

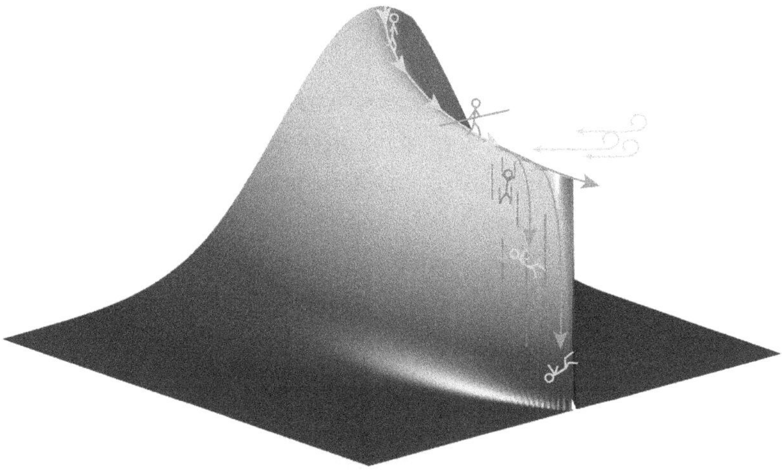

FIGURE 9.2 The 'knife edge' mountain ridge becomes so narrow that it is impossible to stay on the path as the wind rises and the ground slips.

This approach comes from physics and has led to centuries of scientific discovery. But what works for physics does not work for society. Our economic, financial and political systems are more like biology – everything affects everything else, and relationships evolve. 'Everything else remains the same' is simply not possible. Risk would be ruled out by assumption.

None of the scenarios discussed publicly[7] have been assessed in terms of system resilience. We don't know if they are achievable. Many are probably *'knife-edge scenarios'*: fairytales that lie too close to the edge of chaos to be achievable. Knife-edge scenarios require an impossible amount of steering to keep on track, otherwise they fall off the path (especially if there are unexpected headwinds). They are like a ridge walk that becomes so narrow that no one can finish crossing it (Figure 9.2).

For example, a scenario in which we go through a very rapid transition would be a knife-edge scenario, unless it includes measures to absorb financial imbalances, currency risk, widespread insolvencies and more. Few people are asking if these measures are

[7] For example, the IPCC and NGFS scenarios.

included though. Most economic models simply assume we will never need them!

Another example is scenarios where we don't decarbonize quickly but after 2050 use lots of negative emission technologies to bring down global temperatures.[8] Despite standard models telling us this is a good idea, it is obviously hugely risky. How can we be sure policy-makers in the 2070s would spend money on negative emissions? We don't even know if the technology will work. It is crazy that these scenarios are taken seriously.

Policy-makers need to ask researchers if they are confident that their scenarios are not on the knife edge. This will not be easy though. It needs expertise in finance, economics, sociology and more. Getting people with this expertise to work together is a challenge.

Policy-makers will soon face an uncomfortable truth. In Chapter 3, we explained the trade-off between optimisation and resilience. Almost all the computer models used to develop these scenarios are optimisation tools. The scenarios therefore have, by definition, the *minimum level of resilience possible*! Out of the 3131 scenarios from 95 models in the last IPCC database, nearly all of them are on the knife edge! They have not been assessed for stability. And including more scenarios does not make the results more robust if all the scenarios are made the same way.

It would only take a tiny policy error, or a minor pandemic, or a regional war, to knock any of these scenarios off the knife edge. At that point, anything could happen. Social unrest, financial collapse, sovereign insolvency would all be on the table. All the worst possible things that policy-makers want to avoid! Carrying on with the planned emission reductions would be unlikely.

It is frightening stuff. The tools that should be guiding us may be leading us to the precipice. Most policy-makers are not modelling experts, nor should they be. They don't know that the models only tell us nothing will go wrong because they assume nothing will go

[8] See the IPCC 1.5°C report, IPCC (2018a).

wrong. If they realised what was going on, they would surely be asking different questions.

Since risk is not estimated in current scenarios, policy-makers have seen little risk assessment of climate policy.[9] Even if they try to follow a model scenario, they cannot monitor progress anywhere near the level that the model assumes. Each step could push part of our society off the precipice, into chaos.

As discussed in Chapter 3, we should discuss risk in terms of stability and instability. Complexity science tells us that some systems are naturally stable, others are unstable, and we can guess when something may go from stable to unstable. For example, the climate could become unstable if the Amazon rainforest or the West Antarctic glacier collapses. The economy was unstable after the financial crisis. Political relations were unstable in the run up to the Second World War and in the run up to the war in Ukraine.

Surprisingly, this type of analysis is not used much in climate economics. The narrow focus of economics and economic models in optimising things is a major roadblock. It's difficult to imagine such an approach working in other policy areas. Armies would not assume that there is no risk of conflict.

In Chapter 3, we used the example of rail networks, which can run smoothly or with delays, depending on the tightness of the timetable. The financial sector is just like a rail system. Small losses can cause larger losses that cause more losses, in domino effects. Risk is systemic, because highly leveraged companies are a risk not just to themselves but to everyone else too.

Geopolitics is similar. Countries interact and influence each other, and risks stack up. The war in Ukraine provides a good example. Countries had to side either with the EU and the US, or with Russia. Trading patterns are shifting, and energy markets have been upended.

[9] IPCC scenarios were designed to assess the range of possible emission pathways for climate risk assessment. Some financial risk assessment has also been done by the Network for Greening the Financial System (NGFS) using these models but only on the basis that risk originates from sudden policy change, a very narrow source of risk.

Experts around the world provide in-depth analysis on these issues. They use scenarios to think about risks and possible worst-case outcomes. They help policy-makers to prepare for the worst. The aim is to avoid crisis.

They don't give fairytales. But in climate economics that's what we are stuck with. Complex problems are assumed to be simple and given simple solutions. If policy-makers apply a carbon price of X, emissions will fall by Y and GDP by Z. The only uncertainty is the different parameters used in the optimisation models.[10]

The dilemma for policy-makers is obviously quite different. They need to think about risk. The things that matter include social, economic, political and financial instability. Inflation, financial crises, debt crises, currency crises, poverty, inequality and breakdown of socio-economic cohesion ... the list goes on. But the models can't help.

We now discuss how climate change and the zero-carbon transition could affect economic, financial and political stability. To understand the risks, we must first understand how fragile our current systems are to shocks and what size of shock could break the system. Central banks already do this regularly for the financial system. We consider it more broadly.

9.2 ECONOMIC AND FINANCIAL STABILITY

9.2.1 *Physical Risks of Climate Change*

Climate scientists tell us that warming temperatures mean extreme weather events will get worse and more frequent. Temperatures are already warming, so we should be seeing these events occurring in our data.

The awkward problem is that these events do not increase proportionately with rising temperatures. They increase by more.[11]

The pattern of events is like the delays on the London Underground (see Chapter 3). Usually, they are small, but sometimes

[10] See van Vuuren et al. (2020).

[11] See Coronese et al. (2019).

they feed into each other and get really big. The severity of the events can be measured using a statistical distribution. The extreme events are in the 'tail' of the distribution; they are large but happen rarely. For extreme weather events, the tail of the distribution is already 'heavy', meaning that the large events happen more often than we would normally expect. Climate change will make the tail become heavier still.

Figure 9.3 shows the effect for floods. The distribution is linear on the chart when using a log scale. Complexity theory tells us that the system may be near the edge of chaos.

The slopes of the lines in the figure tell us about the frequency of large floods. For deaths, the slope is −1.8, suggesting that disastrous events are not that rare. The risk is that even a small increase in flood intensity could cause cascading failures to occur, causing widespread destruction and high numbers of casualties.

If we separate the data for economic damages into the period 2000–2012 and 2013–2023, we see that the slope has gone down, from −1.6 to −1.4. This means that the tails are getting heavier and the system is highly unstable. Larger events are becoming more frequent. As the climate scientists warned, we are moving closer to the edge of chaos.

Is it chaos though? According to World Bank studies, flood risk leads only to GDP losses of between 1% of GDP for middle-income countries to 12% of GDP for low-income countries. Although 12% loss of GDP is a lot, chaos might be a bit of an exaggeration. And 1% is definitely not chaos.

Looking at how people use the data might explain the discrepancy. The average economic cost of each flood over 2000–2012 is 730 million USD, and 830 million USD since 2012. This is a mere rise of 13% or about 0.1% of global GDP. If the world keeps warming at the same rate, then we could add another 13% for the next 12 years, and so on. Not much would change.

This would be an incorrect use of heavy-tailed statistics. Averages are not sufficient when the tail is becoming heavier. The range of costs in the data is around 3 billion USD, so there is already high

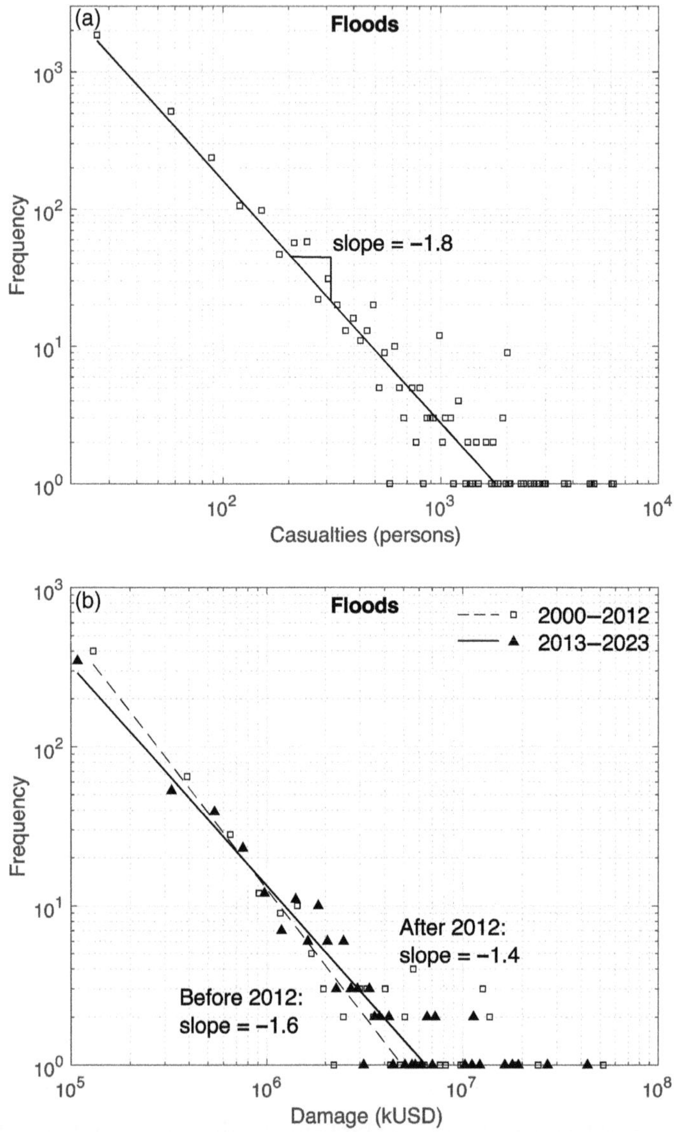

FIGURE 9.3 Floods worldwide in historical data. (a) Frequency–magnitude diagram for deaths associated with floods, since 1900. (b) Frequency–magnitude diagram for economic damage associated with floods since 2000, before and after 2012 for comparison. Data are taken from the EM-DAT International Disaster Database. Data before 2000 may have sampling biases, potentially over-reporting large events and was therefore excluded.

uncertainty. The danger is that we get more and more of the 3 billion USD floods, and worse.

With such a heavy tail, the uncertainty of the average value could be effectively infinite. We cannot rule out the possibility that a catastrophically large flood destroys an entire country. Under these conditions, the average value has no meaning. Fortunately, we can look at something more useful, the median. The median is a mid-point value that half of the events exceed. The median is reliable because it relies on the size of the smaller events. We don't need to know the exact size of the largest events to know the median.[12]

Over 2000–2012, the median cost of each flood is 68 million USD. After 2012, it increases by 67% to 113 million USD. The risk of large-scale destruction has increased massively. One in ten floods will exceed 1.9 billion USD in costs. One in a hundred will exceed 17 billion USD. Five of these floods occurred over 2012–2023. If one of these floods occurred in a small and poor country, it could destroy 50% of GDP.[13] And this is just floods, there are plenty of other types of disasters.

In summary, the possible economic and financial costs are enormous. We should not be saying that governments only need to set aside 13% additional funds for reconstruction. We should be saying that governments will increasingly have less idea how much they will need to pay for flood repairs. They will have less idea how much they will have left to pay for everything else.

Most years, governments will not have to pay much, maybe nothing at all. But the big flood, when it comes, could cause a meltdown of government finances, as happened in Pakistan in 2022. We can see that we have been losing economic resilience since 2012. The situation is already bad. As the tail becomes heavier over time, meltdown eventually becomes inevitable.

[12] The average requires adding small and large numbers, which generates large uncertainties. For example, $10 \pm 1 + 10{,}000 \pm 1{,}000 = 10{,}010 \pm 1{,}001$, which in practice can hardly be distinguished from $10{,}000 \pm 1{,}000$. The median avoids this issue and is much more accurate.

[13] Though such a valuation is very uncertain because there may not be that much monetary value to destroy.

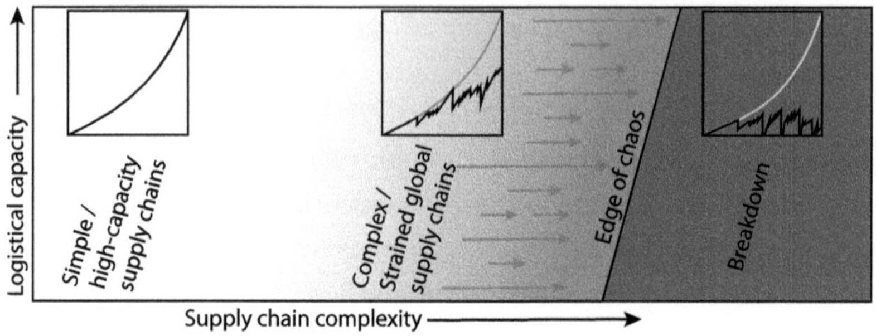

FIGURE 9.4 The stability of global supply chains, depending on how complex they are and the available capacity of global logistics (e.g. ports and shipping routes).

To manage this risk, we must invest to reverse the loss of resilience. The aim is to keep the government budget predictable. For example, enhanced flood defences could mean that, even when water levels increase drastically, damages are much less. Other measures, like not building houses on flood plains, could be simpler still.

The slope of the line is a measure of the global economy's low resilience to climate shocks. We must spend to *turn the line clockwise in Figure 9.3*, reduce the weight of the tail and increase resilience to climate events. Otherwise, countries will end up in an unsurmountable spiral of debt, with crisis following.

But most of all, we must fix our understanding of statistics.

9.2.2 *Supply Chains Near the Edge of Chaos*

Are supply chains on the knife edge, or can they cope with the transition? To understand supply-chain risks, we look at the long-term trend of globalisation, the tightening of global supply chains and recent trade fragmentation. We look at this in the context of the coming zero-carbon transition. We apply the principle of the efficiency–resilience trade-off from Chapter 3 to global supply chains (Figure 9.4).

The supply chains of most advanced modern products are global. They require materials, components and final products to cross borders. They would not exist without free trade.

Free trade, in its idealised form, harmonises regulatory standards between countries and removes tariffs on goods. Companies have bigger markets for their products and can benefit from scale economies. These companies also face more competition, so must keep prices low and innovate where possible. Consumers benefit.

Free trade implies that each country's production becomes more specialised. In fact, this is why most economists support free trade. The results are standardised production in a small number of places. For example, in Europe's single market, many goods are made by gigantic manufacturers in few countries.

Another recent trend is 'just-in-time' manufacturing. This reduces costs because it minimises the need to store goods in warehouses. Performance improves, but it comes at a cost to stability, because a small disruption could leave the company with nothing to sell.

The direction of change is clear. The priority is performance and reducing costs wherever possible. Supply chains become more complex so that costs can be cut. Resilience is sacrificed so that costs can be cut further. This outcome is a feature of the system. It results from companies competing and needing to minimise costs.

This is when supply chains start to look like the London underground. The system becomes fragile and tolerates less and less disruption. It moves closer to the edge of chaos, where one company failing to deliver its products affects many other companies.

Take, for example, the stranding of the Ever Given ship in the Suez canal in 2021.[14] The Suez canal is a critical link for global trade between China and Europe. A queue of 400 ships waiting to pass through the canal formed, with $10 billion worth of goods held up for six days.

Shipping costs respond to capacity bottlenecks, making them volatile in times of trouble (see Figure 9.5). During the recovery from COVID-19 in 2021–2022, demand outstripped capacity, and shipping

[14] See Wikipedia, https://en.wikipedia.org/wiki/2021_Suez_Canal_obstruction.

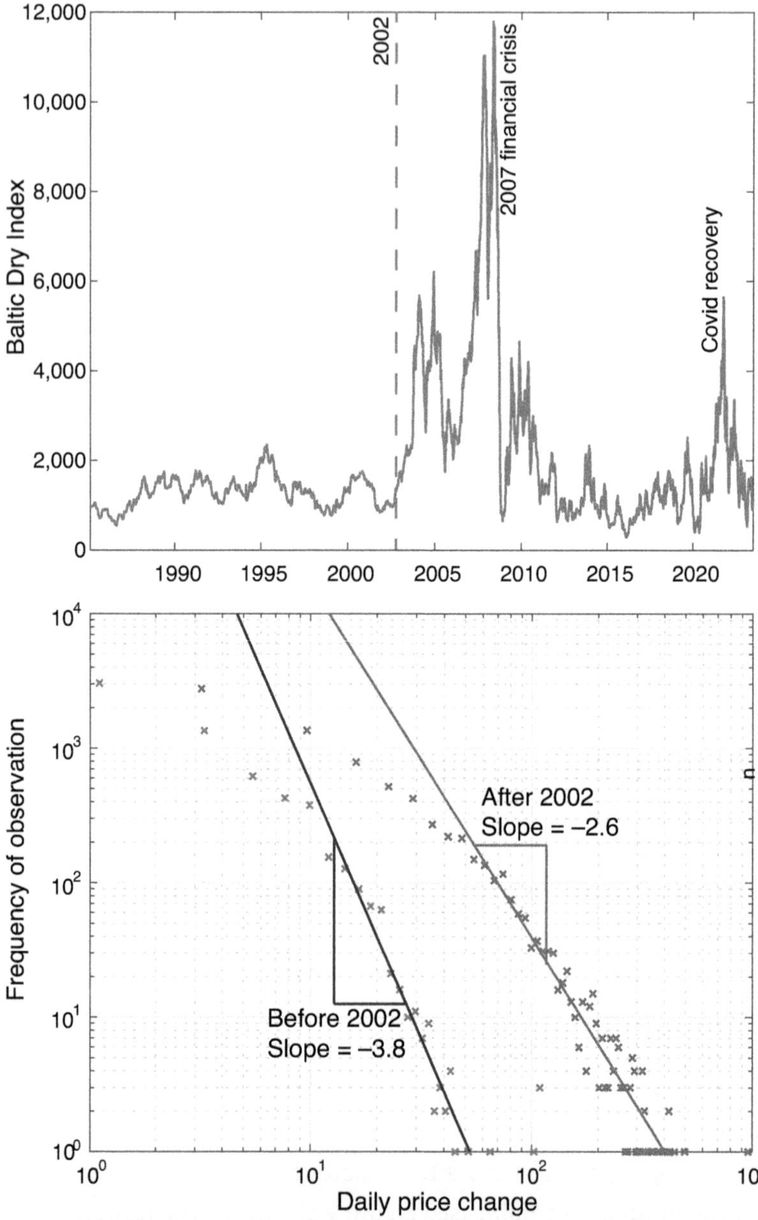

FIGURE 9.5 Indicator of global shipping costs reported daily (called the 'Baltic Dry Indicator') and the frequency of its daily changes. Its volatility has substantially increased since 2002.

costs were highly unstable. Some Chinese goods disappeared from Western shops because it was no longer worth trading them.

The post-Covid period was extreme, but shipping prices have been unstable since 2002. Since 2002, the slope on the chart has changed from –3.8 to –2.6, indicating a much heavier tail of large changes in prices. Global shipping is creeping towards loss of resilience as it tries to handle rapidly rising demands via complex supply chains and just-in-time production. Could additional strain from the zero-carbon transition push it over the edge?

In this book, our theory suggests that the edge of chaos is when the slope of the line goes past –2 towards –1. As we saw above, floods are getting near there already, suggesting an urgent need to increase resilience. Here, we can see that shipping is becoming more unstable, although it remains at a distance from the edge of chaos. But it is close enough to the edge to witness some cascading failures.

There are clearly limits to the declining costs coming from globalisation, because each supply chain failure is itself costly. Spreading production across more factories increases production costs, but it decreases the costs of unreliability. Looking back to Chapter 6, logistics capacity is amongst the bottlenecks for the global economy to solve. New technologies such as 3D printing could reduce the complexity of supply chains and system instability.

It is also clear from announcements in 2025 that free trade is not as attractive for many countries as it was previously and that a breakdown of globalisation appears to have started.[15] The introduction of tariffs and other measures designed to favour domestic production could alleviate the pressure on global logistics. However, these measures could in turn create their own risks that should be monitored going forward.

In theory, the zero-carbon transition should reduce pressure on shipping. Around 20% of shipping freight is fossil fuels, most of which will no longer be needed. However, an oil tanker cannot be

[15] Aiyar et al. (2023).

immediately converted into a container ship, and trade in things like solar panels will increase. The system will again need to adapt.

Ships themselves will need to reduce emissions too. Sailing at lower speeds would reduce emissions but raise costs. Some technological solutions are starting to emerge, but the sector will be placed under further pressure. It seems inevitable that uncertainty and instability will increase at least for a while.

9.2.3 *Transition Risks from Policy*

In Chapter 10, we will discuss low-carbon policies that can reduce risks to society. However, it is important to note that climate policy can also increase the risks as a side effect of accelerating the transition.

Any uncertainty about future policy could lead to instability. No one will invest in something that might be banned from use in a few years' time. Usually though there is signalling about future bans, and companies can adjust (e.g. when old light bulbs were phased out in Europe).

It's not so clear for carbon taxes and carbon markets. For decades, economists and their models have been saying that the best way to reduce emissions is a carbon tax or price covering all activities. In practice, much could go wrong, notably the burden on low-income households. There is limited empirical evidence that carbon taxes actually work.[16] Some have failed spectacularly.

We use the EU's flagship climate policy, its Emission Trading System (ETS), as an example. Figure 9.6 looks at the daily variations in the carbon price set by the EU-ETS. The distribution is super heavy-tailed, with a slope of about −2.1. At −2, the expected value of price changes in the long run becomes infinite, meaning that the price volatility, to be expected on a daily basis, is unbounded. This means that investing in high-carbon, or in zero-carbon capital, can go equally really well or really badly, and no one can tell which and by

16 See Pollitt et al. (2024); Lilliestam et al. (2020); Peñasco et al. (2020).

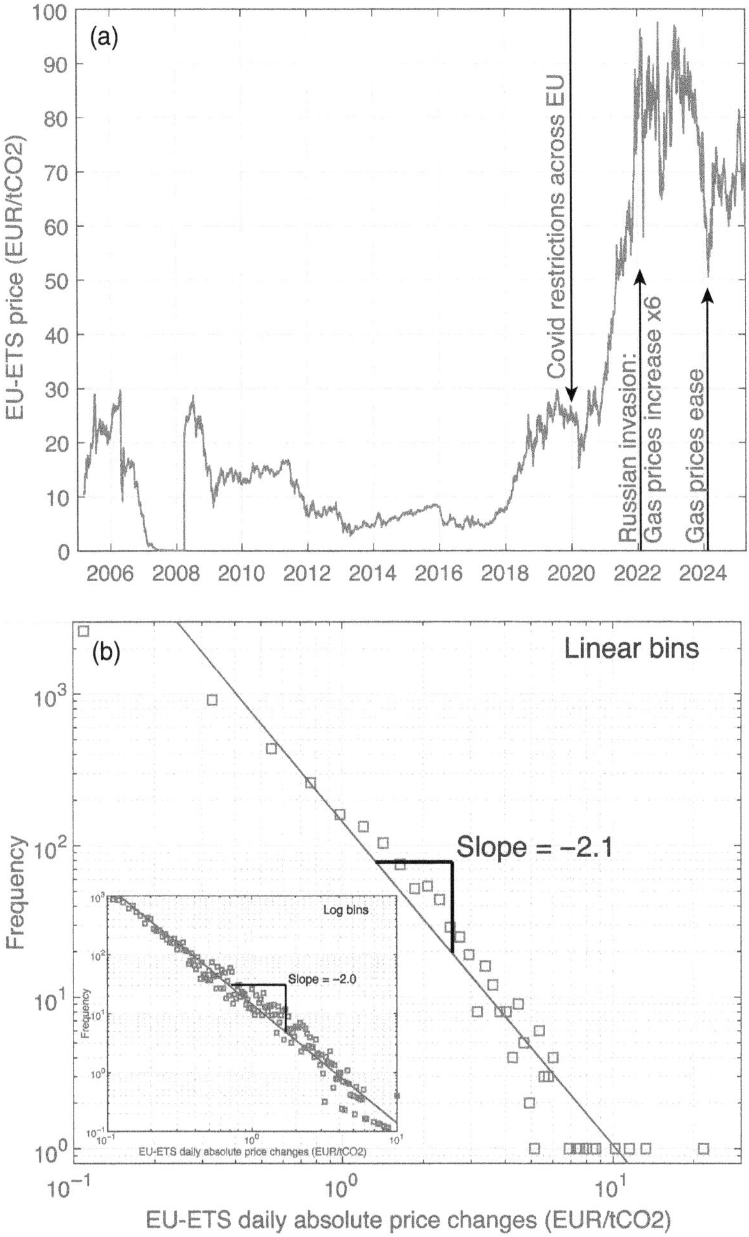

FIGURE 9.6 The heavy tail of the EU-ETS carbon price. (a) The EU-ETS price daily. (b) Frequency–magnitude diagram of absolute price changes. Data from the International Carbon Action Partnership. The main graph uses linear binning, while the inset uses log binning.

how much. The uncertainty deters investment, which doesn't help make progress with decarbonisation.

In addition, the EU-ETS price appears to be driven by world events, not climate policy. For many years, it was very low and had little impact on behaviour. Rose to current levels only after the recovery from COVID-19, at times getting close to 100 EUR/tCO_2.

But the main reason the EU-ETS price increased was the war in Ukraine. When the supply of natural gas from Russia became limited and expensive, European electricity companies switched back to coal. Emissions increased, meaning they needed more permits, pushing up the price for everyone.

The result was that electricity became expensive across Europe, along with gas. There weren't really any climate benefits, and we got a cost of living crisis. It could be argued that the EU-ETS amplifies existing problems, rather than solving anything.

What if Europe had used a carbon tax rather than the ETS? Electricity would still have become more expensive when power companies went back to coal, but the increase would not add to existing volatility in energy markets.

But carbon taxes do not reduce uncertainty to zero. Rates are changed through the political process. The taxes may be abolished altogether (like in Australia). The UK's fuel duty escalator shows how long-term plans can be changed at short notice.

It is telling that all this is missing from economic models. The models usually treat an ETS and a carbon tax the same way. There is no risk of instability in either case. No reason for economists to hesitate before recommending the policy.

The sad fact is that carbon taxes and, especially, emission trading schemes are simply not delivering what policy-makers originally hoped they would deliver. Instead they could be amplifying the ongoing volatility. An ETS can make things worse. At a time when we need to reduce uncertainty, the policy brings more instability into our economic system.

9.2.4 *Transition Risks and Financial Stability*

There are two sources of financial transition risk in the mid-transition period. The more obvious one is that stranded high-carbon assets accumulate and cause a financial crisis. The other one is less obvious and relates to the additional debt that will be needed to pay for the new investment. Lots of companies owing large sums of money to each other increase the risk of future financial crises.

Not all economists believe stranded assets can occur. Many of them believe that the economy creates its own demand and that, if fossil reserves are available, they will be consumed, unless they are priced out of the market. The reality is different. What induces users to buy EVs is usually quite independent from the oil price or the availability of oil reserves. But once people buy EVs, some of that oil will never get to market.

Many companies may be relying on those future oil revenues to remain in business. Stranded assets occur when investors realise that fossil fuel assets, which they used to believe had a certain value, are actually worthless. This can happen suddenly. It just takes someone influential to look carefully at the whole market and decide we don't need it all. And if we invest big in both green and brown at the same time, someone must have made the wrong bet.

Although there has now been much debate on stranded assets, the other risk we face, a debt crisis around zero-carbon assets, has not been widely discussed. Here, it's about companies being in debt and losing their resilience to other financial shocks. It could unravel a bit like the property market in China since 2020. For the climate, the big risk is that a financial crisis, whatever the cause, could hinder further renewable investment and slow the transition. It would of course also have wider economic effects.

Coming back to the efficiency–resilience trade-off, we adapt the previous analysis to the financial system (Figure 9.7). In situations of low debt, the occasional bankruptcy is absorbed by the cash reserves that companies hold. In situations of high debt (and

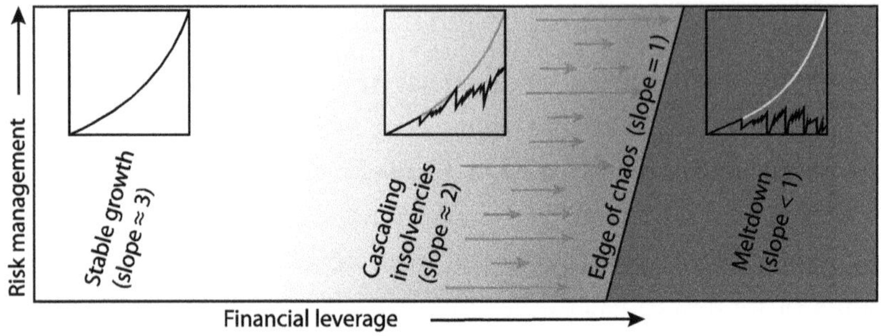

FIGURE 9.7 Economic stability of the financial system, depending on the degree of financial leverage (company debt divided by company value) and the degree of financial regulation. The 'slopes' refer to the slope of the tail of the distribution of fluctuations on a log–log graph.

especially high leverage[17]), companies are more easily pushed into bankruptcy. With all the companies connected, they risk falling over together like dominoes.

The economic historian Carlota Perez tells us that financial crashes have occurred early on in each of the previous great waves. First, investment bubbles form because of over-hype about the new technologies. These bubbles eventually burst when people question how good the technologies will be. There can be substantial losses of financial wealth.[18]

For example, a crash occurred with the development of railways in Britain in 1847. Many rail projects that did not seem profitable were abandoned. In 2001, the dot-com bubble of IT and internet stocks burst when people realised that not all internet companies would make large profits.

To test the potential for financial crashes due to stranded assets or excessive debt (or both), we need to know two things. We need to determine our current level of financial resilience, which is the

[17] 'Leverage' is defined as debt divided by company value. Higher leverage in a company means a higher risk that a sudden loss causes a default on its debt. The same is true at the economy level, since a default by one company is a loss for another company. More leverage thus increases systemic risk of cascading bankruptcies where companies are lined up as dominoes and make each other fall.

[18] See Perez (2001) and Semieniuk et al. (2021).

inverse of leverage, and from that level of resilience, how big a push it takes for the system to fall over. Central banks call this a 'stress-test'.

Understanding Financial Resilience

We illustrate financial resilience using a computer model that imitates investment in companies. The model tracks imaginary investors who are connected to each other by debt relationships (who borrows from whom) and equity relationships (who owns stakes in what).

The model takes into account that investors face risks both from their own activities and from what other investors do. For example, investors that lend money are exposed to the risk of default by their borrowers. Investors that own assets are exposed to changes in prices of their stocks, which are determined by the actions of other investors.

To keep things simple, we set the relationships between investors randomly. However, the ownership patterns in the model are like those in real life.[19] As financial relationships change all the time, the model simulates different profiles for the financial system.

The model builds networks of ownership and debt. We have explored different ways that these networks *naturally develop*. The way that best matches the observed data is called 'preferential attachment', which is well known in mathematics. Each time a new investor is added to the model, it is more likely to link to other investors that are already well connected. This is commonly observed in social networks, and most importantly, in financial networks.[20]

We then test scenarios in the model. The model is broken into time steps. At each timestep, a productive asset is created by the

[19] The simulation is described in detail in Chapter 10 of Mercure (2022), partly inspired by Battiston et al. (2016, 2017). We analysed in detail the real equity network in Semieniuk et al. (2022), and we apply our knowledge of what it looks like (its topology) to creating an artificial one here.

[20] A famous paper describing this is Barabási and Bonabeau (2003).

work of investors lending, borrowing and investing. This involves a three-way transaction:

- Investor A runs a company and raises money on equity markets to build a physical asset (e.g. a factory). He hopes this asset will generate profit for himself and for the equity holder.
- Investor B borrows money from another investor to acquire equity in the company of Investor A, for example, by issuing bonds.
- Investor C lends money to Investor B. This could be, for example, by depositing money at a bank or by buying bonds.

We repeat this process over and over, creating random assets with random ownership, until we have millions of assets. The artificial network grows like a garden of flowers.

Problems arise because investments do not always work out as planned. In the model, we apply random shocks to the value of the assets, for example, of up to 10% of their value. The distribution of shocks that we impose is *not* heavy-tailed (the slopes are lower than –3).

These shocks occasionally make the owners of the assets go bust, especially if they are highly leveraged. Any investors that own equity in those investors or lent them money will make a loss. They could also go bust, and so on. Investors that go bust are removed from the network.

We want to know how big shocks need to be to break the network. Figure 9.8 shows the total value of all the physical assets in the network. The response of the network to shocks is much larger than the shocks we put in. That's because with large shocks there are domino chains of insolvencies that occur. The slopes of the tails we obtain are between –4.5 and just above –2.

For small shocks (less than 5% of asset values), the total value of assets keeps growing, and the slope is –4.5, without investors or companies going bust. However, when the shocks reach 10%, some investors begin to go bust. It depends how many companies the shocks are applied to. Large crashes can happen, and the slope of the size of the crashes gets closer to –2.

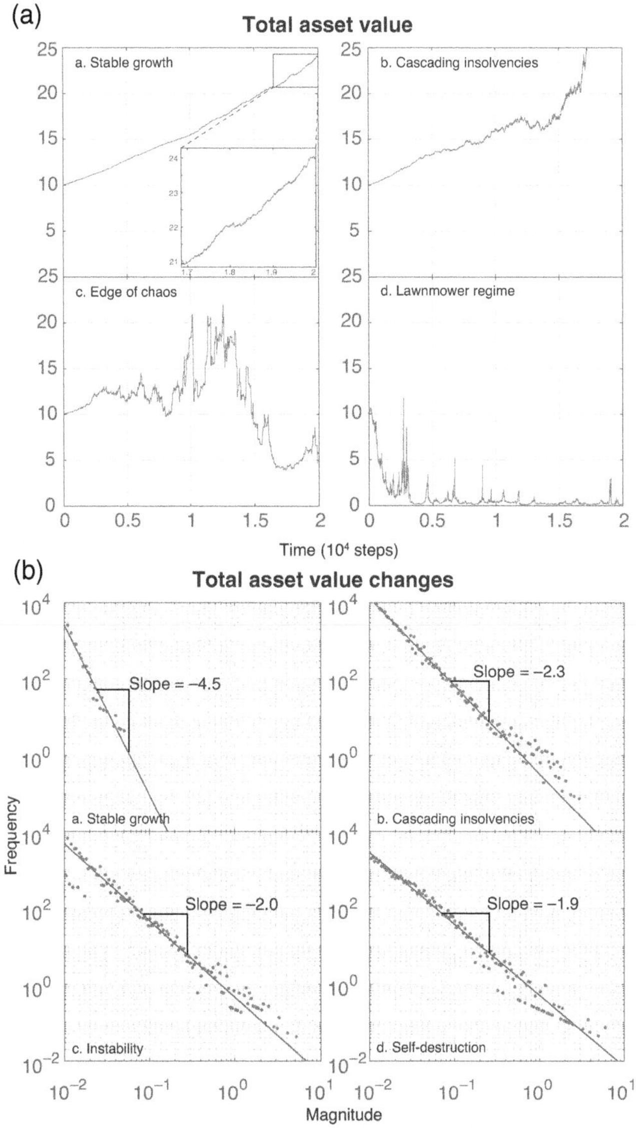

FIGURE 9.8 Simulations of an artificial financial network model of equity and debt interdependencies and insolvencies. (a) The total market capitalisation. Frequency-magnitude distributions of variations in total market capitalisation. Note these estimations use log binning.

There are many ways we can get to beyond –2, but, for example, when the shocks are really high, with 50% of asset values lost applied to 50 investors, we arrive closer to the edge of chaos. The region around –2 begins to be destructive as assets are created and destroyed in equal amounts. The system becomes unstable and stops growing. Beyond that, with shocks of 50% value applied to 500 investors, the system begins to self-destruct. More assets are destroyed than created, and the slope goes into the zone of infinite expected value.

As a reminder, the slope is the degree of resilience of the system. When it is near –3, the system can absorb shocks without a large crash. When it is close to –2, it is too near the edge of chaos, and a small shock could topple it. At –2 and beyond, the average size of the crashes becomes as big as the network itself. The value of the next crash could be anything up to the value of the whole network.

This model illustrates simply the meaning of the measured slope of the tail. We believe that this is representative of the real world: at a slope approaching –2, the financial system is in trouble. Remember that the average size of a crash once the slope goes past –2 is infinity (see Chapter 3).

Having established this scale, how much resilience does the real global financial system have at present?

Measuring Financial Resilience

Figure 9.9 analyses the daily fluctuations in the S&P 500 stock market index, between 1980 and now. The index measures the value of a chosen set of 500 companies, seen as representative of the whole financial system. It matches the measure of value used in the model.

The index has increased in value exponentially, apart from the various financial crises along the way (2001, 2007–2008, 2020). However, the straight line on the log graph shows that the fluctuations are heavy-tailed, with a slope between –3 and –2. The data looks just like what comes out of our toy model.

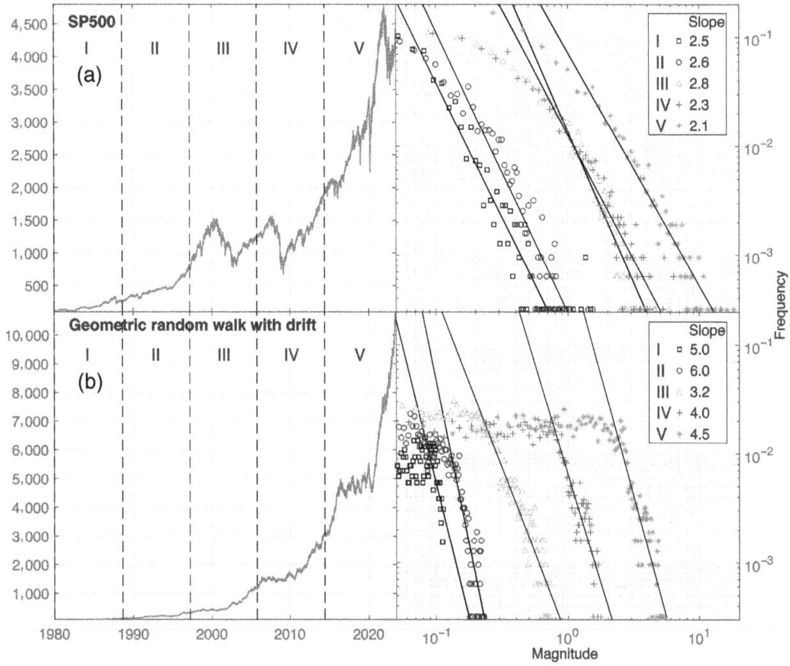

FIGURE 9.9 Fluctuations in the daily S&P 500 stock market index, analysed in five equal stretches of time of 8.7 years between 1980 and 2023 (a), compared against a geometric random walk of similar growth and variance (b). The index has a heavy tail, whereas the random walk (by definition) does not.

Are we becoming less financially resilient over time? Slicing the data into five blocks, we see that, worryingly, we are moving towards the edge of chaos. Volatility has increased substantially. The slope of the distribution has moved back and forth but has started to approach −2 since the 2007–2008 financial crisis. The risk of a financial crash is higher now than it was in the early 2000s. We can also say that the current resilience of the financial system is the lowest it has ever been since 1980 (excluding during financial crises). Near −2, resilience is very low and on the cusp of a state where volatility becomes uncontrollable.

For reference, we compare the data to something called a geometric random walk with drift. This function generates a comparable time series without a heavy tail. It is the most widely used model in standard economics and finance. The value of the index goes up or down randomly by multiplying a random number to the existing value over and over. It is used to estimate the value of share options and other financial assets.[21]

We can see that the geometric random walk model of the standard theory is completely wrong. The fluctuations it generates *look nothing like the real world.* They do not have a heavy tail and give slopes between –3 and –6. The model ignores the key feature of the financial system: its connectivity. It is designed in a way that ignores financial crashes. This is precisely why economists' models failed to see the 2007–2008 financial crisis coming.[22]

Given our gradual loss of financial resilience, how much more strain can the system take, and could the transition cause a financial crash?

Systemic Risk from Stranded Assets

A shock from stranded fossil fuel assets could crash the global financial system. It is important to explore how big a shock might happen in the worst case. Could the zero-carbon transition generate both the shocks and the means to amplify them until the financial system collapses? That's a critical question for central banks and ministries of finance.

To explore this question, we return to the E3ME-FTT model used in the geopolitics exercise in Chapter 8. Fossil fuel demand, supply and trade in seventy countries and regions are estimated in scenarios of countries achieving or not achieving net-zero emissions.

Using the results from the model, we estimate how much money could be lost globally if fossil fuels suddenly became worthless because of a rapid green transition.[23] We used a standard scenario of fossil fuel expansion to describe what many investors may today

[21] See, for example, the textbook by Baxter and Rennie (1996), and critiques of this approach in Cont et al. (2010); Cont and Schaanning (2017). Options and the value of waiting for information are generally priced using the famous Black-Scholes (1973) model, developed on the basis of geometric random walks.

[22] See Cont et al. (2010).

[23] See Semieniuk et al. (2022), which builds on Mercure et al. (2021a).

think the future looks like. We then used another scenario in which fossil fuel demand falls, making the value of fossil fuel reserves much lower. A sudden re-pricing could occur, for example, if investors start to see a clash between the rapid expansion of zero-carbon technologies and continuing investment in fossil fuel production.

The calculations are based on fossil fuels that have not yet been collected or consumed. They represent future revenues and are used to determine today's values of companies on stock markets. Future stranded assets would immediately lead to reductions in company values and could mean bankruptcy if it becomes clear that loans could not be repaid.

We found that up to $11 trillion dollars could evaporate suddenly from global market values, with $1–2 trillion of bankrupt equity (that's the value of companies going bankrupt). Global GDP is about $100 trillion, so losses could be worth 10% of GDP, a huge number. And, according to the model, a 10% shock seems to be large enough to push the economy to the edge of chaos, although it depends a lot on who goes bankrupt and who owns the companies going bankrupt. So, we don't know for sure and need to do more research.

Using databases of share ownership, it is possible to determine where the shock might fall. Ultimately, all activities in the economy belong to either individual people, the government, or pension and other funds. In developing countries that export fossil fuels (e.g. Saudi Arabia, Russia, African countries), the losses are largely taken by the governments. In advanced Western economies (US, UK, EU), the losses are taken by shareholders and pension funds.

This analysis tells us something further. Western economies currently *import* substantial financial risk from developing countries. Many of the assets in developing countries are owned by investors in the West. Therefore, much of the global financial risk of the transition is actually situated in the UK and the US!

And this is just fossil fuel production and reserves. What about transport systems, buildings, infrastructure and all sorts of things that could devalue prematurely with the changing views of investors?[24]

To summarise, we will be harming global financial resilience if we don't get the risk of stranded fossil fuel assets under control. We risk making the entire economy unstable. We need to control investment in fossil fuels to reduce the risk of financial crash. And the risk becomes greater when there is more debt and leverage across the economy. It's not just about limiting climate change. We need to work out *how* to safely transition towards green without crashing the financial system.

9.2.5 How Much Green Lending Is Safe?

All this tells us that the combination of assets losing value and high leverage together are bad for financial stability. But how much lending for zero-carbon activities would actually be safe?

First, how much do we need? Lots of people have tried to guess how much investment will be needed in the zero-carbon transition. Most estimates are bigger than \$100 trillion. That's more than current annual GDP. It is spread across 25 years but is still an unbelievably large amount of money. Governments will provide some of the finance, but much of it will be funded by companies borrowing.

More borrowing means more leverage and therefore more risk. Climate policy can make the investments profitable and reduce risk. However, one question that often comes up is whether the financial system can provide all this funding.

Standard economics says maybe not. In standard economics, banks operate at the limit already. All the available money for borrowing is already used, so we could only invest in zero-carbon things if we cancel some investments in other things like healthcare or houses. That would face opposition and is not good for the economy. Leverage would remain constant.

[24] For a broader discussion of stranded assets, see the book by Caldecott (2018).

In reality, banks create new money when they make loans. The money from the loans is spent and ends up as savings in other banks.[25] As we saw in Chapter 5, this is how the economy grows. But the story is a bit simplistic. It makes it sound like banks can just lend more money and everything will be OK.

The problem is if some of the loans are not repaid. When this happens, the bank relies on money from savers to keep its operations going. But if the savers lose confidence and suddenly want their money back in cash, the bank goes bankrupt (unless it is bailed out by the central bank). And as we know since 2007, because banks lend to each other, if one goes bankrupt, it causes problems throughout the entire banking system.

A rapid increase in lending, particularly to unknown or high-risk activities, will make the economy grow faster, but it also makes a loss of confidence more likely. In addition, the more lending there is, the more entangled everything becomes, and the bigger the house of cards that could crumble.

We know from Figure 9.9 that the normal level of risk in the economy gives a tail slope just above –3. Closer to –4, economic growth is too slow, the cost of excessively high financial resilience. Near –2, growth is very fast, but the risk of financial crash is high too. Past –2, the economy may begin to self-destruct.

There is a connection between the total amount of lending that happens for decarbonisation and the change in slope towards –2 that we can expect to see in global financial value.

In rough terms, we need more than \$100 trillion over 25 years, which is minimum \$4 trillion per year if divided equally. By 2050, we might have increased the debt stock to GDP ratio by at least 25%.[26] For reference, the global private debt to GDP ratio is now

[25] Recap from Chapter 3: In standard economic theory, banks allocate savers' money to borrowers. In reality, the causality is reversed; banks lend money which ends up as savings. The collective action of the banks determines the money supply (see Werner, 2014, 2016; McLeay et al., 2014).

[26] Global GDP is of around \$100 trillion, growing at 3% per year, which therefore just about doubles by 2050, when we need to reach zero emissions. If investment starts at

around 220%. The question is whether the additional debt from climate action is the straw that breaks the camel's back.

We don't know the exact answer to this, but we can say that the estimates of lending required to decarbonise are probably high enough to put global financial systems at risk, pushing the tail slope beyond –2.[27] It doesn't mean this level of lending is not feasible. What then needs to be done is to become more careful regarding who we lend to and what for, and to become more prudent in our lending. This is to avoid the 2008 kind of scenario.

Booms and busts are a feature of the economy and are closely tied to the great waves. Uncertainty offers the chance for profit – and for disaster. We can see that the finance is there, if people believe it can be profitably used. But more finance means more risk.

Chapter 10 discusses ways to reduce the risk. But even this simple analysis points to a conclusion. The risk is highest when finance expands fastest. Spreading out the necessary investment and starting as soon as possible would reduce the risk of crisis.

9.2.6 *Stability of Macro-Financial Balances*

In Chapter 8, we described the quest for foreign currency, especially US dollars. We showed how running out of US dollars could lead to a

$2.6 trillion and grows at the same rate of 3% per year, we reach $100 trillion by 2050. However, we'd be paying back debt too over the period. By 2050, for twenty year loans, about half the debt might already be repaid, with therefore $50 trillion left to repay over $200 trillion of global GDP, that's an addition of 25% to the global debt-to-GDP ratio. To achieve $200 trillion of zero-carbon investment by 2050, we would start at $5 trillion per year, grow at 3% per year and add about 50% to the global debt-to-GDP ratio (depending on the interest rate).

27 To be more precise, according to data from the Bank for International Settlements (https://data.bis.org/topics/TOTAL_CREDIT), global public and private credit (loans and bonds) went from $160 to $231 trillion between 2014 and 2023, while GDP increased from $80 to $105 trillion. That's a debt-to-GDP ratio going from 200% to 220%, an increase of 20 percentage points. During that period, the tail slope went from –2.3 to –2.1, a change of 0.2 (see Figure 9.9). With an additional 25% in debt-to-GDP ratio, assuming that rising leverage is the main source of loss of resilience, the tail slope potentially goes past –2 to –1.9, into the territory of infinitely large crashes.

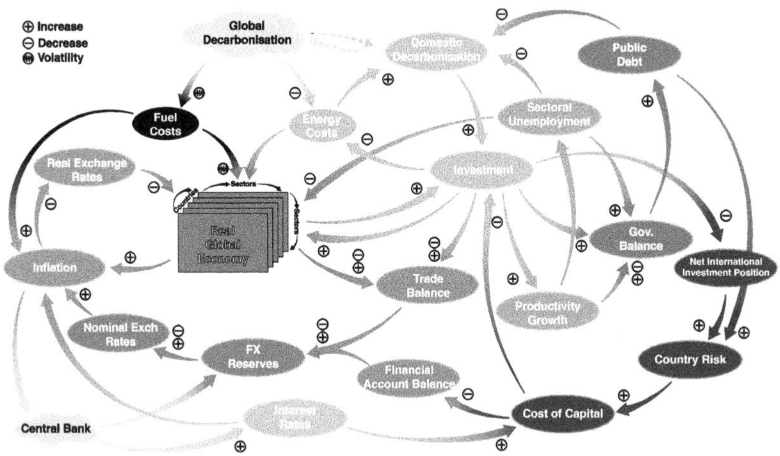

FIGURE 9.10 The feedbacks controlling the stability and value of currencies and other macro-economic quantities. See Espagne et al. (2023).

currency crisis. Here, we discuss how financial instability could spill over across borders.

With a few colleagues from the World Bank, IMF, Banque de France and others, we built a diagram that shows the relevant links between countries (Figure 9.10). The key indicators are *macro-financial balances.*

The zero-carbon transition will affect macro-financial balances, even in countries that don't reduce emissions. We already said why in Chapter 8. Because fossil fuels and fossil equipment will disappear from trade, trade patterns will change and financial flows will be redirected.

In fact, the change is already happening, and technology trends will change macro-financial balances, whether we have more climate policy or not. But as we also already described, it is in most countries' interests to reduce fuel imports. Either way, things are not going to stay as they are.

A plausible disastrous chain of events could be as follows. Decarbonisation creates lots of uncertainty for investment in fossil fuel extraction and makes fuel prices unstable, because demand and supply don't match well. Uncertainty increases and assets get stranded. There may be armed conflict causing supply problems. Meanwhile, investment in renewables and zero-carbon technology increases rapidly, and their costs become lower than those for the old technologies.

National trade balances and financial balances change. On both counts, countries that produce fossil fuels lose out while fossil fuel importers gain. Fossil fuel exporters lose both exports and significant foreign investment into their fossil fuel equipment and infrastructure.

Financial balances are also affected by interest rates and other lending costs that reflect how risky investors think the country is. One possible outcome is cascading debt crises in fuel exporting countries. Fossil fuel exporters have little choice but to replace lost export revenues with foreign currency debt in order to obtain basic supplies. However, this is clearly only a short-term solution that could eventually lead to crisis.

The situation that led to hyperinflation in Venezuela provides a vivid example of what the countries at risk must avoid (Figure 9.11).[28] For decades, Venezuela's economy has been largely based on oil extraction. Its socialist administration has used oil revenues to fund social services for households.

However, the economy became dependent on the global oil market. When oil prices went up, lots of US dollars came, and things were good in Venezuela. When oil prices went down, it was difficult to pay for imports, and things were not so good. Decisions made by OPEC directly affected the Venezuelan economy.

The path to hyperinflation was circular. The state oil company pumped oil out of the ground and exported it, bringing in US dollars (USD). It exchanged the dollars for Venezuelan Bolivars (VES) at local banks and gave the Bolivars to the government. The government used the Bolivars to provide social services to households (like healthcare). Some of these services required imported goods (like medicine), so local companies got dollars from local banks to buy imports.

[28] See Barredo-Zuriarrain (2022).

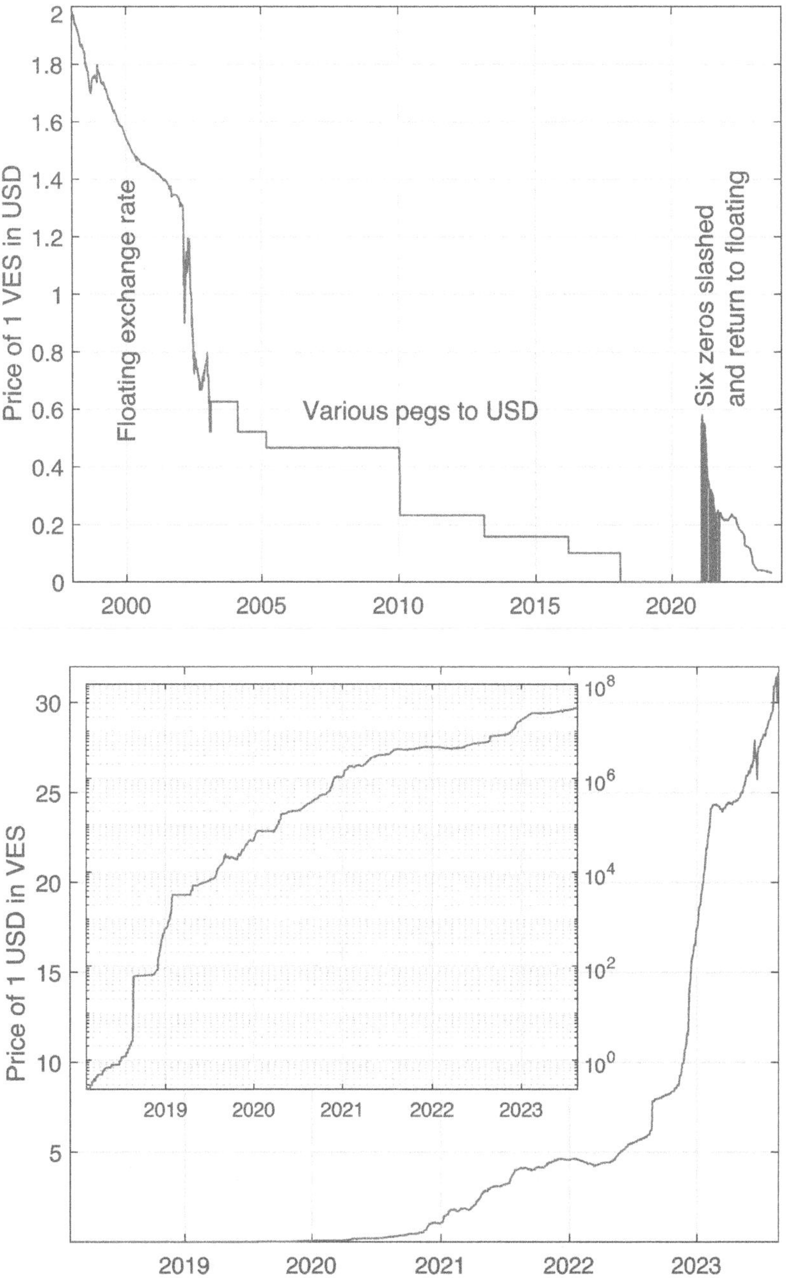

FIGURE 9.11 Hyperinflation in Venezuela.

So, Venezuela got dollars from oil sales and used them to buy medicine and other goods. The government also fixed the exchange rate between USD and VES. Some of the money it got from the state oil company was used to subsidise domestic oil prices.

This all worked while Venezuela got more dollars from oil sales than it needed to buy medicine. It was fine when global oil prices were high. Even short periods of slightly lower oil prices were fine, because extra dollars could be kept back from the good times.

After 2008 though, oil prices fell from well over $100 per barrel to less than $40 per barrel. They stayed below $70 for almost two years. Stocks of dollars started to run out, and companies started to have difficulties getting hold of them. The companies buying medicine went to unofficial sources, who provided dollars at a higher exchange rate. Their costs went up, and they charged the government more.

The government was then faced with lower oil revenues and higher costs for social services. It borrowed VES from the central bank to cover the gap. The result was more VES chasing fewer US dollars. The cost of buying dollars increased further.

This feedback loop eventually caused the currency to crash. The process started slowly in the late 1990s and early 2000s but became astronomical later (Figure 9.11). It remained uncontrolled during the late 2000s and 2010s. Since 2019, you would have needed 100 million VES to buy 1 US dollar. To keep the numbers manageable, six zeros were cut from the currency unit in 2021.

There were other factors too. The state oil company borrowed directly from the central bank, leading to uncontrolled money printing. Subsidising fuel prices for households did not help. Ultimately, however, the problem was the need to maintain social spending even when oil prices were low. A shortage of US dollars brought down the economy.

The zero-carbon transition could see permanently lower oil prices, or maybe an alternation between high and low, depending on the degree to which demand and supply mismatch, and whether we divest from fossil fuels too quickly or too slowly. Many countries will find they can no longer export oil at all. Venezuela was an extreme case, but other countries could find themselves in similar situations. The people in these countries have got used to buying things from abroad cheaply. But when the dollars run out, there will be trouble.

Ultimately, the issue was that this institutional system had very little resilience to changes in the oil price. This is the kind of institutional setup that all countries should avoid. Relying on oil revenues, which are high but volatile, to fund essential public services, which need stability, is a very bad idea, unless a large buffer, for example, a sovereign wealth fund, is used to absorb the roller-coaster effect. Very few countries have such funds, and there is therefore a great risk that many countries in Africa and South America follow the fate of Venezuela.

9.2.7 *The Problem of Economic Diversification*

Volatility in commodity markets does not only affect developing economies. Take, for example, the province of Alberta in Western Canada. It bounces between wealthy and broke, due to the mad swings of the oil market, and oil production in the tar sands being marginally profitable, just like in Venezuela. At oil prices higher than $50, huge royalty revenues accrue to the provincial government. At low oil prices below $50, up to 25% of the provincial budget can evaporate (not including possible losses of tax revenues due to reduced employment and economic activity). On average, oil raises comparable revenues (about $18bn) to all provincial taxes combined ($25bn).[29] This means that the volatility of oil markets makes the government budget just as volatile.

Carrying out a quick analysis of royalty revenues from the official statistics (Figure 9.12), we find that the volatility is about 60% of the revenues themselves. Those variations are, as we would expect, highly heavy-tailed. Uncertainty is substantial given there is not a

[29] For the data, see www.alberta.ca/historical-royalty-revenue-data and www.alberta.ca/budget.

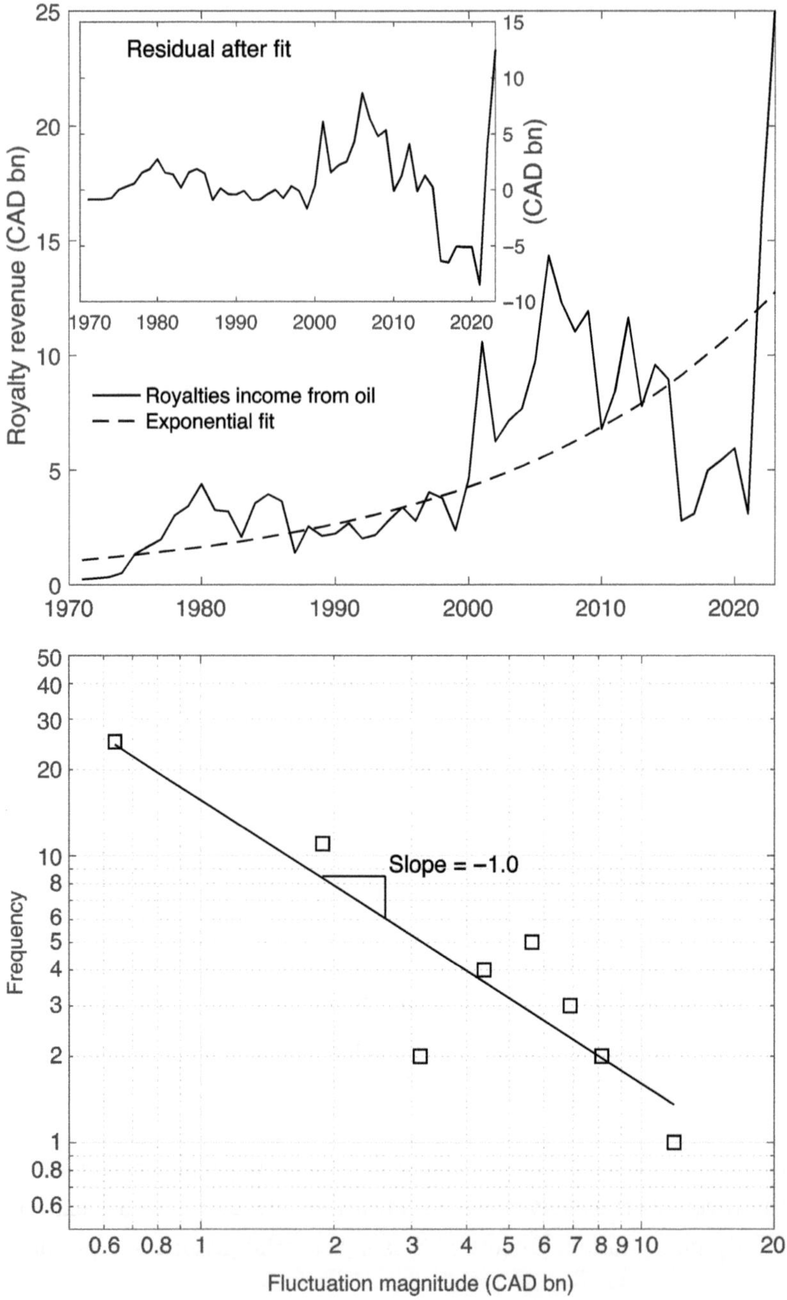

FIGURE 9.12 Highly volatile government revenues from oil and bitumen for the Canadian province of Alberta. We add an exponential trend fit and calculate the frequency of variations in ten equally spaced bins.

lot of data, but the variations appear to have a log–log slope of about −1. This means that each year, the government of Alberta can only ever have a vague notion of what the revenues from the oil sector will be. It therefore cannot predict what its budget will be. It's an endless chaotic boom–bust situation that makes everything difficult to plan.

It is well known that volatile revenue sources can poison economic development and can cause the resource 'curse'. That's where underinvestment occurs in all other industries, leading to lack of economic diversification. There is an inability to focus on anything else.[30] Economies with great oil resources have often failed to translate that wealth into economic development and, worse, appear to do the opposite.[31]

A more resilient and diversified industry than just oil and gas would be desirable in Alberta. If major economies worldwide go ahead and transition to EVs (e.g. China, the EU), Albertan bitumen will be the first production kicked out of the global oil market, and there will be little left to support the regional economy.[32] But the region is rich in renewable energy resources, featuring large expanses of sparsely populated land and a sizeable population of chemical engineers. It seems plausible to move to a green hydrogen and ammonia-based chemical industry and other green chemical or materials industries that could benefit from proximity with large-scale green hydrogen production. This wouldn't solve all of Alberta's economic challenges in the transition, but it could be a start.

What leads to successful economic diversification, especially in areas of low industrial resilience, nobody can really say for sure. There is no recipe guaranteed to work every time. It involves hard and persistent work on getting new activities started where we expect great but declining activities to come to an end. We need to invest

30 See Ross (1999); Savoia and Sen (2021).

31 See Burgis (2015).

32 See Mercure et al. (2021a).

in regions too narrowly focused on coal, oil and gas, to do something else before the general decline sets in. Once the disease of industrial decline begins, investment becomes harder and harder to attract, so it becomes increasingly difficult to turn things around the deeper we sink in it.

9.3 POLITICAL INSTABILITY

9.3.1 Cascades in Conflict and Political Dynamics

As already discussed in Chapter 8, the zero-carbon transition will drastically change the political power of countries and social groups. This could cause major political instability across and within countries. We explore this under the lens of the edge of chaos.

Political instability and wars rarely occur in isolation. Both are caused by previous events, and both lead to future events. For example, a revenge attack is motivated by an earlier attack and could lead to further revenge attacks. Events are clustered and can occur in avalanches, like dominoes.[33] They have instabilities like those of delays in the London underground.

Conflicts and protests are usually driven by longstanding grievances. For example, the issues leading to multiple protests during the Arab spring included an unsustainable cost of living, inequality and local governance.[34] People's feelings about these evolve slowly, leading to internal societal pressure that may not be obvious. This pressure can ignite into protests from relatively minor events, snowballing into major movements, sometimes revolutions.

Figure 9.13 shows the statistical characteristics of recent attacks in Nigeria and Ukraine.[35] Figure 9.13(a) shows the timelines of casualties. The clusters show the nature of attacks and

[33] See Kushwaha and Lee (2023).

[34] See https://en.wikipedia.org/wiki/Arab_Spring.

[35] Individual events with or without casualties are reported by the Armed Conflict Location & Event Data Project. We analysed them for their criticality and instability behaviour. See Kushwaha and Lee (2023) for a similar network analysis of these data.

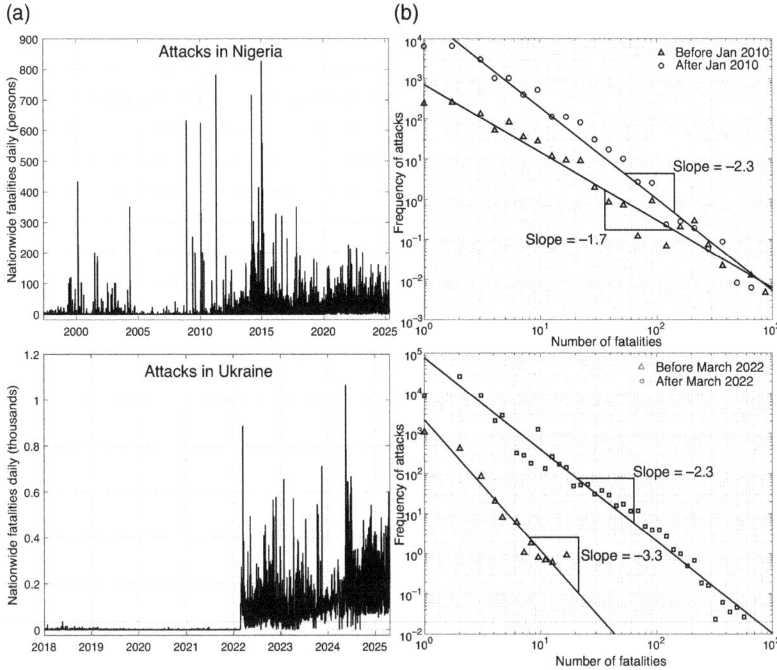

FIGURE 9.13 Frequency distribution of fatalities in conflicts in Nigeria and Ukraine. (a) Timelines for the nationwide numbers of deaths daily. (b) Distributions of deaths per event on log scales, with linear fits. Data from the Armed Conflict Location & Event Data Project (ACLED), processed by the authors. Slopes near −2.0 signal systems with divergent statistical moments, where the expected number of deaths can be any number. Note these estimations use log binning.

counterattacks. Figure 9.13(b) shows distributions of the numbers of casualties.

The intensity with which attacks lead to counterattacks determines the cascading mechanism in these conflicts. Just as with the London underground, the frequency distribution of casualties is a straight line on a log-based chart.

Although Ukraine's war with Russia started in 2014, the intensity of battles increased dramatically when Russia fully invaded in early 2022. The slope of the line moved from −3.3 to −2.3. Battles are fierce and unrestrained. Any minor event can escalate into an explosive battle.

Nigeria has had a long, drawn-out conflict between the government and various rebel groups like Al Shabaab or for control of oil in the Niger Delta.[36] The situation has involved a simmering of instability for some time, with a slope of −1.7 before around 2010. After 2010, however, although the intensity of attacks has increased, their intensity has become less explosive than before, with a slope of −2.3, similar to Ukraine's full-on war. This shows that the intensity of events occurring and their explosiveness are two independent things.

We have not really tried to connect the wars in Ukraine and Nigeria with climate change or climate policy. It would be hard to prove causality when there are so many other factors. But both seem possible. Russia could lose its dominance in EU and global energy markets (see Chapter 8).[37] Pressures on natural resources partly drive conflict in Africa.

The point is not so much that climate change and climate policy will lead to war. It's that they could lead to conflict, and once conflict starts, it is difficult to stop. We are already too close to the edge of chaos.

9.3.2 *Economies on the Edge of Revolution*

In Figure 9.14, we show more data on cascading political failures, looking at protests, riots and strikes. Like wars, protests can gather momentum into something bigger. The slope of the distribution tells us about their state of criticality. Here, we compare France and South Africa.

In France, there is a longstanding tradition for demonstrations, strikes and riots. Between the pandemic and summer 2023, some protests were about climate policy. The protesters became known as the Gilets Jaunes because of the hi-vis jackets (literally 'yellow vests') they wore.

[36] See Burgis (2015).
[37] See, for instance, Kuzemko et al. (2022).

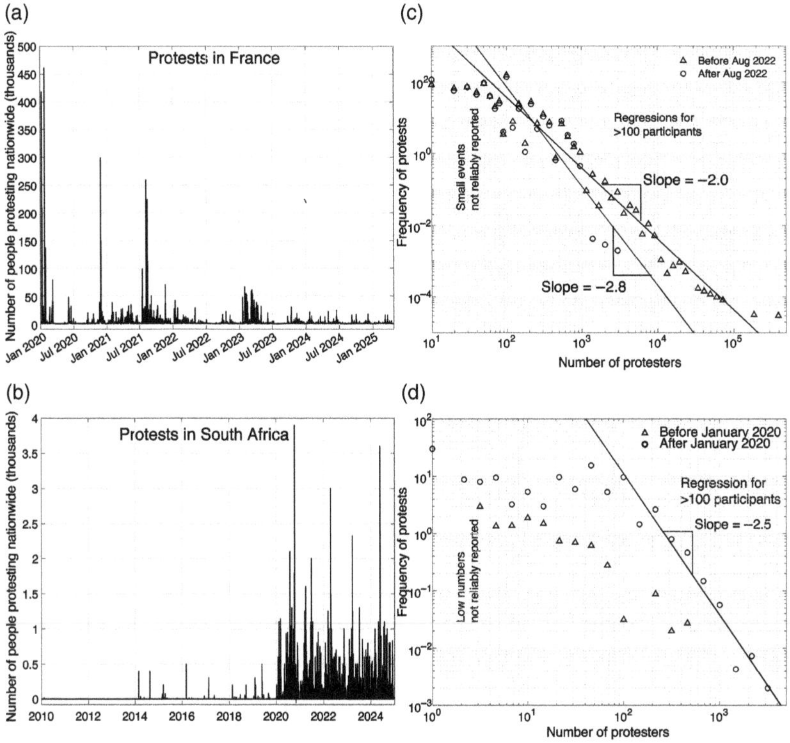

FIGURE 9.14 Number of people protesting each day in France (a) and South Africa (b), and the corresponding frequency–size distribution of individual protests (c, d) since the start of 2020 (France) and 1997 (South Africa), when the data begin. Data source is the Armed Conflict Location & Event Data Project (ACLED), processed by the authors. Crowd sizes appear irregularly reported for events involving less than 100 people, which explains the breakaway from linearity for small events.

The Gilets Jaunes were originally a mixture of workers and low-income people who were affected by a proposed increase in fuel taxes. For example, they included truck drivers and farmers. Over time, more people joined the protests, and the subject of the protests changed. They were no longer just about climate policy.

We find a slope of −2.0 covering a wide range of data, up to around August 2022, when there was an election. This suggests a political situation in France that has been right on the edge of instability, and we could not at the time guess the size of the next protest.

This is the kind of situation that brings down entire governments. It is the stuff of revolutions. After the election, political pressure eased a little, and the slope settled on −2.8. All of a sudden, much less explosive.

We show the same analysis for South Africa. The protests here have been about poverty, poor public services, repeated power cuts, poor governance, inequality and other social issues. They have also been weaponised by various elites using social media.[38] COVID and its resulting restrictions in economic activity drastically increased the pressures that people felt. The system has settled on a slope of −2.5,[39] with some cascading political instability, but not as unstable as France was.

We also checked data for strikes and protests in the UK, where multiple strikes over pay and working conditions happened between 2021 and 2023. However, the distribution is not linear on a log–log graph and not critical. This finding suggests that the UK has some policy flexibility, including for climate policy. France does not.

9.3.3 Fragmentation Risk and the Rise of Populism

Both climate disasters and economic transformation upset people. Over time, they can bring a country to the edge of political chaos. Measures to increase resilience and redistribute wealth may offset some of the strain (Figure 9.15).

In France, inequality has increased in recent decades. Workers and ordinary people have been under economic pressure for some time. Making fuel more expensive may have been the straw that broke the camel's back. We are still seeing the effects of the backlash. Populist parties dominated the 2024 elections, from both the political left and right.

There are lessons for other countries. Climate policies that cause economic hardship bring a country closer to the edge of chaos.

[38] See, for instance, Lockwood (2022).

[39] We don't yet have enough data since the start of the pandemic in 2020 to measure the slope accurately.

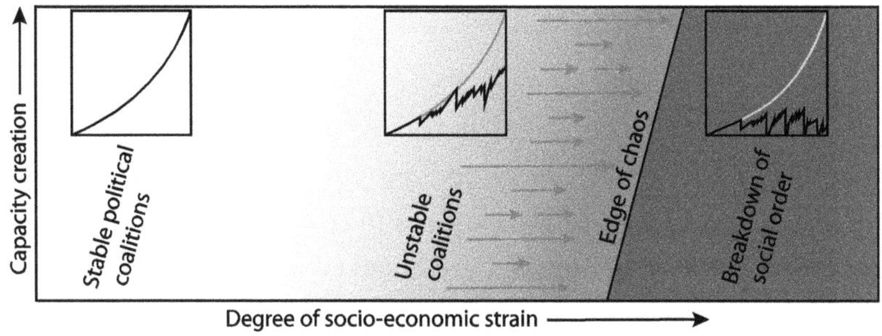

FIGURE 9.15 The regimes of political stability according to the degree of social and economic strain and discontent. Building economic capacity, institutions and infrastructure, as well as improving living standards, increases resilience.

France does not have high inequality, but higher fuel prices were enough to do it.

There are lots of other things going on too of course, not all linked to climate change. All western countries have regions that have suffered from deindustrialisation. We saw in Chapter 7 what this means for the people left behind. These problems are not going to go away and could easily get worse. Fuel taxes may trigger the protests, but the real issues are much deeper.

Our conclusion is that the political backlash from implementing the 'wrong' climate policies could make it impossible to implement the 'right' ones. As we will see in Chapter 10, not all climate policies are equal. Price-based policies are blunt and may not be very effective. But any successful climate policy will create sunrise and sunset industries. This structural change must be managed appropriately, or countries' instititions and their willingness to pursue the transition will fall apart.

Bad climate policy can make the ground fertile for populism. Right-wing leaders know very well how to use this, as we know from history. Left-wing leaders are getting in on it now too. Both will use people's grievances to get into power. Populist leaders will do little to address climate change because they see only the costs and not the benefits. If we get to this point, we've lost. This is how climate policy can shoot itself in the foot and become self-destructive.

9.4 WHAT IF IT ALL GOES WRONG?

In Chapter 1, we showed that the transition could accelerate economic growth. We provided historical evidence in Chapters 4, 5 and 6. In the present chapter, however, we showed that the transition's success hangs by a thread. There are lots of vulnerabilities due to the people left behind and to badly designed policy. The plunge into chaos is close.

The risk is not just social and economic destruction. Politicians could try to slow or delay or even reverse the transition itself. Jair Bolsonaro allowed widespread destruction of the Amazon rainforest. Donald Trump was too late to bring back coal, but there are other parts of the economy where we still need policy to support the transition. We will not get it from leaders who play on people's grievances.

Financial crises could delay the transition too. Remember that we need more than \$100 trillion of financing by 2050. If banks lose confidence in zero-carbon technologies, that money will be harder to come by. It probably won't derail the transition, but it could delay it for long enough that we end up with climate disaster.

Then, there is the risk of disruption to international trade, which is already a sensitive issue. We are currently seeing a backlash against Chinese dominance in zero-carbon products. High tariffs on Chinese EVs will slow adoption. This is only the tip of the iceberg though. Disruption will make products more expensive and could make them unavailable altogether. Either way, we will see delays in the transition.

The story is the same for all these risks, and they all affect each other. Instability leads to more instability. There are politicians waiting to take advantage. They will even try to create instability themselves. Their promises could be largely empty as they cannot change the trajectories of the sunrise and sunset industries. They may, therefore, do their best to delay things instead, like Trump tried to do with coal.

The amount of time left to reach net-zero goals is really limited. We have until 2050 for a 50/50 chance of not exceeding 1.5°C of global warming. There are lots of hurdles in the way. And the slower we go now, the faster we have to go later – which increases the risk of instability.

We have a major policy design problem that we must solve urgently. It is about how to keep the economy stable while rapidly transforming it. This will *not* be achieved using just a high carbon price. That's a recipe for disaster.

In Chapter 10, we make our proposal for effective and resilient climate policy. We think it's our best chance of avoiding disaster.

10 Rethinking Climate Policy

10.1 WE NEED TO RETHINK CLIMATE POLICY URGENTLY

10.1.1 Do We Need to Start All Over?

This book makes the case for a radical rethinking of climate policy. Building on the previous analysis, this chapter describes what the policy would look like.

There are two main policy goals. First of all, we need policies to speed up the zero-carbon transition. We need these policies to avoid possible chaos from a changing climate. Second, we need policies to make the transition bearable. These policies will avoid chaos and increasing social and economic strain during the transition.

Past climate policy has focused, or we could say obsessed, with efficiency. In standard economics, climate policy tries to maximise our benefits from energy use. Economists say that this is only feasible with pricing instruments like taxes or emissions trading. But we learned in this book that optimising the economy minimises its resilience and makes it fragile. It brings our economy right to the edge of chaos where everything breaks down.

Here, we are proposing the opposite, to focus on economic resilience instead. Why? Because both climate change and the transition will impose enormous strain on the economy, the financial system, people and politics, but we can't tell exactly how much. The faster we go, the more strain and uncertainty. How can we hope to get through this if we minimise resilience?

Getting the transition going requires policy strategies that push the system over the initial hump, after which it rolls down the hill on its own. We are less concerned about getting stuck with inefficient energy subsidies. The policies we propose aim to get the transition moving and keep it on track. Once it's rolling, the priority is to prevent it rolling off the path and crashing.

As we discuss in this chapter, some new policies may help to achieve both goals of accelerating the transition and increasing resilience. Carbon pricing could play some role, if used in the right way. But we should be clear from the start that carbon pricing will probably play only a minor role in the whole thing. It has been at best a damaging distraction over the past decade.

We put more emphasis on regulation and investment. These policies can give us rapid progress, not only in near-term emission reductions but also in the technological advances we need to reach zero emissions. Importantly, these policies can be used to improve economic resilience.

Sections 10.2 and 10.3 describe the policies we need to meet the two goals. We don't need to start again. We know about the necessary policies already. We know what has worked up to now and what has not. The question is how to put the right policies in place so that they can work together.

Failure could look very ugly. Chaos threatens, either from climate change itself or from the disruption to society from rapid change. In both cases, the most vulnerable people stand to lose the most. Section 10.4, therefore, takes a step back. We discuss how to coordinate the policies and how to make them work for everyone.

However, before all that, there is one important question, which is how to move on from where we are stuck now. We need to start thinking about the problem differently.

10.1.2 Abandon the Old Ideologies

In any climate policy discussion, we must be clear that only net-zero emissions will do. Anything less is not good enough. To get to net-zero, we need transformational change, not marginal change. The old ideas based on marginal change no longer cut it.

We already saw in Chapter 2 that de-growing the economy won't get us to net-zero. By reducing our wealth, we may repent for our carbon sins, but it will not create a zero-carbon economy. Process innovation and higher efficiency will reduce emissions a bit but not get us to net-zero. And reduced investment, which necessarily happens during de-growth, would slow or even stall the development of the zero-carbon technologies that we need.

The old thinking in economics dates back to the early twentieth century and was applied to climate change in the early 2000s. Back then, we did not have zero-carbon solutions. Instead of promoting EVs, we pushed fuel standards in petrol and diesel cars. Driving less, heating less and even eating less were the best tools we had to reduce emissions. There was a vague idea that capturing carbon might also help.

Economists used their theories to recommend carbon prices because, in their models, carbon prices allow the market to determine the least-cost way to reduce emissions. But these theories are based on marginal change. If our target was to reduce emissions by 5%, they may have been useful.

Net-zero targets changed the game. We need to cut all emissions, so searching for the least-cost emissions to cut isn't very useful. Throw in that we don't know how some technology prices will change, or even what new technologies will arrive, and the least-cost idea seems silly.

Net-zero targets also killed the idea that slowing economic activity would get us to our climate goals, unless we wanted to reduce our economies to zero.

Whether we like it or not, only *zero-carbon* solutions will get us there. Once we are using zero-carbon technologies, we can use as much as we want without increasing emissions, although we yet need all the pieces to complete the puzzle. The constraints come from other resources, like land or material requirements. This is not to say that efficiency does not matter. We need everything we can get to reduce current emissions, and reducing energy demand certainly helps. The key point is that efficiency is at best a stop-gap measure.

As described in Chapter 6, it turns out that getting rid of combustion will reduce energy demand anyway. We can still do the same amount of cooking, heating and travelling, but we will not need the 50% of energy lost in combustion. Smartification will further reduce our energy consumption.

This is good. We don't need to reduce our affluence to the level of cave men to save the climate. We can avoid the toxic politics of suggesting so, especially from advanced economies telling poor countries to weaken economic development.

We can probably also forget about the long and unsuccessful quest for large-scale negative emission technologies. Taking carbon dioxide out of the air is definitely good, so the aim is reasonable. However, most of the technologies have made little or no progress in the last decade.

The reason may be that the business case for these technologies relies too much on the old thinking. The technologies depend heavily on carbon prices and, especially, on carbon markets. As we know from Chapter 9, these markets are unreliable. The technologies also rely on bespoke infrastructure and often cannot be mass-produced. They therefore don't get cheaper.[1]

There may be exceptions. Enhanced weathering removes carbon dioxide from the air but can also be used for improving soil quality. Reforestation could help preserve biodiversity. However, these approaches cannot capture carbon at the rate we are emitting. They are complements, not substitutes, for getting rid of combustion.

We could continue to waste vast amounts of time, energy and political capital by trying to get people to use less energy. The same for trying to find ways to capture emissions. And why? Combustion technologies are on the way out anyway.

So, before we get into the specific policies, it's time to throw out the old way of thinking. Let's focus on the things that matter: rapid emission reductions while building social, economic and financial resilience.

[1] See Malhotra and Schmidt (2020).

10.2 RETHINKING POLICY TO MAKE THE TRANSITION HAPPEN

Moving on from the old way of thinking means focusing more on technology and less on traditional optimisation economics. The basic idea is we need to get the right technologies in the right places. It sounds easy, but there are several barriers on the way. The aim of the policy is to knock down these barriers.

First, the technologies need to exist. Fortunately, in most cases, they already do. Renewables can give us carbon-free electricity, and EVs can use that electricity to get us around. There are still gaps, however. Getting aeroplanes to fly long distances without using jet fuel is hard. We don't know how to make cement without releasing carbon dioxide. We, therefore, still need policies to *get the technological train moving*.

Second, people and businesses need to know about the technologies. That doesn't just mean they need to have heard of them. They need to trust the technologies to deliver what they need. There is an important role to *create an informed public*. People usually trust their friends and family, so the more people go green, the more trust is built and others can follow.

Third, people must be able to buy the equipment. There are two important policy aspects here. There could be existing rules that prevent the technology from being used, so there is a policy need for *getting regulations right*. Financing new equipment may be an issue too, so we may need policy for *greasing the wheels of private finance* and *rethink public finance*. To get dollars to the right places, we must *reform international climate finance*.

Finally, people must *want* to use the technology. This means that, among many other things, it would help if it was cheaper than current alternatives. The technological train may get us most of the way there, but there is still a role for *the carbon pricing hammer*, which might at the very least prevent us from backsliding into old bad habits. Net-zero means there is no going back.

We cannot stress enough that it only takes one barrier to prevent change from happening. Different policies are needed to overcome barriers of different kinds, and there is no single silver bullet. We need *policy mixes for market creation.*

10.2.1 Get the Green Technology Train Moving

As discussed in Chapters 2 and 6, historically, a lot of technological change has been started by governments. Often, it was for military purposes. Britain converted its navy to use oil rather than coal, which prompted a wider use of oil engines. The US Department of Defense paid astronomers to develop CCD imaging, from which digital cameras were later developed.[2]

Governments tend to lead because no one else will do it. No other institution has deep enough pockets to take on the risk of creating entire economic sectors. If we had left it to the market, previous technology revolutions would probably never have happened.

The case of EVs is insightful. People will not buy EVs if they don't think they will be able to charge them. Companies will not build charging points if they cannot be sure that anyone will use them. Without intervention, nothing happens.

We need to think about it in terms of risk. It is a chicken and egg problem. No one wants to take the plunge first. Public investments can get things going. Building an entire charging network would be expensive, but the public doesn't need to do it all. Once companies can see what is going on, they will take over. The public investment is therefore needed only at the start and need not be substantial.[3]

It's the same in almost every sector. The state invests and sets the direction of movement. It 'crowds-in' private investment through its leadership. Large investment may not be needed, but there are many ways to help. They include training the workforce, setting up regulatory agencies, creating initial demand and building initial infrastructure.

[2] For oil, see, for example, Ediger and Bowlus (2019). For imaging, see Mazzucato (2013).
[3] See Mercure et al. (2025b).

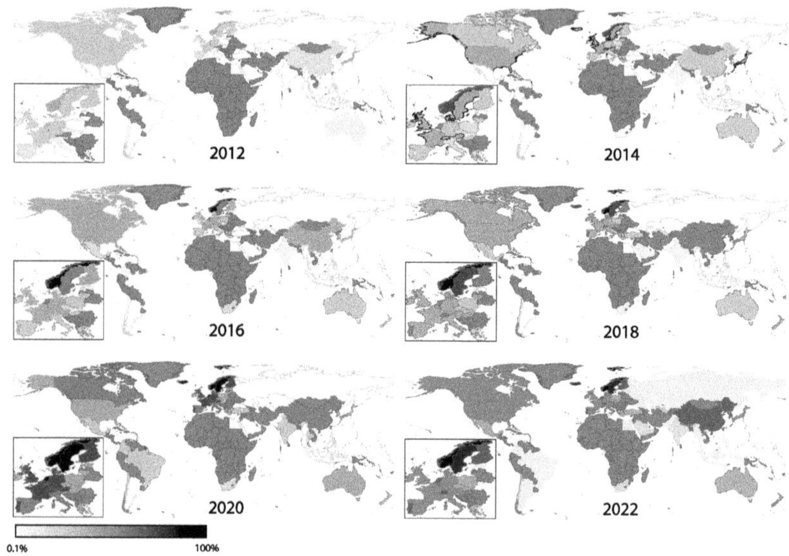

FIGURE 10.1 The spilling out of EVs between countries, from core innovating regions towards neighbours.

This is why technology development is like a train. Once it is built and sent in the right direction, it becomes very difficult to stop. Policy is only needed to first get the train moving.

This thinking also helps with the debate about who will pay for decarbonisation. Low-income countries argue that they did not cause climate change and should not pay the bill. They, in any case, have limited resources to do so. They look to developed countries to provide the finance.

The estimated sums involved are enormous and would never be covered by aid budgets. However, these estimates include all the investment required. In reality, governments require only a small share of it to start things off. Then, the private sector can take over, with less and less need for external finance.

Coordination between countries is important too. New products quickly cross borders, as Figure 10.1 shows for EVs.[4] In this

[4] Maps are from Mercure et al. (2025b). The spatial diffusion literature includes Grübler (1998); Bento and Fontes (2015).

example, the core regions with the innovation are the EU, the US and China. People buy EVs in these countries, bringing down production costs and showing how the technology works. People in neighbouring countries soon learn and start buying EVs too.

The follower countries may see faster growth. They can skip teething problems and learn from previous mistakes. We saw this with solar PV, where Germany led the way but has long been overtaken by other countries, and with wind power in places like Portugal.[5] Many other technology transitions have followed a similar pattern.

It works better though if countries can align product standards. If the same product can be sold in different countries, then it probably will be. And here, developed countries can offer support to the developing world without paying huge sums. If governments in rich countries pay for zero-carbon technologies to be developed and mass-produced, they open up options for everyone.

The story of rich countries causing climate problems for poor countries can be turned on its head. The rich countries can offer solutions. This was the story promoted by the UK when it hosted the climate conference in Glasgow (COP26) in 2021. It was called the 'Breakthrough Agenda': rich countries should invest to bring costs down, so that developing countries can get on board the moving train.

We don't yet have all the technologies we need to reach net-zero goals. We need new technologies that don't currently exist. We are also still relying on technology development to make some of the things we need cheaper. Companies see much of it as too risky to invest themselves. The green technology train still needs a bigger push from policy to reduce that risk.

10.2.2 Creating an Informed Public

It might sound obvious that people won't buy something they've never heard of, but that is part of the challenge we are facing. Closing

[5] See Nemet (2019); Bento and Fontes (2015).

knowledge gaps will be critical for getting the right technologies in the right places.

The problem extends beyond just having heard of the technologies. Most people know what a solar panel is. They may not, however, know what the solar panel can do, or how to install it. Just as important as having heard about the technology, they also need to *trust it*.

The issue of trust is especially important because most zero-carbon technologies require a big upfront investment. Whether it is solar panels or heat pumps on buildings, EVs or efficient industrial systems, all come with a big initial cost. No one will spend much money without confidence they will get something back later on.

Almost by definition, there is uncertainty about new technologies and a lack of trust. Incumbent manufacturers may also spread disinformation about new products, as we have seen repeatedly for EVs and heat pumps. Policy-makers must respond to these challenges.

There are different ways to do this. For large industrial plants, it might make sense to send expert advisors to help directly. Simple information campaigns can be effective at reaching households and smaller energy users if they are well targeted. Regulatory agencies are essential for building trust, by ensuring that lemons are not being sold to households and that the new technologies really do achieve what they claim.

Setting targets and spending rules can help to build trust too. For example, demonstrating that a technology works for government activities can give confidence it will work elsewhere too. Setting targets like the phasing out of fossil fuel cars by a certain date gives a clear signal that the new technology is expected to become the dominant one by then.

Ultimately, information flows through many different channels. The mass media can reach large numbers of people, so may be good for raising initial awareness, but messages through personal contacts often have more impact. Social media has blurred the distinction between the two and has become a key tool of persuasion in the modern world, but disinformation has also become widespread. It may need to become a deliberate government policy to tackle problems of information about zero-carbon options head on.

None of this is easy, but there are people that can help. Communications and marketing experts face these challenges every day. They can help to make a climate-informed public.

10.2.3 *Getting Regulations Right*

Regulations do two main things. They set the rules of the economic game, and they ensure that products and institutions can be relied upon and are safe. Commercial exchanges in markets also follow rules that are set by regulations. For example, electricity markets have detailed rules that companies must follow.

Regulations can also help to build trust. If we pay more for a washing machine that has an A+++ energy efficiency rating, we assume that someone measured its energy consumption. We also assume that the insulation material we install in our homes has been thoroughly tested for fire risk.

Economists generally don't like regulations. They say they are inefficient and costly, compared to taxes. Politicians don't like them either, because they force people and companies to fill out paperwork and follow rules, which no one likes doing. That's why politicians sometimes brag about how many regulations they've scrapped.

But without regulations, nothing would work, and people wouldn't trust anything. And with the creation of new goods, markets and technologies comes new rules. We need to be sure that the new products are safe and really do reduce emissions.

As we discuss in Section 10.3, there is a role for regulation to keep us away from the edge of chaos. Sometimes, however, government regulation can prevent people from doing climate-friendly things. Usually, these regulations can be changed, but it takes time and delays the transition. Seeing off these issues before they arise could help a lot.

An obvious example is the case of onshore wind power in the UK. Wind power became the cheapest way to generate electricity, but no one could build new windmills on land because of planning rules. Planning rules of course have a purpose and should not be ignored. However, the rules effectively banned wind power and were not particularly helpful to the British countryside. It didn't matter how cheap wind power was if no one could get planning permission to build.

Similar planning rules can make it difficult to upgrade heating systems, improve windows or fit insulation in historical buildings. Again, it is important to respect listed buildings, but obtaining permission is usually painfully slow. Although it may be possible to use heat pumps in old buildings, getting permission takes time and money.

Planning rules are always influenced by politics, but many other barriers occur simply because of neglect. In some countries, it is difficult to connect solar farms to national grids, because regulations are outdated. Regulations on steel quality may make it impossible to use steel produced by electric arc furnaces.

A good start would be preparing a list of all the existing rules that prevent people and businesses from reducing emissions. Then the same for the new regulations needed. Some existing regulations may be there for good reasons, but many will be either outdated or intended for other purposes. If so, they can be updated. A path for reform must follow. Let's stop scoring climate own goals.

10.2.4 Greasing the Wheels of Private Finance

Restrictions on borrowing can be even more annoying than government regulations. In theory at least, bad rules should at least apply to everyone equally. But financial constraints apply mostly to the poor. It simply isn't fair.

In the past few years, electric cars were a good example. With much lower running costs, they can offer better value for money than oil-based cars. But only people who could pay the high upfront cost could get them. The rich got cheaper and cleaner transport, while the poor had to get by on the old technologies. And, as we found out in Chapter 5, it gets worse for poor people if they don't have a charging point at home.

Government subsidies for electric cars, therefore, mostly benefited rich people – at least at first. The moving technology train means that soon everyone can benefit, as electric cars become cheaper to buy as well as run. However, subsidies will probably be gone by then.

Heat pumps have the same problem. They are another way for the rich to get subsidies and save money, while the poor make do with old technologies. Tenants may somehow need to convince their landlords to upgrade their heating systems.

There are examples in the corporate world too. Energy-efficient technologies reduce companies' energy bills and make them more competitive. But they need to invest first, and they need access to finance to do that. Big companies (e.g. Tesco) are at the front of the queue to benefit because banks are used to working with them. Small ones (e.g. the corner pub) must make do.

We cannot escape that banks lend where they see profit. The issue of how poor people can access finance goes well beyond climate change. But it seems especially unfair when both the poor people and the planet are denied the benefits. And most people think small businesses deserve more support, not less.

Can policy help? Governments can usually borrow money much more easily and cheaply than companies. They can also encourage private banks to lend through loan subsidies or guarantees, and some schemes have been highly profitable for banks.

The important point is to understand what the financial constraints are. Barriers because of wealth require different solutions to barriers because of size. When poor, facing higher fuel taxes doesn't provide better access to loans, quite the reverse.

Many countries use publicly owned development banks to serve the needs not covered by commercial banks. This could really help, if the development bank is well-guided.

However, there won't be a one-size-fits-all policy solution that cuts across technologies, sectors and countries. The policy needs will probably change over time. But whichever way is chosen, the wheels of finance need greasing if they are to support our policy goals.

10.2.5 Rethink Public Finance

Government budgets have been very tight since bailing out the banks after the 2008 crash, and again after the Covid pandemic. We went for austerity after spending to keep the economy afloat. Since the aftermath of the financial crisis, countries have become particularly concerned with the levels of public debt.

Greece, Italy, Spain and much of southern Europe were on the brink of insolvency, and Northern Europe wasn't so keen on bailing out what they thought was uncontrolled public spending in the South. But once they got Greece to halve the size of its government, many people were thrown into poverty.

Tight public finances mean that after half of government revenues gets spent on public health, education, social services and pensions, there is usually not a lot left for investment in public infrastructure, technology and R&D. However, there is a major difference between spending on operational expenditures and spending on investment: investment is often profitable.

Economists will say that if the investment is truly profitable, the private sector will take it on; therefore, it's not the role of the government to take this on. They also argue that the government taking on such investments bears the risk of state capture by private interests.

The reality is that much of the zero-carbon technology we need is profitable, and despite that, it's not really happening. It would seem like the private sector is just lazy. Companies probably have their own reasons not to get involved in certain types of projects, but in the end, they have to get done. But public finances being so tight, the government is waiting for companies to do it, and companies are waiting for the government to do it.

Take, for example, public chargers for EVs. It's clear there are not enough of them outside of big cities. In some towns, there aren't any at all. There are EVs nonetheless in those towns, as motivated people go to all sorts of lengths to get their EVs charged elsewhere. Clearly, companies are not bothered to deliver for those people, even though charging points are largely profitable.

The public sector could do this profitably. But the investment competes with spending on education and health, and in a drive to reduce deficits, investment typically gets thrown out, on the grounds that the private sector can take it on. But given it is profitable investment, although it bears some risk, it shouldn't technically count as deficit. It doesn't for companies, why should it for the state?

Brazil has got around this problem by separating public investment from public spending, getting the investment done by its national development bank called BNDES. The bank is capitalised by the government, but is profitable, which means it does not add to the deficit. It is also run slightly separately from the government, so it is not as constrained by politics, and its spending does not compete with priorities like health and education.

BNDES' aim is to invest in the gaps left by private banks, and there are lots of them. This includes zero-carbon problems, infrastructure, agriculture, but also R&D and support for building new industries. It imposes requirements to ensure that the money is used to build sustainable businesses in the country, rather than funding imports. This is how, for example, a globally competitive wind industry was developed in Brazil. This could be done in the UK and every country in the world.[6]

10.2.6 Reform International Climate Finance

For many developing countries, rethinking public finance is not enough. They still need dollars to pay for the zero-carbon

[6] See Grubb et al. (2021a) for a case study on Brazil's wind industry, which may not have happened without the structure imposed by BNDES. The UK set up the British Business Bank in 2014, but it remains small with respect to total fiscal expenditure (about 1%), in contrast with the BNDES (Carreras, 2020).

technologies. African countries and Caribbean islands don't produce solar panels, nor EVs or heat pumps. It would be good if they could, but, in the near term, they will have to get them from abroad. And for that, they need hard currency.

Currency risk, meaning unexpected changes in exchange rates, is the main problem. It puts off international climate investors from lending dollars to these countries. There are not a million ways to solve the problem. Currency risk must be 'hedged' by providing insurance. Financial facilities must be created that offer currency hedges to investors to reduce the risk. It would need substantial initial investment.

For example, the World Bank lends US dollars to developing countries using its own currency risk hedging mechanism. This is great for World Bank loans, but it doesn't help other investors. Something equivalent but much bigger is need to do this at global scale. We need an international facility to offer insurance against currency risk. The World Bank Group's 'Multilateral Investment Guarantee Agency' (MIGA) offers such a mechanism for political risk, but nothing exists at scale for currency risk.

There is also 'country risk'. This is currently in the hands of rating agencies. When a rating agency like Moody's downgrades a country, some investors pull out. The country loses access to some of its dollars, and currency risk increases. The rating agency's judgement becomes a self-fulfilling prophecy.

Often, there is little the country can do. The government can balance its budgets and even set carbon taxes, but it doesn't get US dollars.

And then the US Federal Reserve might increase interest rates. When this happens, investors take their US dollars away from developing countries. This is bad already, but if the rating agency then issues a downgrade, more dollars disappear. It can spiral into crisis.

Under these conditions, it should not be surprising that developing countries do not use their US dollars to buy zero-carbon equipment. Any additional borrowing could push the country closer to crisis. The system clearly needs reform.

Mia Mottley, the Prime Minister of Barbados, agrees. She has gone on record saying that the global financial system must be reformed if we are to tackle climate change. Certainly, the debates at climate conferences would be a lot easier if access to US dollars was not such a barrier.

10.2.7 The Carbon Pricing Hammer

It is always funny to think back to how our lives were different even 20 years ago. Back in 2007, when the UK's Climate Change Act was adopted, most people were familiar with the internet, but smartphones were new. Zero-carbon technologies were also in a different place. We could have set a super-high carbon price, and the result would not have been lots of solar panels, cheap EVs and offshore wind power. Emissions might have fallen a bit, but mainly because we would have hammered our economy without transforming it. And we would have definitely harmed our ability to do so.

The hammer analogy is accurate in other ways too. For two decades, economists have talked about 'getting the prices right'. Some economists still think only a carbon price can solve all our problems. Carbon pricing is the hammer, the only tool in their climate toolbox. Therefore, these economists can only see nails.

The awkward truth is that, increasingly, the prices are already right, and still not that much is happening. Solar power is now the cheapest form of electricity generation (increasingly even including battery costs) in many countries, but the rate of uptake is still often moderate. There have also long been cost-effective energy efficiency measures not taken up.

But for all that, the EU's emissions trading scheme (the EU-ETS) has had some (though limited) successes. It killed coal power in the UK and dealt coal a heavy blow across the EU. This was easy because natural gas power stations were ready to take up the slack. Increasingly, wind and solar do this job too, although largely because of other European policies.

There is, therefore, some role for carbon pricing. When the technologies are widely available in the market, it may make the crucial difference for getting them used. It may also be helpful in countering the lower oil and gas prices we could see when we use less of them.[7] It could raise revenues for governments that can be used to improve resilience. And most importantly, it can ensure we don't slide back into fossil fuels, shutting the door behind us.

It is all quite niche though. And the hammer is not a precise tool. When we tax carbon, we tax almost everything. We, therefore, cannot set a high tax rate without creating inequalities and upsetting people, who then strike back at the next elections. The weak get hammered even more than the strong.[8] And we are doing our hammering in the dark: we hit everything, hoping that *something* comes out of it. There are no guarantees it will work.

Could carbon pricing be less like a hammer? When we take the technology perspective, there is no reason to have the same carbon price on all sectors nor in all countries. As the EU-ETS showed, it doesn't make sense to have the same carbon price for electricity generation (easy to transition) as for cement (technically difficult). A high tax on a sector that hasn't yet found a way to decarbonise is not helpful. It may make it more difficult for companies to find solutions.

The problem is that carbon pricing is well and truly stuck in the old way of thinking. If we could just get over the offence made to economists, targeted sectoral carbon prices could in fact be really useful. That would allow the carbon price to be high where it needs to be high and low where it needs to be low. But this is a debate that's not even started yet.

10.2.8 Devise Policy Mixes for Market Creation

If this all sounds ambitious, it's because it really is. We need new thinking. We need alternative policies. Policies that will drive transformational change. Policies with more of a technology focus.

[7] Although, as discussed in Chapter 8, fossil fuel prices could both go up and down with decarbonisation, or even become very volatile, depending on whether expectations lead to excess or insufficient production capacity, or alternating between the two.

[8] See Grubb et al. (2014); Sharpe (2023).

We need zero-carbon technologies to get us out of trouble, and the aim of policy is to help them do that. How much help the technologies need depends on how well developed they are. For technologies at an early stage of development, markets don't yet exist, pricing is all over the place and investment is scarce. Uncertainty is high and confidence is low, because quality is not monitored or regulated.

Take, for example, the steel industry. If we go beyond recycling scrap, green steel doesn't yet have a market. It needs green hydrogen, which also doesn't yet have a market. We don't know the price of either of these things. Without an established green hydrogen market (with reliable demand and supply), potential producers have low confidence in how much they could sell. They, therefore, don't invest. Steelmakers have low confidence in getting the green hydrogen they need. They also don't invest.

Without intervention, both green steel and green hydrogen go nowhere. Recently, however, the German government has set up an institution that guarantees to buy and sell green hydrogen at fixed prices. This gives companies confidence to invest, and a market is created. A similar thing is happening in India.[9]

The trick is to find as many users of green hydrogen as possible (fertilisers, air travel, long distance freight, steel). Then, demand can be scaled up, and costs can be reduced. If the market becomes large enough, and costs low enough, the old technologies can be pushed out. Can green hydrogen prices come down by enough to unlock all this? We don't know, and we need to find out.

It's a similar coordination game in many other sectors. By definition, markets don't exist for new technologies. Markets are not created by magic. They need rules that are set by the government. They need someone to enforce the rules. They need a combination of policies.

At least in early development, regulation to create the rules of the game is the priority. Although prices do matter at the start,

[9] For Germany, see www.bmwk.de/Navigation/EN/hydrogen/national-hydrogen-strategy.html. For India, see https://mnre.gov.in/national-green-hydrogen-mission/.

guaranteed income is more important. Once technologies are produced at volume, prices start to come down anyway. We've done it already for renewables and for EVs. We need to do it now for the other sectors lagging behind, like aviation, steel, chemicals, fertilisers and freight transport. Because it is too unstable, carbon pricing doesn't appear to help (see Chapter 9).[10]

Sometimes, the chicken and egg problem is so severe that no one will start the process. Here, there is a clear role for government to be the first buyer, as is happening with German green hydrogen. This can kick-start the technology development process, reducing prices for others. Other policy examples include electrifying public vehicles, installing the first EV charging points or installing zero-carbon heating systems in public buildings. Doing this gives a reason for the private sector to develop capabilities (such as installing heat pumps), which later become used by private companies and individuals.

More broadly, effective policy mixes will involve several moving parts, with separate instruments taking charge of:

1. Creating a market for a new clean product with its rules of operation and compliance, such as with a facility that buys and sells;
2. Creating an incentive for people to engage with the clean product, such as with a subsidy;
3. Kick-starting the diffusion process for the product to expand production, such as with public procurement;
4. Regulating the phase-out of the dirty products, such as with energy/carbon efficiency regulations that enforce product standards.

The critical point is these four elements *reinforce* each other. A subsidy or carbon tax won't be effective if a market is not created. The creation of a market will not be successful if no one can afford the

[10] Feed-in tariffs and contracts for difference, in the case of renewables, which absorb market risk from electricity prices, have been hugely successful (Grubb et al., 2021a; Anadon et al., 2022). For EVs, subsidies helped until battery costs came down enough to begin removing subsidies. We have yet to see evidence that carbon prices support technological change (Lilliestam et al., 2020).

product. Building the market with public procurement can increase production capacity and bring costs down for everyone else. Regulating out old products forces companies to innovate and develop new solutions.

Economists recognise some of these issues as market failures. The coordination problem is well known, as is under-investment in new technology. However, it's not clear whether that way of thinking is useful. It assumes that markets already exist and that problems can be solved through price adjustments. We are creating the economy of tomorrow, and this is never something that could be delivered by the market alone, or by subsidies and taxes.[11]

Finally, in contrast to current economic wisdom,[12] general public R&D subsidies help with new technology but not market creation, increasing returns or even spreading knowledge. R&D subsidies were important decades ago at the early stage of creation of new technologies (e.g. wind power dates from the 1980s), but here we are talking mostly about market-shaping policies for existing technologies. Support needs to be targeted.

10.3 ACTIVELY MANAGE RISK AND CREATE RESILIENCE

We start to hit on a paradox. We want to prevent climate chaos, so need the zero-carbon transition to move as fast as possible. However, a faster transition means more risk for financial, economic and social-political instability. We need policies to manage that too.

This section explores some of the key policies. We start with directing investment to the right place and *guiding an orderly phase-out of brown*. Then, we discuss the risk of *capacity constraints* and the need to *diversify production*. Lastly, we look at how to manage risks of *financial instability* and the need to *spread the new wealth*.

[11] See, for instance, Kattel et al. (2018).

[12] For example, in Acemoglu (2002); Acemoglu et al. (2012); Aghion et al. (2021).

10.3.1 Guide an Orderly Phase-Out of Brown

An obvious target for resilience policy is the place where we know for sure there will be pain: the decline of old industry. The first step to take is also obvious, limiting the amount of investment that goes into it there. Today's investment could be tomorrow's stranded assets.

The financial sector is already well aware of the risk of stranded assets. We commonly hear fund managers talk of 'peak oil demand'. We know that the losses could run to trillions of dollars.[13] A sudden destruction of wealth on this scale is clearly a risk to financial stability, as we discussed in Chapter 9.

Banning investment into sectors like fossil fuels has an appeal as a simple solution but is not really doable in practice. Even if we somehow blocked Europeans and Americans from investing in oil, other countries could carry on. We can't even stop a coal mine being built in Australia, even less in India or Indonesia, and we certainly cannot stop companies from investing in new equipment for current mines.

In short, as long as there is demand for fossil fuels, we don't lose the brown industry overnight. So, if we want people still to get to work, some investment will remain necessary.

But how much investment is too much? How can we direct companies to invest sensibly? Technically, it is true that carbon prices could help to direct investment. Expectations of high future carbon prices, if they could be trusted, could in principle be powerful. But as discussed in Chapter 9, the carbon price tomorrow could be anything from zero to any value. Carbon taxes can also be abandoned anytime at any time. We've made little progress in decades towards comprehensive global carbon pricing, except in sectors where it already existed.[14] It would be dangerously deluding ourselves to think that these expectations could be achieved.

We see three key factors. First, policy-makers must communicate sensible long-term plans for the transition. Second,

[13] See Mercure et al. (2018b); Semieniuk et al. (2022).

[14] See Agnolucci et al. (2024).

technological change must become obvious. Third, companies must believe what governments say and what they see around them.

The risks for ordinary people are even more important. It means avoiding Thatcher and the coal mines all over again. It means getting rid of combustion without getting the ugly symptoms of post-industrial decline or creating new inequalities on top of existing ones.

In one of their more useful contributions, economists talk about problems with the 'mobility of labour'. Simply put, these are the things that stop workers moving to new jobs. The most important ones are a lack of access to suitable training and industries not developing in the communities that need the jobs.

This points towards policy solutions. Offering retraining is an obvious one, but it requires support as well, because people cannot work while in full-time training. What gets taught is obviously an important issue too.

Where industries should be situated is more controversial. Most people are attached to where they live and would prefer not to move. But bringing new jobs to declining areas is difficult – and becomes more difficult over time. It is important to step in before the long-term effects of decline begin to appear and act on economic diversification. It is feasible though, because as we described in Chapter 7, it's been done before.

There is no silver bullet here. Every town has its own advantages that could attract companies. Each town must play to these advantages, but they also need help from central governments to capture new opportunities. Having a local labour force that is available and willing to work, even if training is needed, should be a bonus. Active engagement between local government and companies is important for saving those who are left behind.

When all else fails, the social support described below is a last resort. Inevitably, some people will come to rely on it, as some people do already. The goal of policy should be to avoid whole communities becoming dependent, and for that, they must be supported in moving on from old industries.

10.3.2 Beware of Capacity Constraints

As discussed in Chapters 3 and 5, the concept in standard economics standard economics context that the economy tends towards full capacity is pretty strange. In reality, full capacity happens when things go wrong (e.g. after the Covid pandemic). Think about the London underground example in Chapter 3. Companies don't want things to go wrong like that and, therefore, usually do not operate at full capacity. Policy can help them to stay away from the edge of chaos.

In the zero-carbon transition, avoiding capacity constraints in green technologies is both obvious and critical. However, avoiding capacity constraints in brown industries is also important and, in some ways, more difficult.

Take the brownest sector of all, fossil fuels. The whole aim of the transition is to get rid of most of it. Many people would say the faster we get rid of it, the better.

Let's take it to the extreme. What would happen if production stopped tomorrow? The answer is, we would be in trouble. Most of our cars would run out of fuel. We soon wouldn't be able to heat most of our homes. Even those of us that only use electricity might find ourselves cut off for parts of the day.

Maybe that's not realistic. So, what if production dropped by half within a year? There would be frantic competition for the remaining half. Prices would shoot up. The moderately poor would end up spending most of their money on essential fuel. Huge amounts of money would go from ordinary people to rich owners of oil companies. The very poor would have to do without altogether. Inflation would follow.[15]

Not so unrealistic now. When Russian gas stopped flowing to Europe, gas became six to ten times more expensive. Energy companies made historic profits, and a cost of living and inflation crisis started. As always, the poorest were hit hardest. Yes, the

[15] See Semieniuk et al. (2025).

crisis pushed people and companies to greener alternatives (but also towards more coal!), but this takes time. In the short term, Europeans were stuck paying high prices for imported gas.[16]

The European example showed just how bad capacity constraints are for stability, whether in green or brown. First, we need to reduce fossil fuel demand; then companies will reduce supply (and capacity) in response. We must not let reductions in supply capacity get ahead. If we do, the edge of chaos beckons.

For brown industries, this is tricky. Too much investment, and we get stranded assets. Too little, and we get capacity constraints. The international dimension adds further complexity – although no one wants to be left with the stranded assets, a reliable source of fossil fuels is important for military use until we see meaningful technological change in defence.

Because investment in brown industries is usually long-lived, we cannot expect the market to solve this problem on its own. Coordination between government and private companies is necessary to maintain stability. Otherwise, we get price chaos, and then inflation and more inequality.

For green products, the need to avoid capacity constraints is obvious. We can hit capacity constraints because of higher demand as well as lower supply, as we saw in the period after COVID-19 lockdowns. At this time, there were shortages of all sorts of products, including microchips, which led to shortages of cars. Inflation took off, but more notable was the instability in prices of some goods like second-hand cars.

We can relate this to the model of economic growth that we presented in Chapter 5. Rising demand from product innovation pushes the economy towards full capacity and increasing price volatility. Investment in expanding capacity and process innovation pulls the economy away from that volatility. It's an endless tug of war between demand growth and capacity growth. *We build capacity to respond to demand in order for prices to remain stable and avoid inflation.*

[16] See Kemfert et al. (2022).

More capacity always means more resilience. But in a transitioning economy, it's much more complex because the composition of demand changes rapidly. Importantly, demand can change much faster than we can build new capacity. This is why we often see instability during technology transitions.

Green capacity constraints could slow the entire transition. For example, after COVID-19, there was a scarcity in critical minerals needed to manufacture zero-carbon technologies. Soaring prices caused cost declines of green technologies to stop and reverse, for a period.[17] The same could happen again.

Just as importantly, the transition will make people rely on the green technologies. We cannot force people to rely on something that is unreliable!

Again, the market alone will not solve this problem. It takes years to build new mines for critical minerals. Huge price swings in the meantime may benefit a few companies but hurt most people and the poorest people especially. Some guidance from policy-makers is needed.

For example, sometimes experts predict a shortage of a critical mineral, but the private sector will not invest because the risks are too high. We are now seeing an example of such cooperation in critical minerals, partly driven by geopolitics. Here, there is a role for the public sector to play: working with the private sector to reduce the risks and potentially invest directly. Usually, further private sector investment follows, helping to stabilise prices.

Some developing countries already guide their economies using national development banks to avoid price instabilities. Advanced economies have mostly abandoned the practice but could revive it. Development banks are profitable and not a drain on public budgets.[18] Their profits could be used to reduce other transition costs.

[17] See IEA (2021, 2023a); Boer et al. (2021).

[18] Loans from publicly owned development banks do not usually count as deficit on government books, as they can technically be profitable assets. And it is helpful to use a development bank as a vehicle to carry risk, which operates at an arm's length from politics.

Policy-makers must think carefully about where there might be capacity constraints. This sort of industrial policy is frowned upon within traditional economics. However, in practice, it has long been happening in the US, EU and UK, not just in China. Its role has grown substantially in recent years.

10.3.3 Spread the Risk for Sustainable Economic Development

A longer-term aim is *economic diversification*. Financial advisors tell us to diversify our investments to reduce overall risk. The same is true for the economy. Areas that produce lots of different things will not be so vulnerable to future technological advances. Regions that only produce fossil fuels, or manufacture brown products, will be at risk.

The thing is, diversifying an economy is extremely difficult. It means the same as economic development. Achieving development is hard in poor countries. As we saw with Alberta in Chapter 9, it can be hard for advanced economies too. This is mostly a problem of regional (local) economic development.

We know from Chapter 5 that similar companies tend to cluster together. In the upswing of new sectors, they benefit from sharing ideas, expertise and lower transport costs. But we also know that, past the golden age (which is where fossil fuels are), clustering becomes a problem. As with phasing out the brown and ensuring economic capacity, we need policy to guide the economy, because it doesn't find its way on its own.

Again, we get into industrial strategy, which economists have traditionally warned against. And again, we hit against the trade-off between optimisation (why all those firms cluster together) and resilience (avoiding the plunge into oblivion in Chapter 7). The role of policy is to help build resilience.

The need for diversification is obviously most urgent in areas dependent on brown activities, where there is a race to develop new capacity before decline sets in. However, all regions can benefit from spreading the risk. And while the priority in replacing brown is to create jobs as quickly as possible, diversification is about creating lots of different kinds of jobs in the places where the risks of decline are concentrated.

Again, there is no recipe that is guaranteed to work every time, and diversifying requires hard and persistent effort. Regions must start with the advantages they already have and find ways to leverage those advantages to attract investment.

For example, we cannot expect pitmen or oil rig operators to begin writing complex computer code or become artificial intelligence experts. We maybe could expect their children to do so, but this takes a generation. More realistic is that petrochemical hubs could transition to hydrogen as a chemical feedstock, using the current workforce. Then, there are possibilities to move into other aspects of the hydrogen economy, and so on, until hydrogen becomes only a small part of the economy.

In that spirit, it seems reasonable to take each industrial region and assess in which green products it could build competitiveness.[19] And there is no reason to limit the list to green products. There could be strong growth from AI, biotechnology and all the other new products that will generate economic demand.

One important, but often overlooked, factor in diversifying is the need to create a place where workers actually want to live. Diversification likely means attracting some new workers while keeping most of the old ones. Creating an environment that people want to live in, for example, with high-quality public services and low pollution levels, is a necessary condition. Because it drives away investment, industrial decline can make this impossible.

Spreading the risk is clearly important. It allows policy-makers to stay one step ahead of technology trends. It may not sound exciting, and it will be hard work, but it is necessary to ensure long-term resilience.

[19] See Mealy and Teytelboym (2022).

10.3.4 Ensure Appropriate Financial Supervision

The financial sector remains an important source of instability. We only need to look back to 2008 to see how it can spread chaos. That happened because of large amounts of unsound mortgage lending, a panic in banking and a plunge in house prices. Imagine what climate change and stranded assets could do.

Most people would like to see a financial sector that is both smaller and more heavily regulated. However, some people say that we need big finance to fund all the new zero-carbon technologies. Either way, we need to make sure the financial sector doesn't tip itself over the edge of chaos.

We described what could go wrong in Chapter 9. The financial sector can be the source of trouble, but it can also amplify other problems. Policies are needed to manage both risks.

Current policy often aims at making sure information about climate risk is widely available to banks and other financial organisations. For example, companies increasingly have to disclose their emissions. Stress-testing exercises show climate risks. This is a good starting point.

It does not go far enough though. After all, banks should have known about the risks they were taking on before the global financial crisis. Climate change is far more complex than all of that. Artificial intelligence and the other new technologies are too.

And, importantly, although investors love casinos, we must rein them in. New technology will offer lots of opportunity for risky, speculative betting, which can build a big house of cards ready to collapse. And when it collapses, it brings everything else down with it. Contradictory investment in both green and brown technologies at the same time will create all the conditions needed for a financial crash. We need to control this.

First, we must take control of the current accumulation of 'systemic' risk. But we're going in the wrong direction, as we increase deregulation of the financial sector. Wealthy people like doing this because it allows bankers and rich entrepreneurs to make money more quickly. If we put in charge people with too great an interest in deregulation, chances are it brings us right to the edge of chaos.

Second, policy can tackle some of the specific risks. For example, at some point in the transition, investors will realise that oil has no future, as they already have done for coal in the US and Europe. The value of oil companies will quickly fall to near zero. Are banks and pension funds sufficiently prepared?

Any financial company that can be expected to go under in this scenario must be called out and made to change its behaviour.[20] Building systemic risk where trouble can already be foreseen is irresponsible. Similar scenarios for climate-related extreme weather events and risks from other transitions can be created, and the same approach can be applied.

More general policy is also needed to limit the financial sector amplifying other risks. Many countries have reserve requirements, and some have restrictions on bank lending.[21] As we move into a period of greater uncertainty, there is a case for tighter regulation.

The argument that stricter regulation would limit green investment is probably not true. Regulation aims to limit unacceptable behaviour and financial products risky at the whole system level, while green investment is not particularly risky.

Ultimately, we cannot avoid the performance–stability trade-off, and we will need to prioritise stability more than in recent decades, in anticipation of the extra strain being put on the system.

10.3.5 *Spread the New Wealth*

Finally, we need to ensure that there are no people left behind. We need this to maintain social stability. We need to look after the people who lose their jobs through no fault of their own. If all else fails, we need a strong safety net. We can do that by sharing some of the new wealth that will be generated.

[20] That's the purpose of doing banking 'stress tests', to test the resilience of individual banks in the context of a hypothetical crash (BoE, 2022).

[21] Liquid money set aside by companies to absorb unforeseen losses.

In theory, some of this is easy. As we saw in Chapter 1, we should all get cheaper electricity and transport. But this won't happen if electricity companies and EV charging networks keep prices high. Instead, a few rich shareholders will get all the benefits.

A combination of price regulation and competition policy can deal with these issues. This means regulators will need to be on the ball. In transitions, things change quickly, and companies will do everything they can to make large profits. For example, while most countries already regulate electricity providers, companies that provide public charging for EVs are mostly not regulated. The result is high prices.

There are also tricky issues in electricity markets, like in the UK, that rely on the 'marginal' cost approach. These markets combine cheap electricity from renewables with expensive electricity from natural gas. But, the electricity price is set by the expensive bit generated from natural gas.

This means that ordinary people don't see the benefits of cheap renewable electricity. Instead, they go to the electricity companies and their shareholders. A few people gain and most lose out. Climate policy is blamed for high bills. Market reform is sorely needed.

More broadly, we must ensure that everyone can get the benefits. Although everyone uses electricity, the biggest cost savings will be for people who use heat pumps and EVs. This needs to be everyone, not just rich people. The wheels of finance must be greased appropriately.

Even if we manage all of this, there is still the question of the people left behind, those that lose their jobs and the people in the towns that lose their main employers. This is where the social safety net comes in.

Money helps of course, both for the people that receive social benefits and for the wider community in which they spend it. We already mentioned retraining, which is an important part of the story, if not always easy. Funding for new businesses is always useful. It may be possible to create government jobs in some places – after all, the government will be taking on new responsibilities during the transition.

What is missing though is the human touch. These people are not problems that can be solved by throwing money their way. A public presence that listens and responds to their needs can help to hold communities together. It may even find new ways to generate wealth in the areas left behind.

Unfortunately, doing this is labour-intensive and expensive. Many people will argue that the time and money would be better spent elsewhere. There are two problems with this argument. First, these areas will have people available to do the work. Second, the aim is not to maximise economic production, but it is to avoid creating new inequalities and marginalisation. Not least, because those at the losing end could otherwise make the whole plan fail. We do not want big holes in our safety net.

10.4 THE NEED FOR POLICY COORDINATION

None of this is going to be easy. We need multiple overlapping policies from different government departments that will complement and, sometimes, contradict each other. Compared to the idea of setting a carbon tax and hoping for the best, it seems hopelessly complex.

One thing that should be clear by now is that an industrial strategy is needed. Ultimately, we want a new green economy that we can work in and live by. Any region that destroys the old industries but does not attract the new industries could have a problem. It could be headed into decline, while missing much of the investment boom of the low-carbon transition. This means ageing infrastructure, lack of jobs, declining investment and difficulties to move forward. It's a bleak de-growth scenario.

Since the 1970s, most economists have viewed industrial strategy as a bad thing. There is too much temptation for governments to give money to the wrong people. Better to trust the market instead. More recently, however, industrial strategy is becoming more popular. Ironically, governments have led the way, and economists have grudgingly followed.

In truth, as we have described throughout this book, some industrial policy has always been there, quietly happening in the background. It has usually been called different things, like innovation policy or national security.

In the UK, industrial policy has focused on addressing clean growth, artificial intelligence, shaping future mobility and population ageing.[22] In 2017, this approach was officially called the UK's industrial strategy. The title was abolished a few years later, but most of the policy remained in place.

In the US, an explicit industrial strategy was adopted with Joe Biden's Chips Act and Inflation Reduction Act, something that would have been unthinkable just a few years earlier. In the EU, the Carbon Border Adjustment Mechanism is part of a much broader set of policies that tackle industrial competitiveness. China does not try to hide the sectors it wants to prioritise for economic growth.

Around the world, the pendulum has thus swung against the traditional economic view of letting markets decide. Industrial policy is the new fashion. In time, industrial strategy might be linked formally to theories of economic growth like the one we described in Chapter 5.

If we are to put all the policies outlined above into a single package, it will probably need to be through an industrial strategy. How else could we coordinate between the various government departments, private companies, financial sectors and other interested parties?

However, current industrial strategies fall well short of what is required. They do recognise that the road from innovation to market is long and difficult.[23] They also recognise that other countries are

22 See the UK's 2017 industrial strategy, www.gov.uk/government/publications/industrial-strategy-building-a-britain-fit-for-the-future. Since late 2023, the website warns the reader that this policy has been abolished.

23 See Grubb et al. (2014); Sharpe (2023).

trying to get there first. They even go beyond the traditional narrow focus on economic growth to recognise climate targets. But they are focused entirely on performance and not on stability.

It's an improvement, but we have not yet fully escaped the old way of thinking. We are missing two important lessons from complexity theory, that everything is connected and that complex systems like our economy are unstable. We need to bring other people into the discussion, for example, financial regulators and social security departments.

Maybe, it's no longer called industrial strategy. Transition strategy might be a better name, but it doesn't really matter. What we need is everyone working together towards a common goal. That goal is a decarbonised world in which everyone is better off.

Conclusion

Given all our great technological progress and the profitable potential of green opportunities, why are we designing such poor strategies towards zero-carbon economies? It's time to share reflections after finishing writing this book. As practitioners, we both spend most of our time travelling and talking to officials in ministries of finance, central banks and other ministries, academics and campaigners. What's going on?

In the last few years, the narrative around reducing emissions has gone upside down as we discovered that zero-carbon technologies were now cheaper than fossil fuels. That in itself should have been enough, we would have thought, to start seriously moving on from fossil fuels and build a sustainable economy. It's not just to save the planet anymore; it also makes money.

But it seems that we endlessly get bogged down into endless conversations and do nothing. Each climate conference, one after the other, seems to make less progress than the previous one. We get stuck into horrible debates about why advanced economies do not finance the transition in developing economies. But advanced economies need to get their own houses in order. The investment needed is huge. But the curious thing is, it's all profitable investment, and banks are desperate for investable opportunities, so where's the problem? We seem perfectly able to finance fossil fuels at that scale, which are now increasingly *more* expensive than green technologies. That seems to make no sense.

Could it be the fault of economists if we make little progress? After all, some have repeated for decades that the transition was not worth investing in because the damages from climate change did not justify the costs (using numbers plucked out from the air). Others have moralised about the 'sin' of borrowing, repeating over and over like a mantra that we can't afford the loans, neither in the UK nor elsewhere.

Austerity policy was supposed to get us out of the high debt hangover from bailing out banks during the financial crisis. But economies across Europe never really got back to normal. Spending less doesn't necessarily reduce debt if it harms the ability of the economy to create wealth. Now, outdated spending rules in governments, such as in the UK, prevent them from investing in the greatest economic opportunity of a generation, and the source of the next great wave of economic growth.

As a result, nobody can agree who will invest in this big opportunity. But oddly, we are still able to we still throw endless money at old technology, spending rules or not, which we know is now headed towards decline. We invest in assets that are at risk of becoming stranded. It's because we do the halfway house, where we finance just enough growth in green technology, to make brown investments questionable, from a financial risk perspective. But at the same time, we throw money at brown technology too and find ourselves in a contradiction. We are unable to scale up the green finance and get on with things.

Poor and developing countries, may not be able to invest the US dollars. But the economic opportunity is not any less profitable in these countries. It's because we like to rate those countries as risky, and are unwilling to hedge that risk, that we refrain from investing in the huge economic opportunities. They need their dollars for oil, essential supplies and interest on existing debt. There should be win-win opportunities for international finance.

And we have the arrogance of telling off those countries for borrowing abroad, when they need the dollars just to get by, mostly for oil. Most of their dollar revenues are paid to advanced economies as interest on existing loans, and the rest goes to essential supplies.

We are wasting the growth opportunity of a generation because we repeat the mantra over and over that it is too expensive to move on from fossil fuels.

Meanwhile, the transition is slowly but surely progressing, enough to pile up financial and geopolitical risk around the world. Big oil producing countries can see the risks ahead. Energy markets are unstable. Inflation returns. There is a cost of living crisis. And we throw up our hands in the air asking what to do.

Sometimes, it seems that it might have been arguing back to economists that we should have done first. Getting that out of the way could well have been the key to getting the transition going. We can still do it; it's never too late to have that debate.

The reality is, costs come down as we invest. So the story is not really about cost, it's about where we want to be during the next generation. If we invest in a low-carbon future worldwide, it will become cheap to continue going that way and in fact end up much cheaper than fossil fuels. But we need to get the technological train moving. We are sitting on the fence, going neither forward nor backward.

As we get moving and leave behind fossil fuels, we will grow the economy and improve living standards. But there are going to be great challenges, and maybe that's what the conversation needs to be about. A rapid economic transformation will stretch the economy to breaking point, creating a risk of economic and financial instability. Wealth will become ever more concentrated in ever fewer hands, increasing inequality and political vulnerability. These risks have a big chance of making the transition backfire.

Allowing markets to decide everything will not make those risks go away, nor will it help get the technological train moving. Allowing free markets to decide instead of policy-makers is only just a way to procrastinate and not take responsibility. Not much new will come out of markets on their own. We need a direction in innovation and technological leadership.

Sitting back is also a way to let someone else decide for us. Currently, it's China calling all the shots but whoever ends up producing the new technologies will gain economic power. Of course, China knew that solar energy and EVs had a chance of becoming the next big thing and invested in them big early on just in case. It adapted those industries from the West and made them cheap. Now, China reaps the rewards for having done so. Catching up will be hard, even more so for countries that sit on the fence.

Meanwhile, low-regulation free markets increase the economic risks that come with the zero-carbon transition, rather than decrease them. Wealth ownership naturally concentrates in ever fewer hands if we don't intervene. Banks get bigger; corporations increase power. Money drains from the real economy into the financial economy, creating bubbles while repeated cost of living crises arise.

Further deregulation and cutting through red tape to reduce costs and accelerate growth increase the risk of disasters, crashes and price instability. This is not very compatible with a rapid economic transformation in which we stretch the capacity of the economy to its limits.

The cost of the zero-carbon economic transformation is the risk of instability, and we need to prepare for that. The costs, if there are any, are about the measures that we need to take to improve economic resilience. We must improve the ability of the economy to survive shocks of all kinds: stranded fossil fuel assets; climate disasters; over-investment in technologies that turn out not to work very well. We must duplicate production capacity and distribute it around the world, and reduce reliance on a single source for manufacturing all products.

But lastly and most importantly, the zero-carbon transformation is an opportunity to provide new worthwhile occupations and livelihoods to our children, so that they can have fulfilling lives. No point sending people back into coal pits digging, or drilling on off-shore oil platforms, or pumping petrol into people's cars. These are occupations of a bygone era. Investing in where we want to go makes it cheap to go there, with more rewarding livelihoods and more time left for meaningful lives.

Appendix A: A Method to Measure Economic Resilience

In this book, we make extensive use of measurements of heavy tails in different datasets to say something about economic resilience. The method was introduced using rail networks as an example. We then establish our view on economic resilience and what it means in the context of a rapid low-carbon transition.

It is worth describing in this appendix the origins and soundness of this method, as it is not something widely used in economics. The method actually finds its origin in physics, evolutionary biology and complexity science.

Complex systems in which the method applies are those that have many moving parts that influence each other and where cascading failures occur. That's the domino problem, where the risk of one domino falling over because of its neighbours falling over is much greater than the risk of falling over for other reasons. In such a situation, dominoes rarely fall over on their own; they do so in groups. The economy generally falls in this category, because most of its internal parts and organs are deeply interlinked with others, so that when one component fails, other parts fail too. Understanding resilience, therefore, requires to look at the system as a whole.

The question in this appendix is why this method works. *Why does looking at the slope of frequency–magnitude diagrams on log–log graphs tell us anything about performance and stability?* Earthquakes, and the Gutemberg–Richter law that describes them, give a good illustration of why we actually observe a straight line on a log–log graph in complex systems.[1] Let's talk about that first. Then, we need to talk about what the measured slope means.

[1] See Bak et al. (2002).

THE ANALOGY OF EARTHQUAKES

Earthquakes happen because the slow movement of tectonic plates relative to each other builds up pressure inside the rocks at the boundaries. Past certain thresholds of pressure, rocks fracture and the Earth's crust moves suddenly to release that pressure, sending around small shockwaves that we feel as small earthquakes. Those shockwaves travel and push other high-pressure points to fracture, which sends off more shockwaves, amplifying the original one. The result can be anything between a relatively large earthquake and a small one that disperses quickly.

The Gutemberg–Richter law describes the relationship between the number of earthquakes and their magnitude and indicates that they should align along a straight line on a log–log graph. This law is incredibly precise and remains empirically verified over at least eight orders of magnitude! In other words, for earthquakes of magnitude between 2 and 9 on the Richter Scale, a logarithmic metric measures relative movements of the ground from 10^0 to 10^8, measured on a seismometer. The slope of the line in volcanic areas is usually near –1.0 on a $\log_{10}$ scale. In mathematics, this is called a 'power law' function of tremor magnitude M, where –1.0 is the 'exponent':

$$F(M) \propto \left(\frac{M}{M_0}\right)^{-1.0} \tag{A.1}$$

F is the frequency of earthquakes that exceed the value M, M is their magnitude and M_0 is a reference magnitude value setting the measurement scale (e.g. 1 mm). The exponent of –1.0 means that earthquakes of magnitude 2 are ten times more frequent than those of magnitude 3, which are ten times more frequent than those of magnitude 4 and so on.

Many other things work just like earthquakes, for example, financial crises. Per Bak, a Danish physicist working in the US, developed a general theory that explains problems like earthquakes.

His theory applies to all kinds of things, including traffic jams, evolutionary leaps in biology, the travelling of signals in the brain and shocks in supply chains in the economy. They all have their own version of the Gutemberg–Richter law.[2]

The theory was first developed in 1987 using the idealised model of the 'sandpile', where sand slowly drips on a table, as it would in a hourglass. It gradually builds a conical pile, at an angle that gradually increases. However, past a certain angle, it becomes unstable and begins to collapse, build up again, and collapse again, and so on. There are large and small sand collapses, that each grain of sand added to the pile can trigger. Each grain of sand added can find its place or trigger an avalanche.

Using a very simple computer algorithm, Bak and colleagues showed that the frequency–magnitude cumulative distribution of sand collapses follows a straight line on a log–log graph with a slope of −1.0 (in two dimensions). The sandpile always builds itself up to a precarious point, which Bak called 'self-organised criticality' (SOC), where the system is said to be 'on the edge of chaos'.

Bak also measured and simulated all sorts of other problems, always finding straight lines on log–log graphs and measuring slope exponents. This applies with the conditions that:[3]

1. A slow force exists that builds pressure (e.g. demand in the economy against capacity).
2. Items are strongly interlinked, where failure in one can cause failure in another.
3. Failure happens when force applied on one item exceeds a threshold (e.g. financial losses leading to insolvency).

Systems that meet these conditions can be expected to show heavy tails in their fluctuations or dynamics of failures.

[2] See Bak's book that summarises all this, Bak (1996), and various papers (Bak et al., 1987, 1988, 1993; Bak and Sneppen, 1993).

[3] See Watkins et al. (2016).

THE MEANING OF THE MEASURED SLOPE

Although there has been controversy on the general nature of self-organised criticality to describe real things,[4] it nonetheless provides a reliable theoretical basis to measure the stability of any complex system. From all the known examples of self-organised criticality, on the edge of chaos, the slope of the cumulative distribution on a log–log graph is typically near −1.

Meanwhile, looking at economic resilience using time series, it is common to see times of relative calm and times of upheaval. This can happen within days, or within years, at many time scales. It is straightforward to measure this by looking at relative changes in price time series, where straight lines on log–log graphs (or 'heavy tails') are actually the norm rather than the exception.

'Tail heaviness' is therefore easy to measure using the slope of a straight line on a log–log graph. We also often see related symptoms of self-organised criticality, what's called 'clustered volatility' and 'memory', especially in financial time series. Tail heaviness is a good measure of volatility.

The observation of heavy tails, however, clashes with the standard economic and financial theory, which assumes that they don't exist and therefore offers no explanation for them. In reality, they are ubiquitous. The question is therefore what the tail heaviness value really means. It makes complete sense to measure the degree of instability using the slope, but Bak's theory does not offer any real explanation for the meaning of the slope value when the system is not exactly on the edge of chaos.

We acknowledge that the tail slope value can be an inaccurate rough measurement. There exist more sophisticated ways to estimate tail heavinesses.[5] Frequencies could follow lognormal or other heavy-tailed distributions, but the amounts of data we have at hand typically do not allow to see the difference clearly. But the

[4] See Watkins et al. (2016).
[5] See Clauset et al. (2009).

goal here is not accuracy or even to prove that the data we are looking at truly follow power laws. These details are not really important, what matters is how heavy the tail is and how frequent the big disasters are, irrespective of the real mathematical distribution they might follow. For that, our method is suitable, and what it tells us is the relative weight of probability between small and large events.

Although not discussed extensively in the SOC theory, different values of the slope have radically different interpretations regarding the *moments* of the distribution, that is, the average, standard deviation, skewness and so on. Let's show here why. We take a power law frequency distribution function of fluctuation magnitude M with slope (exponent) α:

$$f(M) = \frac{\alpha - 1}{M_0}\left(\frac{M}{M_0}\right)^{-\alpha}, \quad \alpha > 1, \qquad \text{(A.2)}$$

where the factor $\frac{\alpha-1}{M_0}$ ensures that probabilities sum to 1. Typically, α will be in the range between 1 and 3 (if $\alpha \leq 1$, the function cannot be normalised). α is what we measure on a log–log graph.

The average is:

$$\int_{M_0}^{\infty} f(M) M dM = \frac{\alpha - 1}{M_0} \int_{M_0}^{\infty} \left(\frac{M}{M_0}\right)^{-\alpha} dM = \left(\frac{\alpha - 1}{\alpha - 2}\right) M_0 \qquad \text{(A.3)}$$

However, this only has a solution if $\alpha > 2$. If α is equal to 2 or between 2 and 1, the average is infinity.

Of course, if we take a finite time series of tail heaviness of 2 or less (such as earthquakes), and take an average, it will only give infinity if one of the values in the dataset is infinity. But what's important to understand with this calculation is that for a large amount of data, the likelihood that the dataset includes very large numbers is high, and these large numbers bias heavily the average towards high values. This means that the longer the time series, the higher the average becomes. In other words, the average depends on how long we wait; it is not stable when $\alpha \leq 2$. That's because if we wait long enough, a 'big one' will inevitably come.

One example of this is if we were to measure the average net worth of the audience at a business conference where people gradually come in to join. If we wait long enough, there is a chance that Bill Gates or Jeff Bezos comes in, at which point the average might go up a factor of 100 or even 1,000. The value would increase over time, as the occasional rich person joins. That's because wealth is distributed following a Pareto distribution, that is, a power law, with the exponent between −1 and −2.[6]

The same phenomenon happens with the standard deviation:

$$\int_{M_0}^{\infty} f(M)M^2 dM = \frac{\alpha - 1}{M_0} \int_{M_0}^{\infty} M^{2-\alpha} dM = \left(\frac{\alpha - 1}{\alpha - 3}\right) M_0^2 \qquad \text{(A.4)}$$

provided that $\alpha > 3$, since for $\alpha \leq 3$, the result is, again, infinity. This means that the standard deviation, our measure of uncertainty, drifts slowly towards infinity as we add more data into the dataset.

These results provide boundaries over what the slope that we measure on log–log graphs mean. At $\alpha > 3$, the system is predictable as it has a well-defined average and standard deviation. This means that the next disaster that can be expected has a magnitude that is predictable and bounded.

For $2 < \alpha \leq 3$, the average exists, but it is unreliable, because the standard deviation, which is a measure of uncertainty, is infinite. This means that we know very little what to expect next: volatility could be very small or very large. Many economic systems and indices fall in this category.

At $\alpha \leq 2$, the average itself, for an infinitely long time series, is infinite. In practice, it means that the measured average will drift upwards over time. Not only does the system have no predictability, but the next disaster to expect is largely unbounded: it could be of any magnitude. Earthquakes fall in this category, as well as climate change impacts.

Finally, we note that the fitting method we use to find α is not very accurate, usually because we don't have enough data. Therefore,

[6] See, for instance, Saez and Stantcheva (2018).

we cannot interpret α with absolute certainty. For example, we may not be able to really tell the difference between $\alpha = 1.9$ and $\alpha = 2.1$ because of the uncertainty on the linear fits we make to the data. But there is nonetheless a very clear difference, for instance, between systems in the range $\alpha > 3$ compared to $\alpha \simeq 2$, or if α consistently drifts from 3 towards 2. In this case, α is a good metric for resilience.

Most economic variables find themselves on the spectrum between –3.5 and –2, with occasional variables above –2 (for instance, Bitcoin). Our interpretation is that across the spectrum, a tail heaviness lower than –3 indicates a system with substantial resilience, but given that we observe few such systems, we assume that they are rare because such levels of resilience are expensive. Similarly, at the other end of the spectrum, few systems lie above –2, and our interpretation is that the high level of volatility becomes too expensive for business. In theory, the edge of chaos lies at –2. However, practically, it doesn't matter where it is; our observation across many economic variables is that systems above –2 are typically in trouble as they become too unstable to function properly.

Appendix B: A Dynamic Input–Output Model of Economic Evolution

As described in Chapter 5, our model of economic growth is described using a progression of three steps:

1. Explaining growth on the basis of lending for investment, detailing what economic flows, which originate from lending and investment, go to wages, profits, banks and loan repayments (Figure 5.5);
2. Exploring how sectors substitute each other, on the basis of creative destruction (Figure 5.6);
3. Exploring how the structure of the economy autonomously evolves as new industries are born and old ones decline, with dynamic relationships between them (Figure 5.7).

In this appendix, we provide equations for reproducing Figures 5.5–5.7, based on Figure 5.3. While the main text describes qualitatively what we understand happens in the economy over time and with investment, it doesn't provide in detail how we implement this world view in practice with numbers.

B.1 REPRODUCING FIGURE 5.5

This model is made up of two components (1) a growth of lending component and (2) an investment breakdown component. The growth component simulates the growth of financing power of industrialists due to their previous successes at generating returns to their investors. In this model, purchasing power originates from bank lending having a residence time in the economy before being cancelled out by loan repayments.[1] This involves a growth of lending from financial institutions, creating the purchasing power via credit, as

[1] See Pollitt and Mercure (2017); Mercure et al. (2019).

their trust in their borrowers grows. At this stage, the model does not involve any sectoral detail or possible growth or decline of particular industries.

The model focuses on a virtuous cycle between industrial input costs coming down due to cumulative investment, leaving excess purchasing power as profits for industrialists and banks, motivating more lending and investment. Stage 1 of the model is described by two variables as functions of time: cumulative investment $N(t)$ and an indicator of industrial costs (inversely proportional to productivity) $C(t)$. The Δ symbol means a change in those quantities over a time period Δt.

Variables

$N(t)$ = cumulative investment
$C(t)$ = input cost to industry
Z = carrying capacity

Equations

Cost reductions (or productivity growth) originate in this simple model from an economy-wide learning curve with learning exponent b, which can be written as

$$C(t) = C_0 \left(\frac{N(t)}{N_0} \right)^{-b} \quad \Rightarrow \Delta C(t) = -b \frac{\Delta N(t)}{N(t)} C(t). \qquad \text{(B.1)}$$

Investment from lending increases following cumulative past investment. In principle, this leads to a rising exponential, damped by a number of factors:

$$\frac{\Delta N(t)}{\Delta t} = aN(t) \left(\frac{Z - N(t)}{Z} \right) C(t)(1 + \epsilon), \qquad \text{(B.2)}$$

where ϵ is noise that modulates the rate of return, reflecting that some projects do well while others do not. To carry out the calculation, these two equations are estimated in alternation.

In this equation, some factors damp what would otherwise be exponential growth. This includes first cost reductions, given that as input costs come down, the value of investment necessarily comes down over time. But we've also introduced a carrying capacity Z, that is, a factor that reflects a self-limiting aspect of economic growth. The environment and population may not be able to sustain or justify endless demand growth. This is notably the case if population peaks, imposing limits on aggregate demand (as happened, e.g. in Japan). These factors together cause in Figure 5.5 a slowdown of growth, consistent with what's observed in advanced economies.

These two equations form a closed set of finite difference equations that we can estimate on a chosen time step (the length of which is arbitrary, here, we assume years). Costs reduce due to increasing cumulative investment, and investment increases due to declining costs generating profits.

This is where the second stage of the model comes in. In Stage 2, we introduce the fact that projects take years to generate return, expressed by Figure 5.3. In the model, this means that at each time step in the simulation with the two equations B.1 and B.2, the investment timeline and project life cycle of Figure 5.3 apply up to a number of years ahead. We've assumed ten-year long uniform projects, but this can be done with various durations or ranges of durations. What's important is that they overlap, in other words, projects 2 and 3 might start and end only one year after project 1 starts, and therefore the profits from all projects become added.

Thus, in the simulation, we add $\Delta N(t_0)$ times the values from Figure 5.3 at time t_0 and later times $t_0 + t$ up to ten years. One project commits profits to accrue up to ten years later. By the time any project is completed, the economy will have grown slightly due to the investment in and income generated by other projects. Loan repayments are taken out from revenue streams, while wages consist in money circulating in the economy for the duration of each project. We calculate this by accounting for investment, debt servicing, interest paid, profits and operational expenditures (wages) in separate accounts, which are shown in Figure 5.5.

B.2 REPRODUCING FIGURE 5.6

In this second modelling stage, we assume that sectors succeed each other through creative destruction due to cost reductions, a model borrowed from earlier work.[2] Here, we create new sectors every twenty-five years. Cost reductions occur sector by sector according to random learning rates. New sectors arising begin to capture market shares if they are profitable, or disappear if they are not. The succession of sectors generates a different storyline each time the model is run, which depends on those random numbers.

The succession of sectors occurs as follows. Investors are assumed to make a choice between all the sectors they could invest in and compare. To do this, we carry out pair-wise comparisons between every possible pair of sectors. We look at pairs because we assume that most investors do not consider all sectors simultaneously. Some investors are assumed unaware of new sectors emerging, or have no interest in them, proportionally to their existing market share. In other words, a winner-take-all dynamic emerges, where larger sectors attract proportionally more investment than smaller sectors, but only if they are profitable.

Variables

i, j = sectors of production
F_{ij} = preference matrix between pairs of options i, j
S_i = market share of technology i
τ_i = life expectancy of technology i
σ_i = width parameter of cost distribution for technology i

Relationships

$\sum_i S_i = 1$
$F_{ij} + F_{ji} = 1$

Equations

The pairwise comparison works via an ordinary binary logit of the sector input cost (or profitability) difference $C_j(t) - C_i(t)$:

[2] See Mercure (2012, 2015, 2018).

$$F_{ij}(t) = \frac{1}{1 + \exp\left(\frac{C_j(t) - C_i(t)}{\sigma_{ij}}\right)}, \qquad \sigma_{ij} = \sqrt{\sigma_i^2 + \sigma_j^2}. \tag{B.3}$$

The implicit assumption is that sectoral input costs are Gumbel-distributed with width parameter σ_i, and F_{ij} expresses the resulting logit preference of agents for sector i over j, with $F_{ij} + F_{ji} = 1$ (e.g. 30% go for i, 70% go for j).

As investors compare options, they make choices in what to invest between every possible pair. Denoting $S_i(t)$ as the share of the total of investable projects occupied by sector i, the change in this due to investors changing their choice is

$$\frac{\Delta S_{ij}(t)}{\Delta t} = S_i(t)S_j(t)F_{ij}\frac{1}{\tau_i}, \tag{B.4}$$

where τ_{ij} is the average time it takes to switch from i to j, for which we can use the average lifetime of projects, in this case ten years. This equation expresses the fact that investors changing their minds from investing in sector i towards investing in sector j depends on (1) how many investors used to invest in i and (2) the capacity of sector j for receiving investment and expanding.

This then requires to be aggregated to obtain net contributions to sector i from all other sectors. This requires to sum over all sectors j:

$$\frac{\Delta S_i(t)}{\Delta t} = \sum_j S_i(t)S_j(t)\left(F_{ij} - F_{ji}\right)\frac{1}{\tau_{ij}}, \tag{B.5}$$

This equation is occasionally called the 'replicator equation', or 'Lotka-Volterra', in evolutionary biology, as it is used to model evolving populations in ecosystems.[3]

What attracts economic activity towards some sectors and away from others are the increasing returns that arise as the scale increases. In this model, costs come down following sector-specific learning curves (with rates chosen randomly), rather than an economy-wide one. Sectors doing well attract economic activity at

[3] See Hofbauer and Sigmund (1998).

the expense of those not doing well. The result is a succession of diffusion of various technological sectors as they come into fashion and disappear again.

B.3 REPRODUCING FIGURE 5.7

Here, we use multi-sectoral input–output analysis to determine the interdependences between sectors. Some sectors depend on or feed other sectors. For example, a food processing sector cannot function without an agriculture sector to provide its basic inputs, while the agriculture sector needs the food sector to take its output, otherwise it would disappear. Thus, these sectors induce growth in each other, rather than compete. Meanwhile, other sectors compete directly for the same market share, such as coal and electricity as inputs for making steel.

As in the previous model, new sectors are created every twenty-five years, but this time, they come along with new interdependencies with other sectors. At the same time, old sectors become more efficient in their use of input resources due to their learning curves. Therefore, older interdependencies decline in relative volume, as new ones appear. The volumes associated with new interdependencies will grow rapidly in absolute terms, while volumes in old interdependencies will peak and decline.

Following a standard input–output model, we use a matrix that indicates what each sector uses as inputs and what portion of their outputs are inputs to other sectors as opposed to being consumed as end products.

Variables

δ_{ij} = Kronecker's Delta: equals 1 if $i = j$, 0 otherwise
q_i = vector of quantities produced
p_i = vector of prices
A_{ij} = transaction matrix between sectors (square)
a_{ij} = input–output matrix

Definitions

$a_{ij} = \frac{A_{ij}}{p_i q_j}$ = IO matrix

$\sum_i p_i \delta_{ij} q_j$ = total production (prices times quantities, $\neq$ GDP)

$\sum_{ij} p_i a_{ij} q_j$ = total intermediate production

$\sum_j a_{ij} q_j = \alpha_i$ = intermediate input quantities for production q_j

$\sum_i p_i a_{ij} = \overline{p}_j$ = unit prices of intermediate products

$\sum_j a_{ij} p_j = \tilde{p}_i$ = components of production costs in industry i

Relationships

$\sum_j (\delta_{ij} - a_{ij}) q_j = d_i$ production according to demand d_i

$\sum_j p_i \delta_{ij} q_j - p_i a_{ij} q_j = V_i$ = sectoral profits (surplus, always > 0)

$\sum_j p_i a_{ij} q_j = Y_i = I_i + G_i + C_i$ = basic macroeconomic identity

Equations

The Lotka–Volterra equation for the evolution of production capacity (the investment equation) is modified from equation B.5 in two respects, as follows:

$$\frac{\Delta q_i}{\Delta t} = r_i q_i + \sum_j \left(q_i T_{ij} q_j + q_i a_{ij} q_j \right) \tag{B.6}$$

where $T_{ij} = \frac{F_{ij} - F_{ji}}{\tau_{ij}}$. First, it is in absolute terms, rather than relative shares of the market, which means that a growth term is included (the first term, with sectoral growth rate r_i). Second, we must add the sectoral interdependencies via the input–output matrix a_{ij} (the third term). The second term remains the same competition interaction between sectors (eq. B.5), where $F_{ij} = F_{ij}(p_i - p_j)$ and $F_{ji} = 1 - F_{ij}$ are binary logit functions of price difference $p_i - p_j$ between the sectors competing.

Thus, in short, we have a growth term, a creative destruction term and an interdependency term. Sectors have three possible sources of growth. They can grow out of the final demand for their product. They can grow out of eating away at some other sector's demand. Or they can grow because they provide the inputs to another sector whose demand is growing (and conversely for sectoral decline).

The prices change according to the learning-by-doing relationship, $p_i = \left(\frac{N_i}{N_0}\right)^{-b_i} p_0$, where $N_i = \sum_t q_i(t)$ is cumulative production in the sector since the start of history, N_0; p_0 is a reference point in time and b_i is the learning exponent (related to the learning rate). This leads to the equation

$$p_i(t + \Delta t) = p_i(t) - b_i \frac{\Delta N_i(t)}{N_i(t)} p_i(t). \tag{B.7}$$

Price and quantity changes lead to a gradual change in the input–output matrix a_{ij}, which we work out using the following equation. The transaction matrix at time t is

$$A_{ij}(t) = p_i(t) a_{ij}(t) q_j(t), \quad a_{ij} = \frac{A_{ij}(t)}{p_i(t) q_j(t)} \tag{B.8}$$

The change in the transaction matrix due to a change in prices and quantities is

$$A_{ij}(t + \Delta t) = A_{ij}(t) + \Delta A_{ij}(t + \Delta t). \tag{B.9}$$

We can convert this into the corresponding input–output table:

$$a_{ij}(t + \Delta t) \simeq \frac{p_i(t) q_j(t)}{p_i(t + \Delta t) q_j(t + \Delta t)} a_{ij}(t) + \Delta a_{ij}(t + \Delta t). \tag{B.10}$$

At the limit where Δt becomes quite small, the second term becomes small compared to the first. Under this approximation, we can just re-scale the input–output coefficients by the changes in prices and quantities.

However, the number of rows and columns in the transactions and input–output matrices change as new products are introduced, creating new sectors and new interdependencies. For example, IT systems are gradually introduced, and slowly, all sectors begin to use computers to improve their productivity. We, therefore, use the term Δa_{ij} to represent the addition of those new interdependencies, the new connections that didn't exist before. In this model, we create new rows and columns using self-consistent random numbers.

Thus, here, the model works via the iteration of three steps. First, equation B.6 evaluates the changes in production by sector as the economy grows and evolves. Equation B.7 evaluates the resulting changes in sectoral input costs and prices, which we assume proportional here. And lastly, equation B.10 evaluates what changes in the input–output table are consistent with the changes in prices and quantities generated by the B.6 and B.7 equations. The calculation then goes back to equation B.6.

References

Abernathy, William J., and Utterback, James M. 1978. Patterns of industrial innovation. *Technology Review*, **80**(7), 40–47.

Acemoglu, Daron. 2002. Directed technical change. *The Review of Economic Studies*, **69**(4), 781–809.

Acemoglu, Daron, and Restrepo, Pascual. 2018. The race between man and machine: Implications of technology for growth, factor shares, and employment. *American Economic Review*, **108**(6), 1488–1542.

Acemoglu, Daron, Aghion, Philippe, Bursztyn, Leonardo, and Hemous, David. 2012. The environment and directed technical change. *American Economic Review*, **102**(1), 131–166.

Ackerman, Frank, and Heinzerling, Lisa. 2002. Pricing the priceless: Cost-benefit analysis of environmental protection. *University of Pennsylvania Law Review*, **150**(5), 1553–1584.

Aghion, Philippe, Antonin, Céline, and Bunel, Simon. 2021. *The Power of Creative Destruction: Economic Upheaval and the Wealth of Nations*. Harvard University Press.

Agnolucci, Paolo, Gencer, Defne, and Heine, Dirk. 2024. Total Carbon Pricing for Energy Consumption: The Importance of Energy Taxes and Subsidies. *Energy Subsidy Reform in Action Series*; ESMAP Technical Report. World Bank.

Aiyar, Shekhar, Chen, Jiaqian, Ebeke, Christian H., Garcia-Saltos, Roberto, Gudmundsson, Tryggvi, Ilyina, Anna, Kangur, Alvar, Kunaratskul, Tansaya, Rodriguez, Sergio L., Ruta, Michele, et al. 2023. Geo-economic fragmentation and the future of multilateralism. *IMF Staff Discussion Notes*, **2023**(001), 42p.

Aklin, Michaël, and Mildenberger, Matto. 2020. Prisoners of the wrong dilemma: Why distributive conflict, not collective action, characterizes the politics of climate change. *Global Environmental Politics*, **20**(4), 4–27.

Anadon, L., Penasco, C., Sharpe, S., Mercure, J.-F., Grubb, M., and co authors. 2022. *Ten Principles for Policymaking in the Energy Transition*. Technical report. Economics of Innovation and System Transition (EEIST).

Ansari, Esmail, and Kaufmann, Robert K. 2019. The effect of oil and gas price and price volatility on rig activity in tight formations and OPEC strategy. *Nature Energy*, **4**(4), 321–328.

Arntz, Melanie, Gregory, Terry, and Zierahn, Ulrich. 2017. Revisiting the risk of automation. *Economics Letters*, **159**, 157–160.

Arthur, Brian. 2014. *Complexity and the Economy*. Oxford.

Arthur, W. Brian, Ermoliev, Yu M., and Kaniovski, Yu M. 1987. Path-dependent processes and the emergence of macro-structure. *European Journal of Operational Research*, **30**(3), 294–303.

Arthur, W. Brian, et al. 1994. *Increasing Returns and Path Dependence in the Economy*. University of Michigan Press.

Autor, David H. 2015. Why are there still so many jobs? The history and future of workplace automation. *Journal of Economic Perspectives*, **29**(3), 3–30.

Bak, P., Tang, C., and Wiesenfeld, K. 1987. Self-organized criticality: An explanation of 1/F noise. *Physical Review Letters*, **59**(4), 381–384.

Bak, Per. 1996. *How Nature Works*. Springer Verlag.

Bak, Per, and Sneppen, Kim. 1993. Punctuated equilibrium and criticality in a simple model of evolution. *Physical Review Letters*, **71**(24), 4083.

Bak, Per, Tang, Chao, and Wiesenfeld, Kurt. 1988. Self-organized criticality. *Physical Review A*, **38**(1), 364.

Bak, Per, Chen, Kan, Scheinkman, José, and Woodford, Michael. 1993. Aggregate fluctuations from independent sectoral shocks: Self-organized criticality in a model of production and inventory dynamics. *Ricerche Economiche*, **47**(1), 3–30.

Bak, Per, Christensen, Kim, Danon, Leon, and Scanlon, Tim. 2002. Unified scaling law for earthquakes. *Physical Review Letters*, **88**(17), 178501.

Bank of England. 2015. *The Impact of Climate Change on the UK Insurance Sector*. Technical report. Bank of England, www.bankofengland.co.uk/prudential-regulation/publication/2015/the-impact-of-climate-change-on-the-uk-insurance-sector.

Barabási, Albert-László, and Albert, Réka. 1999. Emergence of scaling in random networks. *Science*, **286**(5439), 509–512.

Barabási, Albert-László, and Bonabeau, Eric. 2003. Scale-free networks. *Scientific American*, **288**(5), 60–69.

Baram, M. S. 1980. Cost-benefit analysis: An inadequate basis for health, safety, and environmental regulatory decision-making. *Ecology Law Quarterly*, **8**(3), 473–531.

Barredo-Zuriarrain, Juan. 2022. Credit-fueled demand and shrinking aggregate supply: A study on the hyperinflation in Venezuela. *Review of Political Economy*, **36**(1), 304–324.

Bateman, I. J., Carson, R. T., Day, B., Hanemann, M., Hanley, N., Hett, T., Jones-Lee, M., Loomes, G., Mourato, S., Özdemiroglu, E., Pearce, D. W., Sugden, R., and Swanson, J. 2002. *Economic Valuation with Stated Preference Techniques: A Manual.* Edward Elgar Publishing Ltd.

Battiston, Stefano, Farmer, J. Doyne, Flache, Andreas, Garlaschelli, Diego, Haldane, Andrew G., Heesterbeek, Hans, Hommes, Cars, Jaeger, Carlo, May, Robert, and Scheffer, Marten. 2016. Complexity theory and financial regulation. *Science,* **351**(6275), 818–819.

Battiston, Stefano, Mandel, Antoine, Monasterolo, Irene, Schütze, Franziska, and Visentin, Gabriele. 2017. A climate stress-test of the financial system. *Nature Climate Change,* **7**(4), 283.

Baxter, Martin, and Rennie, Andrew. 1996. *Financial Calculus: An Introduction to Derivative Pricing.* Cambridge University Press.

BEIS. 2017. *Industrial Strategy: Building a Britain Fit for the Future.* Technical report. Department for Business, Energy and Industrial Strategy.

Benson, Christopher L., Triulzi, Giorgio, and Magee, Christopher L. 2018. Is There a Moore's Law for 3D Printing? *3D Printing and Additive Manufacturing,* **5**(1), 53–62.

Bento, N., and Fontes, M. 2015. Spatial diffusion and the formation of a technological innovation system in the receiving country: The case of wind energy in Portugal. *Environmental Innovation and Societal Transitions,* **15**, 158–179.

Black, Fischer, and Scholes, Myron. 1973. The pricing of options and corporate liabilities. *Journal of Political Economy,* **81**(3), 637–654.

BoE. 2018. *Transition in Thinking: The Impact of Climate Change on the UK Banking Sector.* Technical report. Bank of England, www.bankofengland.co.uk/prudential-regulation/publication/2018/transition-in-thinking-the-impact-of-climate-change-on-the-uk-banking-sector.

BoE. 2022. *Results of the 2021 Climate Biennial Exploratory Scenario (CBES).* Technical report. Bank of England, www.bankofengland.co.uk/stress-testing/2022/results-of-the-2021-climate-biennial-exploratory-scenario.

Boer, Lukas, Pescatori, Mr Andrea, and Stuermer, Martin. 2021. Energy transition metals. *International Monetary Fund working papers.*

Bolton, Patrick, Despres, Morgan, Pereira Da Silva, Luiz Awazu, Samama, Frédéric, and Svartman, Romain. 2020. *The Green Swan: Central Banking and Financial Stability in the Age of Climate Change.* Technical report. Banque de France.

Burgis, Tom. 2015. *The Looting Machine.* HarperCollins Publishers.

Byrne, David. 2002. Industrial culture in a post-industrial world: The case of the North East of England. *City,* **6**(3), 279–289.

Caldecott, Ben. 2018. *Stranded Assets and the Environment: Risk, Resilience and Opportunity.* Routledge.

Carlson, J. M., and Doyle, John. 2002. Complexity and robustness. *Proceedings of the National Academy of Sciences of the United States of America*, **99**(suppl 1), 2538–2545.

Carreras, Marco. 2020. Investigating the Role of BNDES as a Tool to Transmit Countercyclical Policy Decisions: Evidence from 2002-2016. *SSRN.*

Castelo-Branco, Isabel, Cruz-Jesus, Frederico, and Oliveira, Tiago. 2019. Assessing Industry 4.0 readiness in manufacturing: Evidence for the European Union. *Computers in Industry*, **107**, 22–32.

Chester, D., Lynch, C., Szerszynski, B., Mercure, J.-F., and Jarvis, A. 2024a. Heterogeneous capital stocks and economic inertia in the US economy. *Ecological Economics*, **217**, 108075.

Chester, Daniel, Lynch, Cormac, Mercure, Jean-Francois, and Jarvis, Andrew. 2024b. Stranded human and produced capital in a net-zero transition. *Environmental Research: Climate*, **3**(4), 045012.

Clark, Alex, and Zhang, Weirong. 2022. Estimating the employment and fiscal consequences of thermal coal phase-out in china. *Energies*, **15**(3), 800.

Clauset, Aaron, Shalizi, Cosma Rohilla, and Newman, Mark E. J. 2009. Power-law distributions in empirical data. *SIAM Review*, **51**(4), 661–703.

Cont, Rama, and Schaanning, Eric. 2017. Fire sales, indirect contagion and systemic stress testing. *Norges Bank Research Working Papers.*

Cont, Rama, Moussa, Amal, and Santos, Edson B. 2010. Network structure and systemic risk in banking systems. *SSRN.*

Coronese, Matteo, Lamperti, Francesco, Keller, Klaus, Chiaromonte, Francesca, and Roventini, Andrea. 2019. Evidence for sharp increase in the economic damages of extreme natural disasters. *Proceedings of the National Academy of Sciences*, **116**(43), 21450–21455.

Cosme, Inês, Santos, Rui, and O'Neill, Daniel W. 2017. Assessing the degrowth discourse: A review and analysis of academic degrowth policy proposals. *Journal of Cleaner Production*, **149**, 321–334.

Criscuolo, Chiara, Gal, Peter, Leidecker, Timo, Losma, Francesco, and Nicoletti, Giuseppe. 2021. The role of telework for productivity during and post-COVID-19: Results from an OECD survey among managers and workers.

Dahl, Erik J. 2001. Naval innovation: From coal to oil. *Joint Force Quarterly*, **27**, 52.

De Ponti, Tomek, Rijk, Bert, and Van Ittersum, Martin K. 2012. The crop yield gap between organic and conventional agriculture. *Agricultural Systems*, **108**, 1–9.

De Stercke, S. 2014. *Dynamics of Energy Systems: A Useful Perspective (IIASA Interim Report No. IR-14-013).*

Dennis, Norman, Henriques, Fernando, and Slaughter, Clifford. 1956. *Coal Is Our Life: An Analysis of a Yorkshire Mining Community*. Tavistock London.

Diesendorf, Mark, and Wiedmann, Thomas. 2020. Implications of trends in energy return on energy invested (EROI) for transitioning to renewable electricity. *Ecological Economics*, **176**, 106726.

Dosi, G. 1982. Technological paradigms and technological trajectories. *Research policy*, **2**(3), I47–62.

Dosi, G., Freeman, C., Nelson, R., Silverberg, G., and Soete, L. 1988. *Technical Change and Economic Theory*. Pinter Publishers.

Doyle, John, and Carlson, Jean M. 2000. Power laws, highly optimized tolerance, and generalized source coding. *Physical Review Letters*, **84**(24), 5656.

Ediger, Volkan Ş., and Bowlus, John V. 2019. A farewell to King Coal: Geopolitics, energy security, and the transition to oil, 1898–1917. *The Historical Journal*, **62**(2), 427–449.

Eichengreen, Barry, and Hausmann, Ricardo. 1999. Exchange rates and financial fragility. *NBER Working Papers*, 7418. doi:10.3386/w7418.

Espagne, E., Mercure, J.-F, Oman, W., Semieniuk, G., Pollitt, H., Volz, U., Campiglio, E., and Svartzman, R. 2023. Cross-border risks in the low-carbon transition. *IMF Working Papers*.

Farmer, J Doyne, and Lafond, François. 2016. How predictable is technological progress? *Research Policy*, **45**(3), 647–665.

Felipe, Jesus, and McCombie, John S. L. 2014. The aggregate production function: 'Not even wrong'. *Review of Political Economy*, **26**(1), 60–84.

Fisher, Irving. 1932. *Booms and Depressions*. Adelphi.

Franta, Benjamin. 2021. Weaponizing Economics: Big Oil, Economic consultants, and climate policy delay. *Environmental Politics*, **31**(4), 555-575.

Freeman, C., and Perez, C. 1988. Structural crises of adjustment: Business cycles and investment behaviour. Pages 38–66 of: Dosi, G., Freeman, C., Nelson, R., Silverberg, G., and Soete, L. (eds), *Technical Change and Economic Theory*. Pinter Publishers.

Freeman, C., and Louçã, F. 2001. *As Time Goes By*. Oxford University Press.

Funtowicz, Silvio O., and Ravetz, Jerome R. 1994. The worth of a songbird: Ecological economics as a post-normal science. *Ecological Economics*, **10**(3), 197–207.

Galgóczi, Béla. 2014. The long and winding road from black to green: Decades of structural change in the Ruhr region. *International Journal of Labour Research*, **6**(2), 217.

Gao, Caixia. 2021. Genome engineering for crop improvement and future agriculture. *Cell*, **184**(6), 1621–1635.

Geels, F. W. 2002. Technological transitions as evolutionary reconfiguration processes: A multi-level perspective and a case-study. *Research Policy*, **31**(8–9), 1257–1274.

Geels, F. W. 2005. The dynamics of transitions in socio-technical systems: A multi-level analysis of the transition pathway from horse-drawn carriages to automobiles (1860–1930). *Technology Analysis & Strategic Management*, **17**(4), 445–476.

Geels, Frank W., and Schot, Johan. 2007. Typology of sociotechnical transition pathways. *Research Policy*, **36**(3), 399–417.

Gherhes, Cristian, Vorley, Tim, and Brooks, Chay. 2020. Making sense of industrial decline: How legacies of the past influence the development of entrepreneurship cultures in formerly industrialized places. *Entrepreneurship & Regional Development*, **32**(9–10), 899–921.

Graeber, David. 2014. *Debt-Updated and Expanded: The First 5,000 Years*. Melville House.

Graeber, David. 2018. *Bullshit Jobs: A Theory*. Simon & Schuster.

Grubb, Michael, Bashmakov, Igor, Drummond, Paul, Myshak, Anna, Hughes, Nick, Biancardi, Andrea, Agnolucci, Paolo, and Lowe, Robert. 2018. An exploration of energy cost, ranges, limits and adjustment process. *UCL-ISR*.

Grubb, Michael, Chapuis, Thierry, and Duong, Minh Ha. 1995. The economics of changing course: Implications of adaptability and inertia for optimal climate policy. *Energy Policy*, **23**(4–5), 417–431.

Grubb, M., Drummond, P., Mercure, J.-F., Hepburn, C., and co authors. 2021a. *The New Economics of Innovation and Transition: Evaluating Opportunities and Risks*. Technical report. Economics of Innovation and System Transition (EEIST), www.eeist.co.uk.

Grubb, Michael, Drummond, Paul, Poncia, Alexandra, McDowall, Will, Popp, David, Samadi, Sascha, Penasco, Cristina, Gillingham, Kenneth, Smulders, Sjak, Glachant, Matthieu, et al. 2021b. Induced innovation in energy technologies and systems: A review of evidence and potential implications for CO2 mitigation. *Environmental Research Letters*, **16**(4), 48.

Grubb, M., Hourcade, J.-C., and Neuhoff, K. 2014. *Planetary Economics*. Taylor Francis/Routledge.

Grubert, E., and Hastings-Simon, S. 2022. Designing the mid-transition: A review of medium-term challenges for coordinated decarbonization in the United States. *WIREs Climate Change*, **13**(3), e768.

Grübler, Arnulf. 1990. *The Rise and Fall of Infrastructures: Dynamics of Evolution and Technological Change in Transport*. Physica-Verlag.

Grübler, Arnulf. 1998. *Technology and Global Change*. Cambridge University Press.

Grübler, Arnulf, and Wilson, Charlie. 2013. *Energy Technology Innovation*. Cambridge University Press.

Grübler, A., Nakicenovic, N., and Victor, D. G. 1999. Dynamics of energy technologies and global change. *Energy Policy*, **27**(5), 247–280.

Grubler, Arnulf, Wilson, Charlie, Bento, Nuno, Boza-Kiss, Benigna, Krey, Volker, McCollum, David L., Rao, Narasimha D., Riahi, Keywan, Rogelj, Joeri, De Stercke, Simon, et al. 2018. A low energy demand scenario for meeting the 1.5 C target and sustainable development goals without negative emission technologies. *Nature Energy*, **3**(6), 515–527.

Haldane, Andrew G., and May, Robert M. 2011. Systemic risk in banking ecosystems. *Nature*, **469**(7330), 351–355.

Hall, Charles A. S., Lambert, Jessica G., and Balogh, Stephen B. 2014. EROI of different fuels and the implications for society. *Energy Policy*, **64**, 141–152.

Hallegatte, Stephane. 2014. Economic resilience: Definition and measurement. *World Bank Policy Research Working Paper.*

Hanley, Nick, and Barbier, Edward B. 2009. *Pricing Nature: Cost-Benefit Analysis and Environmental Policy*. Edward Elgar Publishing.

Hofbauer, Josef, and Sigmund, Karl. 1998. *Evolutionary Games and Population Dynamics*. Cambridge University Press.

Holling, Crawford S. 1973. Resilience and stability of ecological systems. *Annual Review Ecology, Evolution, and Systematics*. 4, 1–23. https://doi.org/10.1146/annurev.es.04.110173.000245.

Hubbert, M. K. 1962. Energy resources. A report to the Committee on Natural Resources. *National Academy of Science, Government Printing Office*, Publication No. 1000-D.

Hynes, William, Trump, Benjamin D., Kirman, Alan, Haldane, Andrew, and Linkov, Igor. 2022. Systemic resilience in economics. *Nature Physics*, **18**(4), 381–384.

IEA. 2020a. *Oil Market Report 2024*. IEA/OECD.

IEA. 2020b. *World Energy Outlook 2020*. IEA/OECD.

IEA. 2021. *The Role of Critical Minerals in Clean Energy Transitions*. IEA/OECD.

IEA. 2022. *Solar PV Global Supply Chains*. IEA/OECD.

IEA. 2023a. *Critical Minerals Market Review 2023*. IEA/OECD.

IEA. 2023b. *World Energy Balances dataset 2023*. IEA/OECD.

IEA. 2024. *World Energy Balances dataset 2023*. IEA/OECD.

IPCC. 2018a. *Special Report: Global Warming of 1.5°C*. Cambridge University Press.

IPCC. 2018b. *SR15 Scenarios Database*. Technical report.

IPCC. 2021. *Climate Change 2021: The Physical Science Basis*. Cambridge University Press.

Ives, M. C., Righetti, L., Schiele, J., De Meyer, K., Hubble-Rose, L., Teng, F., Kruitwagen, L., Tillmann-Morris, L., Wang, T., Way, R., and Hepburn, C. 2021.

The prospects for Paris: Behavioral insights into unconditional cooperation on climate change. *Oxford INET Working Paper Series No. 21-04.*

Jackson, Tim. 2009. *Prosperity without Growth: Economics for a Finite Planet.* Earthscan.

Jennings, T., Tipper, H. A., Daglish, J., Grubb, M., and Drummond, P. 2020. *Policy, Innovation and Cost Reduction in UK Offshore Wind.* Technical report. Carbon Trust.

Johnstone, Phil, and Hielscher, Sabine. 2017. Phasing out coal, sustaining coal communities? Living with technological decline in sustainability pathways. *The Extractive Industries and Society*, **4**(3), 457–461.

Kagerman, H., Wahlster, W., and Helbig, J. 2013. Securing the future of German manufacturing industry: Recommendations for implementing the strategic initiative Industrie 4.0, final report of the Industrie 4.0 Working Group.

Kahneman, D., and Tversky, A. 1979. Prospect theory: An analysis of decision under risk. *Econometrica*, **47**(2), 263–291.

Kaldor, N. 1957. A model of economic-growth. *Economic Journal*, **67**(268), 586–624.

Kattel, Rainer, Mazzucato, Mariana, Ryan-Collins, Josh, and Sharpe, Simon. 2018. The economics of change: Policy and appraisal for missions, market shaping and public purpose Policy Report. *Institute for Innovation and Public Purpose.*

Katz, J Sylvan. 2016. What is a complex innovation system? *PloS One*, **11**(6), e0156150.

Kemfert, Claudia, Präger, Fabian, Braunger, Isabell, Hoffart, Franziska M., and Brauers, Hanna. 2022. The expansion of natural gas infrastructure puts energy transitions at risk. *Nature Energy*, **7**(7), 582–587.

Kemp, Luke, and Cline, Eric H. 2022. Systemic risk and resilience: The bronze age collapse and recovery. Pages 207–223 of: *Perspectives on Public Policy in Societal-Environmental Crises: What the Future Needs from History*. Springer International Publishing Cham.

Klepper, Steven. 1997. Industry life cycles. *Industrial and Corporate Change*, **6**(1), 145–182.

Klingebiel, Ronald, and Rammer, Christian. 2014. Resource allocation strategy for innovation portfolio management. *Strategic Management Journal*, **35**(2), 246–268.

Knobloch, Florian, Hanssen, Steef V., Lam, Aileen, Pollitt, Hector, Salas, Pablo, Chewpreecha, Unnada, Huijbregts, Mark A. J., and Mercure, Jean-Francois. 2020. Net emission reductions from electric cars and heat pumps in 59 world regions over time. *Nature Sustainability*, **3**(6), 437–447.

Kondratieff, Nikolai. 1928. *The Long Wave Cycle.* Russian Association of Social Research Institutes.

Krugman, Paul. 1991. Increasing returns and economic geography. *Journal of Political Economy*, **99**(3), 483–499.

Kushwaha, Niraj, and Lee, Edward D. 2023. Discovering the mesoscale for chains of conflict. *PNAS Nexus*, **2**(7), pgad228.

Kuzemko, Caroline, Blondeel, Mathieu, Dupont, Claire, and Brisbois, Marie Claire. 2022. Russia's war on Ukraine, European energy policy responses & implications for sustainable transformations. *Energy Research & Social Science*, **93**, 102842.

Lafond, F., Greenwald, D., and Farmer, J. D. 2020. 'Can stimulating demand drive costs down? World War II as a natural experiment. *INET Oxford Working Paper No. 2020-02*.

Lafond, François, Bailey, Aimee Gotway, Bakker, Jan David, Rebois, Dylan, Zadourian, Rubina, McSharry, Patrick, and Farmer, J. Doyne. 2018. How well do experience curves predict technological progress? A method for making distributional forecasts. *Technological Forecasting and Social Change*, **128**, 104–117.

Lambert, Jessica G., Hall, Charles A. S., Balogh, Stephen, Gupta, Ajay, and Arnold, Michelle. 2014. Energy, EROI and quality of life. *Energy Policy*, **64**, 153–167.

Lasi, Heiner, Fettke, Peter, Kemper, Hans-Georg, Feld, Thomas, and Hoffmann, Michael. 2014. Industry 4.0. *Business & Information Systems Engineering*, **6**(4), 239–242.

Lenton, Tim, Watson, Andrew, and Watson, Andrew J. 2011. *Revolutions that Made the Earth*. Oxford University Press.

Lenton, Timothy M., Held, Hermann, Kriegler, Elmar, Hall, Jim W., Lucht, Wolfgang, Rahmstorf, Stefan, and Schellnhuber, Hans Joachim. 2008. Tipping elements in the Earth's climate system. *Proceedings of the National Academy of Sciences*, **105**(6), 1786–1793.

Lilliestam, Johan, Patt, Anthony, and Bersalli, Germán. 2020. The effect of carbon pricing on technological change for full energy decarbonization: A review of empirical ex-post evidence. *WIREs Climate Change*, **12**, 681.

Lockwood, Sarah J. 2022. Protest brokers and the technology of mobilization: Evidence from South Africa. *Comparative Political Studies*, **55**(4), 628–656.

Mah, Alice. 2009. Devastation but also home: Place attachment in areas of industrial decline. *Home Cultures*, **6**(3), 287–310.

Malhotra, Abhishek, and Schmidt, Tobias S. 2020. Accelerating low-carbon innovation. *Joule*, **4**, 2259–2267.

Malthus, Thomas Robert. 1872. *An Essay on the Principle of Population or a View of Its Past and Present Effects on Human Happiness, an Inquiry into Our*

Prospects Respecting the Future Removal or Mitigation of the Evils Which It Occasions by Rev. TR Malthus. Reeves and Turner.

Markkanen, Sanna, and Anger-Kraavi, Annela. 2019. Social impacts of climate change mitigation policies and their implications for inequality. *Climate Policy*, **19**(7), 827–844.

Martin, Ron, Sunley, Peter, Tyler, Peter, and Gardiner, Ben. 2016. Divergent cities in post-industrial Britain. *Cambridge Journal of Regions, Economy and Society*, **9**(2), 269–299.

Mass, William, and Robertson, Andrew. 1996. From textiles to automobiles: mechanical and organizational innovation in the Toyoda enterprises, 1895–1933. *Business and Economic History*, **25**(2) 1–37.

Mazzucato, Mariana. 2013. *The Entrepreneurial State: Debunking the Public vs. Private Myth in Risk and Innovation*. Anthem.

Mazzucato, Mariana. 2018. *The Value of Everything: Who Makes and Who Takes from the Real Economy*. PublicAffairs.

Mazzucato, Mariana. 2021. *Mission Economy: A Moonshot Guide to Changing Capitalism*. Penguin UK.

McGlade, Christophe, and Ekins, Paul. 2015. The geographical distribution of fossil fuels unused when limiting global warming to 2 °C. *Nature*, **517**, 187–190.

McLeay, M., Radia, A., and Thomas, R. 2014. *Money Creation in the Modern Economy*. Technical report, Bank of England. www.bankofengland.co.uk/publications/Pages/quarterlybulletin/2014/qb14q1.aspx.

Meadows, Donella H., Meadows, Dennis L., Randers, Joergen, and Behrens III, William W. 1972. *The Limits to Growth*. Technical report, Club of Rome.

Mealy, Penny, and Teytelboym, Alexander. 2022. Economic complexity and the green economy. *Research Policy*, **51**(8), 103948.

Meinshausen, M., Meinshausen, N., Hare, W., Raper, S. C. B., Frieler, K., Knutti, R., Frame, D. J., and Allen, M. R. 2009. Greenhouse-gas emission targets for limiting global warming to 2C. *Nature*, **458**(7242), 1158–1162.

Mercure, J.-F. 2012. FTT:Power: A global model of the power sector with induced technological change and natural resource depletion. *Energy Policy*, **48**(0), 799–811.

Mercure, J.-F. 2015. An age structured demographic theory of technological change. *Journal of Evolutionary Economics*, **25**, 787–820.

Mercure, J.-F. 2018. Fashion, fads and the popularity of choices: Micro-foundations for diffusion consumer theory. *Structural Change and Economic Dynamics*, **46**, 194–207.

Mercure, J.-F. 2022. *Complexity Economics for Environmental Governance*. Cambridge University Press.

Mercure, J.-F., and Lam, A. 2015. The effectiveness of policy on consumer choices for private road passenger transport emissions reductions in six major economies. *Environmental Research Letters*, **10**, 064008.

Mercure, J. F. A., Knobloch, F., Pollitt, H., Lewney, R., Rademakers, K., Eichler, L., van der Laan, J., and Paroussos, L. 2016. *Policy-Induced Energy Technological Innovation and Finance for Low-Carbon Economic Growth. Study on the Macroeconomics of Energy and Climate Policies.* Technical report, European Commission. https://ec.europa.eu/energy/sites/ener/files/documents/ENER%20Macro-Energy_Innovation_D2%20Final%20%28Ares%20registered%29.pdf.

Mercure, Jean-Francois, Knobloch, Florian, Pollitt, Hector, Paroussos, Leonidas, Scrieciu, S. Serban, and Lewney, Richard. 2019. Modelling innovation and the macroeconomics of low-carbon transitions: Theory, perspectives and practical use. *Climate Policy*, **19**(8), 1019–1037.

Mercure, Jean-Francois, Pollitt, Hector, Edwards, Neil R., Holden, Philip B., Chewpreecha, Unnada, Salas, Pablo, Lam, Aileen, Knobloch, Florian, and Vinuales, Jorge E. 2018a. Environmental impact assessment for climate change policy with the simulation-based integrated assessment model E3ME-FTT-GENIE. *Energy Strategy Reviews*, **20**, 195–208.

Mercure, J.-F., Pollitt, H., Geels, F. W., Zenghelis, 2025. The effects of low-carbon transitions on labour productivity: Analysing UK electricity, heat, and mobility with a techno-economic simulation model. *Climate Policy*, **25**(8), 1–18. https://doi.org/10.1080/14693062.2025.2522836.

Mercure, J.-F., Pollitt, Hector, Viñuales, Jorge E., Edwards, Neil R., Holden, Philip B., Chewpreecha, Unnada, Salas, Pablo, Sognnaes, Ida, Lam, Aileen, and Knobloch, Florian. 2018b. Macroeconomic impact of stranded fossil fuel assets. *Nature Climate Change*, **8**(7), 588.

Mercure, J.-F., Salas, Pablo, Vercoulen, Pim, Semieniuk, Gregor, Lam, Aileen, Pollitt, Hector, Holden, Philip B., Vakilifard, Negar, Chewpreecha, Unnada, Edwards, Neil R., and Vinuales, J. E. 2021a. Reframing incentives for climate policy action. *Nature Energy*, **6**(12), 1133–1143.

Mercure, Jean-Francois, Sharpe, Simon, Vinuales, Jorge E., Ives, Matthew, Grubb, Michael, Lam, Aileen, Drummond, Paul, Pollitt, Hector, Knobloch, Florian, and Nijsse, Femke J. M. M. 2021b. Risk-opportunity analysis for transformative policy design and appraisal. *Global Environmental Change*, **70**, 102359.

Mercure, J.-F., Lam, A., Buxton, J. E., Boulton, C. A., Akther, A., Lenton, T. M. 2025b. Evidence of a cascading positive tipping point towards electric vehicles, *Nature Communications*, https://doi.org/10.1038/s41467-025-66945-9.

Miyoshi, H., and Kii, M. 2011. *Technological Innovation and Public Policy.* Palgrave Macmillan Asian Business Series.

Nakicenovic, N. 1986. The automobile road to technological-change – Diffusion of the automobile as a process of technological substitution. *Technological Forecasting and Social Change,* **29**(4), 309–340.

Nemet, Gregory F. 2019. *How Solar Energy Became Cheap: A Model for Lowcarbon Innovation.* Routledge.

Nijsse, F. J. M. M., Mercure, J.-F., Ameli, N., Larosa, F., Kothari, S., Rickman, J., Vercoulen, P., and Pollitt, H. 2023. The momentum of solar energy. *Nature Communications,* **14**(1), 6542.

Nordhaus, William D. 1993. Optimal greenhouse-gas reductions and tax policy in the 'DICE' model. *The American Economic Review,* **83**(2), 313–317.

Nordhaus, William D. 2010. Economic aspects of global warming in a post-Copenhagen environment. *Proceedings of the National Academy of Sciences,* **107**(26), 11721–11726.

Nordhaus, W. D. 2013. *DICE-2013R Model.*

Nordhaus, William D. 2017. Revisiting the social cost of carbon. *Proceedings of the National Academy of Sciences,* **114**(7), 1518–1523.

Pathan, Misbah, Patel, Nivedita, Yagnik, Hiteshri, and Shah, Manan. 2020. Artificial cognition for applications in smart agriculture: A comprehensive review. *Artificial Intelligence in Agriculture,* **4**, 81–95.

Perez, Carlota. 2001. *Technological Revolutions and Financial Capital.* Edward Elgar.

Peñasco, Cristina, Anadón, Laura Díaz, and Verdolini, Elena. 2020. Systematic review of the outcomes and trade-offs of ten types of decarbonisation 2 policy instruments. *Nature Climate Change,* **11**(3), 257–265.

Polanyi, Karl. 1944. *The Great Transformation.* Beacon Press Boston.

Polewsky, Max, Hankammer, Stephan, Kleer, Robin, and Antons, David. 2024. Degrowth vs. green growth. A computational review and interdisciplinary research agenda. *Ecological Economics,* **217**, 108067.

Pollin, Robert. 2019. Advancing a viable global climate stabilization project: Degrowth versus the green new deal. *Review of Radical Political Economics,* **51**(2), 311–319.

Pollitt, H., and Mercure, J.-F. 2017. The role of money and the financial sector in energy-economy models used for assessing climate and energy policy. *Climate Policy,* **18**(2), 184–197.

Pollitt, Hector, Mercure, Jean-Francois, Barker, Terry, Salas, Pablo, and Scrieciu, Serban. 2024. The role of the IPCC in assessing actionable evidence for climate policymaking. *npj Climate Action,* **3**, 11.

Potter, Antony, and Watts, H. Doug. 2011. Evolutionary agglomeration theory: Increasing returns, diminishing returns, and the industry life cycle. *Journal of Economic Geography*, **11**(3), 417–455.

Reinhart, Carmen M., and Rogoff, Kenneth S. 2010. Growth in a time of debt. *American Economic Review*, **100**(2), 573–578.

Richardson, Katherine, Steffen, Will, Lucht, Wolfgang, Bendtsen, Jørgen, Cornell, Sarah E., Donges, Jonathan F., Drüke, Markus, Fetzer, Ingo, Bala, Govindasamy, von Bloh, Werner, et al. 2023. Earth beyond six of nine planetary boundaries. *Science Advances*, **9**(37), eadh2458.

Rockström, Johan, Steffen, Will, Noone, Kevin, Persson, Åsa, Chapin, F. Stuart, Lambin, Eric F., Lenton, Timothy M., Scheffer, Marten, Folke, Carl, Schellnhuber, Hans Joachim, et al. 2009. A safe operating space for humanity. *Nature*, **461**(7263), 472–475.

Romer, Paul M. 1986. Increasing returns and long-run growth. *Journal of Political Economy*, **94**(5), 1002–1037.

Ross, Michael L. 1999. The political economy of the resource curse. *World Politics*, **51**(2), 297–322.

Saez, Emmanuel, and Stantcheva, Stefanie. 2018. A simpler theory of optimal capital taxation. *Journal of Public Economics*, **162**, 120–142.

Savoia, Antonio, and Sen, Kunal. 2021. The political economy of the resource curse: A development perspective. *Annual Review of Resource Economics*, **13**(1), 203–223.

Schumpeter, J. A. 1934. *The Theory of Economic Development – An Inquiry into Profits, Capital, Credit, Interest and the Business Cycle*. Harvard University Press.

Schumpeter, J. A. 1939. *Business Cycles*. McGraw-Hill.

Schumpeter, J. A. 1942. *Capitalism, Socialism and Democracy*. Martino Publishing.

Schumpeter, Joseph A. 1947. The creative response in economic history. *The Journal of Economic History*, **7**(2), 149–159.

Semieniuk, Gregor, Campiglio, Emanuele, Mercure, Jean-Francois, Volz, Ulrich, and Edwards, Neil R. 2021. Low-carbon transition risks for finance. *Wiley Interdisciplinary Reviews: Climate Change*, **12**(1), e678.

Semieniuk, G., Holden, P. B., Salas, P., Vercoulen, J.-F., Mercure, P., Lam, A., Pollitt, H., Chewpreecha, U., Edwards, N. R., and Vinuales, J. E. 2022. Stranded fossil-fuel assets translate into major losses for investors in advanced economies. *Nature Climate Change*, **12**(6), 532–538.

Semieniuk, G., Weber, I. M., Weaver, I. S., Wasner, E., Braun, B., Holden, P. B., Salas, P., Mercure, J. F., and Edwards, N. R. 2025. Best of times, worst of times:

record fossil-fuel profits, inflation and inequality. *Energy Research & Social Science*, **127**, 104221.

Shaikh, Anwar. 1974. Laws of production and laws of algebra: The Humbug production function. *The Review of Economics and Statistics*, **56**(1), 115–120.

Sharpe, Simon. 2023. *Five Times Faster*. Cambridge University Press.

Solow, R. M. 1957. Technical change and the aggregate production function. *The Review of Economics and Statistics*, **39**(3), 312–320.

Stankiewicz, Rikard. 2000. The concept of 'design space'. Pages 234–247 of: *Technological Innovation as an Evolutionary Process*. Cambridge University Press.

Steffen, W., Richardson, K., Rockström, J., Cornell, S. E., Fetzer, I., Bennett, E. M., Biggs, R., Carpenter, S. R., de Vries, W., de Wit, C. A., Folke, C., Gerten, D., Heinke, J., Mace, G. M., Persson, L. M., Ramanathan, V., Reyers, B., and Sörlin, S. 2015. Planetary boundaries: Guiding human development on a changing planet. *Science*, **347**, 1259855.

Steinbeck, John. 1939. *The Grapes of Wrath*. The Viking Press.

Stern, Nicholas. 2007. *The Economics of Climate Change*. Cambridge University Press.

Stern, Nicholas, Stiglitz, Joseph, and Taylor, Charlotte. 2022. The economics of immense risk, urgent action and radical change: Towards new approaches to the economics of climate change. *Journal of Economic Methodology*, **29**(3), 181–216.

Thaler, Richard H. 2016. Behavioral economics: Past, present, and future. *American Economic Review*, **106**(7), 1577–1600.

Thirlwall, Anthony Philip. 1979. The balance of payments constraint as an explanation of international growth rate differences. *BNL Quarterly Review*, **32**(128), 45–53.

Thorleifsson, Cathrine. 2016. From coal to Ukip: The struggle over identity in post-industrial Doncaster. *History and Anthropology*, **27**(5), 555–568.

Tol, Richard S. J. 2024. A meta-analysis of the total economic impact of climate change. *Energy Policy*, **185**, 113922.

Turner, Royce Logan. 1985. Post war pit closures: The politics of de-industrialisation. *Political Quarterly*, **56**(2) 167.

Utterback, James M., and Abernathy, William J. 1975. A dynamic model of process and product innovation. *Omega*, **3**(6), 639–656.

Van de Graaf, Thijs, and Bradshaw, Michael. 2018. Stranded wealth: Rethinking the politics of oil in an age of abundance. *International Affairs*, **94**(6), 1309–1328.

Van de Graaf, Thijs, and Sovacool, Benjamin K. 2020. *Global Energy Politics*. John Wiley & Sons.

Van den Bergh, Jeroen C. J. M. 2011. Environment versus growth – A criticism of 'degrowth' and a plea for 'a-growth'. *Ecological Economics*, **70**(5), 881–890.

van Vuuren, D.P., van der Wijst, Kaj-Ivar, Marsman, Stijn, van den Berg, Maarten, Hof, Andries F., and Jones, Chris D. 2020. The costs of achieving climate targets and the sources of uncertainty. *Nature Climate Change*, **10**(4), 329–334.

Varshney, Rajeev K., Bohra, Abhishek, Roorkiwal, Manish, Barmukh, Rutwik, Cowling, Wallace A., Chitikineni, Annapurna, Lam, Hon-Ming, Hickey, Lee T., Croser, Janine S., Bayer, Philipp E., et al. 2021. Fast-forward breeding for a food-secure world. *Trends in Genetics*, **37**(12), 1124–1136.

Walsh, David, Taulbut, Martin, and Hanlon, Phil. 2010. The aftershock of deindustrialization – Trends in mortality in Scotland and other parts of post-industrial Europe. *The European Journal of Public Health*, **20**(1), 58–64.

Watkins, Nicholas W., Pruessner, Gunnar, Chapman, Sandra C., Crosby, Norma B., and Jensen, Henrik J. 2016. 25 years of self-organized criticality: Concepts and controversies. *Space Science Reviews*, **198**(1–4), 3–44.

Way, Rupert, Ives, Matthew C., Mealy, Penny, and Farmer, J. Doyne. 2022. Empirically grounded technology forecasts and the energy transition. *Joule*, **6**(9), 2057–2082.

Weitzman, Martin L. 2009. On modeling and interpreting the economics of catastrophic climate change. *The Review of Economics and Statistics*, **91**(1), 1–19.

Werner, Richard A. 2014. Can banks individually create money out of nothing? – The theories and the empirical evidence. *International Review of Financial Analysis*, **36**, 1–19.

Werner, Richard A. 2016. A lost century in economics: Three theories of banking and the conclusive evidence. *International Review of Financial Analysis*, **46**, 361–379.

Wohlers. 2021. *Wohlers Report 2021: Additive Manufacturing and 3D Printing State of the Industry.* Technical report. Wohlers Associates.

Yelle, Louis E. 1983. Adding life cycles to learning curves. *Long Range Planning*, **16**(6), 82–87.

Zenghelis, Dimitri, Fouquet, Roger, and Hippe, Ralph. 2018. Stranded assets: Then and now. In: *Stranded Assets and the Environment: Risk, Resilience and Opportunity*. Routledge.

Ziegler, Micah S., and Trancik, Jessika E. 2021. Re-examining rates of lithium-ion battery technology improvement and cost decline. *Energy & Environmental Science*, **14**(4), 1635–1651.

Author Index

Subject Index

For EU product safety concerns, contact us at Calle de José Abascal, 56–1°,
28003 Madrid, Spain or eugpsr@cambridge.org.

www.ingramcontent.com/pod-product-compliance
Ingram Content Group UK Ltd.
Pitfield, Milton Keynes, MK11 3LW, UK
UKHW020838290926
15470UKWH00004B/1422
* 9 7 8 1 0 0 9 7 0 8 3 7 1 *